P9-CBB-654

The Smart Consumer's Guide to

Home Buying

Peter A. Schkeeper, PE
Licensed Professional Engineer
Red Bank, New Jersey

Jack P. Friedman, Ph.D., CPA, MAI, CRE, ASA
Real Estate Consultant and Author
Jack Friedman & Associates
Dallas, Texas

Jack C. Harris, Ph.D.
Consultant and Former Research Economist
Real Estate Research Center
Texas A&M University

BARRON'S

About the Authors

Peter A. Schkeeper, PE, is a building inspection and forensic engineering consultant to individuals and corporations. He has performed thousands of home inspections. This book is his first for Barron's. Jack P. Friedman is a real estate consultant and author who has written a number of books for Barron's. Jack C. Harris is a consultant who retired as a research economist at Texas A&M University. He has also written a number of books for Barron's.

Acknowledgments

The charts on pages 287–290 and 511–512 are reprinted courtesy of the United States Department of Housing and Urban Development.

© Copyright 2008 by Barron's Educational Series, Inc.

All inquiries should be addressed to:
Barron's Educational Series, Inc.
250 Wireless Boulevard
Hauppauge, New York 11788
www.barronseduc.com

Library of Congress Catalog Card No. 2007009077

ISBN-13: 978-0-7641-3571-2
ISBN-10: 0-7641-3571-6

Library of Congress Cataloging-in-Publication Data
Schkeeper, Peter A.
    The smart consumer's guide to home buying / Peter A. Schkeeper,
Jack P. Friedman, Jack C. Harris.
    p. cm.
  Includes index.
  ISBN-13: 978-0-7641-3571-2
  ISBN-10: 0-7641-3571-6
    1. House buying. I. Friedman, Jack P. II. Harris, Jack C., 1945– III. Title.

HD1390.5.S34 2008
643′.12—dc22   2007009077

Printed in Canada
9 8 7 6 5 4 3 2 1

Contents

Introduction

T hink of buying a home as a romantic journey, and at the same time, a business venture. It's romantic because you want to love the place if you're going to live there in happiness, but like any romance, there can be high maintenance if you want to keep the spirit alive and well. Home buying is also a business venture because a home is often the largest single investment that most single individuals or families will ever make. A home can also be the cornerstone of your investment program or retirement plan. We'll show you how to take command of the process as chairman of the board and chief executive officer of your home-buying venture—as it is a business that needs constant supervision. Our goal is to help you develop objectivity and realistic plans in your personal home-buying adventure and guide you over the humps that seem determined to get in your way. We plan to make you a smart consumer.

Many of our chapters are titled with a question you need answered. What we do in these pages is fine-tune every aspect of home buying to provide solutions to obvious, everyday situations and to questions you probably haven't yet thought about. Our work progresses from getting you ready, to helping you understand what you can afford, through the process of closing and after-moving-in ideas for the future. It reads like a story from front to back, but you can easily use this book as a reference guide for any chapter of special interest.

We're going to take you by the hand through the maze of mortgage shopping to simplify the seemingly insolvable problems associated with buying money. Oh, yes, mortgage money *is* a commodity that's bought and sold everyday and you need to become familiar with its terminology and practices. The recent subprime mortgage market problems make this information particularly important. We'll make you comfortable in the money market so you can ask the right questions of a potential lender and expeditiously answer their questions of you. We present some mathematics, not necessarily to make you an expert, but to at least prepare you for discussions with financial people so you are not misled. We provide you with the information and tools to put you in the financial driver's seat.

While you're behind the wheel, we'll join you for the trip of a lifetime to find your dream house. We'll help you decide what you really need, as opposed to what you'd love to have, and point you in the right direction for the professional help you're going to require along the way. We'll help clarify your thinking on new versus old, one style or another, neighborhoods, town planning and zoning, and the perils of a fixer-upper. We'll cover a lot of territory on this trip, known in the world of real estate as "location, location, location" where you can "look, look, look." We'll be with you every step of the way.

Even after you find the perfect house there are still a million details no sensible buyer can afford to overlook. We'll guide you through the negotiating process. We'll discuss utilities and maintenance and the absolutely non-negotiable necessity of a professional home inspection. Finally, we'll take you on a side trip through remodeling and the ups and downs of condominium ownership to the star-kissed dream of owning the ideal vacation home.

We've included a glossary with translations from "techno-speak" into English, where necessary. Web sites are listed throughout our chapters for additional information. Checklists and worksheets are provided for use in your search and evaluation. Our information is as current as our publication date, so use of our referenced web sites will help you obtain the latest information. Organizational concepts, including use of loose-leaf notebooks and zip-top tote bags as portable files, will help you to become and stay focused.

Because we are addressing a national audience our book may seem a bit general in references to local situations. Local regulations and laws vary widely throughout the country, so we have outlined how to obtain local professional assistance when needed and have identified where you may obtain local knowledge directly applicable to your needs.

Happy reading and welcome to the world of the landed gentry! Are you ready for the trip of a lifetime? Let's go!

Chapter 1

Am I Ready to Buy a Home?

*A*lthough owning a home is often called the "American Dream," it is not the best alternative for everyone. Some people have found that owning a home, in the wrong situation or at the wrong time, can become more of a nightmare than a dream. One of the first things you need to think about is whether owning a home is right for you at this time in your life. If so, are you prepared to make the type of commitments required to make **home ownership** a reality?

First let's look at what type of home buyer you are. People who buy homes can be divided into three general groups according to their primary motivation for moving. **Relocatees** are moving because they need or want to locate in a different place—maybe to change jobs or just because they prefer a different town or neighborhood. Not everyone in this group buys—some rent an apartment or house, at least temporarily, but many buy because they prefer the advantages of owning. Relocatees often are under time constraints because they have to complete their move within a specific period. They may make several house-hunting trips and buy a home before they actually move to their new location, or they may move first and search the market while living in temporary accommodations. Either way, relocatees face a difficult job in finding the right home. Their task is often complicated by having to sell a home in their current location.

Upgraders buy to improve their housing situation. They may need more space, or, as empty-nesters, less space. They may want a more modern home or a more traditional home. They may want to move to a more compatible neighborhood or a more prestigious one. Sometimes, they decide to build a home—one that has everything they have always wanted in a house but could never find on the market. These buyers, unless their present condition is unbearable, can afford to take their time searching the market and may be able to drive a hard bargain if market conditions permit.

Most of the time, it is the upgraders who provide homes for the **first-timers.** Essentially, first-timers are upgraders who are buying their initial home. They may be relocating or could be moving up to better housing, but their main focus is on becoming home owners. They may be tired of renting or dealing with landlords and living in someone else's property. They might feel that owning is a step that coincides with their advancing financial status or the arrival of new family members. Undoubtedly, they are convinced that purchasing a home is a sound investment decision. First-timers can afford to take their time in finding a home, assuming they are not also relocatees, but they often have significant financial constraints that handicap their search for a home.

Of course, you realize that these groups are not mutually exclusive. A couple might be relocating from a small rental apartment to a new town where they will buy a more luxurious home. What distinguishes each group, and why we are taking the trouble to introduce them, is their primary reason for being in the market for a home. That reason will affect how they approach the market and how they decide on the home they will buy. It is helpful to realize which group you are part of before you think much further about the actual purchase. Each group will take different measures to prepare to enter the market.

If you are a relocatee, you will need as much information as possible about the market, because presumably you start out knowing very little about neighborhoods and local service providers in the area to which you are moving. Further, you will want to get this information expeditiously. You may not have the luxury of contemplating the pros and cons of ownership: you are facing a deadline. If time is too short and you really know nothing about the area, it may be better to rent a home until you can collect more information, despite the inconvenience of having to move more than once. A bad purchase decision will turn out to be much more inconvenient in the long run.

If your main object is to upgrade, you will want to make sure your purchase is truly an improvement. You will need to give some time to decide what is most important to you and which features are worth the additional expense. You may also want to time your purchase to take advantage of interest rate fluctuations or at least not get caught by spiking interest rates.

First-time buyers need a lot of information about affordable homes and financing. You will want to know about loans especially suited for a first home purchase. At the same time, you will want to assure yourself that the home you buy will hold its value and preserve (and hopefully increase) your equity. There are financial hurdles for the first-timer that require special preparation.

While most home-buying books are oriented toward the first-time, and presumably novice, home buyer, we offer information in this book that will be helpful to all three types of buyers. Most relocatees and upgraders should be familiar with what it takes to purchase a home and be acquainted with what it means to be a home owner. Those types of buyers mainly need information about the area and house to which they plan to move. They are "ready" to buy when they have enough information to ensure that their new residence will be satisfactory. If it has been a long while since they last moved, there probably have been some major changes in the financial market that will require research. Even veteran home buyers may benefit from reviewing much of this book.

First-timers, in addition to gathering information, should consider whether owning any home is the right choice for them.

The Attraction of Owning a Home

Besides the vague promise of the "American Dream," there are some very real advantages of owning a home. These provide perspective when personalizing the decision to become or to remain a home owner. Let's look at the list of most-often cited advantages:

- **Pride of ownership.** Sure, you are proud of owning something so large, expensive, and vital as a house. But this aspect is more than vanity. **Pride of ownership** means that you are accepting a more prominent role in your community (i.e., not as a fly-by-night renter). You take responsibility for the appearance and upkeep of your property. Your home becomes an expression of your tastes and values.

- **Selection.** Although you can find detached, single-family homes for rent, they may be in short supply in the neighborhoods where you want to live. For the most part, single-family rental homes are something of an oddity in the housing market. Most investors do not buy single-family homes to rent them out because they have to pay a higher price to outbid those who want to live in the home. When they are available, such homes often are available only temporarily, and not in the better locations and maybe not in the best of condition. To get the type of home you want, you may need to buy rather than rent.

- **Ability to remodel.** Landlords are not always keen on their tenants' making significant modifications to the premises. Understandably, they do not know how long you will rent and may find it difficult to interest another tenant in a home with all the rooms painted black. One of the great things about owning a home is the ability to change it according to your own tastes (although there may be restrictions on what you can do to the exterior, even if you do own the home).

- **Control.** When you own, you not only have the right to remodel the home, but you have more control over your destiny (at least as far as where you live is concerned). You do not have to worry about needing to move when your lease expires. You don't have stipulations attached to your ability to live in the home. As long as you make your mortgage payments and obey the law, you can enjoy your home indefinitely.

- **Predictable costs.** When you buy, you lock in the main cost of the home at the purchase price. Depending on the loan you get, you may lock in the loan payments as well, although the total monthly payment may increase if it includes a provision for taxes and insurance. There are no unexpected rent increases. Many home owners find that their monthly payments actually decrease in significance as their income rises over the term of the loan.

- **Investment.** The value of the home may increase over time, so that when you are ready to move, you are able to sell it for more than you paid. Though you have to repay the outstanding principal of the loan, you get to keep all of the gains from the increased value. If you borrowed money to buy the home, your rate of return on your initial investment is magnified. Even if the value of the home does not increase, you may have some gain because of the portion of your loan payments devoted to principal reduction.

- **Taxes.** The federal income tax code has provisions that give special advantages to home owners. Interest paid on a mortgage loan for a home you live in can be used as an itemized deduction against taxable income. Property taxes paid on the home are eligible as well. These deductions may help lower the cost of home ownership, though the benefit of all **itemized deductions** is tempered by the standard deduction available to all taxpayers. Local governments often provide a **homestead exemption** discount on property taxes due on owner-occupied homes. The potentially most important break, however, is the fact that for most people, gains on resale of a residence are exempt from taxation if you live in the home for at least two years.

The Home-Ownership Commitment

With all these advantages, how could owning a home not be the best choice for everyone? All these benefits come at a price and may not materialize if you make a bad purchase. Let's run through the list once more.

- Pride of ownership entails a significant commitment to one location. If the neighborhood turns out not to be as you expected or your preferences change, you may not be satisfied with your home. Neighborhoods change over time and can decline in quality (e.g., houses in need of repair, more unkempt lawns, higher crime rates). That is a risk all home owners face.

- Selection presumes that you want a single-family home and the family-oriented lifestyle it facilitates. If you want low-maintenance housing, you may prefer an apartment, and these are more plentiful in the rental market. Also, access to facilities like swimming pools, clubs, and tennis courts often is more affordable in a rental complex.

- If the home you buy is not in good shape, the ability to remodel can morph into the need to make major repairs. Houses are complex structures and a lot can go wrong. Further, not all of these things are obvious before you buy, even to trained observers.

- Control also brings a responsibility for the consequences of everything in and around your home. If someone is injured on your property due to negligence, you are liable. As an owner, you may not be dependent on a landlord for upkeep, but you may be just as dependent on a cadre of repair and remodeling service providers.

- The cost of acquiring the property is fixed, but that is only one aspect of the total cost of ownership. Property taxes, insurance, and maintenance are much less predictable and certainly not fixed. Also, there is always the possibility of something important failing (such as a leaky roof) and in need of repair or replacement.

- It is possible to lose money on a house. Contrary to what many believe, houses do sometimes decline in value. You could find yourself in a buyer's market when it is time to sell. And not all homes keep up with the general trend in prices. However, the biggest investment drawback of housing is the fact that you have to tie up a large amount of money (possibly your whole life savings) in one asset. In investment terms, this means a lack of **liquidity** (it is hard to sell the property quickly) and a lack of diversification (you are dependent on one asset). That is why home buyers expect to make a higher return compared to depositing the money in a bank account.

- If you do not have enough deductible expenses to make itemizing beneficial, the tax deductions are of no value. Also, the value of deductions decreases as your marginal tax rate falls. That is why tax deductions are more useful to those with high incomes. The deferral of resale profits is only good if you have a gain. If you lose money on the sale, those losses will not reduce your income taxes.

If this sounds a bit pessimistic, consider that more than two of every three households in this country own their home. Furthermore, the percentage that are home owners has risen steadily over the last century. The trend reflects the growing prosperity of the American population, as well as the fact that people tend to choose home ownership when their income and wealth allow. A lot of your neighbors consider owning a home to be worthwhile. You should, however, decide whether to own a home based on your own circumstances.

Gathering Information About a New Home

No prospective home buyer can have too much information about the neighborhood and city that may become her new home. The most essential information is gathered through personal experience—actually driving through the area, preferably at different times of day and on different days of the week, to observe the ordinary life of the area. Try to observe the way most residents regard their homes. Do they just use them as places to sleep in between commutes to work and other places? Or do they pursue activities around the house—gardening, walking, home improvement projects, or socializing with their neighbors? There is no best answer to these questions, but you will probably prefer to live in a neighborhood where the neighbors do things that you like to do.

Check out traffic patterns during rush hours. Are some streets less desirable because of this traffic? Would it make it difficult to get in and out of your driveway or make it unsafe for your children to play in the yard? Are there safe ways to walk around the neighborhood or for children to go to school? Where are parks and other recreational attractions? Once again, the way you judge these things depends on your personal taste.

If you are moving to a different town, you will want to know about local taxes and services. Information in **real estate** listings that show the amount of taxes paid by the seller are not always good indications of what you will owe if you buy the house, because the seller may qualify for special treatment that is not extended to a new owner. A good start is to do an Internet search on the name of the town. Most cities, even small ones, have official sites that provide information on taxes, utilities, and local regulations. If you are moving to a new state, you might search through that state's government sites. Look especially at the revenue department, as it will show the type of state taxes you will have to pay.

There are web sites that provide statistical profiles of cities at *www.usacitylink.com* and *www.moving.com/Find_a_Place/* and individual neighborhoods at *http://realestate.yahoo.com/Neighborhoods*. Such information most often is from general sources, such as the U.S. census, but may give you some useful decision-making help, particularly if you are comparing a number of localities. In addition, you can get data on local schools at *www.schoolmatch.com* and how the cost of living in the area you are considering compares with your current home at *www.bankrate.com/brm/movecalc.asp*.

You can also get data on housing values or prices in the area you are considering. If you are working with a real estate agent, ask her to look up recent sale prices for homes in the neighbor-hood. She may be willing to put together an analysis for you and should at least be willing to give you a sample of recent sale prices. On the other hand, if you are looking at a number of areas or do not yet have an agent, you still can access data on home values. Several web sites such as *www.zillow.com*, *www.realestate. yahoo.com/Homevalues*, and *www.homegain.com*, provide value esti-mates of individual homes in localities all over the country (rec-ognize that these data are provided free of charge and their accuracy is not guaranteed). To access the data, input the address of a home along with its ZIP code. One nice feature of most of these sites is that they also give you values for surrounding homes, so you can get an idea of how values are distributed through the community. This is particularly useful for those who are mindful of the old real estate adage about buying the highest valued home on the block (i.e., the notion that if you own the most expensive house on the block, its value appreciation will be retarded by the other less valuable homes).

When I was trying to buy a home in a distant town, one particular real estate broker did something that proved very help-ful. Without knowing me or how real my intention was to buy, she began emailing me descriptions of all new listings on the mul-tiple listing service (MLS) each week. There was enough informa-tion to get a comprehensive feel for the market. Each description included a little photo, the size and age of the house, the asking price, and other features. I was so impressed that I ended up buy-ing a home through that broker.

Buying Your First Home

Buying a home is like three major purchases combined into one. First, you are choosing a physical structure that will provide shel-ter and facilitate the things you like to do when at home: relax, prepare and enjoy meals, entertain yourself, and maybe pursue hobbies and get some work done. That is the aspect of a home that is familiar to most people. Second, you are selecting the place where you will put down stakes for a while. Unless you plan to hibernate in your house, the neighborhood can be important to your enjoyment of your new home. Even if you do not plan to interact with your neighbors, the location will affect the time required to commute to work and take care of routine shopping and errands. The neighborhood can have a major impact on whether your home increases in value over the period you own it.

The third facet of the purchase is getting the right financing. This part not only determines how much the house will cost, but also can affect your peace of mind while owning the home. Loan shopping can be almost as complicated as the home search. At the same time, most people do not know enough about the mortgage market to make good choices without doing some research. Recognize that there are professionals who operate in the housing market and in the loan markets that can be invaluable to your ability to make an informed decision. You should first know the basics of mortgage financing so you can better take advantage of the services of these professionals, as well as protect yourself from the occasional dishonest agent.

Real estate agents can show you what is available in the market, but they cannot decide for you, or even recommend, the "best" home. From a moderately long-term perspective—you probably are going to live in the house for several years—think of what you really need from a house. The list should include how much space you need, how much land you want, and the kinds of rooms and amenities you expect. Make a "must have" list, then a luxury list. You may not be able to afford everything you want, so this prioritized list will help you with any unavoidable trade-offs. If you have not lived in a lot of houses, you might not have strong opinions about these things, but you know what you like and dislike. Make those things explicit.

Location is important enough that you probably should settle on a neighborhood before you even look at a house. Like the house purchase, take some time to think about what is important to you about where you live. Locate the places you visit frequently—your job, the homes of your friends and relatives, food stores, and recreation facilities—and decide how important it is to be close to each one. Think about what makes an environment pleasant to you. For example, some people are rediscovering the old-fashioned pleasures of large trees and sidewalks. Others like large lawns that help to insulate you from your neighbors. You may be able to get an idea of what type of families live in an area just by driving through at various times of the day. Some neighborhoods tend to attract young couples with small children, couples with older children, professionals, or retired people. Real estate agents should be able to give you some information (be aware that they are prohibited by law from giving data or opinions on an area's composition or trend in racial or ethnic makeup).

Look at how houses in the neighborhood are maintained to detect any signs that the area is declining. How many of the homes are offered for rent? Established neighborhoods usually enjoy a long period of vitality during which home owners invest in keeping their homes in good condition, mainly because they believe that the area has a future. When that faith is no longer widespread, homes are allowed to deteriorate at a greater rate. Such an area most likely is doomed to continued decline.

Getting That First Loan

Arranging **financing** is one of the biggest hurdles for the first-time home buyer. Most people buy a home with a combination of a mortgage loan and cash. The mortgage loan market has developed to the point where only a relatively small amount of cash is required. Keep in mind, however, that the less cash you invest, the higher will be your monthly payment. Nevertheless, many people find it easier to get a larger loan than to come up with more cash.

Potential sources of **down payment** cash should be identified before you approach a lender. These sources might include personal savings, financial assets that can be sold, and gifts from relatives. Knowing what you have to work with will help you choose the right type of mortgage loan. Plus, the lender will want to know where your cash down payment is coming from. In planning this part of the financing, keep in mind that you will need to retain some cash for incidental costs connected to the purchase (**closing costs**) as well as for any emergency expenses that might come up.

Before you go to a lender, get a copy of your **credit report**. You are allowed a free copy of your credit report once a year. Actually, that should be "reports," because there are three separate credit-rating agencies, and each compiles a different report. There are companies that will provide you a copy of each report and explain how to read one. You can access reports at *www.annualcreditreport.com*. You may also go to each of the credit agencies' sites at *www.experian.com*, *www.transunion.com*, and *www.econsumer.equifax.com* where, in addition to getting a report, you may be able to provide feedback if you find errors on your report.

The credit report has information on how many lines of credit and loans you have and your history in paying off loans and other obligations. This includes not only whether you have paid your bills, but how promptly you did so. Lenders will order these reports, and the information will weigh heavily on your ability to get a loan, as well as the loan terms offered. You will want to be concerned with two things when looking through your report.

Your Rights Under the Federal Fair Credit Reporting Act

When you review your credit report, or just begin to investigate your credit status, keep in mind that federal law provides you with a set of rights to aid in your task of gauging your credit rating. Here is a summary of your rights under the law:

- Notification of any instance in which your credit report has been used to deny the granting of credit, insurance, or a job. You have the right to know which credit agency provided the data.
- A free copy of your credit file every year, as well as whenever you are denied a loan, insurance, or a job because of information in your file.
- Access to your credit score, though not necessarily free of charge.
- Response to your identification of data on your report that you believe to be inaccurate or incorrect. The credit reporting agency must investigate your claim(s) unless they can show them to be frivolous. If the investigation finds your claim to be true, the agency must correct the report in a timely fashion.
- Purging of old information that would lower your credit rating. If you have slow or missed payments that are more than seven years old, they should not be included in the report. Personal bankruptcies are deleted after ten years.
- Limited access to your report. No one should be allowed to see your report unless they have a valid reason, such as in response to your application for credit, a job, or an apartment lease. You must give written consent for your employer or potential employer to access the data.
- Right to sue a credit agency or user of data that violates your rights under the Act.
- For detailed information and procedures in exercising your rights, go to *www.ftc.gov/credit*.

First, make sure that the information is accurate. If you see something you know to be contrary to fact (such as an outstanding loan that you have paid off), you can challenge the report and ask to have it corrected. Mistakes do crop up on these reports, and they

What's in Your Credit Report?

When you get a copy of your report, here is what you should see:

- Personal information: your name, current and previous addresses, Social Security number.
- Any civil judgments, tax liens, and bankruptcies.
- A list of your active credit accounts, including bank credit cards and store accounts.
- Your record of late payments, missed payments, and delinquencies.
- How long you have been using credit.

Be alert for the following when reviewing your report:

- Anything that you know to be wrong—an account that you never opened, one that you know you have closed, any payments that were not credited and that you have evidence of having paid. Accounts that you never opened could be a sign of identity theft— someone opening an account using your identity.
- Any of your personal data that is incorrect.
- Persistent history of late payments, especially involving penalties for missing due dates. If these data are accurate, you probably will not qualify to get the best terms on your loan.
- A habit of making the minimum payment on credit cards, thereby creating a growing balance, will diminish your credit rating.
- More than a few active credit cards and more than four or five store accounts will have a negative effect on your credit rating.
- Outstanding debt that is a large percentage of the credit extended to you. If you are "maxing" out your credit cards, lenders will not be eager to extend credit to you on favorable terms.

If you find negative information on your credit report, and it is correct, you have two choices. You can defer the home purchase decision until you can improve your credit rating, or you can plow ahead and accept whatever loan terms you are offered. Changing your credit rating may take several years of diligence on your part, but it will save you a lot of money over time and make the purchase easier. If you decide to go ahead, contact a lender early to see what type of loan you can get with your current credit history. Be careful of taking on more debt.

can be detrimental to your chances of getting a loan (as well as affect other things like the insurance premiums you pay). Second, view your creditworthiness from the standpoint of the lender. If you discover that you have a lot of open credit lines that you may have forgotten about (e.g., that store credit card you applied for in exchange for a discount on your first purchase), you might want to close some of these and thereby improve your credit rating. Lenders do not like to lend money to someone who has too many opportunities to go further into debt.

You may also wish to get your **FICO score**. This is a measure that supposedly indicates the likelihood that you will faithfully pay off a loan. These credit scores are derived from the information in your credit report using a special statistical program. In one simple number, the score helps lenders categorize you on the basis of the risk that you will default on a loan. Scores go from 300 to 850, with those above 760 qualifying for the lowest interest rates and cash requirements. Those with low scores (below 500) may qualify only for **sub-prime loans**, with much higher interest rates and down payments. You cannot get your FICO for free (at least not without signing up for a service that may be free for a short trial period), but there are companies that sell the information for a nominal fee at *www.myfico.com*. Knowing your score is not as important as reviewing your credit report, but it will clue you in to how much difficulty you may have in finding an affordable loan.

You may also want to get **prequalified**. When you apply for a mortgage loan, the lender will determine how much loan you qualify for based on your credit rating, current income, and debts. Prequalification is a preliminary estimate of how much loan you might be able to get. A lender, or even your real estate agent, may run this analysis for no charge (for a web site with a prequalification calculator, see *www.dinkytown.net/java/LoanPrequal*). This information allows you to go into the housing market with some idea of what you can afford. No need to waste time looking at homes that are well beyond your reach.

Market Hybrids

Before you decide that owning a home is not for you, consider the following alternatives to traditional home owning. In today's market, it is possible to combine some of the benefits of owning a home with some of the features of renting. If you find that home ownership in general works for you except for a few things that create issues, you might want to consider one of these hybrids.

- **Buy a condo apartment.** You like everything about home ownership except that you like to play tennis and swim but do not want to invest in a court and pool. Or you want to live in an urban setting with good access to restaurants and nightlife attractions. You do not mind living in an apartment but just don't want to deal with a landlord or pay rent. You also are attracted to the financial benefits of owning. A **condominium** apartment gives you ownership of your housing unit while you share the grounds and facilities with other home owners. Since **condos** can be developed on smaller pieces of land, they are feasible in high-density urban areas. Your ability to customize and use your property is constrained a bit, and an owners' association controls the use of grounds and facilities shared by the home owners. You have a voice in what the association does, and written **bylaws** govern your rights as a home owner. Though some condos are developed chiefly as a "cheaper" way to become a home owner, price should never be the primary basis for choosing this alternative. Low-quality condos often fail to maintain their attractiveness when markets cool and can then represent a risky investment. Condo living is a distinctly different experience from the typical suburban home (for more information on buying a condominium, see Barron's *Keys to Purchasing a Condo or Co-op*). You should make sure the condo parameters are acceptable to you before buying.

- **Buy a manufactured home.** A factory-built home (the obsolete terms "mobile home" or "trailer" are commonly applied to these units, although **manufactured housing** is the terminology applicable to all homes built in a factory since federal standards took effect in 1973) can provide the amenities and services of a site-built home at a lower cost. It also allows you to live in your own home without having to buy the underlying land, although this option does make you somewhat dependent on whoever owns the land. Many such homes are located in rental communities that may offer some of the amenities found in condominium communities. If you do not own the land, you will have limited value increase, since most of a home's appreciation is generated by its location. Of course, you can also place one of these units on land you own, assuming it is allowed by local land use regulations.

- **Lease option.** Suppose you find a home you like but are not sure you want to own it. Possibly you also don't have quite enough cash for a purchase right now or your credit rating needs rehabilitation. If the housing market is slow, you may find the owner willing to give you a **lease with the option to buy** at a future date. You get to live in the home, pay rent, and presumably try out the home as a place to live, with limited obligation on your part. The option feature may provide for a fixed price, so that you have some protection from appreciation while you are trying to accumulate a down payment. Some sellers even apply part of the rent to the eventual purchase price. You have the benefits of low-cost entry and the freedom to walk away at the end of the lease while gaining a quasi-ownership position in the home.

- **Buy a duplex.** A **duplex** has two separate dwelling units in one structure (there also are "triplexes" and "quadraplexes" with three and four units, respectively). If you buy the structure, you can live in one side and rent out the other. You have the control benefits of a home owner with the investment and taxation benefits of a landlord. However, you sacrifice some of the privacy of a single-family home owner and you have to take on the responsibilities of a landlord. Some duplex buyers find that the income from the second unit pays the mortgage for the whole property, providing nearly free housing to the owner.

Home-Buyer's Checklist

Before you proceed with your search for a home, ask yourself the following questions:

- Am I ready to commit to one location for the next five years or more?

- Can I raise enough cash for a down payment? Figure at least three percent of the price of the home.

- Are there any special loan or grant programs that are available to people like me? Programs may carry eligibility requirements based on your income, status as a nonhome-owner, or where the home is located. A good source of information on special programs is your local housing counseling agency. See *www.hud.gov/offices/hsg/sfh/hcc/ hcs.cfm* for a list of **HUD**-approved agencies in your area. These agencies also provide consumer education courses that may be required to participate in loan programs.

- Have I ordered a copy of my credit report from at least one of the three credit agencies? Have I reviewed the information to see if it is accurate?

- Have I been prequalified so that I have an idea of how much financing I can get? This number gives you a guide to how much home you can buy.

- What type of homes are available on the market in the area where I wish to move? Are they what I had in mind when I decided to consider buying a home?

Chapter 2

What Are My Needs?

*I*n this chapter, we will guide you through reality checks on several levels—needs versus wants, practicality versus pie-in-the-sky, and everything in between.

A young couple we know suffered total frustration in their search for "The House" for the family they were about to establish—daddy, mommy, baby, and nanny. Marc and Katy were career-driven and very successful in the world of finance; he worked near the New Jersey shore and she, in the Big Apple, New York City. Katy would not be giving up her career, so room and privacy for a live-in nanny was a basic need, as was proximity to fast train or ferry service into the city. And, of course, the best possible school system had to be there for the future child or children.

Were Marc and Katy expecting too much? Maybe. The New Jersey shore is a pricey place to live. For reasons no one will ever know, Marc and Katy lost out on at least six dream houses they had bid on—all within one short year. Life works in mysterious ways, however, and their ill-fated search became moot when Katy was transferred to an even better job on the West Coast. Marc packed his laptop and off they went to blissful center-city life with a view of the Golden Gate Bridge in San Francisco.

Not all happenstance works out as well, so we're here to help you in your search—with eyes wide open.

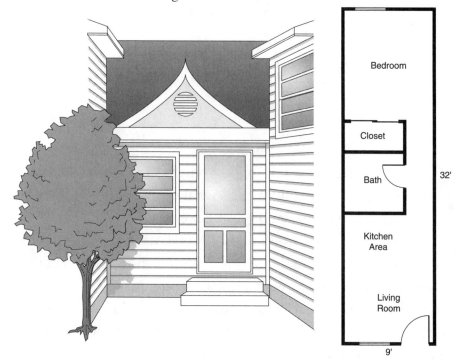

Figure 2–1: Small Home

Do you need a large house, or will a small one do?

Needs Versus Wants

Home buyers come in all shapes and sizes, all with distinct, diverse needs and wants. Homes are definitely not a one-size-fits-all market. In this chapter, we'll guide you in identifying your home needs.

How much house do you really need? We will present information and questions. Your answers will help you feel confident that you have considered all of the important factors. Work sheets will be provided to record your specific needs. These work sheets are not fixed, as your information will vary with changes in your life. We recommend that you prioritize your needs using an ABC system. "A" would be a most important necessary need. Only a few need categories will have A's. "B" would be important, but not essential, and "C" would be desirable.

Ask yourself, "What are my basic needs?" This is the starting point for knowing how much house you really need. Ask yourself, "How do I wish to live?" This is *your* lifestyle. Depending upon location requirements you may be able to afford a house with more than your basic needs. Adding your desires (wants) to your needs helps you to better distinguish between potential houses. *Needs* are those things you cannot do without as opposed to *wants*, which you'd love to have but may have to put on hold for the time being. This is particularly true for first-time buyers. A house that meets both your needs and wants is the ultimate home, the golden ring on life's carousel.

As we go through life developing partnerships and/or families, our needs and wants change. Regardless of the type and location of a house, there must be a required number of bedrooms, bathrooms, and other rooms beyond a kitchen and living room that will meet your basic needs. As your interests change so will your home priorities. The appeal of a log cabin in the woods can create driving passions for some. Others will seek the white picket fence surrounding a neatly packed Cape Cod-style home within walking distance of a local village.

This chapter will help you to evaluate your needs. You will also learn about additional wants that would add to the quality of your home life. Having those needs and wants well defined puts you in a stronger position to evaluate potential houses. This will speed your decision process when you are ready to make your home purchase. You will also learn to determine your wants. Later, as you go along, you'll want to prioritize your needs and wants. Wants may well add to the quality of your life, but they are the "icing on the cake" and may have to be deferred. You may be pleasantly surprised, though, as you house shop, that some of your priority "want" items are already in place.

The homework outlined in this chapter can be ongoing throughout your home-buying career. Yes, home buying is like a career. It is best done after thorough study. The more study you perform, the smarter consumer you become. You'll find that our homework is far from onerous. It will be a valuable learning experience and fun at the same time.

It is often said that purchasing a house is the biggest investment anyone will ever make. That does not mean you have to do it only once. The more knowledge you have about home buying, the easier it will be for you to recognize economic opportunity to increase your home enjoyment. Home and building ownership can also be a great wealth builder. We'll talk about that as we go on.

No two buyers' needs are the same but some basics are common to all. People living in tents do not expect running water and sanitary facilities to be located within the living quarters. This could be fine for a camping trip but not for your basic home. City versus country will be discussed. The basic needs for living in New York City are far different from the needs of those who choose to live in rural areas. Needs are the fundamental elements necessary for you and your family to function. Water and nutritious food are examples of what we need to live. Ice cream is very desirable but not an essential food source. Unlike food, where some say, "If you like it, it must be bad for you," evaluating our home needs may be more like comparing whether we can live with vegetables and chicken or must we have caviar and gourmet food. You need to understand and be realistic about your basic needs. You must keep needs separate from nonessential wants. When comparing homes within your budget we will consider your desired wants. But, by fully understanding your basic needs, you will find a larger quantity of home choices that meet those needs.

Needs vary with life conditions. As your life changes, your needs will also change. Family size, lifestyle, quality of schools, job travel and commuting, first home versus upgrading and expansion or downsizing, care for dependent parents, and physical limitations or disabilities all play a part. As your financial resources improve, your view of basic needs may change. Sometimes when we move from a lower cost area to a higher cost area we need to reduce our wants to more basic needs to get a home we can afford. Starter-home needs are quite different from second- or third-home needs. Life partnerships and family-building can have dramatic effects on our home needs. Parents and relatives may become dependent upon us, thus increasing space or special facility requirements. Important core lifestyles or cultural and religious requirements will affect our basic needs. As we build a family, space requirements will change. Health issues are further examples of what can potentially create dramatic different housing needs. Certain illnesses require specialized housing needs. Older people have needs far different from those of young people. Accessibility requirements are not generally met in the typical home, such as wheelchair access to the living space and bathrooms. Some of these may require extensive renovation, but happily, some features are easy to change, such as when a lever is required for door handles versus a knob.

How many times have you heard "Write it down"? It's good advice. Writing helps thinking. As you proceed through this book and develop a full understanding of the home-buying process and identify your specific needs and wants, writing down information will be important. Writing your thoughts will help you to achieve clear thinking. Keep a notebook. Jot down *everything* you think you need and would like to have at this stage in your home buying. You can use the work sheets we have provided in this book. The more "homework" you do in preparation for your home purchase, the greater the probability that you will achieve your goals.

Try brainstorming. Brainstorming is a creative-thinking concept that will allow you to create many ideas without being judgmental. Make lists and lists of ideas about each topic we present. Initially, do not judge any of those ideas. After an intense session of brainstorming, put your notes aside. Allow your mind time to rest without thinking about any of the ideas. After a period of time, new ideas will pop into your head. Make note of these new ideas! Later, you can develop criteria to help you select which ideas are most important in your search for a home. This process is very powerful. Your notebook of random, spontaneous notations and ideas will become your sacred home-buying journal. While you are in your brainstorming phase, do a lot of reading to stimulate your thinking about needs and wants and how you want to prioritize them.

An Internet search under "home plans" can connect you with an almost unlimited number of web sites with house plans where you can review features and layout possibilities. Home-plan web sites will show you square feet and room sizes, whereas most used-home real estate sales information leaves out square feet and may not show room sizes.

Wants can make life easier and more fun. Having a garage may not be one of your basic needs, but when the garage comes with a house you like, it sure makes life easier. It also helps protect your car, which is probably your second most expensive possession. Garages are enjoyable, especially when you also have an electric garage door opener for rainy days. This is just one example of how wants can make life easier and more fun. Having a swimming pool or an entertainment room are additional wants that can make life more fun, but generally cannot be considered basic needs. Learning to differentiate needs and wants is not easy.

If you are currently renting, there may be features in your rental unit that you have taken for granted but are not basic needs. For example, a starter home may not have a provision for in-house laundry facilities. For some people, having a laundry room is an essential need and for others it will be a want. Physical fitness, hobbies, and leisure interests can have quite an effect on what features you need in a home. Gardening is a passion for some people that will determine the type and size of property needed. Storage for hobby equipment, including boats or vehicles on the property or in a garage, can be very important to others. Having a kitchen that allows entertaining large groups may be just what your family lifestyle needs.

Pets place certain demands on a home. A cat or dog can fit into just about any home situation where not prohibited by apartment owners or community associations. Larger animals are another story. Horses, for example, need housing and space and would be restricted from areas that do not have the proper zoning. Livestock, too, require land, specialty out buildings, and appropriate zoning. Having a boat moored in your backyard requires waterfront property. Spectacular views may require a hillside location. Some people dream of airport access for their private airplane. That may be pie-in-the-sky, but whatever your aspiration, living in a home that helps us live our life's dreams is a great goal that, within reason, can often be achieved.

Your stage of life is a determining factor in finding the perfect house. From just starting out, to settling down in that ideal retirement home, will have a large affect on how you define your needs. Today's ever-increasing size of new houses makes it difficult for anyone to obtain a smaller, new, starter, detached single-family house without having it built. This was not always so.

After World War II there was a rush to build homes for the returning servicemen and servicewomen. Large developments were created with essentially the same home framing structure, varied only by some appearance modifications. This allowed mass production techniques to be used. Levittown, on New York's Long Island and in Pennsylvania, come immediately to mind.

Thousands of houses sprang up on huge tracts of previously undeveloped or farm lands. Those houses were modest by today's standards. There were no "McMansions" in Levittown! These small houses, however, served a great purpose in meeting basic needs. Often, they started at only about 850 to 1,000 square feet (79 to 93 square meters) without a garage on a lot 50 feet wide by 100 feet deep (15 meters wide by 30 meters deep). Some styles had a stairway to an unfinished attic that would allow expansion. In areas where basements could be constructed the basement was an additional source of expansion. The main floor would have a living room, eat-in kitchen, bathroom, and two bedrooms. The front door would enter the living room and the side or rear door would enter the kitchen. Except for a manufactured home, this is about as basic as one can get. In this size house there may not be room for a dishwasher in the kitchen and there is probably no room for a laundry on the main floor. A laundry could be located in a basement, when one exists. Even after sixty years, these sturdy little post-war houses continue to serve today's starter-home needs.

Plans are readily available for constructing a starter home, providing a lot can be found. The cost of land, however, can be prohibitive, particularly when a desirable location is sought. Manufactured homes, condos, and older homes may be the necessary starting point. The value of real estate is so high that it can easily frighten people seeking their first house. The more homework you do to develop you basic needs and plan your search, the easier it will be to make a purchase with confidence. As with most things in life, getting that start is so important. Once you have achieved some momentum in the experience of home buying, moving up and getting closer to your dream home becomes easier.

Intermediate home buying, for those of you who already have purchased at least one house, provides valuable experience when evaluating your current needs and wants. Some people move every five to seven years while others spend almost a lifetime in one house. The more experience you get, the greater challenge you can undertake. Unless you are forced into an urgent house search, taking time to evaluate market conditions in desirable locations will help you determine what additional desires can be added to your home needs.

Downsizing can be a daunting challenge. Empty-nesters, whose children are grown, many times find that there is no longer a need for the larger house. They often consider moving to a smaller home for one important reason—to save money on taxes, insurance, and utilities. Relocation to an expensive market area is another major cause of seeking a smaller house. Here it is particularly difficult to redefine needs, because the sacrifice of some things becomes necessary. Start by making a list of what you can or may have to give up. If Aunt Betty's huge mahogany dining table won't fit in your new dining area, you may want to give it to a relative who's still living in the old family mansion, just to keep it in the family. If this is not feasible, temporary storage may provide a transition where you postpone actually giving up cherished possessions.

There has been a tremendous surge in the availability of self-storage facilities where you can have independent access to rented space for short or long periods of time. The space may be a garage-like box, or extremely spacious. Many storage facilities also offer interior storage rooms with heating and air conditioning available. Moving companies often rent storage space for short or long terms. Self-storage also comes in handy for first-time buyers who have too much "stuff" for their small starter houses.

Time urgencies can be the impetus we need to get moving. Time is a gift we all share equally. Knowing what you need and want and preparing financially for a home purchase requires greater effort when time is of the essence. Some of us appear to be lucky, like the person who always gets an upfront parking space in busy malls. You've seen him—he's the fellow who manages to grab the last empty seat in the airline waiting room during a blizzard. For most of us, though, better planning is what we count on to bring results from realistic expectations and confidence when making quick decisions. This book will prove useful, particularly when you are crunched for time. You will have your basic needs and wants defined. You will think through your financial condition. You will develop a knowledge base. You will develop a plan and strategy for obtaining your first or next house. The confidence that comes from this homework will help you to make quicker decisions.

When you are short of time, an immediate move can create great pressures and increase the risk of making mistakes. Sometimes, stepping back and renting is a necessary option to allow adequate planning time for a successful home purchase. The work sheets will be particularly useful, even for an emergency relocation. Any level of thinking about basic needs will help us keep calm during the often frustrating process of finding a desirable house. Short term or long term, having time to develop plans can be a luxury when not squandered. Using ideas presented in this book will allow you to continually refine your home-buying plan.

Goal Planning

Know where you are heading by setting goals. When you take a road trip to a particular destination, the destination is one part of a goal. The time it takes to get to the destination and the comfort level may also be part of the goal. Living in a dream house can be one of the most rewarding experiences in life. That is why we are learning about goals to improve our home-buying experience. Having not just a house, but living in a home that we love, is powerful and comforting. Our physical, emotional, and spiritual well being can be positively enhanced by the home we create. Size and

Figure 2–2: Cape Cod-Style Home

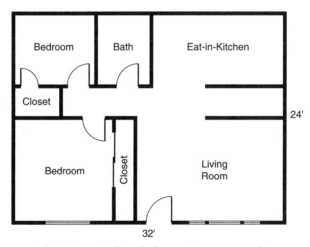

The Cape Cod-style house is very popular.

appointments are not the be-all-end-all for everyone. Where we are in our stage of life will affect our perception of perfection. So unless we are going to rely on luck, let's plan to achieve that goal. It's the quality of life that we are learning how to achieve. We may need to make many turns on the highway of our home-buying experiences to get to our destination. Let's also try to enjoy the journey, so we can find happiness at each stage of home ownership.

Above and beyond the sheer enjoyment of the quality of life a dream house can provide is the advantage of wealth-building through home ownership. Householders can accrue wealth through our current tax system, which encourages home ownership with its significant tax savings. When market value increases we gain even more wealth. As with any market-driven system it is also possible that house values can decline, so careful financial analysis, discussed in Chapter 3, is very important. Wealth-building is an important goal for many reasons. It is not merely accumulation of money for a flamboyant lifestyle. It is part of our long-range plan for our children's college education. It is our safety cushion in case of a fall. Retirement or work sabbaticals without accumulated wealth could stretch our finances to the breaking point. Medical emergencies without accumulated wealth could wipe us out. Setting our near-term and long-term goals helps us to put into perspective the home-buying process while maintaining a balance in our life.

Quality of life has many interpretations. For some, it's luxurious surroundings or mere acquisition. For others it's the wherewithal to travel. For still others it has no monetary connotations—it's strictly emotional. For these people, quality of life means simple enjoyments like:

Waking up to a sunrise view;
Having some outdoor space;
Looking out to a horizon;
Having space, woods, farmland;
Being close to our place of worship;
Having walking paths nearby;
Looking out on water;
Looking out over hillsides;
Having a swimming pool;
Having a gym;
And so on.

For a Harley Davidson motorcycle rider it may be the Harley slogan: "Live to Ride and Ride to Live."

Living, on or off a Harley, can be uncertain. Having children, medical emergencies, divorce, caring for an aging parent—all bring change in our lives and our quality of life. Unfortunately, we cannot predict many of life's changes but we'll be in a better position if we have done some advance preparation. Thinking about our life and any potential changes may influence our home-buying needs. Factor into all of this the possibility of relocation, because relocation can either open up great opportunities or be a constraint. The career of a working partner or spouse can be a constraint. The happiness and welfare of children in high school can provide a serious challenge when trying to relocate.

Family

One constant, perhaps, in our quality-of-life goal is family, but family is no longer just the happy TV father who always knew best, the self-effacing mommy, and the two adorable children. That ideal family would be the prime reason for buying a single-family home, preferably with a yard. How your real family is composed—probably both daddy and mommy work and maybe there are three or four children—will determine the type and size of the house to meet today's family needs. The size of the yard will or will not allow for expansion or adding such luxuries as a swimming pool.

Family today can mean single, married, partnered, or just sharing quarters with a housemate. Single life affords the greatest latitude for independent decisions. Unless a single person is buying a co-op in the city where only a single bedroom or efficiency can be afforded—and even then with severe belt-tightening—a two-bedroom, eat-in kitchen and living room would meet the very basic home requirement. Those post-World War II Levittown-style

Cape Cods or ranchers just fit this minimum size. Today's new houses are seldom small enough for starter homes with expansion capabilities. Manufactured houses can be obtained in small sizes and, of course, mobile homes can be even smaller.

Married couples must consider family planning to develop their home needs. Joint ownership requires agreement, at least in principle. Not all married couples have joint ownership for a variety of reasons, but they often have children. Children are delightful, but they can be demanding. Babies may be just fine sleeping in the parents' bedroom but you will quickly need to set up a separate room, if only to give the sleeping partner some peace. Many families have one room for the girls and a separate room for the boys. As the family grows, bathrooms or the lack thereof, can create potential conflict. Obviously, one bathroom is essential. A second may be needed. As financial strength grows, a third bathroom may become desirable. Any more than that number are luxuries.

Married people with children often have still-living parents as well—parents who, if they move in with you, create special needs that can seriously impact on quality of life for everyone in the family. Is the house large enough to accommodate additional people? Will more bathrooms be needed? Will a separate kitchen be important? Is there room for personal space—an extra living room or den? What about storage? It will be important to also to consider the need for barrier-free living with limited or no stairs. The mother-daughter house style with separate living space within the same house can be a real plus. This can be something to plan for when an addition appears to be needed. If that's the case, be sure the property is large enough for such an addition. In other parts of this book we discuss zoning and building requirements to think about when considering an addition. Finally, the layout of the house will affect the design of any addition. Using an architect to create concepts will be worth the monetary outlay.

Partnerships may or may not involve children, but in all other respects, partners share a home life like married couples. Legal ownership may vary so decision making may be more one-sided. Partnerships of any kind may bring the need for individual space within the home adding a room requirement for that space. Often this might be a bedroom used as a den or office. A workshop or sewing room might also double as individual space.

Housemates may be home-ownership partners or tenants, so here, too, the decision process will be affected by the ownership arrangement. Will you need separate bedrooms for each housemate? Will you need separate bathrooms? Will there need to be another personal room for each housemate, such as a living room or den? The mother-daughter home is sort of a housemate arrangement where there may be a separate kitchen and entrances. Basements might be used for living space, but unless they have windows suitable for fire exits, this is not the safest condition for bedrooms.

Ethnic, Religious, and Cultural Importance

Ethnic, religious, and cultural affiliations can be important considerations in finding the right house. Early waves of immigration to America had strong religious and ethnic influence on neighborhood settlement, and in many neighborhoods, that group solidarity is still very strong. Being with people of like background may still be a priority and this need could exceed all other needs for some people. People who need close association with others in their religious or ethnic group will have significant limitations on where they can live. This will affect the availability of houses to select from.

On the other hand, the United States has historically been the "melting pot" that welcomed immigrants and encouraged them to become part of mainstream America. Many people today actively seek out areas where they can raise their children in a climate of diversity. For these people, living in a neighborhood where there are cultural and religious differences would be a priority.

Community involvement is a strong need for some people, so the aspects of the community where they will seek involvement become important considerations.

Are there hospitals, libraries, and museums that depend on volunteer workers? Are there Boy Scouts, Girl Scouts, or other youth groups that need adult volunteers? The list could go on ad infinitum, but for newcomers who want to be involved it is worth researching. Clubs and service organizations may also need to be considered. Some organizations have regular meetings where attendance is mandatory. Proximity may be important.

Physical Limitations

Physical limitations—your own or those of anyone in the family—must be taken into consideration. Many of us experience some form of physical limitation. It's important to consider these limitations when buying a new home. Wheelchair dependency is one very obvious example.

The inability to climb stairs is another obvious limitation for certain individuals. When this is the case, we want to consider ranch-style houses that have no basements and allow easy access to the main floor. When it is necessary to live in a house that has stairs, there are devices available that eliminate the need to climb those stairs. An expensive option would be an elevator, but there are far less-costly chairlifts that can be attached to the side of the stairs.

For people with limitations, accessibility requirements can range from the need for wheelchair access, not only into the house, but also throughout the interior. This requirement would necessitate modifications to most existing homes—like widening doorways and locating light switches or controls within the reach of a seated person. The entire home may not need to meet the accessibility requirements, but at least certain essential areas of the home would have to accommodate specific accessibility needs. Bathrooms, the main living space, and entry/exit provisions are most critical.

Does anyone in the family have asthma or any other environmental sensitivity that could include allergies to materials that may be within the house or on the property adjacent to the home? Houses that have resident pets may require special cleaning and removal of absorbent materials. Certain seasonal allergies, such as those that come from pollen, may affect your choice of the area where you wish to live. People particularly vulnerable to certain insect bites will need to be careful about the area where their otherwise perfect dream house is situated.

Figure 2–3: Waterfront Sunset

Do you want to live near an ocean or lake?

Lifestyle

Beyond all of these specific areas of concern is "How do I want to live?" This opens broad vistas—thinking about our desired lifestyle will not only influence the type of house we want but also specific locations. Our own lifestyle interests often change over time. Spending a little effort at the start to understand your current and anticipated interest will help you plan your ideal home and location.

Are you a country mouse or a city mouse? An urban cowboy or a countrified city dweller? City life with its hustle and bustle of activity can be very exhilarating. Closeness to transportation, shopping, theater and a wide variety of social activity is at your fingertips in a city. If the pace of the city is a little faster than you'd like, there are many growing communities away from large cities that have active downtown areas close to where you can have the privacy of a yard. At the other end of the spectrum there is country living with wide, open spaces or heavily treed areas that offer the most privacy and quiet.

City mice, country mice, or mice in suburbia all want downtime at home to unwind from the workaday world. Downtime duration depends on commuting time. How long will it take you to get to and from your job? A ten-minute drive to your local downtown would be ideal. An hour or two on a train or bus, however, could be daunting no matter how much you love your work. On the other hand, that hour or two could be part of your downtime. Lots of commuters relish that time to read, play cards, chat, or just snooze their way to and fro. It's something you have to think seriously about or you're not going to be a happy camper.

Another mental exercise is realizing whether you are a morning person or a night person. Do you need unbroken eastern exposure to awaken with the sun? Is a lot of sky exposure important to your well being? If that's the case, you may well be a country mouse. If you couldn't care less about morning sun but would rather bask in the glare of neon, you are, no doubt, a city mouse. If you are in between, take suburbia.

What about sports? Spectator or participant? Are you active in sports? Do you need to live where there are regular basketball teams or soccer teams that you can join? How close to the sport activity of your choice do you wish to live? Are you an avid fan? How close do you wish to live to your team's home field? Is it worth a lengthy trip to cheer the home team on? Do you yearn to have a basketball court or tennis court on your own property? Is jogging one of your activities that necessitate closeness to a track or will you be happy with safe streets to run on? Fishing, hunting, boating, skiing, and other sports that require special locations will influence where you live and, not incidentally, how much space you require for storage of special sports equipment.

What about entertainment? Do you attend opera or go to the theater on a regular basis? Is it important that you be close? Restaurants, gyms, clubs, theater, and so on offer attractions that vary in importance. How important is it to you that you are close to certain entertainment activities? Make a list of your entertainment priorities and be sure to evaluate each potential location for how best these needs are met.

How important is dedicated space for hobbies? Model aircraft-building may not need much in specialized house requirements, but it would be nice to have a workroom where you can leave in-progress projects on a worktable rather than have to clear off a temporary work space on the kitchen table before tomorrow's breakfast. Antique auto restoration could require an extra-large garage and special electrical needs. Gardening is a hobby that can even enhance the quality of food we enjoy. For city dwellers there are gardening devices that can work on small apartment decks, but you can grow herbs in pots on a windowsill, anywhere. Having beautiful flowers and shrubbery may require a larger property size and desirable soil conditions.

Work

And then there is work. Work is the means by which we earn money to live. Work pays the bills. It may hold high priority in controlling your life, but it is not your entire life. It's a big part of that life though, and depending on the type of work you are now doing or might do in the future, work seriously determines where you live and what kind of home best suits you. Getting to work could be a nightmare or a pleasant journey. People who change jobs more frequently may well end up as unhappy campers. The home place that may be ideal for your present job may not work well for your next job. When both partners work it becomes even more complex. Compromising to achieve a reasonable commute is probably needed.

There is hope. Perhaps you can work from home. Zero commuting time is available for those of us who have a home office. Having a quiet space in your own home for a full-time or part-time office can be very good. But when you sleep, eat, entertain, and work at home you may become totally overwhelmed by living in a 24-hour office. It can take enormous discipline to balance one's life with a home office. That being said, a home office may be particularly helpful when starting a new business or when telecommuting with a distant office. Local zoning can be an issue that restricts certain home-office activities. Condo living may have restrictions. Check out local ordinances and any community association regulations.

Perhaps you'd like to live on a farm and enjoy the "earthy" life. It isn't quite that easy. Farm living is like having a home office with the additional burdens of the need for maintaining specialized out buildings and a large property area. Zoning is always important. A well for water and septic systems for sewage treatment will probably be needed. Farm life is not for everyone. It is hard work. Like living the life of a fisherman, Mother Nature controls many of the factors that determine success. Sometimes people who own farm property choose not to work the land and lease their property to other farmers who may want to get back to that same land. This provides both the satisfaction of farm life and the tax advantage. Also, there is some income from the land rental. Another approach is to acquire a home adjacent to a farm where you have the open space nearby. Always consider, though, what may happen if the farm is sold and becomes developed. Living adjacent to Green Acres can provide similar benefits to living adjacent to a farm but with greater confidence that the property will never be developed. **Green Acres** are lands designated by law to be maintained free of development in perpetuity to preserve diminishing open space.

Transportation

If you have to travel to work, is getting there half the fun? When we discussed commuting a few pages back, we talked about how people change jobs more frequently these days. It becomes important to understand the kinds of transportation that you might like to have available in your new home location.

Of course, you can always take to the road. One of the great strengths about living in the United States is our highway system. There are major highways going north and south, and east and west. There are toll roads and toll bridges that will affect the cost of travel. Using these highways requires an automobile, motorcycle, or truck. Of course, not everyone who buys a house has a vehicle for every commuter in that house. Getting an understanding of the highway traffic patterns in the areas where you wish to live is very important. In areas near busy commercial centers, slowdowns and backups at bridges or tunnels can be infuriating, but are a fact of life. You may have to build such tie-ups into your commuting schedule. If bicycles were allowed on highways, commuting would be a lot easier and faster at peak rush-hour times. Forty thousand Frenchmen can't be wrong—Parisians who still go everywhere on two wheels.

Public transport may be your best option. Buses operate in many communities and of course, use highways. This makes them subject to the same traffic delays as automobiles, but at least you're not the one steaming behind the wheel. There is another plus when commuter parking lots are available for bus riders. If you have to bus into an inner city, you can park your car and leave the hard part to the bus driver. Trains are more limited in where they operate but generally are very clean and dependable. Subways are a special form of train transport available in certain cities and, again, generally run on time. Taxicabs operate almost everywhere and are convenient for short transportation needs.

School

One of the strongest and highest priority factors in establishing the location of the family home is the quality of its school district. Parents want the best possible education for their children in elementary, middle, and high schools and are often willing to forego their less important wants to meet this need. It may be desirable that educational facilities for family members are nearby. Knowing the family's educational requirements, and what facilities are conveniently available in areas where we wish to live, is very important.

Grade-school education may be at a public school, a parochial school, or a private school. Considering the children's needs during the time you anticipate living at your next home is an important factor in your location decision. Unless you are sending your children to a boarding school, this may be one of your highest priorities in determining preferred locations. Seldom do you have a large area to choose from when seeking a particular school system. Transportation may be another limiting factor. Does the school district provide school bus service or must you escort the kids to and from school? This can present problems when both parents are working. The quality of public education is vital to most parents. Testing is becoming more popular throughout the country. Test results may help influence our desired locations. There are disputes about the quality of the testing, though, so you'll want to learn as much as possible about various school districts. You can learn the relative performance of a district by contacting your state's department of education. They can tell you not only the district's academic standing but also how finances are administered by the local board of education. Information is plentiful and available from local communities and state agencies.

Also consider your children's out-of-school activities. Are parks and playgrounds nearby? What kinds of programs do they offer for children alone or with other family members? Are there museums? What programs do they offer? Does the town or county have a better-than-adequate library system? Positive answers to all of these questions work together to create cultural advantages. Life without them can be restrictive.

When college is desired for one of the working adults in the home, convenient location may be particularly important. Today, there are learning programs that may have only limited classroom requirements. What courses of study are you considering and what schools offer those programs? Does your employer participate in graduate education with particular colleges or universities? Is a community college part of your picture? Is there a college nearby?

Special education requirements may also be part of the picture. When a physical limitation or a learning disability requires special education programs for one of your household members, some school districts are better equipped than others to handle your specific needs. Search them out and put that information into the equation of your home location needs.

Medical

We have seen earlier that physical limitations must be considered for older people; medical needs must also be considered. Regular, periodic medical tests and treatment of anyone in the family should cause you to look closer for sources where those needs can be satisfied. What are your special requirements? Where can you get the needed assistance? How important is it to be close to the source to satisfy those needs? Proximity to diagnostic and/or treatment centers may well determine where you choose to live.

Storage Requirements

Having taken care of human needs, let's take a look at how other factors can dictate which house you buy. What do you need to store in your new home? Can it be boxed? Will humidity control be important? Perhaps the storage is only a temporary condition. People downsizing may need off-site storage. Certain hobbies generate significant storage requirements and, depending upon your home-purchasing power, off-site storage may be necessary. Perhaps it's a motorcycle or recreation vehicle that you wish to store in a sheltered environment when you cannot get a house with a garage.

Home storage can be in a garage, attic, or basement. How much you have to store and how important it is that stored items are not exposed to water or wide-ranging temperatures will affect the amount of livable space that can be assigned to storage. Not all homes have garages with extra space, usable attic space, or usable basement space. Something as simple as buying or building a prefabricated shed may solve a storage problem. A shed can certainly serve as storage space for some recreation vehicles and garden equipment.

If your storage needs are greater than any at-home possibility, consider the off-site self-storage facilities we discussed earlier. They may be the answer. Costs are generally manageable. If this is not a feasible solution, you may need to decide what you can live without. You may have to be ruthless.

Figure 2–4: Expanded Estate

You should think about whether you will need to expand the size of your home in the future when making a purchase decision.

Expansion Requirements

When you think you've found the perfect house in the perfect location, ask yourself, "Can this be forever? Will this perfect house still be perfect later on?" Anticipating the future is far from an exact science, but you can try. If this is your first home with a growing family, you may want to try to project what your family needs may be as the children grow. Does the house lend itself to expansion? If you are a downsizing empty-nester, be careful of how far down you want to or should go. The extent to which your needs may expand or diminish will affect your choice.

A growing family can offer exciting challenges in creative space utilization. Will you need bedrooms large enough for two children to share, or will more bedrooms be required in the fore-seeable future? The number of bedrooms is one of the most basic home-size determining factors. Expanding leisure activities and the equipment they require may be a deciding factor. Skiing in the winter, boating in the summer, biking, recreation vehicles, starting a home business, and other expanding life interests all create the demand for space. Sometimes the space requirements are quite specific. A growing woodworking hobby not only creates demands for space, but also for electrical power. If you seem to be running out of space, you can always move. But if you live in a house you love, in a place you love, yet feel that the walls may be closing in, expansion may be your only option.

My Home Improvement Skills

How much of the house expansion are you willing or qualified to undertake? Just as first-time buyers are admonished to "beware the handyperson special," expanders and renovators must determine whether they are up to the job. Ask yourself, "How much of a fixer-upper am I? Do I have the skills and interest to tackle home-improvement projects or even a small expansion project? Will I have the interest to learn and become proficient at these skills?" These are important questions for the individual considering purchasing a "handyperson special" or a home with great expansion qualities. If your honest answers are "no," pass it by. Even one "no" is enough. If you can honestly and confidently answer "yes!" then go for it.

Today's handyperson has Home Depot®, Lowe's®, and a host of other home-improvement centers, all ready to become your new best friend. Unlike a few years ago, today there are tremendous resources available to the handyperson. We've even heard of dating opportunities leading to marriages from chance encounters in Home Depot®, resulting from the home do-it-yourself passion in both women and men. There are many books and workshops that can teach almost anyone with the interest and some basic skills. In the state of New Jersey, home owners can design their own homes and do all of the work to obtain the necessary building permits, providing they can demonstrate to the local construction officials that they have the necessary basic skills and that the design conforms to applicable building codes.

Not everyone who can cut lumber and frame can do electrical wiring and plumbing, so it may be necessary to subcontract certain skills. By law in most places electrical work must be contracted out to a licensed electrician. But a great deal of savings (and personal satisfaction) can be realized from doing much of your own work. Proceed carefully, because getting a professional craftsperson to correct your mistakes may cost more than having the professional do the work in the first place.

If you feel you are all thumbs and have no home repair or servicing skills, don't even try to do it yourself. Learn to find, hire, and manage honest workers. But be wary. Just because someone has a truck with a sign does not mean he is right for your job. If you insist on buying that charming historic home with age wrinkles and maintenance needs, then be prepared to get good help. Check out your local consumer affairs office to see if there have been complaints against the contractor you have in mind. Ask for references. He may not refer you to an irate client, but you can still learn a lot by talking with a satisfied client. Maybe not everything was flawless. Perhaps there were long delays. Talk with the client's neighbors. Find out all you can before you sign a contract. In any case, it's money you'll be spending and not your precious free time.

Remodel Versus Moving

When it's time for something newer or for expansion, one question becomes "Do I remodel or just move?" If it is not necessary to find a new location, let's first explore other aspects of remodeling as an option. You already know the strengths and weaknesses of your existing house. You have done a study to determine your needs and desires. Can your neighborhood location market a higher-value house? If expanded space is necessary, will that be possible within the footprint of your existing house or will you need to use more of your property area? If more property area is needed, will the local zoning allow such expansion? Once you have determined that your investment in the expanded/remodeled house will obtain at least equal market value and you have no zoning problems, you are ready to consider expansion. There is an exception to the market-value criteria. That is when it's not financially possible for you to buy a new house that will meet your needs, but when you do have sufficient resources for expansion.

If we seem to have been putting you through your paces, the exercise should prove to be worth the effort because as it is said, "Home is where the heart is."

Home-Buyer's Checklist

- Have I fully clarified needs versus wants in terms of space and house features?

- Have I identified family and lifestyle considerations, including physical limitations and medical needs?

- Are my goals for work, transportation, and education realistic?

- Have I brainstormed realistically with other family members about location needs?

- Am I honest in assessing my home-improvement skills that may be needed in expansion and/or remodeling?

Work Sheets

Location	Needs	Wants
Commute	_____	_____
Schools	_____	_____
Medical	_____	_____
Ethnic/Religious	_____	_____
Environmental	_____	_____
Community	_____	_____

Housing/Property	Needs	Wants
# of people	_____	_____
# of Bedrooms	_____	_____
# of Kitchens	_____	_____
Repair/Remodeling	_____	_____
Accessibility	_____	_____
Expansion potential	_____	_____
Storage	_____	_____
Property	_____	_____

Appendix: Home-Buying Plan Notebook with Tabs

Here's an idea to help you organize your planning and home-buying record keeping. Few people have extra office space to organize and store the vast amount of information you will accumulate. Some people are happy with a large box and a bunch of file folders. We think we have a better idea. Our chapters have been organized to help you evaluate choices. We have provided work sheets and checklists that will help you organize your information and make decisions. We suggest you consider loose-leaf books to organize this information. Within the loose-leaf book, use tabs such as the Ready Index® Reference Dividers from Avery where you can organize the contents into 5, 8, 10, 15, or 31 sections. Even if you do not have a computer to label the table-of-contents page you can write your section headings. If you have subheadings, then you can insert another set of tabs. You might have a loose-leaf book where the basic information is organized into 8 sections, each of which has a 31-section set of tabs for detailed information about that particular section. When you consider different homes you may want a home-search section for up to 8 communities, with tabs 1–15 or 1–31 to include information about each particular home within that community. You can be very creative by using loose-leaf books with multiple tabbed sections. All of your supplies can be obtained at an office supply store. Look over the different kinds of loose-leaf book information holders, as well as business card holders.

To organize your loose-leaf books and additional supplies we suggest you consider obtaining one or more extra-large zip-top tote bags, such as you can get from Lands End® or L.L. Bean®. These make a great portable office file to hold loose-leaf books, along with a camera, a three-hole punch, and any other equipment you may want to assist you with your home-buying project.

Devote one loose-leaf book to overall management of your project with sections such as: calendar; note pages; contact lists; needs analysis; mortgage information, maps and community information. As your search expands you will want another book for the houses you are considering and eventually you will want a book just for the house on which you are making an offer. It's easy to add sections. Remember that this is to help you organize your information, so have fun using loose-leaf books.

Chapter 3

Can I Afford to Buy a Home?

*B*efore you get too serious about house hunting, you need to address the question of how much you can afford to pay for a home. What exactly does it mean to say you can "afford" a home? To answer that question, you have to be specific about what you want and need. The fact is that there probably is a house for sale in your area that anyone with reasonable credit and a steady income could buy. The problem is that almost no one would want to own that home. It may be in very poor condition, may be located in a rough or run-down neighborhood, or may have some type of stigma attached (e.g., site of a notorious murder). When I worked as a housing economist at Texas A&M University, I compiled a housing affordability indicator for the state of Texas. I was often asked by news reporters to estimate how many families could afford a home, but no objective answer could be given to such a question. The real answer is almost all of the families. But that answer is totally meaningless since many would not want the house they could afford.

So, to get back to our question: Can *you* afford a home? First, you need an idea of what it will cost to buy an acceptable home. There are actually two parts to that question. Unless you are a millionaire (in which case, you probably would not be reading this book), you won't be paying cash for your home. That means you will be shopping for financing as well as for a home. The price of the house and the terms of the loan together determine the cost of the home. Later, we will see how the two interact.

Although you can get loans for 100 percent of the price of a home (especially if you are a military veteran), you will need some cash for the purchase. The more cash you can invest, the easier it will be to get a loan and the less burdensome will be your monthly payment. We will look at how those two factors interrelate in this chapter. First, let's look at the constraints that determine what you can afford.

What It Means to Be Able to Afford a Home

The three basic factors in your ability to afford a home are (1) the price of the home, (2) how much cash will be required, and (3) the monthly payment on the loan. As you may suspect, the three are linked together so that when one factor changes, so do the other two. Each is limited by your personal and financial situation and governed by conditions in the market. Nevertheless, it is possible, with a little market information, to make estimates of these factors sufficient to give you a "go/no go" indication for your future as a home owner.

The first factor is the cost of the home. As we said before, there probably is a home you could easily afford, but it might not suit your needs. You will need to specify your needs to the point that you can identify homes that meet those needs. Then you can find asking prices for similar houses that are on the market. That will give you a threshold amount for entering the market. In some cases, sellers will be amenable to concessions, such as paying some or all of your costs associated with getting a loan. Such concessions are in lieu of a lower price, but they may be helpful in fitting the financing to your situation.

The second factor is the amount of cash you can raise and afford to invest in the purchase. Despite how good an investment the home purchase turns out to be, you will not be able to access the cash you invest until you sell the house. This is likely to be at least several years, or you probably would not be thinking of buying a home. This is not like putting cash into a bank account; it is more like putting it into a certificate of deposit with a hefty penalty for early withdrawal. It is true that you may be able to borrow on your **equity** through a **home equity loan**, but you probably will not be able to borrow an amount equal to the entire equity. Therefore, the amount of money you can raise and afford to salt away for as long as you own the home, forms the upper bound of your down-payment investment. The lower bound is the minimum that the lender requires. This depends on the type of loan you get, but you might use three percent as a starting estimate. The more you invest in cash, the less your mortgage loan will cost.

The last part of the affordability picture is the **mortgage loan**. Lenders have a maximum amount they will lend on a home, based on its **market value**. In most cases, they require some type of **mortgage insurance** or guarantee to lend more than 80 percent of value on an owner-occupied home. This mortgage insurance is not an exotic thing: it is, in fact, used by the overwhelming majority of first-timers as well as by many upgraders and relocatees. Insurance is offered by private companies (i.e., **private mortgage insurance**) and the federal government (i.e., FHA insurance). The federal **Department of Veterans Affairs (VA)** offers home-loan guarantees (**VA loans**) as a benefit to qualified military veterans. All these insurance programs have the effect of reducing the amount of cash down payment you need to finance the purchase. Your ability to use mortgage insurance will depend to a great extent on your credit rating. If you fall into the sub-prime risk category, you will not be able to get a loan without a substantial down payment.

In addition to the limit imposed by the **loan-to-value ratio (LTV)** criterion, the lender will also qualify you for a specific amount of loan. The amount of loan you qualify for depends on the interest rate on the loan, estimates of the cost of taxes and insurance, your current income, and how much debt you already carry. The lender will calculate the maximum monthly payment you can "afford" based on a specific percentage of your income. Another estimate is made based on the income you have left over after you meet existing debt obligations. The smaller of the two becomes the maximum loan payment allowed. Part of that payment will go to maintain an account for paying annual property taxes, premiums on hazard insurance, and mortgage insurance premiums. The rest is devoted to paying the interest and principal on the mortgage loan. The lower the interest rate, the more loan you can get for the same monthly payment. This loan amount becomes a guideline to how much the lender will loan you. The difference between the loan amount and the cost of the house is the amount of cash down payment you must supply.

The three factors are highly interrelated. If you cannot make the numbers fit, you must find a cheaper home, come up with more cash, or find a loan with a lower interest rate. For planning purposes, you can calculate the largest loan you think you can get and the highest down payment you think you can arrange, and that will determine the most expensive house you can obtain. You might also do another estimate based on the amounts you feel comfortable borrowing and investing. That will become your baseline number. From there, you will see if any homes in that price range are acceptable.

What the Market Has to Offer

Okay, let's say you have a good idea of what you need in a house and a list of locations that would be acceptable. You want to know if you can afford to buy the home you want. You need to do two things: find out what homes are on the market and what the sellers are asking for them. Fortunately, there are several ways you can get this information.

The traditional ways to search the market are to peruse the classified ads in the newspaper and to contact a real estate agent. These options are still available, while the Internet has added new outlets for market information. The trade-off in selecting a method involves time and effort versus precision. The Internet offers speed and convenience and the total absence of any implied or specified obligation. The information, however, may not be the most reliable or current. For an initial, ballpark estimate of what homes costs, the more convenient sources probably will do nicely. On the other hand, if you are not a do-it-yourself type of person and would like someone to help direct your search, by all means contact a real estate agent. Unless you sign a contract with an agent, you have no legal obligation to stick with that agent, no matter how much market information she provides. If the agent is especially helpful and you like her, you probably will use her to make your eventual purchase.

Many **real estate agents** maintain Web sites that list homes for sale through the **multiple listing service (MLS)**. This refers to a cooperative arrangement among local real estate agents whereby **listings** (i.e., a real estate term for homes that an agent has contracted to sell) are pooled and any member of the multiple listing service can earn a commission by presenting a willing and able buyer for one of the homes. The MLS usually represents a little over half of all the homes on the market, and it has most of the more broadly appealing homes. Because the listings are pooled, the MLS represents a centralized database of information that allows members to conduct intelligent searches for their clients. It also allows you to look at what is on the market through the web sites of member agents. Don't expect to find the detailed information you would find at the broker's office, but it should be sufficient to provide a first screening of the market. The **National Association of Realtors**® also has a site that allows searches in your locality at *www.realtor.com*. This site operates very much like the local sites. In many markets, there are web sites that cover homes that are offered without an MLS-member agent. These so-called **For Sale by Owner** or **FSBO** homes are listed on the sites by the owners.

MLS and FSBO sites might not be very specific about the exact location of the home; usually there is no address listed. You may be able to get the city or county and possibly the name of a subdivision.

If you don't have access to the Internet, you can find similar data in newspaper classified ads. The newspaper probably will have almost all the FSBOs and a sampling of agent listings. The Sunday paper will be especially rich with such ads. The ads will give asking prices and possibly the address of the home (more so for FSBOs than agent listings).

A visit to a local real estate agent is another good way to gather information. You will want to explain to the agent that you are looking for very preliminary data so that you can decide whether you can afford a home. Be warned that some agents will try to influence your decision right away. On the other hand, some agents may not be interested in working with you until you are more serious about buying. If you are fortunate, you will find an agent who will be of great assistance in your search of the market. That agent may even be willing to work up an estimate of what your cash investment and monthly payment would be if you were to buy a specific home. This assistance can be invaluable as long as you understand what the agent is doing. Such a preliminary session is a good way to find an agent for when you begin a more detailed home search.

Keep in mind that with all these sources, the price indicator is the amount that the seller is asking for the home. Only in the most active markets do buyers pay the **asking price**. In most cases, the seller has boosted the price a bit in anticipation of negotiating with the buyer. You might take these offering prices as a "worst-case scenario" while hoping to get a better deal when you seriously enter the market.

Getting the Money Together

After perusing the market, you now have some idea of how much you will have to gather to buy a home. To determine whether you can afford to buy the home you want, you have to figure out if you can afford the mortgage loan it will require. The first step is to identify possible sources of cash. The more cash you can put together, the more affordable will be the loan.

Before we get into this subject, let's clarify one point. Is it possible to buy a home if you have no cash? You may have seen references to "no money down" deals, as well as promotions that promise the acquisition of wonderful homes with no cash investment. In today's market, you actually may find financing that will cover 100 percent of the sales price. If not, you may be able to find a seller who is willing to lend you the down payment. Even in these cases, however, it is rarely possible to buy with absolutely no cash investment. You will probably have to pay some closing costs, or be required to prepay some expenses such as the first year's insurance premium. The point is that there is cost involved in avoiding a down payment. The loan, and consequently the monthly payment, will be larger, and that may make it harder for you to qualify for the loan. The premium you pay for mortgage insurance may be larger, and your loan may have a higher interest rate. If the seller is providing some of the financing, it may be in lieu of a price reduction that you would get with no special financing. Getting sellers to consider such deals requires a market that favors buyers to some extent, and that usually means price concessions. You may determine that financing help is more valuable than a lower price, and you may be right. Just realize that there is a cost to going into the purchase with little or no cash.

At this point, you should make an estimate of your **net worth**. Basically, that is the sum of everything you own of value minus the amount that you owe. You will have to do this exercise when you go to apply for a loan. Do it beforehand to size up your financial position and to locate whatever resources you may bring to bear on the purchase.

Your net worth is an accounting of your wealth, not your income (that will come later). It is money, near-money, and whatever you have that might be turned into money. Include the following types of wealth:

- Any cash you have on hand

- The amount you have in bank accounts (checking and savings)

- Other bank accounts, such as certificates of deposit (CDs), minus any penalties imposed for early withdrawal of principal

- Any money market accounts at brokerage houses or mutual funds

- Money owed to you by those who you reasonably expect to pay you back

- The current market value of any securities you own: stocks, bonds, mutual funds

- The value of any individual retirement accounts (IRAs) that allow you to withdraw funds, penalty free, if used to buy a home

- The market value of anything that could be sold to raise cash—automobiles, boats, furniture, collectibles. Do not include clothes and personal items that would command little as resales.

- The market value of any real estate you already own.
- The value of any business that you own.

Deduct from these amounts the outstanding principal of any loans you currently have open and the current balance on credit cards and lines of credit.

For purposes of looking for sources of down-payment cash, evaluate each of the above potential sources in terms of your willingness and the advisability of selling the asset. If you decide you can part with any of these assets, figure in the cost associated with selling. For example, selling real estate usually requires paying a sales commission to a broker.

You do not need to look solely to your own resources for a down payment. You may have relatives who wish to encourage your purchase of a home or just want to help you get started financially. They may be willing to contribute or lend you money or may agree to cosign the loan (more helpful if you have poor credit or haven't established a credit rating). Before you chalk up any of these sources, check with a mortgage broker to see if any would not be allowed for the type of financing you think will be most likely for your situation. Lenders do care about where you get your down-payment cash. If your down payment comes entirely from a gift, the lender may be concerned that you don't have enough of your own money in the home. The more you have to lose, the more you will be encouraged to continue making payments when your budget gets squeezed. If you are borrowing part of the down payment, that represents another debt obligation that should be reflected on your loan application. Lenders should be very forthcoming with any such hesitations, and you should know about them before proceeding.

If you are a first-time home buyer or if you are willing to buy a home in a designated neighborhood, you may be able to get a grant for the down payment. Local and state governments have programs to assist people in buying a home. You will have to buy a home within the area where the program is targeted, and there may be other qualifications, such as a limit on the income you can have to participate. You can find out about these programs in two ways. You might simply run an Internet search on "down-payment assistance" and see if there is a program in your area. Or you can contact an authorized housing or credit counseling agency in your area (see Chapter 1 for a link to HUD's list of approved agencies).

There are a number of private, not-for-profit organizations that provide down-payment grants. One of the largest is the Nehemiah Down Payment Assistance Program at *www. getdownpayment.com*, which contributes up to six percent of the purchase price for home buyers who fit its qualifications (you do not have to be a first-time buyer). Other nonprofits operate programs whereby home sellers contribute to the down payment through the offices of the organization. The effect is tantamount to a reduction in price without the effects such a reduction would have on the loan amount. In all these cases, be sure to be aboveboard with the lender and get advance indications that these arrangements will be acceptable.

If you are selling a home while in the process of buying a new one, you may have proceeds from the sale to apply to the purchase. Find out the approximate market value of your home. You may visit some of the home price web sites mentioned in Chapter 1 (*www.zillow.com* may have specific data on your home) or consult with a real estate agent to have a comparable market analysis done. The agent should be willing to do this analysis free of charge with the implied obligation that you will use the agency's services when you are ready to sell.

Once you have an estimate of your home's value, you can use that to indicate what you would get when you sell it. From that amount, deduct 8–10 percent for selling costs. Find out from your mortgage lender how much you owe on the mortgage loan (don't forget to include any home equity or second mortgage you may have) and deduct this amount from the sales proceeds. The result is what you can expect to have left available to plug into the new home.

With all these sources of cash, keep in mind that you will need some money to move, as well as to fix up anything that needs it when you move into the new home. Also take into account that you should retain some cash reserves for emergencies. You want to be covered in case someone gets sick or injured.

How Much Mortgage Loan Can You Get?

The difference between the cost of the house and the amount of cash you have to invest is filled by one or more mortgage loans. A mortgage loan differs from other types of loans in that the loan is secured by the property you are purchasing. In other words, the lender does not have to depend on your word alone to assure that the loan will be repaid. If for some reason you are unable or unwilling to make your payments on time, there is a legal procedure through which the lender can take over the property or have it sold to satisfy what you owe. That is the main reason the terms on mortgage loans can be much more liberal than on a credit card or other unsecured loan.

The loan terms you get will depend on two main factors: the economy and your personal risk assessment. The primary effect the economy has on your loan is to set the interest rate. Interest rates rise and fall according to the supply and demand of money in the market (i.e., the "capital market"). Rates also vary for different kinds of mortgage loans. In almost all cases, "fixed-rate" loans will be more expensive than "adjustable-rate" loans. These types of loans will be described in Chapter 5. For now, it is enough to know that the amount you can borrow may change for different types of loans.

The better you look to the lender, risk-wise, the lower your interest rate will be and the more likely you are to get a low down-payment loan. A lot will depend on your **credit score**. We introduced this concept in Chapter 1 as a number that condenses the information on your **credit report** to predict how likely you are to default on the loan. It may make you uncomfortable that someone has reduced you to a number, but the fact remains that the lender has to make a judgment on the risk of extending you a loan based on some criterion. Credit scores are not perfect, but they are an improvement over judging you based on more superficial criteria, such as your race and social class. Indeed, you can take steps to improve your credit score.

In Chapter 1, we recommended that you get **prequalified** in order to see how much you could borrow based on your income and existing debt. Actually, having a lender prequalify you is only one of the ways to find out what you can afford. First, your real estate agent can work up an estimate similar to that of a lender. Prequalification does not delve into your creditworthiness; rather, it assumes you qualify for the best terms available in the market. It is simply a mechanical application of standard lender criteria.

There are a number of sites on the Internet that allow you to calculate the maximum loan you qualify for and use that amount to estimate the top of your price range. Some of these are explicit about the interest rate applied and the income ratios used to link income to loan amount. Others are more of a black box. All are easy to use and probably are worthwhile. However, the

Getting a Copy of Your Credit Score

Your credit score is a number that is statistically derived from information in your credit report. The score has significant influence on your ability to get a mortgage loan, as well as the terms offered on the loan. Despite the importance of the number, it is not as important to obtain a copy of your score as it is to review your credit report. There are two good reasons to get a copy of your credit report: to see thether there are credit problems that you might be able to improve and to clear up any inaccuracies in the report. Your credit score, on the other hand, only reveals your credit status and does not provide any clues to upgrade your credit standing.

To clear up any confusion about your score, you should realize that each of the three credit agencies creates its own version of your score. If you are going to get a copy of one, you should get copies of all three because you don't know which one your lender will use. Your mortgage loan score will differ from the score used by your insurance company, and that might differ from one that a prospective employer might see. All of these scores are based on the same set of data, but they are intended to predict a different type of risk: the probability that you will default on your loan versus the probability that you will file an insurance claim or do something detrimental to your employer. Despite the differences, each of these scores may go under the general term **FICO score**. This acronym stands for **Fair Isaac Company**, the firm that developed the technique for computing credit scores. At the same time, each of the three credit agencies has its own name for its version of the FICO score.

Unlike your credit report, you do not have a right to a free copy of your credit score. However, there are plenty of offers to give you a free score on the Internet. To get your "free" copy, you will probably have to sign up for a trial subscription to a credit-monitoring service. The service tracks your credit report and lets you know if anything pops up that might damage your credit rating. After a month of free service, you will begin to incur a monthly fee unless you take measures to extract yourself from the service.

exercise will be more useful to you if you understand exactly what the calculators are doing. That way, you can better understand the results printed out on the screen and you can do your own custom analysis.

Mortgage loan prequalification is based on the procedure used by loan officers to determine whether a loan applicant can afford the amount of loan applied for. Essentially, the officer calculates the highest monthly payment you can make as a specific percentage of your monthly gross income. Lenders making **conventional loans** apply a ratio of 25–28 percent to make this calculation. For government-insured **FHA loans**, the ratio is 29 percent. Then a second calculation is made of your total debt payments as a percentage of your gross income. The total debt is the prospective mortgage loan payment plus those payments on loans you already have. This "back-end" ratio is 33–36 percent for conventional loans and 41 percent for FHA loans. Although these ratios are not as strictly applied as in the past, they serve to define your borrowing limits under normal circumstances.

The process is not mysterious and can be applied by anyone who knows how to calculate a monthly loan payment. There are a number of ways to find loan payment amounts: a book of tables (see *Barron's Real Estate Handbook,* for example), a financial calculator, or one of the mortgage calculators available on the Internet.

Here is the basic procedure for loan qualifying. First, the **loan officer** helps you identify your qualifying monthly income. This includes the salary or wages of you and any other family member providing steady income. Also include any income sources that can be counted on regularly (e.g., Social Security, pensions, and investment income). Apply the lender's qualifying ratio to income to calculate the maximum allowance for the monthly loan payment. From this amount, subtract an estimate of what it will cost to maintain an **escrow** account. This account collects money sufficient to pay property taxes and home-owner's insurance premiums. An amount is paid into the account each month equal to one-twelfth of the annual cost of taxes and insurance. If you need to buy mortgage insurance, there may be a premium added to your monthly payment, so that will have to be subtracted as well. The remainder is the highest amount you can pay for principle and interest on the loan. The amount of loan this payment will support depends on the term of the loan and the interest rate.

How Your Credit Score Affects Affordability

The interest rate offered to a mortgage borrower with a low credit score may be almost twice that of the one given to a top score. FICO scores range from 300 to 850 and you will need to be above 760 to get the best interest rates. If you are near the bottom of the range—the so-called "sub-prime" risk category—you may have to go to a lender who specializes in high-risk loans.

There is a web site with a calculator that lets you see how your score may affect your ability to buy a home. Go to *www.myfico.com/myfico/CreditCentral/LoanRates.asp*. When you select a type of loan, a geographic area, and the amount of loan you need, it will calculate monthly payments and total interest paid for different ranges of credit scores. The results are based on current rates offered in the market.

Let's work an example of a prequalification analysis. Then we will do some examples using online loan-qualifying calculators. Suppose we have a couple with a monthly salary of $5,000 plus $1,500 in additional income, for a total of $6,500 per month. They have an outstanding auto loan that requires $500 in monthly payments and are paying about $300 per month on their credit cards. They are seeking a 30-year fixed-rate loan, and the current interest rate is 6¼ percent. They estimate that an escrow account for taxes and insurance would run about $350 per month for the price range of home they would buy.

First, we find that the lender will allow loan payments to be as much as 28 percent of monthly income. That means that our couple qualifies for a loan with a monthly payment of no more than $1,820 ($6,500 times 0.28). Subtracting the escrow payment leaves them with $1,470 for principal and interest. Our mortgage calculator shows that, at 6¼ percent interest for 30 years, they could borrow $238,752.

Next, apply the back-end ratio, in this case 36 percent, according to the lender. The portion of monthly income that can be used for debt payments is $2,340. Our couple has $800 in existing payments, leaving $1,540 for the mortgage payment. Back out the escrow of $350 and they have $1,190 for principal and interest. This would support a loan of only $193,271. Since the lender uses the lower of the two loan figures, this example shows how existing debt can limit the amount that can be borrowed.

Now, let's use the online calculators to see how they compare to our homemade analysis. We will use the same couple as above. Let us say they can manage only $5,000 to invest in their home purchase. First, we will run the analysis through the calculator provided at the Mortgage 101 site at *www.mortgage101.com/ Calculators/Afford.asp?p=mtg101*. The calculator requires us to input income, existing debts, local ZIP code, and the estimated percentage down payment. We have to do a little trial and error to get the down payment, which in this case comes out to be 2 percent. Here's the result of the analysis:

Monthly payment:

Principal and interest	$1,422.62
Taxes	311.32
Home owner insurance	65.96
Mortgage insurance	184.79
Total	$1,984.69

Loan amount	$230,986.00
Down payment	4,714.00
House value	$235,700.00

The house value represents the most expensive home the couple could buy under the assumptions used. Let's try a different calculator to do the same analysis. This one is provided by Guardian Loan Company at *www.Guardianloancompany.com/pages/learning/qualifying.asp#*.

Monthly payment:

Principal and interest	$1,209.79
Taxes	165.80
Home owner insurance	82.80
Mortgage insurance	81.87
Total	$1,540.26

Loan amount	$193,770.00
Down payment	5,000.00
House value	$198,770.00

As you can see, different calculators give differing results, primarily because they use different ratios and other assumptions. The online calculators do not seem to have a problem with our couple's existing debt. There are other calculators on the Internet besides these two, so you might as well use as many as you care to and develop a range of values to guide your search.

Suppose our couple has been saving up for some time to buy the home and now have $25,000 for the down payment. Here's how our two Web calculators alter the analysis:

	Mortgage 101	Guardian Loan
Monthly payment:		
Principal and interest	$1,396.59	$1,189.89
Taxes	332.85	179.60
Home owner insurance	70.52	89.80
Mortgage insurance	94.79	80.32
Total	$1,894.75	$1,539.61
Loan amount	$226,800.00	$190,519.00
Down payment	25,200.00	25,000.00
House value	$252,000.00	$215,519.00

One of the oddities of these calculators is that they seem to indicate that someone making a higher down payment would qualify for a smaller loan. In reality, most lenders would be more willing to make a larger loan to someone who is putting up more cash. If you can provide a down payment equal to 20 percent of the price, you should be able to avoid mortgage insurance, thereby being able to devote more of your payment to principal and interest on a larger loan.

Even if you have confidence in the results from online calculators, you still may want to do the math yourself. It is not difficult, particularly if you can calculate mortgage payments. As an example, suppose our couple is uncomfortable with the idea of having a mortgage payment that takes up almost a third of their gross income each month. They want to know how much loan they could get for a monthly payment of $1,200. Because they probably will be buying a less expensive home than that envisioned in the earlier analysis, they project taxes to be $200 and home-owner insurance to cost $50 per month.

If they have only $5,000 for a down payment, they will have to buy mortgage insurance. The monthly premium is estimated at $95. First, calculate how much of the $1,200 monthly payment can be devoted to principal and interest:

Total payment	$1,200
Less: Taxes	200
Less: Home owner insurance	50
Less: Mortgage insurance	95
Principal and interest	$855

At $6\frac{1}{4}$ percent interest for 30 years, a monthly payment of $855 will support a loan of $138,862. Add the $5,000 down payment and they can buy a home worth $143,862.

How much more home could they buy with a $25,000 down payment? Let's say they find out that the increased down payment will reduce their mortgage insurance to $45 per month. The calculation of principal and interest is as follows:

Total payment	$1,200
Less: Taxes	200
Less: Home owner insurance	50
Less: Mortgage insurance	45
Principal and interest	$905

The higher payment supports a loan of $146,983. With a $25,000 down payment, they are in the market for a home costing up to $171,983.

A final note on pre-qualifying. While getting prequalified is valuable only as a source of information, getting **pre-approved** can overcome a potential hurdle to buying a home. Pre-approval

Can You Improve Your Credit Score?

Suppose you find that your credit score is low enough to jeopardize your chances of buying a home.

Recognize that your score is based on your credit history as portrayed in your credit report. Also recognize that there are no gimmicks that can make a poor credit history turn into a good score. You can improve your credit history, and thereby your score, by adopting good credit-management practices, but it will take time to counteract any mistakes you have made in the past (see Chapter 1 for ways to improve your credit report).

If you don't have a score, that means you haven't used credit long enough to establish a rating. To calculate a score, the credit agency needs at least one credit account that has been open for six months, and there should be some activity in the account (charges and payments) within the last six months. If you don't have any credit accounts, the best way to establish credit is to take out a loan that you know you can repay and make the required payments on a timely basis. Don't go overboard; just take on something well within your means.

When you review your credit report, you may be surprised to find out you still have accounts that you have forgotten or thought you had closed. Accounts you do not use should be closed by writing the company and specifically requesting that the account be terminated.

In general you want to have no more than a handful of accounts, and any balance you maintain should be well below the limit placed on the account. It will not improve your score to open new accounts and spread your outstanding balance among them. The opening of new accounts will offset the lower balances in each one. It also won't help to get a **consolidation loan** in order to cancel existing accounts (although it might lower your costs). Paying down your total debt is the best way to raise your score. Incidentally, do not be afraid to shop around for a mortgage loan, even though lenders may order a copy of your credit score when you inquire. Such inquiries will not affect your score unless it is apparent that you are trying to open new credit accounts to raise your debt level.

requires the services of a lender, who will pull your credit report and score to assess the risk of making a loan to you. There may be a fee involved in getting pre-approved. The lender will indicate what types of loan you can get and the amount you can qualify for. You can then go into the housing market with more confidence that you will be able to get financing (it is not uncommon for home sales to fall through because of the buyer's inability to get a loan). In a seller's market, where there are many buyers for each available home, being pre-approved may provide you some advantage. Pre-approval, however, does not **lock in** the interest rate, so you could still find the home unaffordable should interest rates increase between the time you are pre-approved and the time you make an offer on a home.

Buyer Costs Other Than Down Payment

Although all transaction costs are negotiable, there are some costs that normally are the responsibility of the buyer. All of these can be paid by the seller if they are so negotiated in the **contract**. Recognize that any costs accepted by the seller that normally would be paid by the buyer probably will be in lieu of a reduction in the sales price of the home. Many buyers prefer a higher price if the seller will pay more of the transaction costs. It saves on the amount of cash the buyer must front for the purchase. It can cause problems, however, if the home does not **appraise** at the negotiated price. In addition, not all sellers will be willing to pay additional closing costs, particularly if they are trying to extract as much cash as possible from the sale (after all, they probably are buying another home themselves). In your pre-house search planning, you may want to factor in the payment of transaction costs common to home sales.

Work Sheets
Determining Whether You Can Afford a Home

Typical asking price for suitable home $ _____

Expected discount through negotiation

     (0–15 percent of price)   − _____

Threshold price of home   _____

Potential down payment cash sources:

	Value	Percent you can apply to down payment	Cash available for down payment
Cash/bank accounts	_____ ×	_____ =	_____
CDs	_____ ×	_____ =	_____
Money market funds	_____ ×	_____ =	_____
Stocks/bonds	_____ ×	_____ =	_____
IRA/retirement account	_____ ×	_____ =	_____
Possessions	_____ ×	_____ =	_____
Real estate	_____ ×	_____ =	_____
Other	_____ ×	_____ =	_____
Total cash available for down payment		$	_____

Threshold price $ _____

Less: Down-payment cash   − _____

Required loan   = _____

Threshold price $ _____

Estimated monthly taxes and insurance (1–3 percent)   × _____

Annual costs of escrow   = _____

Monthly escrow (annual cost ÷ 12)   = _____

Estimated principal and interest payment for required loan $ _____

Monthly escrow   + _____

Required monthly payment   = _____

Your monthly income before taxes × 100   / _____

Monthly mortgage payment burden   = _____ %

Required monthly payment $ _____

Existing monthly debt payments   + _____

Total debt payments   = _____

Monthly income   / _____

Total debt burden   = _____

Here is a list of expenses you should anticipate:

- **Home owner's insurance premium.** If you get a new policy, you will have to pay the first year's premium at closing. If you are assuming the policy of the seller, you will have to pay a prorated amount to the seller, who has already paid for the full year.

- **Earnest money.** A deposit of 1–5 percent of the sales price is commonly required when an offer is presented to the seller. The deposit will be credited to your down payment if you complete the sale. However, you will have to write the check when you make your offer.

- **Loan application.** A fee ($300–$500) usually is required at the time you apply for a mortgage loan. The fee pays for an appraisal of the home you are buying, copies of your credit report and score, and other expenses for processing your application.

- **Loan points.** These fees, each point representing one percent of the loan amount, are collected by lenders as a requirement for making the loan. Points are not used as much today as in previous years, but they can allow you to get a lower interest rate if needed to qualify for the loan you want.

- **Inspection fees.** If you want a professional inspector to examine the house before you buy, you will have to pay a fee of $300–$750. This usually is collected at the inspection.

- **Mortgage insurance premium.** Some mortgage insurance policies require payment of a lump-sum premium at closing. However, it is common to pay a monthly premium over the term of the loan, in addition.

- **Title insurance.** This special insurance protects an owner from valid claims to title of the property. Sellers commonly pay for a policy that protects the mortgage lender from loss. Buyers have an option to buy such insurance for themselves for an additional fee.

- **Attorney's fees.** Each side in the transaction normally has an attorney who reviews the documents to see if everything is legal and in their party's best interest. Figure a few hundred dollars to cover this cost.

Home-Buyer's Checklist

- Make a detailed list of the features that you want in your new home. Also think about how much space and how many rooms you will need.

- Check the web sites of local real estate brokers or the National Association of Realtors® to see how much sellers are asking for homes that match your criteria. Read the classified ads in the newspaper for the area you are moving to for more information on asking prices.

- Consider contacting a real estate broker in the area for assistance in pricing the market.

- Prepare a net worth statement listing your assets and debts. Consider what you could use to raise a cash down payment.

- Calculate how much mortgage loan you may qualify for, or have a lender or real estate agent prepare such an estimate.

- Calculate how much loan you can get for a monthly payment that fits your budget.

- Make an estimate of all the cash requirements of the purchase, other than the down payment.

Chapter 4

What Should I Know About Mortgages?

T he search for the proper loan can be almost as complicated as finding the right house. The reasons are many.
Financing will determine to a great extent your ability to
afford a home (Americans became home owners in large numbers only after loans became available that covered most of the
purchase price and provided a long time to repay the loan). So
choosing the right loan can be crucial. Also, there are a number
of different types of loans available, each with advantages and
drawbacks that make them ideal for specific circumstances.
Finally, there are a number of ways the home buyer can get a loan,
and the terms may differ from one source to another. To make
things even more complex, you can't compare these sources
solely on the basis of lowest interest rate, as other factors such as
speed of loan approval are important.

If you have plenty of cash and can qualify for a loan with
ease, you face a much easier task in getting financing. However, it
still is a good idea to know how a mortgage loan works and how
the mortgage market operates. That largely is the goal of this
chapter. First, we will describe the anatomy of a mortgage loan
and show how the basic terms of the loan can be varied to create
a whole menu of loan variations. Then we will describe the market for mortgage loans and indicate how market forces affect the

terms you get on your loan. Finally, we will look at a few special aspects of mortgage loans.

Inside a Mortgage Loan

The fundamentals of loans are simple. The lender gives you a sum of money in return for a promise to repay it some time in the future, along with an additional amount to make it worthwhile to the lender. With a mortgage loan, the promise is detailed in the **loan contract**. This contract contains a statement that you recognize your debt to the lender for a specific sum of money, a description of how interest will be charged, a schedule for paying interest and loan principal, and other conditions that you must satisfy to keep the loan viable.

What distinguishes a mortgage loan from most other loans is the **mortgage note**. This document pledges real property (in most cases, the property whose purchase you are financing with the loan) to support your obligation to the lender. The mortgage describes the legal procedure by which the lender can gain satisfaction of the loan if you fail to comply with the terms of the loan contract. That satisfaction usually comes in the form of selling the property and paying off the lender's claim with the proceeds. The security provided by the mortgage is the reason that lenders are willing to advance large amounts of money to ordinary individuals at relatively low interest rates. The important thing to understand is that failure to live up to the loan contract (most specfically, to make the payments on time) could result in your losing the home as well as damaging your credit rating. Later in this chapter, we will look more closely at what could happen if you **default** on the contract.

Interest

All loans require the payment of **interest**. Think of interest as the rent you pay to use somebody else's money. When a lender releases an amount of money, that loan **principal** begins to earn interest until all or a portion of the principal is repaid. Three things determine how much interest is earned: (1) the amount of principal outstanding (i.e., not yet repaid), (2) the interest rate, and (3) the period of time that has passed since the principal was released. For most mortgage loans, the principal is released by the lender on the day of **closing** when the buyer takes title to the property. Each dollar released earns interest from the day of closing until it is paid down, usually as part of the monthly payment.

Here is a simple example to show how loan principal earns interest. Let's say I lend you $100 at five percent interest. If you pay back the entire $100 after a year, you will owe $5 in interest (the total payback would be $105). Say you paid me $50 at midyear. That $50 earns interest for only six months and earns $1.25 in interest ($50 × .05 ÷ 2). The remaining $50 would earn 5 percent interest for the full year, which is $2.50. You would pay $51.25 at midyear ($50 principal plus $1.25 interest) and $52.50 at year end ($50 principal plus $2.50 interest).

Most mortgage loans require a payment at the beginning of each month. The payment includes an amount equal to the interest earned on the outstanding principal during the previous month (interest for the period between the closing day and the beginning of the next full month is paid most often at closing— that is why there is no payment during the first full month of the loan term). Most, but not all, mortgage loans require that a portion of each payment be devoted to paying down the outstanding principal. That way, when the payments end, the loan is paid off completely. Because of the gradual reduction in outstanding principal (referred to as **amortization**), the amount of interest due is slightly less each month. This reduction means that if the payment is the same each month, the amount used to pay down the principal increases each month. In the first several years, very little of the principal is retired. Most of the principal is repaid in the last years of the loan term.

Example of How Much of Principal Is Retired Each Year
Loan Amount: $100,000   Term: 30 Years   Interest Rate: 6%

Year	Principal Outstanding ($)	Principal Retired During Year ($)
1	98,772	1,228
2	97,468	1,304
3	96,084	1,384
4	94,615	1,469
5	93,054	1,561
6–25		
26	25,529	5,483
27	19,708	5,821
28	13,528	6,180
29	6,966	6,562
30	0	6,966

The traditional mortgage loan has a **fixed rate** of interest that applies for the 15- to 30-year **term** of the loan (when we refer to the term of the loan, we mean the life span of the loan as defined in the loan contract; thus a 30-year loan has a term of 30 years even though typically the loan will be repaid much earlier than that). Recognize that, when the interest rate is fixed, the lender cannot increase the interest rate, even if market rates go up. On the other hand, the borrower may be able to get a new loan at a lower rate and repay the existing one if market rates go down. That is one reason why long-term, fixed-rate loans carry relatively higher interest rates than a comparable **adjustable-rate loan**.

Partly because lenders became less willing to commit to a rate fixed for a long period and partly because they began to offer lower interest rates to borrowers who allow the interest rate to vary, **adjustable-rate mortgages (ARM)** have become a fixture in the mortgage market. Borrowers may be able to get ARMs with initial interest rates (remember, the rate can change over the term) several percentage points lower than comparable fixed-rate loans. When the interest rate on an ARM changes, the monthly payment changes to reflect the new rate. An ARM borrower could find the monthly payments, which seemed so low at first, rising dramatically if market interest rates go up. Nevertheless, when rates on fixed-rate loans are high, ARMs tend to pick up considerable market share. In Chapter 5, we will take a closer look at ARMs and all their variations.

Another thing that can vary on mortgage loans is the way interest is paid. More specifically, loan payments can be designed to include all interest accrued plus a provision for principal amortization, only the interest accrued, or something less than the accrued interest. In the first case, the loan is called a **self-amortizing mortgage**, since the regular loan payments are sufficient to completely pay back the loan principal. The loan whose payments only cover the interest accrued is called an **interest-only loan**, for obvious reasons. Interest-only loans require a payment of principal at the end of the loan term or anytime the borrower wishes to retire the loan. In most cases, this **balloon payment** is made by refinancing the debt with a new loan.

If the payment is less than the interest accrued, the unpaid amount of interest is plowed back into the loan and the outstanding principal increases. Because of the growing principal, this is called **negative amortization**, compared to the normal amortization used to gradually repay the loan. As you can imagine, negative amortization cannot go on indefinitely or the loan would never be repaid. Indeed, loans that allow negative amortization do so only under extraordinary circumstances. For example, there is a mortgage loan that provides for monthly payments that start low and increase by a specific percentage amount each year for the first several years of the term. For the first year or two, the payments are set lower than the required interest, creating negative amortization. By the time payments are set to a constant level, they are raised to be sufficient to fully amortize the principal outstanding over the remaining term.

Some ARMs have limits on the percentage change in the monthly payment amount after the interest rate has been adjusted. This limit can create negative amortization when the interest rate rises sufficiently. Flexible-payment or **option ARMs** allow the borrower to opt for a minimum payment in lieu of their regular monthly payment. The choice works like a credit card account, where the borrower can choose to make a nominal minimum payment. Like the credit card, the mortgage loan principal outstanding will increase whenever the minimum payment is chosen because the nominal payment amount is too low to cover the interest owed. Like the credit card holder, borrowers who consistently opt for the minimum payment will find their debt level increasing.

Saving on Interest

You can go in the opposite direction from negative amortization and choose to pay off the loan on an accelerated schedule. Some borrowers take out loans with relatively short terms—15 to 20 years—because the loan is paid off faster and total interest paid is less. Other borrowers who desire to retire the loan early make discretionary payments to principal whenever they have some extra money to invest. Such payments go entirely toward retiring loan principal. Since the amount of the monthly payment is not changed, the amortization schedule is shifted forward, resulting in a loan that amortizes before the end of its term. A third way for loans to be retired early is to arrange a biweekly schedule for loan payments. These loans require payment every two weeks of an amount equal to one-half a normal loan's monthly payment. Since there are 26 two-week periods in a year, the borrower is in effect making a thirteenth payment each year, and it goes directly toward retiring principal. These loans are aimed at borrowers who get a paycheck every other week, so that the mortgage payment can be automatically deducted from the paycheck.

The table below shows the loan amount and how much interest is paid over the term for a 30-year self-amortizing loan, an interest-only loan, and a 15-year self-amortizing loan.

Comparison of Different Types of Mortgage Loans
$100,000 Loan Amount at 6% Interest

Item	Amortizing Loan 30-year term	Interest-Only Loan 30-year term	Amortizing Loan 15-year term
Monthly principal and interest	$599.55	$500.00	$843.86
Total interest paid over term	$115,838.00	$180,000.00	$51,894.00

The table indicates how an interest-only loan can reduce your monthly payment but at the cost of more interest.

Comparison of Different Types of Mortgage Loans
$100,000 Loan Amount at 6% Interest

Item	Amortizing Loan 30-year term	Interest-Only Loan 30-year term	Amortizing Loan 15-year term
Monthly principal and interest	$599.55	$500.00	$843.86
Total interest paid during first five years	$29,027.00	$30,000.00	$26,641.00

The tables also show the effect of changing the loan term. As the term increases, the payment is lower. Two things limit the benefits of stretching the term. First, few lenders make mortgage loans for terms longer than 30 years. To get a longer term, you would have to go outside the mainstream of the mortgage market and probably end up paying a much higher interest rate. In addition, the effect of term length on payment amount diminishes as you go beyond 25 years. The table on the following page illustrates this effect.

Years ago, mortgage loans with 15-year terms became popular. They offered lenders a way to avoid a really long-term commitment to a fixed-interest rate, while giving borrowers more stability than they could get with an ARM. Lenders pushed the loans by offering lower interest rates compared to longer-term fixed-rate loans. At one point the push was so aggressive that it became possible to get a 15-year loan with a lower monthly payment than a 30-year loan for the same amount. If the interest rate is low enough, this situation can occur. Check the market rates and don't just assume the payments will be higher with a shorter term.

Comparison of the Effect of Loan Term on Monthly Payment
$100,000 Loan Amount at 6% Interest
Self-Amortizing Loan

Term in Years	Monthly Principal and Interest ($)
10	1,110.21
15	843.86
20	716.43
25	644.30
30	599.55
35	570.19
40	550.21

Note that in this description, we have been careful to use the term "monthly principal and interest payment" rather than just "monthly payment" or "loan payment." The reason is that most mortgage loans include more in the monthly payment than just principal and interest. Some loans require the borrower to take out a mortgage insurance policy that helps protect the lender from losses in case the borrower fails to make the loan payments. There are different ways to pay the premiums on this insurance, but when they take the form of monthly payments, they are included in the loan payment. Lenders also may require maintenance of a special account—called an escrow account—that is used to pay **hazard insurance** premiums and property taxes when they come due. If there is a condo or home-owners association that requires a periodic assessment, that may be included as well. The rationale for these charges is that the timely payment of such expenses is crucial to protecting the property's value. If the property were destroyed and the loss were not covered by insurance, the possibility of default by the owner would be very high. Likewise, if the home were condemned because of nonpayment of taxes or **foreclosed** by delinquent homeowner fees, the lender would lose its collateral. At any rate, the term "monthly payment" includes the entire amount collected by the lender, which often is more than just principal and interest.

How the Mortgage Market Is Organized

There was a time, not too long ago, when getting a mortgage loan was pretty simple (not necessarily easy, but simple). You would go to a special bank-like institution called a "savings and loan association" and apply for a loan to buy a home. This institution specialized in mortgages, mostly on homes, and they basically offered one type of loan—a long-term, fully amortizing, fixed-rate mortgage loan. You filled out an application and signed forms to allow the association to verify your financial information. Approval usually took about a month to six weeks. Before you bought the house, you might have already been familiar with the association if you had opened a savings account there. The association would hold your loan in its portfolio of investments and use deposits like your savings account to fund these loans. It basically was a Norman Rockwell type of world where everyone was reasonably honest and interest rates stayed low and steady.

Well, it turned out that not everyone was totally honest, and interest rates could move upward. As a result, savings and loans became a casualty of the 1980s. Fortunately for home buyers, a whole new way of providing mortgage loans developed during this time. Subsequent housing booms and growth of the mortgage market have pushed the dark days of the late 1980s out of our memory. The savings-and-loan world seems like something out of an old black-and-white holiday movie.

Today, you have a number of viable choices when shopping for a mortgage loan. Most people use the services of a **mortgage broker**. Just as a real estate broker finds property for sale, so a mortgage broker finds loans available in the market. The broker does not actually make the loan but can do all the paperwork necessary for you to apply for the loan. A broker is a good choice if you would like to look at a broader array of loan types than just one lender could provide. Mortgage brokers are all over the Internet, so comparing loan terms between different brokers is easy.

Another popular choice is the **mortgage banker**. You may not be able to tell the difference between a mortgage broker and banker, but they operate quite differently. Both originate loans and sell them to investors. The mortgage banker services loans for investors, whereas brokers do not service loans. After the loan is "originated" (i.e., that the loan application is processed, approved, and funded), it is sold to investors who specialize in buying existing loans. The mortgage banker may collect a lot of similar type loans into a "pool" and sell the entire batch to a large investor. This type of mortgage-banking operation has replaced the older originate-and-hold-in-portfolio practice of the savings and loan association.

Banking institutions still make mortgage loans. The distinction between a bank and a savings and loan association is no longer very important. Banks, associations, and credit unions frequently make mortgage loans and can be a good source of adjustable-rate mortgages (ARMs). These institutions rely on deposits as their primary source of funds. A lender who uses deposits to make long-term, fixed-rate loans runs the risk of being caught short when interest rates rise. This is because higher yields have to be paid on the deposits to keep them from being withdrawn. The loans, however, keep producing the same income, no matter what interest rates do. Profit is squeezed and can even disappear (this is what first doomed the savings and loan associations in the early 1980s; later it was bad loans that did them in). What the deposit-funded institutions tend to do is to sell off their fixed-rate loans to investors, just as mortgage bankers do, and retain the adjustable loans in portfolio.

Incidentally, many real estate brokers have a mortgage banking or brokerage business operating in their office. This provides convenient "one-stop shopping" for people using the broker to find a home. The broker may offer the lending operation as a side business or may just have an arrangement with an independent mortgage lender to use the space. You are not required to use this lender, but there is no reason to avoid seeing what he has to offer, as long as you shop enough alternative sources to know what is available elsewhere in the market.

Sometimes there are special loans available for qualified borrowers (e.g., first-time buyers or moderate-income families) that offer special terms more favorable than those available elsewhere. Most often, these loans are offered through the regular channels of brokers, bankers, and banks. The loans are funded by government, nonprofit, and private organizations that buy the loans after they are originated and set certain criteria on how the loans are made and who is eligible for them. If you think you qualify, ask your lender of choice about such loans. If you want an excellent source of information on what is currently available, consult with an HUD-approved housing counseling agency (see page 19). These organizations help people find a way to buy a home. They also provide counseling and educational programs on personal finance and budgeting to help people prepare to buy something major like a home. In fact, such counseling and education is required to participate in many of the special loan programs.

Application

Let's say you have selected a lender and are ready to apply for your home loan. You have with you a copy of your sales contract and a net worth statement. You also have a good idea of what you will use as a cash down payment. The loan officer (the person who helps you apply for a loan, whether the lender is a bank, a mortgage banker, or a mortgage broker) will show you the various types of loans available and indicate the current terms. You will get some information that will help you choose a loan and plan for the eventual closing. This includes a booklet prepared by the federal government that explains the various costs that must be paid at the closing (see Chapter 13). You will get a truth-in-lending disclosure of the true interest rate on the loan—the so-called **APR** or **annual percentage rate**. This may differ from the **contract interest rate** stated in the loan contract because it takes into account any **points** that you may have to pay to get the loan. We will see what points are and how they affect the loan in Chapter 5. Finally, you will get a "good-faith estimate" of what your total costs will be to close the loan. The lender is required to provide this estimate within three days of loan application, supposedly to help you make your loan decision. Since you have already paid your application fee and signed a contract, the information probably will not be helpful in choosing a loan. It will, however, help you plan for the closing by giving you a better idea of what the costs will be, and you may try to find service providers who can beat these estimated prices. The good-faith estimate is just that—an estimate and not a *guarantee* of the costs.

The application is about five-pages long and includes sections calling for information about the property being mortgaged, your income and assets, your debts and liabilities, and your employment. (To see a copy of the contract form used for most home mortgage loans, go to *www.efanniemae.com/sf/formsdocs/forms/1003.jsp*.) There may be additional documents as well, such as waivers that give the lender permission to verify your employment and bank records. The loan application must be accompanied by a check for the application fee. This fee goes to pay for an appraisal (an estimate of value) of the mortgaged property, for copies of your credit reports and scores, and to defray the costs of processing the application. If the lender is a bank that intends to keep the loan in portfolio, the appraisal may consist of little more than a bank officer going to see if the property exists as you've described. Most of the time, a state-certified appraiser will fill out a form that details his opinion of the property's market value. The loan amount will be based on the lesser of the sales price or the appraised value. Let's look at an example to see how this might be important.

Abby contracts to buy a home for $175,000. She then applies for a mortgage to cover 95 percent of the cost ($166,250). The appraisal comes in at $170,000. The lender makes the loan based on a maximum value of $170,000, which means the loan will be $161,500 to keep the loan-to-value ratio at 95 percent. If Abby wants to go through with the purchase, she will have to come up with almost $5,000 in additional cash down payment.

Processing the Application

Your **credit score** needs to come back strong enough to allow you to get the loan terms you anticipate. If your score is too low, you may have to apply at a different lender who makes **subprime loans**. The loan officer will qualify you based on your income and debt, using the criteria set for the type of loan for which you are applying. Your financial data will be verified. The processing may be completed in as little as a day (using automated loan-origination programs) or as long as several weeks. At the end of the process, you will be informed of the lender's decision; either you are turned down or you are approved for the loan. If you are approved, the lender will issue a **commitment letter** to make the loan within a specified period. Hopefully, this period will be long enough to allow you to close the sale. Most home

Common Mortgage Contract Clauses

Here are some of the provisions you may find in your mortgage loan contract or note:

- **Property description.** Somewhere near the front of the document there will be a legal description of the property being mortgaged. In addition, there will be language that indicates you are pledging this property to back up your promise to abide by the loan contract.

- **Escrow account.** If your lender requires an escrow account for taxes and insurance premiums, it will be described here. Essentially, this clause gives the lender the right to collect a monthly fee from you (as part of the loan payment) in order to maintain an account for paying these expenses when due. The clause may provide for interest to be paid on the account, but usually that is not the case. There probably will be language describing what the lender will do in case the account is insufficient to pay the expenses. Typically, you will be assessed an amount to replenish the account that must be paid in a lump sum.

- **Property maintenance.** These clauses place responsibility on the borrower to keep the property in good condition and to insure it against hazards like fire and natural destruction. There may be other restrictions on how the borrower can use the property. An additional clause will describe what happens in case the property is condemned for public use.

- **Due on sale.** This clause prescribes the rights of the lender in case the mortgaged property is sold before the loan is retired. In general, there are three possible forms this clause may take: (1) The loan could be retained and transferred to the new owner. In this case, the loan is said to be **assumable**. An assumable loan can be of significant value when the home is sold if interest rates on new loans are higher than the contract rate on the existing loan. (2) The loan could be assumed by the new owner with the approval of the lender. This provision may also allow the lender to alter the terms of the loan; and (3) the loan becomes due immediately at the closing of the sale.

- **Prepayment clause.** This provision allows the borrower to pay the outstanding principal in part or in total before it is due. Prepayment allows the borrower to make periodic additional payments to reduce the principal balance at any time during the term. More importantly, it allows the borrower to refinance the loan whenever it is in the borrower's interest (e.g., if a new loan can be arranged at more favorable terms). Some prepayment clauses impose a penalty if the loan is repaid within the first several years of the term. This **prepayment penalty** will be a specified percentage of the remaining principal balance. In some states, such penalties are prohibited by law.

- **Default.** There will be language describing what constitutes default on the loan contract. The most common cause of default is failure to make the scheduled loan payments on time. This clause defines what "being on time" means. In addition, there may be a provision for a late fee on payments not made by the due date each month. The clause also describes what happens if the borrower defaults. Usually, a notice of default is sent by the lender to the borrower, after which the borrower will have a specified period to make up the default. Most of the content of this clause is prescribed by state law.

loan commitments also lock in the terms of the loan so the home buyer can proceed to close without being vulnerable to a subsequent increase in interest rates.

The Fate of the Loan

What happens next depends on the lender. The loan could be held in the lender's portfolio of loans and used to generate income. Otherwise, it could be sold into the **secondary market**. The primary loan market is made up of banks, mortgage bankers, and brokers who originate loans—they find and work with borrowers to generate new loans. The secondary market consists of entities that buy loans that have been originated in the **primary**

market. These entities may be other banks that want to build up their portfolios. They may be investors who are attracted to real estate debt. More than likely, however, secondary-loan purchasers will be one of the major companies that provide a conduit from the primary mortgage market to the greater capital market.

By far the two most important secondary market purchasers of home mortgages are **Fannie Mae** and **Freddie Mac**. These organizations are semiprivate companies whose stock is sold on the New York Stock Exchange, but also have special ties to the federal government (i.e., Fannie Mae was a government agency at one time). The goal of these companies, besides making a profit, is to provide liquidity in the secondary mortgage market—in other words, to make sure there is an active and organized place for mortgage lenders to sell loans. This does two things for local lenders. They can continue to fund their lending activity with short-term deposits because they are not holding the bag on long-term, fixed-income loans. In addition, they can balance out periods when they have a high demand for loans and a low supply of deposits by selling off the surplus loans. Without Fannie and Freddie, the mortgage banking and brokerage industries would not exist as we know it today.

For you, the borrower, the advantages of Fannie and Freddie mean that you are assured of a steady supply of mortgage credit, no matter where you live or how interest rates fluctuate. Under the old savings-and-loan system, the supply of mortgage loans could dry up if there were too much demand in the local area or if interest rates rose too high. Also, Fannie and Freddie have come up with special loans designed to help people buy their first home, and these are available nationwide because of the broad presence of these two companies.

Earlier we called Fannie and Freddie "conduits" to the capital markets. Here is what they do. Once your loan is closed, the originating lender bundles it up with many other similar loans and sells them to Fannie or Freddie. The two companies have already issued guidelines on the characteristics of loans that they will buy. That is why the application you filled out was a form prepared by Fannie and Freddie. There is a statutory limit placed on the size of loans that Fannie or Freddie can buy, so if you are financing an especially expensive home (or most any home in an expensive market), you may not be able to benefit from these companies' participation. Loans that are eligible for Fannie or Freddie purchase are called **conforming loans** and those too large are called **jumbo mortgages**. In general, loans that do not conform carry higher interest rates and other less favorable terms than do conforming loans.

If Fannie or Freddie buys the loan, it will become part of a pool of similar loans, a larger version of the one collected by the originating lender. These pools become the basis for securities that are sold in the capital markets (i.e., the general market for long-term debt instruments like bonds). These markets are large, global, and liquid, thus representing a continuing supply of funds for home buyers. Investors in Fannie and Freddie securities are paid dividends from the income generated by the loans in the pool. As the loans amortize and are retired, investors are returned part of their investment. Fannie and Freddie stand behind the securities to guarantee the payments to investors. There are other companies that organize pools of loans and issue securities based on them. A government agency, **Ginnie Mae**, often is enlisted to guarantee the payments on these securities.

Service

Whether your loan is sold to Fannie or any other investor, you may never know. In most cases, the lender who originated your loan will continue to "service" the loan. That is, it will collect the payments, manage the escrow account, handle any inquiries you may have, and send annual statements so you can know how much interest to claim on your tax return. Occasionally, a loan servicer will sell the service contract to another company (the servicing company gets a fee based on the size of the loan). When that happens, you will be notified by your original servicer to begin sending your payments to a new company. Unless you receive written notice (not just an e-mail message) from your current servicer, you should *never* respond to a company that claims to have taken over your loan account. There are people out there trying to snare the unwary. Otherwise, changing servicers is not a big deal; you merely change the address when sending in your monthly checks. If you pay through automatic bank drafts, you will have to inform your bank of the change.

Insuring Your Loan

The loan-to-value ratio is a key measure of risk to the lender. The ratio is exactly what it sounds like; the amount of the loan as a percentage of the market value of the mortgaged property. If you are buying a $100,000 home with an $80,000 loan, your loan-to-value ratio is 80 percent. This 80 percent ratio is the maximum risk exposure mortgage lenders will accept without special insurance or a guarantee. Since many borrowers are unable to place a 20 percent cash down payment on their first home purchase, a significant percentage of mortgage loans exceed the 80 percent limit. Typically, these loans are insured by the federal government or a private insurance company or are guaranteed by the government.

Home loans insured by the federal **Department of Housing and Urban Development (HUD)** are called **FHA loans** after the section of HUD that handles the program: the Federal Housing Administration. Borrowers who use FHA insurance pay an insurance premium at closing equal to $1\frac{1}{2}$ percent of the loan amount (although due at closing, it is common for the fee to be financed into the loan). If the loan-to-value ratio is greater than 90 percent, there is an additional monthly premium that is paid during the first several years of the loan term. The monthly payment incorporates this premium. If you fail to keep up payments and the lender is forced to foreclose your loan, the FHA will defray any losses incurred by the lender.

There are alternatives to FHA, provided by private insurance companies. This so-called **private mortgage insurance (PMI)** operates much like FHA, although there are a few differences. The FHA is considered more lenient on the loans it will insure, therefore making it a little easier to get approved. PMI companies do not cover the entire mortgage amount, and only reimburse lenders for the amount of the loan over 80 percent of the property value. There is usually a one or two percent up-front premium on PMI and a monthly premium added to the mortgage payment. PMI can be canceled when the loan is amortized below 80 percent of the home's value. There is a limit to the size of loan that FHA can insure. So, if you are buying a home that requires a large loan, you may have to go with PMI.

If you are a military veteran, you may be eligible to get a **VA loan** that can cover the entire cost of the home. Veterans who served full time receive an entitlement that can be used to waive the usual down payment requirement of mortgage lenders. The guarantee is of a specified amount of loan and generally allows the veteran to borrow up to about $240,000 with no cash. Realize that the entitlement is no substitute for cash; it docs not reduce the amount of the loan. It is a guarantee. If you default on the loan payments and the lender forecloses, the federal government pays the lender up to the entitlement amount (in reality, FHA and VA usually just buy the home at the foreclosure sale, thereby reimbursing the lender). If you think you may be eligible and would like more information, contact the **Department of Veterans Affairs** or go to *www.homeloans.va.gov*.

Giving Homebuyers a Helping Hand

In recent times, the federal government has initiated programs to help extend home ownership to those who traditionally have not been able to afford a home—young families, ethnic minorities, and inner-city residents. Through the government's urging, the FHA further liberalized its lending criteria, and Fannie and Freddie created special loan programs aimed at easing loan-qualifying. These loans have relaxed income ratios (or no ratios at all) and low down-payment requirements, and often give applicants credit for evidence of good financial performance that might not ordinarily fit into the credit-rating system. For example, a borrower may improve the chance of getting a loan by showing a history of timely payment of rent.

These loans are aimed at borrowers who want to buy a home but have little cash down payment and may not have established a solid credit rating. Their current income is low enough that the monthly mortgage payment would exceed the traditional criteria lenders apply to such loans. However, the borrower has not shown tendencies toward financial irresponsibility, and is willing to undergo special financial counseling to obtain the loan. If this is the type of loan you think you need, ask lenders in your area about their availability. To become more knowledgeable about the alternatives, if for no other reason than to know the names of the loans, go to the web sites maintained by Fannie and Freddie at *www.fanniemae.com/homebuyers/homepath/index.jhtml* and *www.freddiemac.com/homepossible/*.

Not Ready for Prime Time

If you are new to borrowing and have little credit history, you may find that the only loans you can get will have above-market interest rates. On the other hand, if you have had financial difficulties in the past, you could be classified as a sub-prime credit risk and face significantly higher interest rates. Hopefully, over time, your responsible use of credit will improve your record and eventually qualify you for better terms.

Unfortunately, some sub-prime borrowers fall victim to unscrupulous lenders who take advantage of the borrowers' lack of savvy and low expectations. These predatory lenders practice fraud, and any experience with them will destroy whatever creditworthiness you may have been able to build.

Here are some things to look out for during your search for an affordable home loan. If you find one of these characteristics, the loan may still be legitimate, but be suspicious and find out more before signing up.

- An interest rate 5–6 percentage points above the rate on prime mortgages

- A large number of discount points (most loans today have no more than 1.5 points unless the interest rate is reduced)

- Fees that total more than five percent of the loan amount

- A lender that requires you to take out a credit life insurance policy (such a policy promises to make your mortgage payment if the main income provider dies; usually this is just over-priced life insurance)

- A lender who ignores your credit rating and makes the loan entirely based on the value of the home

- A lender who calls you up or contacts you personally

- Any special terms that are available only for a limited time

- Prepayment penalties that never expire (prepayment penalties compensate the lender if you pay off the loan early in the term)

- A lender who does not qualify you based on your income and does not indicate what your monthly payment will be.

What Happens If You Can't Make the Payments?

You may have thought you could afford the mortgage when you applied, but after a few months or years, maybe something happens that prevents you from coming up with the necessary amount each and every month. It could be that your budget was based on no unexpected expenses popping up, or it could be that a truly catastrophic expense occurred—one that no amount of prudent budgeting could have anticipated. It also could be that you have an adjustable interest rate that is adjusted upward by more than you can handle.

Missing a payment is a serious matter but is not that uncommon. Lenders actually expect some borrowers to fall into difficulty. They have measures to deal with such occurrences. If you find that you cannot make your payment on time, and it will take more than a few weeks to make up the payment, contact the company that services your loan (the company where you send your payments) and see if they have provisions to help you get through the financial straits you have encountered. You do not want to keep the problem a secret from your lender. A costly foreclosure is something to be avoided if possible.

If there is reason to think that your problem is temporary and not chronic, such as a large medical bill that overwhelmed your cash flow, the lender might forbear the missed payment and allow you to make it up over the next few months. Alternatively, you may be able to recast the loan to reduce the payment amount. When the loan has been sold into the secondary market, as is most often the case, the servicing lender may not be able to do anything if the loan holder does not go along.

If you cannot get help from the lender and it is evident that you cannot afford the payments, you should try to sell the home.

If the market is active and favorable for sellers, you may be able to get your equity investment out through the sales proceeds. If market conditions are not favorable, you may find that you cannot afford to sell the home because the costs of selling more than wipe out any gain. This is when people tend to allow the lender to foreclose the loan and take the house.

When the lender forecloses, you are sent a notice indicating that the entire amount of the loan balance is due immediately (this is called **accelerating the loan**). You are given a period to pay off the loan. As most people cannot pay off the loan (if they could, they wouldn't have defaulted), the lender proceeds with the legal process of foreclosing. The procedure differs depending on state law and whether the mortgage contract provides for an alternative to going through the courts. At any rate, the house will be sold eventually and the proceeds divvied up to pay off the loan, any unpaid interest, and the lender's expenses. You get anything that is left. Most often, the lender or loan insurer ends up bidding for and buying the home for the amount owed to the lender. You get nothing (if the home could be sold for more than what was owed, you probably would have been successful in selling before the loan was foreclosed). In some events, the sale fails to cover the lender's losses and you may be served a **deficiency judgment** for the shortfall. You may lose the house and still have to pay.

Tax Breaks

You have probably heard that buying a home helps you save on your taxes. What this statement refers to are the various incentives included in the federal income tax code that favor the purchase of a home. The most potentially valuable of these is the ability to sell a home without having to pay tax on the profits. Also important is the ability to deduct property tax and mortgage interest from taxable income, even though you do not have to pay tax on the "rent" that you pay yourself to live in your home. Owners of rental property can deduct all property-related expenses, but must report rental income as part of their taxable income.

Property tax and mortgage interest are sizable expenses, so the ability to deduct them from tax income is a big benefit. Complicating the picture is the fact that you must itemize your deductions to claim these benefits. When you itemize, you forgo the standard deduction that is available to all taxpayers. That means that a couple filing jointly would have to itemize more than approximately $10,000 in expenses before they benefit from itemizing. For some home buyers, itemized deductions are of little or no value, as they are better off taking the standard deduction. For others, they are indispensable. Before you factor tax breaks into your decision process, make an approximate tally of your tax-deductible expenses to see if you will benefit from itemizing.

Chapter 5

How Do I Choose a Mortgage?

What is the best mortgage loan? That's a bit like asking what's the best house to buy. Of course, it depends on what you want and what is important to you. Just like the right home, the right loan can make your home-ownership experience a happy one or a disappointment.

What can go wrong? Payments that are too high for your budget. A loan that leaves you too vulnerable to fluctuations in interest rates. Loan terms that are not what you expected when you applied. Mortgage loan officers are trained to help you apply for a loan and they can also be helpful in selecting a loan from those available. Realize, though, that the loan officer is interested in getting you the largest loan you can get, not the largest one you can afford. It is up to you to decide how much debt and how big a payment you want to tackle. The income ratios used to qualify you (to the extent they are still used) assume you can devote a large percentage of your take-home income to the mortgage payment. You do not have to borrow up to your limit. Stay within a limit that makes you feel comfortable based on your current income.

Basis for Selection

In a minute, we will look at the variety of mortgage loans that may be available in the current market. First, however, let's review some of the ways that you may base your choice of a loan.

Personalize this list and select the criteria that are most important to you.

- **Largest loan amount for the same monthly payment**. Some borrowers look for the largest loan that a lender will let them have. But the lender is doing you no favor to give you a loan than you can't afford. So this criterion maximizes the size of the loan for a given monthly payment. Obviously, a low interest rate will help. However, there are other ways to keep payments low: lengthen the term, pay interest only, or allow negative amortization. Also, adjustable-rate mortgage (ARM) loans may have lower initial interest rates than comparable fixed-rate loans.

- **Lowest required down payment**. Most first-time home buyers are hard-pressed to come up with a cash down payment, yet a home purchase usually requires a significant amount of cash beyond the down payment. Therefore, many home buyers need to minimize the down payment to have any chance of buying a decent home. Mortgage insurance can lower the down payment, and a government guarantee can eliminate it altogether. It may be possible as well to tack on a second mortgage to make up most of what the first mortgage does not cover.

- **Least amount of interest paid.** Here is a different aspect of affordability—the overall cost of the loan. Some borrowers are appalled at how much a loan can cost over the entire term (i.e., a $100,000 loan at six percent interest requires almost $216,000 in payments over 30 years). Lower interest rates, shorter terms, and loans that provide for accelerated amortization help hold down these costs.

- **Predictability.** If you plan on living in the home for a long time and do not want to take a chance on your loan becoming unaffordable if interest rates rise, you will want a loan with a fixed-interest rate. However, if you are willing to take some risk, there are ways to tame the potential volatility of an adjustable-rate loan, and you may be able to enjoy a lower interest rate. Realize that, even with a fixed-rate loan, your payment can increase as the demands on your escrow account grow.

- **Maximum tax benefits.** Only the portion of your mortgage payment devoted to interest is deductible against your taxable income. While a large percentage of your payment in the first several years is interest, some might want to deduct the entire payment. You can do this if the payments are interest only. If you are making payments with negative amortization, you can only deduct the amount you actually pay, not the amount of interest that accrues each month.

- **Flexibility.** Most mortgage loans allow a certain amount of flexibility in terms of paying back the principal (you can pay down the balance with extra payments whenever you want, in most cases). However, the requirement to make the entire monthly payment on time is pretty inflexible. There are loans available that allow some leeway in the monthly payment for times when money is short.

Today's mortgage market is varied enough to satisfy any of these needs. It can become confusing to make a choice if you don't have a clear idea of what you are trying to achieve, since going for one benefit will require a trade-off on another. In some cases, you do not have a lot of choice, such as the down-payment requirement. If you don't have much cash, that criterion will move to the top of your list. However, if you don't like the idea of going into heavy debt, you might search for a source of more down-payment cash, or you might decide to find a less expensive home. You should exercise a good deal of financial prudence when making such a large investment decision. On the other hand, the home may increase in value and create some equity, even if you have to borrow almost all of the purchase price. Also, hopefully your income will grow in the future and make the payment that initially looked so frightful, much more manageable.

The Temptation of ARMs

If you were offered the choice of two loans—one at six percent interest and the other at four percent—which would you take? To make it easier to decide, consider that a $100,000, 30-year loan at six percent requires a monthly principal and interest payment of $599.55, while that same loan at four percent has a payment of $477.42. Surely you can find a good use for the $122 you would save each month by taking the latter loan.

Of course, that is not the whole picture. Your monthly savings is paid for by your acceptance of a good deal more risk than fixed-rate borrowers undertake. There is no free lunch. That does not mean that ARMs (as adjustable-rate mortgage loans are called) should be avoided by everyone and at all times. As long as you understand the pros and cons, you may find an ARM to be the right loan for you.

How an ARM Works

The difference between an ARM and a fixed-rate mortgage is that the interest rate on an ARM may change periodically over the term of the loan. Although there are many variations, the typical ARM allows the interest rate to adjust every year. Other than that, the loan works just like a fixed-rate loan, with a portion of every payment going to principal reduction so that the loan is amortized over the term.

The loan contract for an ARM defines the method used to adjust the interest rate. The frequency of adjustment is established by the length of the **adjustment interval**. Most common is annual adjustment, but the interval may vary from monthly to several years. A standard **index** that is related to market interest rates is selected to govern the adjustment process. The index will be a statistic compiled by a reputable source that is available to the public and that is updated at least as frequently as the adjustment interval. Most commonly used is the Federal Reserve Bank's constant maturity-average yield on bonds sold by the U.S. Treasury. Since these are reported by maturity, they can be matched to the loan interval—an annually adjusted ARM indexed to the one-year Treasury yield, for example. Other indexes used include the average contract rate on mortgages closed by lenders nationwide, the average cost of funds for lenders nationwide, and the London Interbank Offered Rate (LIBOR).

The idea is that the index reflects current market interest rates and is used to keep the rate applied to the loan from being too far above or below current rates. Here is how the index is used to make adjustments. At loan origination, a relationship is established between the index value and the loan interest rate. This most often is expressed as a constant **margin**. For example, the loan contract may state that the interest rate will be adjusted to be two percentage points above the one-year Treasury yield. So if the yield is three percent when the loan is priced, the loan will carry an interest rate of five percent. When the first adjustment date arrives, and the yield has risen to $3\frac{1}{2}$ percent, the loan will be adjusted to a $5\frac{1}{2}$ percent interest rate. Likewise, if the yield had fallen to $2\frac{1}{2}$ percent, the rate would be lowered to $4\frac{1}{2}$ percent. Since the lender is required to give advance notice to the borrower of any rate change, the index value will be taken a few months before the actual adjustment. It is basically that simple.

A naked ARM, in which adjustments are free to follow anywhere the index takes them, could be a scary situation for the borrower. If some economic force sent interest rates soaring, the loan could quickly become unaffordable. To make ARMs more marketable, lenders commonly apply **adjustment caps** that limit how much the interest rate can change. There are two basic types of caps: an **interval-adjustment cap** and a life-of-loan cap. The interval-adjustment cap tends to smooth over changes in the rate so that a borrower does not have to swallow any big jump in monthly payments all at once. The life-of-loan cap essentially places a ceiling and floor around the rate, so that a borrower knows the rate will not go beyond a specified limit, no matter what interest rates do.

To show how caps affect the adjustments, we need to introduce the concept of the **fully indexed rate**. This rate is what the loan interest rate would be if there were nothing to interfere with the adjustment. If, for example, the rate is set to be two percentage points above the one-year Treasury yield, then the fully indexed rate equals the current value of the yield plus two percentage points. In the absence of an adjustment cap, the fully indexed rate is the rate that applies to the loan. When a cap restricts the amount of adjustment, the rate on the loan may differ from the fully indexed rate. At the next adjustment interval, the rate will be adjusted to equal the fully indexed rate as long as the cap is not exceeded.

It is hard to explain this in a clear way, so let's use an example. The table below shows how the loan rate can diverge from the fully indexed rate when the index change exceeds the cap. Two loans are contrasted. The interest rate on both loans is pegged at two percentage points above the value of the index. One loan is uncapped and the other has an adjustment cap of one percentage point for each annual adjustment interval. The pattern in the index is designed to illustrate the action of the cap. Here are the results for the first five years of the loan term:

Year	Index Value (%)	Fully Indexed Rate (%)	Rate on Capped Loan (%)
1	4	6	6
2	6	8	7
3	5.5	7.5	7.5
4	5	7	7
5	3	5	6

Note how the cap kicks in for Year 2 when the index jumps two percentage points. For Year 3, however, the cap allows the loan rate to rise to the fully indexed rate. This can be a little disconcerting for the borrower as the loan rate goes up despite a drop in market rates. As consolation, the borrower has enjoyed a year of below-market interest rate. The two-percentage-point drop in Year 5 is cut short for the capped loan as caps often apply to both increases and declines in the index rate.

How much rate discount should you get by accepting an ARM? The answer depends on something called the **yield curve**. This curve is the pattern you get when you graph bond yields by length of maturity. Normally, short-maturity bonds have yields that are several percentage points below those of long-maturity bonds. The difference rewards investors for tying up their money for a longer period. However, when the market expects interest rates to rise, the difference will increase as the yield curve becomes steeper. In contrast, when rates are expected to fall, the difference decreases and the curve flattens. In extreme situations the curve can invert, and short-term interest rates will be higher than long-term rates. For the ARM borrower, the normal discount of one to two percentage points can be much higher when the curve is steep, and almost disappear when the curve is flat. Why would someone take an ARM if there is no discount in initial rate? In truth, not many ARMs are closed when these conditions prevail. However, if the interest rate is adjusted downward, as may be expected by the market, it could be a bargain for the borrower.

Sometimes when lenders want to make ARMs more appealing, they will originate the loan at an artificially reduced rate, called a **teaser rate**. A teaser rate is good only until the first adjustment date on the loan. The loan rate will revert back to the fully indexed rate even if the index does not change in value. However, if there is an adjustment cap, it may prevent the full increase up to the indexed rate. Let's use our previous example to show how this might work. In this case, the capped loan is originated at a teaser rate of five percent.

Year	Index Value (%)	Fully Indexed Rate (%)	Rate on Capped Loan (%)
1	4	6	5
2	6	8	6
3	5.5	7.5	7
4	5	7	7
5	3	5	6

Because of the cap, it takes four years for the loan rate to equal the fully indexed rate. To illustrate how a cap can alter the monthly payment, we graph the payment amount for the fully indexed rate, the capped rate, and the teaser rate loan based on the index pattern shown in the above tables. The payments are consistent with 30-year ARMs for $100,000.

Note that the three loans end the period with much the same monthly payment. The effect of the cap is to smooth over any volatility in the index, cutting off the peaks and valleys of the cycle. In effect, caps reduce the risk placed on the borrower by the ARM arrangement. Most borrowers, of course, don't mind volatility as long as rates do not go up. Keep in mind that, in most situations, a rise in interest rates reflects an increase in the rate of inflation. Inflation often is reflected as well in rising income and higher rates of property value appreciation. This is not always the case, but when it is, the borrower may have gains in income and property value to offset the cost of higher mortgage payments.

Figure 5–1: Monthly Payments on ARMs

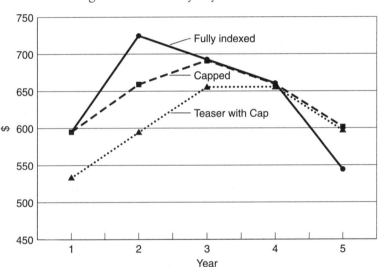

Real-Life Variations

Caps help to make ARM loans more palatable for borrowers, but the market has evolved further to create ARMs that cater more finely to a variety of borrower situations. The most popular ARMs come in two forms: the hybrid ARM and the option ARM.

Hybrid ARMs are a compromise between a fixed-rate and adjustable-rate loan. The loan starts out with an interest rate that is fixed for the first several years, after which the loan converts to an ARM. Typical initial fixed-rate periods are three, five, or seven years. When the loan converts to an ARM, it generally is adjusted annually, indexed to the Treasury yield or the LIBOR. There may be adjustment and life-of-loan caps. The most important feature is the method for setting the rate when the loan converts. A rate based on a fully indexed rate starting on day one of the term might present a huge shock if rates have risen steadily during the fixed-rate interval. Generally, the loans set the margin to equate the fully indexed rate to the fixed rate set during the fixed-rate interval. Combined with adjustment caps, that practice should provide for a smooth transition during the initial years of the adjustable-rate period.

Option ARMs place emphasis on flexibility at the sacrifice of predictability. There is nothing novel about the loan structure; it is a straightforward ARM. The innovation is in the way the borrower makes payments. At the time of each monthly payment, the borrower has the choice of paying an amount based on one of four options:

- **Interest accrued plus principal based on a 30-year amortization schedule.** This is the payment that would be required for a "normal" ARM.

- **Interest accrued plus principal based on a 15-year amortization schedule.** Possibly the borrower is flush with cash and wants to speed up the amortization a bit.

- **Interest accrued only.** This is for those times when money is a little short but not so much that you want to increase your debt level.

- **Minimum payment.** This payment shows good faith to keep the loan viable but is not enough to cover accrued interest. The shortfall is added to the outstanding loan balance in a process known as negative amortization.

An option ARM can be beneficial to borrowers with uneven cash flow, such as the self-employed and employees working on full commission. The borrower essentially decides on a monthly basis how fast to amortize the loan balance. Here are a few more key features of option ARMs:

- The interest rate commonly is adjusted on a monthly basis. Because of the frequent interest rate adjustment and the potentially shifting amortization, the payment level varies significantly from month to month. Adjustment caps are common, as are life-of-loan caps, to place some bounds on the possible jumps in payment level.

- Since there is a good possibility of negative amortization, there has to be some way to insure that the principal is retired by the end of the loan term. This is done in two ways. First, the loan is automatically recast at scheduled intervals—usually once every five or ten years. Essentially, this is like refinancing the loan. The outstanding balance is set to amortize over the remaining loan term. Second, there may be a cap on the outstanding balance as a percentage of the original loan amount. For example, the loan may be set to recast whenever the outstanding balance exceeds 125 percent of the original balance.

Option ARMs are designed for borrowers with sufficient financial discipline and sophistication to stay out of trouble and use the features to their advantage. Such loans often are originated at significantly lower interest rates compared to standard fixed-rate mortgage loans.

How to Choose

ARM loans introduce an element of unpredictability that makes it difficult to compare them to fixed-rate loans. The fact is that there is no way to know exactly how much an ARM will cost, unlike a fixed-rate loan, which can be forecast with certainty. If you are serious about an ARM—and they can provide real advantages to the right borrowers—you will be taking a calculated risk that can be estimated to some extent.

The main reason to accept an ARM over a fixed-rate loan is to get a lower initial interest rate. That low rate may be short-lived if interest rates rise in the early years of the loan term. Unfortunately for the borrower, initial rate discounts are the deepest when rates are expected to rise. When rates are expected to fall, there may be no discount at all. Therefore, choosing an ARM because the rate is much below those on fixed-rate loans is betting against the expectations of the bond markets. The markets can be wrong, but chances are that their expectations about the direction of interest rates will be borne out. If the ARM has caps, especially a life-of-loan cap, it may be a good choice even if rates do rise.

Sometimes a lender can be too aggressive in pricing a capped ARM to the extent that the maximum allowable rate on the ARM is not much higher than that on the fixed-rate loan. Consider this example: You shop around and find the going rate for fixed-rate loans to be seven percent. You also find an ARM with a five-percentage-point life-of-loan cap and one-percentage-point annual cap for a four percent initial rate (not a teaser rate). If you add the life cap to the initial rate, you find that the highest rate the loan could take is nine percent. Because of the annual cap, the fastest the loan could max out would be five years, the rate being effective in year six of the loan term. Furthermore, you are assured of a below-fixed-rate interest rate for at least three years due to the annual cap. So, even under the worst conditions, the loan may be a bargain. Anything less than the worst is to your advantage.

If you know a little about the size of the risk you are taking, should you go ahead and choose the ARM? That depends on your situation. If you are the type of person who worries about things going wrong or feels a lot more pain when you lose money than the pleasure you get when gaining, you probably should stick with fixed-rate loans. If you expect to sell the home after a few years (i.e., maybe it is a "starter home" and you expect to outgrow it, or your job calls for frequent relocation) taking an ARM is not such a risk. If you expect your income to rise over the next several years, your ability to weather higher payments is much greater than if you are on a fixed income. If you are stretching to afford the house and your payment ratio is pushing the limits (at least when there were limits), your capacity to take on higher payments is highly limited. All these factors should come into play when making your decision. Here is a summation of who the ideal borrowers and least appropriate borrowers are for the loans covered in this section:

Fixed-rate mortgage

- Best: long-term horizon, dislikes surprises, when rates are low

- Worst—short-term horizon, when rates are high

ARM with caps

- Best: good income growth prospects, loan payment not burdensome, when discounts available relative to fixed rates

- Worst: main motivation of getting the loan is to qualify for a larger loan amount

Hybrid ARM (starts as fixed rate then changes to adjustable rate)

- Best: expect to hold the loan only through the fixed-rate interval

- Worst: long-term horizon, rates expected to rise

Option ARM

- Best: cash flow varies due to unpredictable income or expenses, good financial management skills

- Worst: attracted to the loan because of the minimum payment option

How Much Down Payment?

The question of how much down payment to make is moot for most first-time buyers and many other home buyers as well. Even the minimal down payment can take a toll on the resources of the average home buyer. Add to that the need to pay for all those incidental expenses involved in buying a home and moving a household, and the question becomes one of minimizing the down payment even more.

Nevertheless, some face a decision about how much cash to invest in the house. Some people delay buying a home until they are in a strong financial position and have ample cash. Others have just sold a home and have a substantial cash profit to reinvest in a new home. For these buyers, the relevant choice is, given the availability of loans that cover the majority of the cost, whether to make a big down payment or invest the cash in some other asset.

Money used to make a down payment on a home essentially is an investment in an **illiquid asset**. That means that if you need to access the money you invested, it will be difficult to free it up.

Doing a Worst-Case Scenario Projection

One way to evaluate the downside risk of an ARM is to project the worst-case scenario. Essentially, you are answering the question "What is the worst that can happen?" The only way this projection can have any meaning is when the ARM is governed by adjustment and life-of-loan caps. The caps allow you to project future interest rate adjustments under the worst-case assumption that interest rates will increase rapidly and consistently during the loan term (even without caps, you can project a bad-case scenario of moderately rising rates even though it might not be the worst that could happen).

As before, let's look at an example. You intend to borrow $100,000 for 30 years. You are trying to choose from a fixed-rate loan at seven percent interest and an annual ARM at five percent initial rate with a one-percentage-point annual cap and a five-percentage-point cap on the maximum rate. You expect it will be at least six years before you refinance the loan. If you take the ARM, how much more would you pay if interest rates take off and the loan adjusts by the maximum amount allowed every year?

The table below shows how the monthly payment would change for the first six years. See Chapter 4 for instructions on how to calculate ARM payments when the interest rate changes.

	Fixed-Rate Loan		ARM	
Year	Interest Rate (%)	P&I Payment (%)	Interest Rate (%)	P&I Payment (%)
1	7	665.30	5	536.82
2	7	665.30	6	598.05
3	7	665.30	7	660.74
4	7	665.30	8	724.59
5	7	665.30	9	789.32
6	7	665.30	10	854.70

Because of the lifetime cap, the payment can be no higher than that in the sixth year. The worst that can happen is that your monthly payment would go up by less than $190. On the other hand, you have a certain savings in the first year of almost $130 per month and at least $67 per month in Year 2. Year 3 is about equal. Only after three years would you have to make a larger payment relative to the fixed-rate loan.

You can project any scenario using this technique. You may want to see what would happen if rates ran up for a few years and then retreated, as often is the case in the real world. You can project a best-case scenario of interest rate declines. Keep in mind that caps often apply to rate reductions as well as rate increases.

A home is an expensive and awkward thing to sell. Awkward because if you sell, you will have to find another place to live. You can access your equity through a **home equity loan**, but that means paying additional interest and the fees involved in getting the loan. If you are buying an illiquid asset, you need to make sure you retain enough cash to handle reasonable unexpected expenses that may occur.

Once you have an emergency reserve in place, deciding what to do with the rest of your available cash should be based on **opportunity cost**. In other words, put the money in the investment that promises the best return adjusted for risk. The return on the down payment is nearly certain—it is the interest rate on the money you will not have to borrow because you are taking out a smaller loan. Ask yourself if you could get as good a return by investing the money elsewhere. Factor in the risk that you have to take to obtain that return or just compare the rates available on risk-free investments like government bonds and insured bank accounts.

If the loan you are using to purchase the house is **assumable** (a subsequent buyer can take over the loan without the interest rate changing), and you expect to sell the house in a few years, you may want to make a minimal down payment. That way, the loan will cover a larger portion of the selling price and be a much more attractive alternative to new financing. That can mean a higher price at resale.

One further factor to consider is the potential extra cost of high-loan-to-value loans. Once the loan amount exceeds 80 percent of the home's value, you will need to pay for mortgage insurance (unless you are eligible for a VA guarantee). The premiums add to the monthly payment. When the loan goes above 90 percent of value, the insurance will be more expensive, whether using PMI or FHA (more on this later). If you are buying a particularly expensive home, it is possible that the loan amount could exceed the loan amounts that Fannie Mae/Freddie Mac can purchase, requiring you to use a **jumbo** loan. These loans generally carry higher interest rates than smaller, conforming loans.

Whither Mortgage Insurance?

If you are not making a substantial down payment (at least 20 percent of the home's value), you will need mortgage insurance to get the loan. You have the choice of a conventional loan insured by a private company (PMI) or an FHA loan insured by the federal Department of Housing and Urban Development. FHA and conventional loans are originated by the same lenders, by and large. When you visit a lender, ask if they offer both types of loans and ask them to compare the insurance premiums and the options for paying them. The differences are subtle and chances are that you, the borrower, won't know the difference. Therefore, you should price both types of insurance and pick the cheaper alternative. However, you should be aware of these differences in case they affect some aspect that is important to you:

- The interest rates applied to FHA and conventional loans may be different. Ask the lender for the current rates on both types.

- The FHA is considered to be more lenient on borrowers with a less-than-sterling credit rating. Since the FHA is a government program intended to help people buy homes, there is public pressure on the agency to approve loans to first-time buyers. If you think you may have trouble getting approved, you may want to first try FHA.

- The FHA allows all or part of the down payment to be supplied through a gift from a relative or employer or a grant from a nonprofit agency. If you are using this type of down payment, check to see if the conventional loan also allows this.

- The insurance premium for FHA is due at closing, but can be financed into the loan and thus paid each month. In addition, if the loan is more than 90 percent of the home's value, there is an additional monthly premium for the first several years of the loan term. PMI premiums can be set up to occur in one lump sum at closing, annually, or monthly.

- By law, PMI must be cancelled when the loan amortizes to 79 percent of value or lower. Likewise, FHA will cancel the monthly premium when the loan balance is 78 percent of the home's value at origination.

- In the past, FHA loans could be assumed by a subsequent buyer without the interest rate changing. Ask your lender if the FHA loan is assumable and what qualifications are applied.

- The FHA cannot insure loans that are larger than a specified limit. This limit varies by area. The limit for any area is at least 48 percent of the current maximum applied to loans purchasable by Fannie Mae. Limits may go as high as 95 percent of the local median house price. If you want to see the current limits for the area where you are buying, check the web site at *https://entp.hud.gov/idapp/html/hicostlook.cfm*. (Note: When entering this address, be sure to type "https://" at the beginning.)

An Alternative to Mortgage Insurance

Competition in the mortgage loan business has encouraged lenders to be more permissive in what they accept as a down payment. As a consequence, some borrowers have found loans that allow much of the down payment to consist of a second mortgage or home equity loan. Borrowers quickly discovered that they could combine a second mortgage with an 80 percent loan-to-value first mortgage and avoid mortgage insurance altogether.

The combination has been dubbed the **piggyback loan** because the second mortgage rides on the first mortgage. Though second mortgages usually carry higher interest rates than first mortgages, the piggyback combination may require a lower monthly payment than a single high-ratio mortgage with an insurance premium. In addition, the interest of the second mortgage is tax-deductible whereas the insurance premium is not (a proposal to make these premiums deductible may be considered by Congress).

Here is an example to show how a piggyback loan might compare with the more conventional PMI loan. Suppose you are trying to buy a home that costs $200,000 and you have $10,000 as down payment. A first mortgage loan for $190,000 goes for seven percent interest and the PMI is $80 per month. Another lender will make you a $160,000 first mortgage for seven percent with no PMI required. The lender will also make a home equity loan for $30,000 at a fixed rate of eight percent. Which should you take?

The first option gives you a monthly principal and interest payment of $1,264.07 (30-year term) and a PMI premium of $80 for a total monthly payment of $1,344.07. The piggyback loan requires a monthly payment of $1,064.48 for the first mortgage and $220.13 for the second mortgage—total payment is $1,284.61.

If you decide to do a piggyback loan, make sure that the lender providing the first mortgage is aware of, and approves of, the second mortgage. An attempt to deceive a lender by claiming your down payment will be all cash could lead to default on the mortgage contract and foreclosure of your loan.

How Long Should the Loan Term Be?

You may find mortgage loans that run as long as 40 years or as short as 10 years. A purely interest-only loan has, in effect, an infinite term, as the principal will not be amortized even though the loan "ends" after a specific number of years. If the loan runs at least 10 years, you will likely move or refinance before the end of the term. Therefore, choosing a term has little to do with how long the lender is committed to the loan (or, as in the case of a fixed-rate loan, how long it is committed to that interest rate). Here are the basic trade-offs:

- **Affordability versus loan retirement.** The longer the term, all other things being equal, the lower the monthly payment (principal and interest). Therefore, if you are stretching your budget to afford the home, you will want as long a term as you can get. However, the longer the term, the longer it will take to pay off the loan. If one of your goals is to be debt-free, you will want the shortest term you can afford. The table below shows an example of how the loan term can affect the monthly payment. Excusing the obvious generalizations, we might expect that younger home buyers would choose a long term to decrease the loan payment, while older buyers might pick a short term so that they can pay off the loan before they retire.

Comparison of the Effects of Changing Loan Term
$100,000 Loan at 7% Interest

Term	Monthly P&I Payment ($)	Interest Paid First Year ($)
Interest only	583.33	7,000
40 years	621.43	6,985
30 years	665.30	6,968
20 years	775.30	6,925
15 years	898.83	6,876
10 years	1,161.08	6,773

• **Total costs versus tax deductions.** The longer the term, the more interest you pay over the life of the loan. This is so, not only because you will be making payments for a longer time (if you take the loan to the end of the term), but also because the loan amortizes more slowly. After the first year, you owe a little more on a longer-term loan than you would if you had taken out a shorter-term loan. With the longer term the payments are lower, but more of that payment is devoted to interest. That may be considered a positive if you are in a high-income tax bracket and need deductions. As the term lengthens, more of the payment is interest and, therefore, eligible for itemized deduction on your income tax return. The difference is not great in the first year, as shown in the table, but it increases in later years. So, if taxes are a major expense for you and you have enough expenses to justify itemizing, you may want a longer-term, or interest-only, loan.

• **Early benefits versus the long run.** The longer you plan to hold the loan, the more beneficial a shorter term will become. As the table shows, you don't save that much in interest for the first year by taking out a shorter-term loan. However, over a period of 10 years, the savings are more meaningful. (You would pay a total of $70,000 in interest for the interest-only loan, but only $59,270 on the 20-year loan). So, once again, we have a trade-off based on how long you expect to hold the loan. Recognize that there are reasons, other than selling the house, that your loan might be retired. The most likely is a refinancing to take advantage of lower interest rates. If you think you will move in a few years or that interest rates will be lower in the future, a shorter-term loan might be your best choice.

Is Negative Amortization a Bad Thing?

As described above, some types of loans make it possible to increase the outstanding principal over time, a process called negative amortization. Obviously, uncontrolled negative amortization can lead to financial trouble, because you are going deeper into debt even while making your loan payments. This brings to mind the specter of the credit card junkie who builds up enormous debt until personal bankruptcy beckons.

Most mortgage loans that allow negative amortization have mechanisms to limit the amount of additional debt that can be incurred. However, that doesn't address the question as to whether it is worthwhile to ever allow the principal to grow. The answer is "yes" and "it depends."

If the buildup is temporary and for the purpose of smoothing over a period of tight cash flow, there should be no problem. One source of potential negative amortization is when an ARM has a percentage cap placed on monthly payments (the payment is not allowed to increase by more than a specific percentage amount) and the cap prevents the payment from fully covering accrued interest. The cap is used to limit the shock of a big increase in the payment. In most cases, the loan will begin to amortize again after the next rate adjustment, so the increase in debt is checked.

A second condition that might affect the advisability of negative amortization is the amount of equity you have built up in the house. If the negative amortization does not wipe out your equity, you are still in sound financial condition. After all, when you take out a home equity loan, you are in effect raising your debt level or "negatively amortizing" your total mortgage debt. The difference is that, in most cases, you can't get a home equity loan unless you actually have sufficient equity to cover the loan.

Choosing a Lender

By now you should feel like you have an idea of what type of loan you need. The next task is to find the best place to get that loan. In Chapter 4, we discussed the various types of lenders who originate mortgage loans. The three most popular sources are mortgage brokers, mortgage bankers, and commercial banks.

Mortgage brokers usually represent several lenders and can offer a variety of loan types. You may be able to compare the rates and offerings of the various lenders. Brokers make their money by collecting a fee from the lender who gets your business. It is similar to buying a house through a real estate broker. The real estate broker represents a number of sellers and is compensated by the seller whose house you buy. Same with the mortgage broker.

Mortgage bankers originate and service loans. Typically, they originate only those types of loans for which a secondary market exists. When the mortgage banker makes a loan with a yield higher than that required by investors in the secondary market, the loan can be sold at a premium. These premiums are how they make their living as well as fees received to service the loans they originate.

Banks make loans for their own portfolios as well as engaging in mortgage-banking activity. They profit when they make loans at a higher yield than the rate they have to pay for deposits and other sources of funds. As you can see, all these sources benefit when you pay a higher rate of interest. This is not some sinister conspiracy; it is the way markets work. As a savvy consumer, you need to do enough research to know what terms are available in the market. Only then can you intelligently evaluate what each lender has to offer. You should also be familiar with the information in your credit report so that you won't be misled into thinking you are a sub-prime borrower, when you are, in fact, eligible for better terms. Armed with this information, you can shop for a loan (remember that getting a number of loan quotes will not affect your credit rating, even if the lenders access your credit record).

If you think you may be eligible for a special loan—your income is below the median in your area, or you have never owned a home—start your search at one of HUD's approved housing counseling agencies. As we have said before, they are the experts on what is available in your area.

One of the most convenient ways to start a search for financing is on the Internet. You will find many choices by doing a search on "mortgage." Some mortgage brokers and bankers operate exclusively online, while many major companies with bricks-and-mortar offices also maintain an Internet presence. You can quickly find out what is available from these sites, or start by looking at benchmark loan rates in your area through sites like *www.bankrate.com*. Thus far, there have been no reports of fraud or predatory behavior by the prominent lenders operating via the Internet.

In your selection of a lender, consider the following criteria:

- **Terms.** Even though most lenders will sell your loan to one of a handful of secondary investors, the rates they offer will vary. Shop around for the best rates with knowledge of the going rate. Realize that **discount points** should be associated with a lower interest rate. Each point should lower the rate by about one-eighth of a percentage point. If you are short of cash or expect to keep the loan for fewer than five years, go for a loan with no points. If the loan is an ARM, find out if the rate is a teaser rate (i.e., one that is below the fully indexed rate).

- **Variety of loan types.** This factor is important if you want to compare different types of loans—fixed versus ARM, conventional versus FHA. Some lenders can provide an objective analysis to help you select the right type of loan. Know something about the loan types before approaching a lender.

- **Processing.** In some cases, the speed with which the lender approves the loan can be important. You may be under some pressure to wrap up the financing and get to closing by a specified date. Of course, it is always good to know as soon as possible whether you will get the loan. You want a lender who is expeditious in processing the loan and definitely will have it done before the loan commitment expires. Lenders usually do not offer guarantees, but check with anyone you know who has applied for a loan recently to see how their lender performed. Local businesses can be checked for complaints with the Better Business Bureau (BBB).

- **Rate locks.** Loan commitments for residential mortgage loans usually lock in the rate for a specified period of time. Customarily there is no fee for this service. The lock is important so that you can complete the transaction knowing that you can afford the loan, no matter what interest rates do in the interim. Ask the lender what the standard commitment includes and how long the rate is locked. For a fee, you can purchase special locks that "float down" whenever interest rates decline during the commitment period. If you are afraid of getting stuck with an above-market rate, you might consider this arrangement.

Most mortgage lenders are honest, but there are a few lurking around to take advantage of consumers unfamiliar with the industry (and why shouldn't you be unfamiliar—you don't get mortgage loans very often). In the past, mortgage bankers who were poorly capitalized (they were operating on a shoestring) had a tendency not to honor their rate commitments when rates increased during the loan approval period. Faced with losing money on the loan, they simply jacked-up the rate. Other shady operators attempt to lure customers with bait-and-switch tactics. They advertise a great rate to get you in the door, then switch you to a more expensive loan.

Home-Buyer's Checklist

- Find out the current rates and other terms for different types of loans available in your locality.
- If you are considering an ARM loan, get details on the frequency of adjustment, the index used, the margin, and any caps on rate adjustments.

- Prepare a worst-case scenario projection of your ARM to get an idea of how high the monthly payment could go and how long it would take to get there.

- Figure out how much you have to devote to a cash down payment. Make sure you retain enough cash to provide a reserve fund against unforeseen emergencies.

- Ask acquaintances and professionals for recommendations on reputable mortgage lenders. Check with the BBB before contacting a local lender.

- Find out the specifics—interest rates, types of loans offered, length of processing, and length and nature of the rate lock—before committing to a lender.

Chapter 6

Where Do I Get Help?

C lick here—the world is at your fingertips. Clicks can tell you a lot of what you want to know but they don't always tell you what you need to know. Bill and Liz found out the hard way.

Bill's job transfer from the Midwest to New York City kindled their dream of a house at the shore yet still within commuting comfort. Bill and Liz were tech savvy but babes-in-the-woods about real estate reality, contracts, and lawyers—and the perils of practical politics. They innocently thought they could click for results without laying out large sums for professional guidance.

They found the house in no time—two blocks from the beach—and the price was right. Was this too good to be true? Yes. Within one year they discovered there was no future for their house. Bill and Liz's dream house was in an older neighborhood destined to be taken over by the city under the Rule of Eminent Domain to make way for high-end, high-rise, highly tax-ratable condos. Despite historical precedent for such municipal action to provide parkland "for the public good," the city had the right and used it, to support private development. The supposedly altruistic goal was to raise the tax base to provide "for the public good."

This wasn't good for any of the residents in the neighborhood and certainly not for Bill and Liz. They hadn't done their homework thoroughly. They hadn't obtained advice from knowledgeable real estate professionals.

Preliminary Research

The Internet has revolutionized information gathering and dissemination. Nothing since the invention of the printing press has made more information available in an instant, literally at our fingertips. The Internet is a terrific source of information, especially for preliminary research, but one can easily get lost exploring the endless sources of data. It might be a good idea to jot down the route you follow so that you'll know how to get there again, because for virtually every question you have there will be another site offering a different answer. There's nothing more frustrating than staring at the screen trying to remember where you found that one priceless nugget of information.

If you do not own a computer with Internet access, your local library or Internet café will have computers to use. There are also many other sources of information we'll explore.

Knowing your source of information is more than just important. Knowing that your sources are reliable is vital. Some sites are very commercial and only seek to sell their services. Others offer opinions that have no basis in fact. The watchwords here are "Watch out." Most communities have web sites that provide information about community services with links to helpful local sites. Larger companies have web sites and many times the links are particularly helpful.

When using search engines, asking the right question can become an art form. You want to weed out lesser commercial sites. Major search engines are at *www.google.com*, *www.yahoo.com*, and *www.msn.com*. In addition to these basic search engines offered by major Internet providers there are also tools that search multiple search engines, such as Copernic Agent Basic or Dogpile, free for download at *www.compernic.com* and *www.dogpile.com*. Don't be put off by silly names. Regardless of what they are called, these multiple search engine tools are advantageous when you get very specific in your search.

Many commercial sites will require that you provide information about yourself prior to getting their "free" information. Just providing a ZIP code is not much to ask but be wary when too much personal information is requested. Caution is needed. Sometimes sites for local communities may appear to be official but are, in fact, commercial sites. Remember the watchwords. Watch out.

Your preliminary research can usually be done without being bombarded by solicitations because your information was provided in order to get some free access. Commercial sites will spend considerable money to get preferential placement on the search engines. Regardless, there is a wealth of information available for your preliminary research without having to give out any personal information beyond the ZIP codes for areas you are searching.

Every aspect of a house can be researched on the Internet. As you go through your home-buying experience, the first place to look for answers to your questions may very well be Internet magazine articles that are also incorporated into various web sites. They often provide 24-carat nuggets of information. Keep a list of your favorite sites.

The Department of Housing and Urban Development site has basic information in English and Spanish at *www.HUD.gov/ buying/index.cfm*. If you are considering buying a HUD house, other areas of their Web site can give you detailed information. We'll talk about this later in this book. The National Association of Realtors® also has a site with links that can be very helpful at *www.realtor.org*. Every state has a state realtor's association with helpful links. For example, New Jersey is at *www.njar.com* with links for information about schools, transportation, and other research tools. States also have governmental sites that you can generally get to at *www.state.xx.us* where the "xx" is the two-letter state designation. The National Association of Home Builders® site at *www.homebuilder.com* is very helpful for people seeking information about new houses.

For local information, newspapers have always been, and will continue to be, a great source of information. They are often also available over the Internet and let you control what you are going to scan and then read. Unlike nationwide papers, such as *The New York Times* or large regional papers, local papers can provide local flavor. Reading old newspapers at a local library may reveal good and bad information about developments that may impact the area where you want to live. If you have time, you may want to subscribe to one or more local papers to get a better understanding of the community life. Where you want to live may be more important then the actual home characteristics. Buying guides, published by local newspapers, run ads for selected areas. While these may not always be current, they give general information about houses and prices in different areas. Frequently, these can be found at local food stores. Keep in mind that ads placed in the newspaper may get online faster than into print so don't wander too far from a computer.

Chambers of Commerce can also be great resources. Their mission is to advance the business of their members and the communities they serve so you can rely on learning all of the positives. Chambers generally can provide packets of information for people who are considering relocating into their areas. This may be information about business, government, and schools. It can be something as simple as the Chamber directory, with all the information in one concise package. If you need more in-depth answers, don't hesitate to ask. You can usually talk with knowledgeable people in any Chamber office to learn more about local conditions. They can refer you to established local businesses that may also help answer your questions.

When you begin to narrow down specific areas, go to the neighborhoods you're interested in to get a feel of what life is like right there on the spot. Talk with people who already live there. Talk with local shopkeepers. Talk with as many people as it takes to find out what you need to know. Remember that market value varies, even in a very small area. That old realtor war cry, "Location, location, location," may seem like a cliché but it does apply. It may even be that a specific corner of a street has greater market value than other locations on the same street. Learning about local market values will help you to make better decisions. Learning about sales histories and trends can also help your understanding of local market conditions. As we have already discussed, this information is usually available on the Internet or in local newspapers.

Should I Look by Myself?

When you already know specifically what you want and where you want to live, you may be in a position to search for houses out on your own. If you have the time and patience, you may do all or parts of the search process that will be discussed further in this chapter. We all learn by doing, so the more you personally study neighborhoods and local market conditions, the stronger will be your knowledge base. When you do not have time or local knowledge of the areas you like, professional assistance is probably needed. How do you find dependable professional help? Family may be a good source of referrals. Family won't knowingly let you down, but networking with friends and co-workers may provide just that extra bit of information that helps you piece the home-search puzzle together.

For Sale by Owner (FSBO)

Sellers trying to save sales commission often offer their houses **For Sale by Owner**, or **FSBO**. Many web sites offer all kinds of services to home owners selling directly to the buyer, including Internet listings. There are benefits to a direct approach if the buyer and seller interact directly. These benefits are true especially when both buyer and seller are knowledgeable about market values and all aspects of home buying and selling. But how will you know if the house is overpriced? If you've done your homework, the whole process will be much easier and you'll be prepared. But, watch out. Those old watchwords again. A buyer's agent may levy a fee that you are responsible for, but it may well be worth it. Don't forget that a direct seller may do less prequalifying of the buyer. She just wants to sell her house without paying a **commission**.

For Sale by Builder

New home-builders have their own sales force and larger builders have web sites. New home-builders use every advertising medium available so you will find information readily available about them. Even if you are not considering buying a brand new house, research into new houses can give you a wealth of current information about the latest technologies, which can prove to be a valuable guide in what to expect.

Larger builders have architects and engineers who wring out all excess from design and construction costs, so along with volume discounts, they can afford to offer competitive pricing. They are a good reference point. You can study their modern layout plans. Learn what features they think are important. Remember, they have already researched what the public wants. They'll also give you clarification of dollars per square foot. This is one of the most important benchmarks when comparing home values. Existing houses generally cost less in terms of dollars per square foot, but again "location, location, location" applies because there will be great differences in dollars per square foot depending upon location.

Working with Professionals

New house or used house—do you still think you can handle it all by yourself? If you have the slightest doubt, you may very well need professional assistance. Whatever your approach to house-buying, remember that professional service is not something you can see, feel, or touch. Retaining professionals can be very challenging. It's not like buying a product, as we shall see. So how do you know who to choose? Do you ask your brother-in-law? Is that attractive ad you saw in the newspaper a good guide? Does a slick Internet presentation give you a clue as to who can provide you with the service you need? Why is there such a broad range in the fees that professionals charge? How can you evaluate one expert against another? One question leads to another. How do you even determine whether you might still be able to handle it on your own?

Often we do not realize we need professional assistance until we're told we have a deadline, and then all of a sudden, it's urgent that we get a professional. Panic sets in and sometimes we just choose the first person, regardless of qualification or expertise. When you have the time, you can do your own homework to learn about various professionals. You can learn about their reputation and how they got where they are. Perhaps you might know clients who can tell you the good and the bad of working with a particular professional.

Are all professionals alike? Does experience really make a difference? When a professional lists multiple specialties, how do you know that your particular needs will be adequately met by that person? How do you know that the professional you retain will even be the one actually doing the work? She might very well assign the details to someone in a back room—an assistant or associate who will be doing the real work. Are you willing to take that chance? How easy will it be for you to talk with the professional you retain? How important is it that the expert you hire has good staff or associates with specialized skills to handle all aspects of your transactions?

In this chapter, we will review a wide variety of professionals whom you may consider in your home-buying and home-ownership experience. These include the realtor or agent who guides you through buying your house to the wide variety of professionals you may need to help you take care of the house and expand or remodel it, if necessary.

An important goal when hiring a professional is to achieve a better result than you could get by doing it on your own. Better may mean more cost-effective. It may mean that you incur less risk. It may mean that the job gets done in a shorter period of time. It may mean that you are better protected against potentially adverse future events. Unlike a product, a professional service is not physically measurable. When you shop for a car you can look at it, feel it, drive it, read reports about its performance, and read records about its maintenance history. This is not possible when you are buying professional services.

It's very difficult to fully understand why professional fees can vary so greatly. Higher fees generally do mean greater experience, which usually means that you are likely to get better results with fewer problems and less risk of error.

A high-paid attorney with in-depth experience in matrimonial matters is not necessarily the attorney who will do well with real estate work. It is experience in a particular area that justifies high fees, and the more experience a professional has, the higher

her fee. Some professionals, like real estate salespeople who work on commissions, earn the same commission regardless of their experience. Different real estate agencies may charge different levels of commission but these agencies may also provide different levels of service. It is essential to fully understand what the agent will be doing for you to earn her fee.

Are fees negotiable? Yes, but it may not be a good idea to negotiate for a lower fee. Concentrate on what the professional will do for the fee. What if the work is delegated to others when lower fees or negotiated fees are involved? To what extent can shortcuts be taken? Be cautious when you try to reduce the fee of any professional. You need to know that a reduction will not affect the quality and quantity of the work. You could say, "Well, that's not professional," but professionals are only human. Unless that person is accustomed to adjusting fees for different clients, her integrity may not be pristine. We will discuss more about this later and in Chapter 12 on negotiations, we will provide additional tips for getting cost-effective professional help.

"Experience, experience, experience" is right up there with "location, location, location." When hiring an expert, look first for experience in the profession. Look secondly for experience in the specific field of work you are hiring the professional to perform. Remember the Family Court lawyer who's not too savvy with real estate. Close familiarity with local conditions is the third form of experience to look for. A wise man once said, "He who has been in business for ten years may have one year of experience ten times." It's not just the number of years someone has been working that counts. It's specific experience in the work you need to have done. Better judgment and a quicker grasp of specific needs and solutions come from experience.

Some of the greatest experience comes from making mistakes, but hopefully not on your job. You do not want to be the source of mistakes that ease the way for future clients. Very local experience can be advantageous when it's specific knowledge of the local real estate market or knowledge of particular local customs. It may be that there are plans not yet published to make changes in an area that would adversely affect any purchase you might be considering. This information is often known only by locally involved professionals. You have to find one who really knows what she is talking about.

You may have to find more than one professional if you are looking at properties in communities that are far apart. However you choose a professional, the watch word becomes "trust." You have to be able to trust her, and she has to be able to trust you. You need a professional that will be easy to work with.

Sometimes a simple phone conversation may be all you need to feel confident. A personal meeting can provide the reassurance that you're in good hands. Knowing one or more referral sources can be the icing on the cake. People you know personally are more likely to give you the benefit of their own experiences. It isn't just how well your professional does the work. It's also how well she will work with you and how well she communicates with you. When transactions progress easily, attention to your needs in a good working relationship is not demanding. When transactions run into snags, the relationship may be jeopardized. No one wants to have difficulty but buying a house can be the time when good people get tested and that is the time you need the best help you can get. Will your professional be available to you during nonbusiness hours and possibly on weekends?

Let's assume now that your new partnership shows every indication of smooth success. Your agent is in full agreement with you and will be available on weekends. There is still one more detail to be ironed out. You have to formalize your arrangement. You need a contract. A contract is a written agreement that defines what the professional is to do and what she is not to do. You can limit your agent's scope of work if that is important. We recommend that you obtain plain-language agreements, in writing, to help avoid any misunderstandings. The contract must define fee schedules that apply. Fees are important but generally not the most important consideration when retaining professional assistance. As we mentioned earlier, professionals generally charge fees commensurate with their experience. If the experience that warrants the higher fee is specifically what you need, then you may benefit disproportionately to the fee. You'll make out like a bandit. Keep in mind that no matter how much time you spend hunched over your keyboard, chances are that you are never going to know as much as this professional. The experience she brings may cost a little more but it may turn out to be your best investment.

Here is a little parable of Brittany and the beautiful house. Driving on a fine spring day, Brittany spots a beautiful house. It's her dream house. She falls madly in love with the house but neglects to do her homework. For Brittany, this is love at first sight, but we all know love is blind. Brittany sees only this beautiful house and the real estate sign on the front lawn with the name of the listing broker. Brittany immediately calls the number on her cell phone to get access to the house. The broker hotfoots it over in his convertible with the key to the lock box in his glad hand. Now Brittany really falls in love with the house as she follows the broker from beautiful room to beautiful room. Her fiancé, Trent, whom she also called on her cell phone, wants only to please her so he supports proceeding with the purchase however the agent directs. The listing agent recommends both the home inspector and the attorney and offers to coordinate their work. Brittany agrees to have the agent retain them both. She would have agreed to anything, so blinded was she.

Hold it for a minute. Let's put Brittany in freeze frame—she may be moving too fast. Does our girl seem capable of good decisions? No way. Has she done her homework? Not on your life. Does she know that the professionals will be looking out for her interests? No, she does not. We won't finish the story because sometimes these stories work out just fine. Sometimes they have horrible consequences. We can only hope that Brittany and Trent came through unscathed and are living happily ever after in their beautiful house with beautiful little Joshua, Caitlin, and Rocky, their beautiful little Shih Tzu puppy.

Of course Brittany and Trent may be a little far-fetched, but it pays to remember **caveat emptor**—"Let the buyer beware." Getting professional help can be like buying fruit at the food market, ranging all the way from fresh and delicious to potentially rotten. To get the best people to help you achieve your goals, you must do your homework. Remember the ABC system and consider similarly evaluating the professionals. For professionals, "A" would be a plus (+) or best qualified, "B" would be adequately qualified, and "C" would be a minus (–) or needs improvement.

Sometimes a second professional opinion is needed. If your doctor told you that you needed possibly dangerous major surgery, you'd get a second opinion without thinking twice. Buying a house is hardly comparable to a life-threatening operation, but it's an expensive proposition that you don't want to end badly. You need to apply the same degree of research in selecting a second professional as you put into choosing the first expert. It may even be desirable for the two professionals to discuss, perhaps in your presence, their respective opinions. Not all professionals will see the same facts in the same light in any particular situation. It can be expensive to obtain second opinions, but depending upon the risk involved, it may be a very good investment.

A word of caution. Be careful in hiring professionals over the Internet. There are professionals, even lawyers who should know better, who solicit work over the Internet without any direct personal contact. Confidentiality that should be important to you may not be protected with Internet-obtained services. They could put you at risk. Another thing to keep in mind is that many professionals must be licensed in the state where they practice. For example, lawyers, real estate agents, architects, professional engineers, and land surveyors must be licensed in the state in which their work is done. If you are ever in doubt that the professional you are considering has the proper licenses, you can probably get confirmation on the Internet at the site for the state licensing board for her professional specialty.

Liability insurance is another area where it is necessary to know that your professional carries appropriate liability insurance. Let's hope it is never needed but in those cases where there is professional malpractice, you want to know it is available. You can always ask for a certificate of professional liability insurance.

Criteria for evaluating a professional include:

- Experience in the profession
- Experience doing the work needed
- Experience in the local area
- References by people you know and trust
- Ease of working relationship
- Will the professional or her staff attend to your needs?
- Availability during off-hours
- Fee

Should I Use a Real Estate Agent?

Real estate sales people are everywhere, but only Realtors® are members of the National Association of Realtors® and subscribe to a strict code of ethics. All states require that real estate agents be licensed. Basically there are two major levels of licensing: real estate sales agents and real estate brokers. A broker can operate a real estate business and hire real estate sales agents. As with any profession there are vast differences in experience and expertise. Not all real estate agents offer the same level of service nor do they charge the same fees.

We'll talk about fee flexibility in Chapter 12 on negotiating. You can easily become overwhelmed by all the choices available. Because buying a home is so complex, you can benefit by having a helpful knowledgeable professional at your side along the way. Will it cost more? Perhaps. But it might also save you money in finding a better deal. You may also save time. And, potentially the most important factor, you might avoid making a mistake by having expert assistance that is truly dedicated to serving your needs.

Local knowledge and expertise in all facets of the real estate transaction are the true tests and benefits of using good real estate agents. They know about almost all properties that are for sale, and good real estate agents know how to put the entire deal together. They are familiar with local zoning and school conditions. They know how to help you obtain financing. And, they can assist with price negotiations. Having an intermediary can facilitate not only the negotiation, but also your own thinking about what is fair. In some states the broker can handle everything from listing to closing. In other states a lawyer or lender may be required to handle the closing.

Let's get down to specifics. How important is the realtor's firm? How important is the particular realtor? Will you need a broker or a real estate salesperson? Do you want a broker who is also a realtor, and a member of a professional organization? Do you need a realtor with a **Graduate Realtor Institute**® **(GRI)** designation? Do you need a realtor who also happens to be an attorney or an engineer? Are you seeking a realtor who works for a discount brokerage firm? Will you be happy with the "next up" real estate salesperson who just happened to be first to greet you when you walked in the door? What are the differences between a seller's agent, a buyer's agent, and a dual agent? It's enough to boggle the mind, but we're here to answer all of these questions.

Because real estate agents need access to a large number of properties, networking with potential sellers has always been the primary source for listings. But with today's instant Internet information it may not seem that the real estate agent is still important. Consider, though, that before a property is made available for sale, someone did some thinking, at least on behalf of the seller. The agent who has the ear of a potential seller learns valuable information about the property well before it becomes public knowledge. Some properties sell even before they are listed. Even when properties are listed, their information can take time to become public knowledge. An agent who shares information with associated agents has the advantage if that particular property is just what you are looking for. Sometimes listings are exclusive to one brokerage firm that offers properties only through their own agents before making them generally available through multiple listing services. Multiple listing services have member brokers who share information and thus have access to a larger number of properties than just the ones listed by their own agents.

Fees are generally paid by the seller and must be stipulated in a contract with a specific real estate agent and a specific brokerage firm within a specific time frame. In addition to broker's commissions, real estate fees often pay for advertising specific properties and the cost of maintaining office operations. Sometimes listing agents have to fund advertising and promotion costs in addition to spending time at open houses and in other promotional activities. When different brokerage firms are involved in the transaction, they split the fees. The buyer's broker is generally paid by the listing broker, not the buyer. Different brokerage firms have different policies about fees and how they are distributed.

As a buyer, you may initially explore available properties with more than one real estate agent, especially when you are looking in widely different areas. You may find yourself working at the same time with different agents in different areas of a state. This is fine, but once you have been shown a specific property by an agent, you have an obligation to work with that agent should you decide to buy that house.

When you call or go into a brokerage sales firm's office and ask to look at properties, there may be an agent who is "next in line" to assist you. If you are not willing to work with that next-in-line person, it would be best to determine exactly who you want to work with before you go into the brokerage office. If you don't have a friend or relative in the field, someone you feel most comfortable with, then referrals from people experienced in working with specific agents can be your best sources. Most real estate brokerages have web sites that identify their agents with information about their experience and expertise. Talk with potential agents. You may be lucky enough to find someone who has the perfect house from the get-go. But most often you can expect to invest a significant amount of time with an agent to find that dream house, so you have to be happy with her.

Don't be surprised if your real estate agent or broker wants to learn everything about what you want—and your ability to pay. The agent is not just being nosy. This is prequalifying homework typically done by the agent to know that there is a potential return for her investment of time. The agent may seek a contract to cover some defined exclusivity in showing you houses.

If you still need more background on any one agent, check out her credentials. GRI membership means that this person has completed at least 90 hours of specialized real estate education. It also means that she subscribes to the code of ethics of the National Association of Realtors®. See *www.realtor.org* for more information.

Something else to consider is the type of brokerage you will be working with. Traditionally, real estate agents and brokers represented the seller, which meant that they worked exclusively to maximize benefits to the seller. Today, we have various forms of agencies—buyer's agents, dual agents, and seller's agents. Some brokerages are exclusively buyer's agents but they are not the most common. You can check them out on the National Association of Exclusive Buyers Agents we site at *www.naeba.com*.

Often a brokerage will both list and sell a property, which maximizes the commission for that brokerage firm. A dual agent represents both the seller and the buyer. The name of the agent on a for-sale sign is the listing agent whose job is to get the best deal for the seller. A buyer's agent has the responsibility to get the best deal for the buyer. It is essential to understand the agency relationship when working with a real estate sales agent. You need to be careful about disclosure to any agent of too much personal information, especially your urgency to make a deal or how high you may be willing to go in price. Your buyer's agent has the obligation to fully protect you, the buyer. Fine, but you still have to keep your eye on what's best for you. A buyer's agent agreement with one agent in an office does not necessarily mean other agents in that office will also act as your buyer's agent. If you are to work with more than one agent in an office, their responsibility to you must be clearly defined in writing.

Evaluating a real estate agent and brokerage firm includes:

- Experience with the category of properties you are seeking
- Referrals from people you know and trust
- Negotiating skill
- Will your agent be a buyer's agent?
- Ease of communication with the agent
- Availability during off hours

Do I Need a Lawyer?

Only lawyers can give legal advice. In some parts of the country, real estate agents or banks can complete the closure process and lawyers are not required. However, retaining a good real estate lawyer can be very helpful. If you have confidence in your own understanding of how best to protect your own interests, you may feel that you do not need a lawyer. For most of us, hiring an attorney is very important and is best done before we are ready to sign any kind of contract. There may be ramifications to house buying that can impact other areas of our lives for which we'll need legal assistance. Like wills and taxes. Sometimes an attorney's paralegal, who handles routine paperwork, can be your new best friend. But it's still important to know that good lawyer oversight is provided. When brokers or lenders handle closings they work much like a paralegal handling administrative functions. But again, only a lawyer can give legal advice. If you don't already have an attorney, the web site of The American Bar Association at *www.findlegalhelp.org* can help you find the legal assistance you may need and may also provide guidance if you choose to handle things yourself.

Buying a house is probably the most complex, and perhaps the largest financial responsibility you are ever likely to undertake. Getting sound advice is vital. People who try to buy and sell houses without real estate agents increase their need for good legal advice. Even when you work with an excellent broker you'll benefit from sound legal advice. In areas where lawyers are required to perform closings, you have no choice. You have to hire a lawyer. Where closings are done by brokers or lenders you may still want to retain a lawyer to protect your interests. Look for an attorney with specific experience in residential real estate.

Where do you begin? Do you need someone in a large firm, a mid-size firm, or will an individual practitioner be best? This is a very important question. The more specialized knowledge you need, the more specialized the lawyer must be. It stands to reason that a big firm has more experts who can muster vast resources quickly for a very large project. This may be the way to go. But then again, an individual practitioner may very well give you the greatest personal attention. The mid-size firm provides a balance of both. As with any professional service the individual person with whom you will be working most directly is very important. This has to be someone you can have full trust and confidence in. She must be someone who will recognize when specialized knowledge is needed and gets help from a specialized law firm or from specialists within her own firm.

If you're buying in an area where there may be future development, a lawyer who fully understands zoning and other developmental constraints is needed. Properties with environmental problems that could have long-reaching ramifications demand specialized knowledge. A prime example of where specialized knowledge is needed is coastal waterfront property that requires in-depth understanding of tidelands instruments.

Evaluating a lawyer includes:

• Experience in residential real estate
• Referrals from people you know and trust

- Ease of communication with the lawyer

- Ease of communication with the paralegal

- Will specialized knowledge be required?

- Trust

Home Inspector

Many popular magazines have ads for home inspector courses and franchises that imply a quick route to riches. Beware. Selecting a good home inspector may make a profound difference. The job of the **home inspector** is objectively assessing the true condition of the home you are buying to the extent possible from visual inspections. A key difference between home inspectors is knowledge and experience. The greater the knowledge and experience, the less likely they will overlook indications of problems. The greater the knowledge and experience, the greater likelihood that the inspector will be able to guide you in understanding the significance of material defects and provide recommendations. Your home inspector is a very key member of your professional team. It should not be left to an inexperienced friend or relative who may be available at a good price. Friends and family can help but unless they are professional home inspectors they may incorrectly identify or overlook problems. Your needs must be properly served.

A licensed professional engineer or architect who performs building inspection engineering has a higher level of education, experience, and problem-solving expertise. The most comprehensive set of standards for residential and small commercial building inspections is that provided by the **National Academy of Building Inspection Engineers (NABIE)**, at *www.nabie.org*.

Please review Chapter 11 before hiring your home inspector. That chapter includes an expanded discussion about hiring a home inspector suitable to your needs.

Mortgage Broker

Banks, independent brokers, real estate firm brokerage, and builders are all sources of mortgages. Banks, real estate firms, and builders will only have their specific products to sell. An independent mortgage broker can shop for a variety of products. A mortgage broker who has an MBA degree demonstrates significant additional education. There are many federal and state regulations and most, but not all, states have licensing requirements for mortgage brokers. Mortgage brokers facilitate the complex process of obtaining a mortgage and help you navigate the obstacles and jump the hurdles so often needed to get a sound mortgage. A good source of information is the National Mortgage Broker's Association site at *www.namb.org*. It is too easy to be seduced by deceptive selling practices including the all-too-easy Internet. Careful selection of your mortgage source and protection of your private information is necessary. A thorough discussion about mortgages is discussed in Chapter 4.

Real Estate Appraiser

Real estate appraisers provide objective reports on estimates of the market value of real estate—land, buildings, and other improvements—but personal property is not in her purview. Typically a lender will retain an appraiser to perform an independent analysis of the property value to determine the maximum amount of loan to consider. This involves a site inspection to perform measurements and document the basic characteristics of the house. Market place comparative analyses and/or cost analyses determine the current market value. Local tax assessments have a relationship to market value, but are not necessarily reliable for current market valuations. On the other hand, however, a real estate appraiser can be your best friend if you want to appeal your property tax assessment. The real estate appraiser can also estimate building replacement costs for insurance purposes, or in divorce and probate proceedings.

Accountant

You may not need an accountant during the house-buying process, but you may need help at tax time. Some accountants work without a license and some are tax preparers. While individuals may not need the year-round services of a Certified Public Accountant (CPA), you may want to look for qualified help before the next dreaded April 15. A CPA can prepare, analyze, and verify your financial documents for tax filing. Some CPAs who are also lawyers specialize in sophisticated tax and accounting matters. All CPAs have credentials to work for public companies. Some specialize in particular industries. Some have expanded into financial and investment planning and into information technology (IT) consulting.

If you think you need help in money matters, be careful. Many self-defined financial advisors are really selling products. Accountants do not sell products. They provide objective advice. Your time of need for tax assistance or investment risk assessment is a good time to consider consulting a qualified, licensed accountant—a CPA.

Architect

You may need an architect if you want a custom house or plan to do expansion or remodeling. Architects design the overall visual quality of homes and buildings. They create the look that provides good feelings. They develop design concepts to meet a building owner's or developer's needs and convert those concepts into blueprints for construction. Architects often supervise construction to assure compliance with their plans and achievement of a target budget. They often specialize in both building plans and architectural style. They frequently work with engineers, interior designers, and other technical specialists who provide design and construction details for various elements of a total project.

Renovation and expansion require special experience in working with older buildings to assure good adaptation of the new to the old, along with any necessary upgrading of an existing building. There are architects, for example, who specialize in historic renovations. You may seek an architect for a totally new project on clear land, for an addition, or for interior modification. Even if you are just looking to open one room to another and think all you need is to have a large beam designed, it can be helpful to bring in an architect to analyze your space and how you live. A professional often sees things that may suggest a very desirable alternative. If your project is major expansion or renovation, be ready to provide the architect with photos of your house and the interior areas where you plan to remodel. A property **survey** is helpful.

All creative projects involve levels of frustration that can try the soul. Generally the more creative the work, the more you may experience frustration. This is because the people associated with getting the work completed will be faced with doing new things. Drawing details may not be perfect, so revisions may be required. Not all craftspeople can translate a creative design from paper to three-dimensional realities. A very creative work may bring new experiences, new feelings, and new frustrations.

If yours is a small project it may not just be consideration of your architect's time to try to meet at her office. You'll be doing yourself the favor of going to see examples of her work. There is an artistic quality to the work of architects so, as in buying any work of art, you will want to see examples of the artist's prior work. You need the comfort of knowing that this artist's style makes you feel good.

You'll feel even better if your architect can provide glowing references from clients who had projects similar to yours within the last five years. You can glean from these a perspective of the architect's work and its consistency. You will also learn the strengths of your architect and how she has made previous clients feel good. Ask them if there are things they would do differently were they to work with this architect again. Get the advantage of their experience.

Engineer

Professional engineers apply the principles of science and mathematics to develop economical solutions to technical problems. Their knowledge and skills provide design, analysis, and evaluation as well as consultation and technical advice for a variety of building design and development construction. These can include foundations, structural beams and trusses, retaining walls, grading plans, soil evaluations, drainage and sewage disposal systems, water supply systems, and house systems involving electrical, mechanical, plumbing, and fire issues.

Engineers are very attentive to detail. They are accustomed to performing analyses and using mathematics in their work. They are masters in utilizing materials to achieve a very specific purpose. Engineers design every system within a house but are seldom the overall designers. Architects of new houses will retain engineering services to design the various systems, including structural design, heating and air conditioning, electrical and plumbing systems, property grading, and drainage systems. In evaluating any one of these systems, engineers are particularly helpful because of their professional attention to detail and analytical approach.

Land Surveyor

Professional land surveyors can provide surveys that are actual maps of existing properties confirming the legal definition of property boundaries and noting any encumbrances (restrictions, easements) or encroachments. A survey can ensure that there are no boundary disputes and guarantee title insurance. Typically the lawyer or closing agent will obtain the survey.

Land surveyors also provide wetland and coastal tideland delineations, flood elevation certificates, perform boundary line adjustments and construction surveys, and, prepare topographic or subdivision maps. They may mark boundaries with pins or monuments. If the property you are interested in is already marked, the extra expense of a survey is still a good investment. Ask whoever is obtaining your survey to have pins or monuments installed if they do not exist. Another very good reason for hiring a land surveyor is to create a fence line before you go to the expense of putting up a boundary fence or installing expensive plantings. It is not neighborly to encroach on your neighbor's property. It can also be very costly if you have to move the fence or redo the landscaping. It's safer to make sure you're on your side of the line.

Builder

You certainly need to consult a builder if you're starting from the ground up. Who do you choose? Builders range from remodelers of existing houses to those who create huge developments. A builder may be part of a large organization with all the advantages of size, but a small builder with limited full-time staff may be able to give you personalized attention and, depending upon the firm's financial and subcontracting resources, the potential for very satisfactory custom work. With any construction project, it's the level of supervision and quality assurance that makes the difference between excellent quality work and a lemon.

Very large developers enjoy the benefit of large organizations with many technical experts. They can engineer the job so that the least amount of material and energy will create a fine product. Large organizations also have the potential for organized and detailed follow-up to correct deficiencies. Outstanding examples of very large successful developers are Toll Brothers at *www.tollbrothers.com* and KHovanian at *www.khov.com*. They offer a wide variety of new construction in specific locations under development. Large builders can offer one-stop shopping for all your home-buying needs, including financing. A word of caution, though. If you buy into a large development, be aware that its very newness and size can put a strain on existing community services, particularly on schools. You have to be prepared for the potential increase in local taxes to cover the cost of needed improvement and/or expansion created by your development.

Consumers and builders alike can find extensive information at *www.nahb.org*, the web site of the National Association of Home Builders.

Handypersons and Trade Professionals

The handyperson is definitely back on the scene. Years ago, before giants like Home Depot® or Lowe's® helped fuel the do-it-yourself movement that swept the country, home owners of the past paid handypersons to do jobs they couldn't or didn't want to do themselves. These artisans of history usually stuck to one calling, like painting or hanging wallpaper, carpentry, and electrical or plumbing work. Unlike the plumber or the electrician, the handyperson, then or now, generally does not have to be licensed. You are definitely going to run into wider variations in quality of skill among today's handypersons who are enjoying a growth spurt in popularity.

With Lowe's® and Home Depot®, today's home owner can be her own handyperson if so inclined. But often she is not. Greater affluence today has freed her from a lot of chores so she hires a handyperson who can come with either a maintenance background or a specialty in one particular skill. Today's handyperson is often a "jack-of-all trades." If she's also a licensed plumber or electrician, so much the better for her and the home owner who hires her. Amateurs have no business trying to do plumbing or electrical work. Call the licensed professional. The need for experienced and honest craftspeople exists. When the job is big enough, such as an installation of a new heating and cooling system, call the heating and air conditioning trade professional. For service of the system, call a licensed plumber or electrician.

People who work in the neighborhood where you live are usually a good first choice in finding the handyperson or trade professional you can count on. They know that neighbors may not only be a source of references, but of future work, providing that the worker continues to provide good service.

Home-Buyer's Checklist

- Have I done the research on the Internet and in person to identify the real estate, legal, and financial assistance that I will need?

- Have I honestly assessed what I am capable of doing and what I'll need help with?

- Should I begin by looking on my own?

- Have I taken best advantage of recommended web sites cited within the chapter and in the appendix?

- Have I identified mortgage and home inspection professionals?

- Am I prepared to work with professional help?

Chapter 7

What Am I Looking For in a Home?

You may think that you know exactly what kind of house you want. Catherine and George did; they just didn't go about looking the right way at first. They wanted history—a house with a past, a house with stories to tell. New houses just couldn't hold a candle to the graciousness of a house that had seen a heap of living. What they hadn't counted on was that history comes with a price—high maintenance. They followed up on "For Sale by Owner" ads for vintage houses and found quite a few that had been lovingly restored—cosmetically. Because they had done their homework they also found that more than a few were in need of serious repair—more money out the window.

Catherine and George realized that they needed a pro team on their side. With a little investigation they found a real estate professional that specialized in historic homes. Even sweeter was their discovery of a building inspection engineer who specialized in "Golden Oldies." End of story? Well, yes, but it took a while. Even with their pro team in place, Catherine and George learned that Rome wasn't built in a day. It still took a while to find a house that had both good structure and cosmetic improvements. Patience and trust paid off.

One of the first things to think about is the type of house you want and the features you want within that house. Then you can consider property features and, finally, location issues, including zoning and area development planning. We'll look at new houses, existing houses, and special types of houses and locations to help you determine what you desire. You may well find, along the way, that you are redefining what you had always thought was written in stone. It pays to keep an open mind.

House Features

House features will depend upon the type of home you want. Let's start by discussing two basic types of houses: detached single family and attached townhouse/condo. Some detached single-family houses are part of a condominium association. Some townhouses are not part of condominium associations. There are many different architectural styles to review. Later we will discuss two- and more-family houses and specialty locations such as historic and waterfront houses. Here we are going to help you define the particular features you want in your next house. We're going to ask you to prioritize these features and remember the ABC's as aids when you have more than one to choose from. You have already considered basic needs and wants, so we will go into more depth here about the features of houses and property that will be important to consider.

The most common type of house is the single family on its own lot. This is your castle where, subject to local zoning and other ordinances, you have the most independence to create your own living space. You also have the greatest obligations for maintenance, insurance, repairs, and other costs associated with independent living. A single-family house has one kitchen and at least one bathroom and one bedroom. More than one kitchen does not necessarily make a house multi-family but usually single-family houses have only one kitchen, unless you're like a family we once knew who had a regular kitchen where you'd expect it to be— plus a summer kitchen in the cool of the basement. That's living!

A detached single-family house is independent of other buildings on the property under and surrounding the house. A detached single-family house is a house you purchase in its entirety, with no shared interests with neighbors for the property under the house. Exceptions we'll talk about later are condominium association detached single-family houses and areas where you have to lease, rather than buy, the land. A single-family house can be detached or attached. **Attached house** means that there is no space between one house and the next. A **townhouse** is a single-family house that can have two or more houses attached.

Do not confuse a single-family attached townhouse with a condominium-attached townhouse that is part of a community association with shared ownership of the structure and property. Townhouses in many cities are individually owned, from the property to the roof, and possibly with air rights as well. They have side walls adjacent to the neighbor's side wall with no space between. Modern building codes require fire-rated side walls for attached construction and certain distances between structures for detached construction to reduce the spread of a potential fire. Frequently the roof of an attached house has a *parapet*, which is an elevation at the side wall to reduce the spread of a potential roof fire. Another example of an attached single-family house is a duplex, which is two single-family houses joined. Attached houses may require an understanding with the neighbor about certain maintenance and certain living conditions. It's best to draw up guidelines for close coexistence to avoid unpleasant surprises later on.

A condominium townhouse is an attached single-family house where the ownership of much of the building and property is shared with other members of the condominium association. See Chapter 8 for more in-depth discussion of various aspects of condo ownership. This type of house is very popular and the major difference between an individually owned single-family townhouse and a condominium townhouse is the form of owner-ship. In some detached single-family condominium houses where the property under the house may or may not be owned by the association, there are financial obligations for shared property. Very little property exists and living is very close together. Larger condo associations may offer on-site recreation facilities like gyms, swimming pools, and tennis courts. Some even have attached golf courses or yacht clubs. Your neighborhood becomes the condominium association. There may be organized activities. Management of the condominium association is over-seen by owners who serve on the association's board of directors while an outside organization generally operates the administra-tive functions.

Single-story houses have only one living floor and may be in a number of styles such as ranch, bungalow, contemporary, and so on. There may be a basement but all living space is located on one floor directly accessible from outside without any stairs or with only one or a few steps. The single-floor house offers the ease of living on one floor without stairs. A popular layout is the L-shape with the garage, laundry, mud room, family room, and kitchen in one leg of the "L" and the bedrooms in the other, anchored by the living/dining areas at the base of the "L". This works well for fam-ilies with small children who don't want to lose sight of mommy. It also offers the advantage of noise control, with active areas well apart from sleeping areas.

Single-floor living is also particularly advantageous for the elderly and those who cannot navigate stairs. Single-story houses invite close contact with nature—it's right outside the door. Or it can be incorporated into the basic layout as an open air court-yard walled by the rooms of the house—the ultimate in outdoor privacy. The single-floor house, typically a ranch, has a larger foundation and larger roof area for the same living space as would a multi-floor house. Don't be confused by the term "raised ranch." This is, indeed, a two-story house.

A two- or three-floor house provides more living space on an equivalent area of land, and frequently offers economies in heating and air conditioning costs. Construction costs, too, can be less due to the smaller foundation and roof area. Bedrooms can be on both the second and first floor, depending upon the size of the house and layout. Some two- or three-story homes will have at least one bedroom on the first level to accommodate people who need to avoid stairs. The larger the house, the more likely it is that there will be multiple floors, at least for part of the house. If this is so, you can create a large two-floor grand entrance that can be very impressive.

A garage—attached or detached—is a much desired feature of any house regardless of the number of floors. An attached garage offers the advantage of direct entrance or exit, a convenience at any time, but especially in bad weather.

Most new houses have attached garages. Gone are the days when the garage had to hug the rear property line. This was the norm in the early days of the last century simply because that's where the barn had been. You'll still find many older houses with garages way out back. This made sense when horses and their aroma were not welcome in the front parlor. It took a while for builders to realize that a garage does not offend the senses as the barn had done.

House Styles

Today's broad variety of house styles offers just as broad a variety in living experiences. Not only can houses differ in appearance, but they can also feel and function differently. Having the opportunity to select the type of house best suited to your particular lifestyle can be a real joy. We shall discuss some basic house styles here and more unusual styles a little later in the specialty house section of this chapter. You can follow up with a web search of "house styles" or a review of architectural books for many hours of pleasant dreaming about the type of house that best suites your personal lifestyle. You don't have to put the dream on hold. Just let it simmer on the back burner for a little while. Life does not always grant our ideal wishes but serious thinking about your dream will definitely hone your skills in the house search-and-selection process.

The Cape Cod style of house became very popular during the 1930s because of its economy of construction and basic weather-resistant form. Sears Roebuck® even offered a mail order version at the time, many of which still exist today. Similar to a bungalow, the Cape is usually one floor that can be, and often is, expanded. After World War II, Cape Cod houses were mass produced for returning GIs and their new families in huge developments—like Levittown—on enormous tracts of land. Its most basic form was a single living floor with an attic and possibly a basement for additional space. The style itself goes back to colonial times on—and it should surprise no one—Cape Cod in Massachusetts. It was a sturdy little house built to weather the changeable climatic conditions of this long arm of land surrounded by the Atlantic Ocean.

The one-and-a-half story version of the Cape with existing attic space is ideal for expansion, using dormers for light and ventilation in one very large second-floor bedroom, or two small ones. Almost all postwar Cape Cods were wood-framed with wood or asbestos-cement shingle siding and wood or asphalt shingle roofs with side gables, making for a strong triangular-shaped structure. The wood-frame house with its steep, gabled roof was economical to build and has proven to be very robust over time. These houses can range from fewer than 700 square feet (65 square meters) to more than 2,000 square feet (186 square meters). Many existing houses have been expanded from their original construction with dormered attic expansions and rear additions. Sometimes open roof-covered porches called "breeze-ways," between the house and detached garage, have been closed-in to create more living space.

Another house style from the past is the Colonial, which takes its name from its origin during colonial times in early America. It is a very livable and practical design. There are many types of colonial houses, but probably most common is the center-hall colonial, typically a two-story square house of eight basic rooms, with or without a basement. Often the living room is to one side of the front entrance hall, flanked by the dining room, with the kitchen and family room at the rear. The second floor typically has four bedrooms. This style house can range in size from about 1,500 square feet (139 square meters) to over 5,000 square feet (465 square meters), significantly larger than a Cape Cod. A colonial's side-gabled roof is less steep than a Cape's. There may be an attached or detached garage.

Contemporary houses do not derive from older times. They are today's houses and do not fit any particular style pattern because they are generally very creatively designed. Usually they are more than one story but, as will be discussed in our ranch section, they can also be single-floor in design. Contemporaries may blend a variety of traditional styles and exciting geometry to express a form of art. Anything goes. Often contemporary houses are abstract shapes with large, open spaces. Steep roof lines and flat roofs may coexist in the same house. Custom construction is typical, with size ranging from very small to very large. Trees growing right in the rooms of the house and gardens within interior open portions of the house are not uncommon to the contemporary style. Again, anything goes.

The ranch house has evolved from the past. Like its great, great grandfather, the homestead of a western rancher, a ranch house has a single floor that can range in style from simple to ultra-modern contemporary. Typically the roof is a relative low-sloped gable. However, flat roofs often exist on the more contemporary designs. The big advantage of the ranch style is one-floor living with ease of entry and no stairs within the house. Like the Cape Cod, size can range from fewer than 700 square feet (65 square meters) to more than 5,000 square feet (465 square meters). Large ranch homes may even enclose an interior courtyard where the outdoors is brought within the house for maximum outdoor privacy. This may have evolved from the Spanish influence in the Southwest. A ranch house may or may not have a basement. This style house does not lend itself to upward expansion without raising and replacing the roof.

One type of ranch, called the "raised ranch," loses the single-floor advantage because while the main floor is still the primary living space, its walk-out basement level also contains living space that sometimes includes bedrooms and entertainment or family rooms. Often there is a basement level, built-in garage for the raised ranch.

The split-level house generally has three living levels but usually with only the height equivalent of two stories. Typically there is a basement-level garage. A split is similar to a raised ranch inasmuch as the basement area includes living space, but it may also have a crawlspace basement area that has no value as living space but is generally good for storage space.

Nostalgia manifests itself in today's renewed interest in Victorian houses, so named for the long-reigning queen of England who gave her name to an entire era. Genuine Victorians are usually historic-age houses more than a century old that ooze individual character. Their "gingerbread" trim can be exceedingly intricate in combinations of sculpted moldings, lacy carved trims, and delicate railings—the fussier the better. Most Victorians also boast comfortable—often wrap-around—porches, high-peaked roofs, wildly varied shingle siding and often, two or more stained-glass windows.

Cape May and Ocean Grove, both seaside resorts in New Jersey, boast extensive numbers of lovingly restored, genuine Victorian houses, as can numerous cities across the country that housed captains of industry and commerce. The boldest, perhaps, are the famous "Painted Ladies" that grace the hills of San Francisco. These old girls can be red, purple, ocher, pink, and green—all on one house!

The charms of Victorians can carry a hefty price tag because of the disarming additional maintenance they require, particularly if they are to be kept in mint condition. New houses can be constructed in the Victorian style by utilizing low-maintenance plastic siding and fake gingerbread. They are appearing in numbers that seem to suggest a hunger for more solid and formal times. Shine on, harvest moon!

Modified or expanded houses have grown as the families who live in them grew—up and out to satisfy the need for more living space. While not a definable style, so many houses have been expanded from their original configuration that it is important to fully understand just how the house has been expanded or modified. A basic knowledge of the original structure and original features will help you to better understand the strengths and weaknesses of the current house. Recently modified or expanded houses almost always seem to look very good. It is often in the unseen connecting joints of an older house with newer construction that potential for surprises exists. Try to understand the logic for the modifications. This may not be apparent from the exterior. Look over the neighborhood for a possible sister house that has not had this level of modification. It can provide helpful clues.

You may be specifically seeking one certain modified house, such as a Cape Cod with dormers and a finished attic. Or a bungalow that now has an attached garage with a large master bedroom suite over the new garage. Another example may be a colonial with a sunroom added to the rear and a finished basement. An existing modified house may be more economical than a built-by-design house with the same features. A not-so-noticeable improvement is a finished basement with foundation walls that have been preconditioned to stay dry and any needed dewatering systems already installed. This can provide excellent space.

Size of Home

The size of a house can be misleading. Frequently total square footage is not published. The larger the area of the house, the more it costs for basic construction. Appointments within the house will vary in cost, just as automobile prices range from economical to luxury. The number of rooms may sound great until you realize how large or small each room is and what storage space is available or lacking. Determining your minimum requirements will be very important. Write this information down and refer to it as an easy-to-use guideline when selecting potential houses to study.

Let's look at typical sizes of moderate homes with one to four bedrooms. Certainly both smaller and larger homes may have the same number of bedrooms, but just as with cars in the luxury class, actual size has little relationship to cost. Again, these are moderate homes.

In a one-bedroom house ranging from 500 to 800 square feet (46 to 74 square meters) one can expect a single bedroom about 12 feet × 11 feet (4 meters × 3 meters), one full bathroom with a combination shower/tub arrangement, plus an open kitchen, dining, and living area. As we progress, you might want to sketch out room sizes on graph paper in a ratio of one square equal to one foot. When we work on furnishing the rooms you can cut furniture pieces by size from your graph paper and actually arrange them in the rooms you have drawn. This process creates a visual aid far better than the mind's eye, which can be undependable.

Let's move on to a two-bedroom moderate house that can range from 750 to 1,500 square feet (70 to 139 square meters). Here one can expect a master bedroom of probably 12 feet × 15 feet (4 meters × 5 meters), with its own bathroom and most likely with a shower. The second bedroom would be about 10 × 10 feet (3 meters × 3 meters). There might be a hall bathroom in the smaller size house and perhaps a powder room in the larger size. In addition, of course, there would be a kitchen and either separate living and dining rooms or a combined living/dining area.

A three-bedroom house might range from 1,200 to 1,800 square feet (111 to 167 square meters). This size would have one master bedroom about 12 feet × 15 feet (4 meters × 6 meters) with a master bath, possibly featuring both tub and shower. The two additional bedrooms could each be about 12 feet × 14 feet (4 meters × 4.5 meters). There may be a hall bathroom and possibly a powder room. In addition there would be an eat-in kitchen, dining room, and living room. Still working with your graph paper?

A four-bedroom house could range from 1,500 to 2,500 square feet (139 to 232 square meters), probably with the same number and sizes of rooms as the three-bedroom house just described—with the addition of a fourth bedroom and a family room.

Now that you can see and compare the room sizes you have so graphically drawn, consider the number of bedrooms you need. Houses are listed regularly by the number of bedrooms, but like overall square footage, room sizes may or may not be listed in advertising information. Keep in mind that the sizes of the bedrooms and amount of closet space will greatly differ. The number of bedrooms and bedroom size need to be considered at the same time. A larger bedroom may accommodate a second bed or a baby area, eliminating the need for an additional room. A small room is usually 9 feet × 10 feet (2.5 meters × 3 meters). Closet space is a critical element of any bedroom's size. Naturally, all bedrooms need at least one window. More than one provides additional light and better air circulation. Let's consider what goes into a bedroom for a better understanding of how room sizes will work for us.

A small bedroom will typically have a single bed, dresser or chest of drawers, a chair, and a small table. Leaving some room around the bed, these items will take about 52 square feet (5 square meters. In a room that is 9 feet × 10 feet (2.5 meters × 3 meters), that leaves an open area of about 4 feet × 9 feet (1 meter × 3 meters). Keep in mind that space in front of windows has very limited use. Depending upon the window position in a room, the useful floor area may be restricted. In order to have a king-size bed with two small chairs and two dressers or chests of drawers, the minimum size of room providing only 6 feet × 10 feet (2 meters × 3 meters) of open space would have to be 11 feet × 12 feet (3 meters × 4 meters). Again, the window layout may require additional space. Generally a room needs to be at least 12 feet wide (4 meters wide) to accommodate two beds. Larger bedrooms generally start at 12 feet × 15 feet (4 meters × 5 meters).

By this time you are a master of graph paper. Now you may begin on furniture according to the following mattress sizes (in inches). Add about eight inches to the length of the bed when a headboard and footboard are used.

Single:	39 inches wide × 75 inches long
	(99 centimeters × 190 centimeters)
Double:	54 inches wide × 75 inches long
	(137 centimeters × 190 centimeters)
Queen:	60 inches wide × 80 inches long
	(152 centimeters × 203 centimeters)
King:	76 inches wide × 80 inches long
	(193 centimeters × 203 centimeters)

How many bathrooms do you need? The bathroom is, essentially, a very private and functional place. One bathroom is a bare necessity, of course, but more than one can be a great convenience. It's amazing how large families in the past managed with just one bathroom, but let's be realistic. No one today wants to take a place in line outside a closed bathroom door. Mercifully, even today's smaller homes usually have one full bathroom and one toilet or powder room. A bathroom that's part of a master bedroom suite is a great convenience. The next level of bathrooms is for two bedrooms to share one bathroom. The height of luxury is a private bath for every bedroom, with powder rooms in various parts of the house for guests.

It's not just the number of bathrooms, but the size that can make a difference. At the very minimum, a bathroom needs a toilet, sink, and a bathtub or shower. If it does not have an outside window, it will need a vent fan to draw moisture and odor out of the house. Often the bathtub has a shower in combination. Having a separate shower is a plus. Often the master bath attached to the master bedroom will have a shower, and the hall bathroom will have a combination bathtub and shower. A third bathroom is generally just a toilet room with a sink, located near the entrance to the house, perhaps off a mud room with an impervious floor, such as tile or vinyl not affected by wetness. If the house has a swimming pool, it is convenient to have a nearby bathroom with a tile floor.

The house for the car or cars—the garage that replaced the horse barn—is in trouble. So many garages are filled with "stuff" that there is no room for even one car, let alone two. One would think that our second most expensive purchase deserves shelter. Most often that is not the case. From basic cars to luxury cars, cars across the United States live on the driveway. The horse was better off. As we accumulate stuff we quickly outgrow storage space within the house, so sheds and attics start to fill. When they hit maximum, the garage gets—all of it. Modern storage devices allow a great deal of wall storage to expand the utility of the garage, so maybe there's hope. An organized garage with room for cars is the great convenience it was designed to be, particularly in bad weather. In any case, an attached garage offers another advantage in that it may become the platform for house expansion at a later date without expanding the footprint of the house.

Let's go downstairs. Full-height basements are another area where the accumulation of stuff can overwhelm the use of space. Will we ever escape the clutter? Some houses have crawl basements that allow access to utilities and perhaps some storage, but are not tall enough for use by many people. A house on a hillside may have a walk-out basement where part of the basement is below grade level and part exits directly to the outside property. Walk-out basements frequently have finished livable areas, such as in a raised ranch as we discussed earlier. Other styles of houses may also have walk-out basements if they are built into hillsides. Portions of basements below grade are typically cooler spaces and are vulnerable to moisture intrusion, so it is important when buying a finished basement to know that all potential moisture intrusion considerations have been given adequate attention.

Moisture accompanied by high humidity has the potential to create mold. In Chapter 17 on expanding the house, we will discuss finishing basements to reduce the potential for problems such as moisture intrusion. Basements frequently have utility rooms with heating and air conditioning equipment, hot water heaters, water supply piping, and other equipment. Basements provide great workroom and storage areas that take pressure off the garage.

Interior Features

Probably the most often-used space in the house—after the bedrooms—is the kitchen, unless you eat out all the time. A comfortable, well-equipped kitchen can greatly enrich your lifestyle, particularly if you like to cook and/or entertain. How many times have you been to a party where everyone congregates in the kitchen, even when other, more comfortable rooms are just down the hall? For millennia, people have gathered around the hearth. It's often the social center of the house.

For growing families, most decisions are probably made after discussion in the kitchen. Most of us will remember from childhood delicious cooking smells that drew us like a magnet to the kitchen. Do you have small children who follow their noses and want to play in the kitchen? You have to know your minimum kitchen requirements and how they may change over the years.

Think about how you live now and how you would like to live in your new home. The ideal kitchen may never be found, ready and waiting for you. It may need to be created. At least give yourself a starting point by defining minimum kitchen requirements. If gas cooking is important, you will need a house that already has gas service or one where you'll be willing to have a propane tank. Some chefs want gas for the stove but electric for the ovens. What specialized equipment will you need to suit your cooking style? Almost as fast as new entertainment technology hits the tech stores, new kitchen appliances hit the chef shops. A computer search will set your head awhirl with endless ideas for your future kitchen. A walk through Home Depot® or Lowe's® will also provide many ideas.

Kitchen size varies greatly, but even in the smallest of houses one can have the feel of a larger kitchen when the dining area is part of the kitchen. Don't overlook windows, counters, and cabinet space—they are very important. A small galley-style kitchen that opens to larger spaces can work very well if everything is reachable from a preparation and cooking area, and guests gather just outside your work area. As kitchens get bigger there may be a cooking area and a separate preparation area. Islands within the kitchen can contribute greatly to a comfortable flow of cooking and people.

If you spend a lot time in the kitchen, consider the compass direction the windows face. When do you need or want the most light, morning or evening? Do you want the kitchen to have the view or should that be the focal point of another room? Do you have a choice?

Finding your ideal kitchen in an existing home will not be likely and many people are not ready or able to renovate their kitchen immediately after purchasing a new home. If the potential is there, you can do it later. Knowing your basic needs can form the criteria for selecting one house over another. This is your starting point. Our work sheet will help you to create these criteria.

We have already discussed the number of bathrooms you may need and their minimum size, basic fixtures, and location in relation to the bedrooms and busy areas throughout the house. There is a great deal more to the bathroom than simple basics. It is a very functional, private place, but it can be spacious and elegant. It can be outfitted with luxurious accommodations—even entertainment facilities for long stay.

If you or someone in the family has special needs, facilities such as walk-in bathtubs may not already exist, but can be added if there's enough room. Wheelchair-accessible showers are seldom already installed, but can be created if the space is available. Knowing that certain special requirements exist will be vital to include in your search criteria. Beyond these, however, are the extra joys we call "luxuries." They are the spice of life when you can afford them.

A large whirlpool tub might be lovely if it already exists, but may not be that high on your list—not yet. As your luxury level increases it may make the list. You might even aspire to your own in-house spa. How about a floor with radiant heat? How about a shower with a steam unit? How about a sauna in the bathroom or at a pool area? How about an indoor lap swimming pool? They all exist but this is approaching serious luxury—and a serious measure of water—liquid or vapor. This kind of luxury requires maintenance of proper humidity controls to guard against mold production. Mold puts a crimp on anyone's luxury.

Another room that needs moisture control and a proper exhaust system is the laundry, no matter what its size or state of sophistication. Many smaller older homes do not have any laundry room. Where they do exist, laundries range from close to non-existent in a corner of the basement, to a large room with built-in ironing boards and storage facilities. In some cases there is only a washing machine that requires plumbing to supply clean water and to take away used water. Portable units with hoses that can be connected to a sink are available so it is possible to have a washing machine in the kitchen with no separate plumbing facilities. Clothes dryers must have exhausts so these are not as portable as washing machines. There are some small, portable, spin clothes dryers, however. Whatever type of dryer you use, you have to be sure that dryer lint is properly exhausted or removed from the house.

Heating Systems

Heating a house is essential. Even in very warm climates there are times when some heat is needed, so heat provisions may be taken for granted. Location, coupled with how well the house is insulated, will determine the overall heat capacity needed. Knowing that you have an adequately sized and properly operating heating system should be determined during the home inspection. Your choice of heat delivery should be part of the overall criteria for your perfect house.

In this section, we will discuss different types of heating systems and the types of energy they use—most typically electricity, gas, or oil. A geothermal heating system that uses a heat pump to transmit energy from the earth into water piping will still need additional energy sources for operation—usually electricity, which is available almost everywhere from public utilities. Natural gas, however, is not piped into all locations. You may need oil or propane gas. You may have a preference for a particular heating system based on your own experience or family health needs.

All houses need some form of heat with a capacity that will achieve 70°F, even under conditions of coldest outdoor temperature. One of the most common forms of heat delivery is forced warm air. This type of system may be combined with air conditioning in that both utilize a blower to circulate warm or cool air throughout the house. Filters are needed for the air-handling unit and they must be changed regularly. Forced warm-air heating systems dry out the air so often humidification systems are needed. This adds a bit more to your maintenance load and scheduling since you need to keep humidifiers clean and turned off during the warm months. Energy for a forced warm-air system may be electric, gas, or oil.

Forced hot-water or steam-heating systems require a boiler typically fired with gas or oil. Coal and wood can also be used in certain boilers. Many people prefer hot-water or steam-heating systems because they gently radiate heat without blowing air that may distribute contaminants. The radiators retain heat, helping to achieve a more uniform temperature without the intermittent blowing of warm air. While forced hot-water systems require an electrical pump to distribute the hot water, a steam-boiler heating system does not need electricity except for operation of a thermostat. Steam systems use gravity to distribute hot water vapor to the radiators.

There are various types of electric heating systems that use electrical components, such as electric-resistance heaters in each room. Radiant heating systems work well to provide even heat by typically circulating hot water through pipes in a concrete floor. Radiant heating can also be installed under a wood floor. This may be especially attractive to families with small children who always play on the floor. The hot water source is from a forced hot-water boiler, which needs controls to prevent the water from getting too hot. Radiant heating can also work with electrical-resistance heating units installed in a floor or ceiling. Radiant heat provides the gentlest uniform heat throughout a room and can be installed with individual thermostat controls for each room.

Cooling Systems

In areas where summer brings uncomfortable heat, air conditioning makes life a lot easier. It allows us to turn away from stifling heat and humidity and continue to function in comfort. It has become so commonplace that air conditioning has become standard, not only in our houses, but also in our cars.

In many houses air conditioning is easily adapted to forced-air heating systems with in-wall ducts already in place. For some people, however, good old AC is not standard. Houses heated by hot water or steam need new ducting for central air conditioning.

For this reason, many older homes that have some air conditioning, like window units, do not have central air because walls in older houses are made of plaster and lath and cannot accommodate air ducts within the walls. Certainly no décor-conscious home owner would tolerate ducts outside the walls, so installing central air in an older house is a challenge. Sometimes the only solution is to go down from the working parts of the system installed in the attic through existing closets to the second-floor bedrooms and the ceilings of the first floor. Happily, this may soon become a moot point because there are now available high-velocity small-diameter air ducts that can be retrofitted into older homes.

The best air conditioning system will have both supply registers and return registers in all rooms that have doors to ensure a steady flow of cool air and to reduce the load on the air conditioner. Window units are available that can be used with typical house electrical wall outlets. In addition to window units there are wall-mounted room air conditioners that do not need ducts. There can be one or more of these interior units for each outside condensing unit.

Property Features

The size of the **lot** and its location will have a substantial effect on the price you will pay for your house. Zoning, which determines what one can do on a particular lot, will be discussed later in this chapter. To the extent that you have choice, developing lot-size criteria will be helpful. Some lifestyle requirements demand a large lot such as when you have horses. You cannot keep horses on a 50 × 100 foot (15 × 30 feet meters) lot! Specialty lots such as waterfront or lots with mountain views may also restrict your choices of size. Whatever its dimensions, your lot will be part of a neighborhood.

Neighborhoods make memories. Whether you're raising a family or moving into your golden years, the area and people around you provide spice for the soup of your life. You can live rural and rustic at great distance from the nearest other human. Or you can be in the thick of things in a townhouse downtown in a hip community brimming with activity at any hour of the day or night. Location, location, location boils down to the neighborhood you choose to live in. Convenience and privacy trade-offs abound. This is probably one of the most difficult decisions to make. After selecting a general area to live in, choosing the most appropriate neighborhood is not easy. What you want may not be available at any price. Nevertheless, identifying desired neighborhood characteristics will be important in your search.

We have already discussed various qualities of life in Chapter 2 on determining needs. They will guide you in developing specific criteria for neighborhoods you might want to live in. To understand a neighborhood it is helpful to spend time there. The name of the game is networking. Talk with people who live there. Read the local papers. Visit the nearest library. Call or visit the local chamber of commerce. They always have a lot of information. Visit web sites for local business, community, and religious organizations. Consider attending local government public meetings. You may even find, as you network, that you already know someone who, in turn, knows someone else familiar with the area.

What utilities are available? Unless you are way out in a rural country area, most houses have access to public water, public sewers, electricity, phone, cable, and natural gas. Let's deal first with the ins and outs of water—literally in and out. The purity of incoming water is not negotiable. We must be able to count on a safe and dependable source. Public utilities usually do a good job of managing the content and quality of water to ensure that it is safe to drink. If your source is a well, you will need to monitor your water quality regularly to know if and when any treatments are necessary for it to be drinkable.

Getting rid of used water safely and efficiently is of equal importance. A public sewer is a great convenience—again, because public utilities usually do a good job. If your house is elevated so that gravity provides the energy for sewage flow, there is very little maintenance except for in-house plumbing fixtures. When public sewerage is not available, you will need a private sewage-treatment facility such as a septic system. These systems need regular maintenance and periodic cleaning. Their life span varies with location and quality of components. Sometimes pumping systems are needed for both public and private sewers.

Electricity is a fundamental utility that is generally available. Your home inspection will reveal whether your system is modern and has adequate capacity, but this is typically not an excessive concern in your house search. In areas that experience regular power outages, having an emergency engine generator could be more than a convenience—it could save your life. Here we come to what type of fuel will be needed. Oil? Natural gas? Propane? Oil is efficient, but its storage can present problems if there is even a small leak in the storage tank. Natural gas, a very effective and generally safe form of fuel, is piped to many houses but not all. The fuel has a pungent odor added to help detect any leak. Another choice could be propane. Both natural gas and propane evaporate when exposed to air so there is not the pollution concern of leaking oil tanks.

With the advent of wireless communication the necessity for the basic phone line has been lessened but not eliminated. Phone service can work when there are electrical power failures because copper phone lines carry enough power to operate a basic phone without any need for additional electricity. So, it is good always to have at least one phone that does not need electricity.

Cable service has become common for TV. This is an area under great development so many changes can be expected in the future.

Zoning

Zoning defines what uses are allowed on any property. Zoning regulations are established by state, regional, and local governments and can evolve and change with time. Monitoring zoning development can help you to know how property usage may change. Industrial, commercial, agricultural, and residential permitted usage is defined by zoning. Zoning typically defines the size of lot, the dimensional restrictions for buildings, and how much space must exist from property lines for certain uses. Zoning will define density or how many buildings of certain types can be put on an acre of land. Mixed use may also be permitted where there are single-family, detached and/or attached, and multiple-family dwelling buildings in the same zone. Restrictions may exist, such as prohibition of a home-based business. It is possible to get approval to deviate from zoning requirements by obtaining a **variance**, but nothing is guaranteed unless a protracted process is followed meticulously. More will be discussed about variances in Chapter 17 on expanding your home. Achieving a basic understanding of zoning will help you to know what you can legally do on your property. Copies of **zoning ordinances** can be obtained at a local library or at the municipal city hall. Your real estate professional can also get this information.

Local and Regional Planning

While zoning defines the existing requirements for designated areas of a town, planning documents may exist at the local or regional level that redirect the future. This could have an impact on a particular property you are considering. For this reason, it is helpful to become knowledgeable about future planning proposals. Investigate what proposals local municipal planning boards are formulating for land use. And don't ignore regional and state planning boards—they can also get in on the act. Learning about proposed plans for areas you are considering will help you to develop a perspective on potential future changes.

New Versus Existing Home

Are you in the market for a new house or an existing house? We shall discuss new houses and then a variety of existing houses, ranging in condition from broom-clean and ready to move in to those that need extensive rehabilitation. When you anticipate moving again in a relatively short period of time—say three years—it will be important to get a sense of the resale market. This may be most dramatic when purchasing a new house in a very large development that is just beginning sales. Having an exit strategy in mind is a sound idea. Let's begin by discussing new and existing houses. Then we'll take a look at a few specialty houses.

The **builder standard** new house will probably be located in a very sizable development that is largely unfinished. If this development is a condominium, then board control will be by the builder until most of the houses are sold. When the development consists of single-family detached houses there may be bonds held by the local government to ensure adequate completion of roads and utilities. Builder standard can be seen in a model home, typically one of the first houses constructed and sublimely decorated to catch—and sometimes fool—the eye of a would-be buyer who sees rooms that may later seem to shrink when his furniture is in place. The model home is designed to sell the rest of the houses in the development.

Even before you set out to visit model homes you can let your fingers do the walking or, in today's style, the dancing, on the keyboard of your computer. When you're looking for a builder-standard home a lot of research can be done right at your computer. Larger builders have web sites that provide a great deal of information about their offerings. Just as with the purchase of a car you will find that there are many options. Be careful about the model on display to know what features are standard and which ones are optional. Builder-standard houses are semi-mass-produced with a basic foundation layout and minimally different exterior features plus a few interior framing layouts. They may offer allowances for plumbing fixtures and floor coverings that permit some customization. For a new home buyer the builder standard generally offers the most value.

In the best of all possible worlds, dreams can come true. Your dream of a custom-built house may range from a unique design where you commission an architect to create for a unique piece of property you already own, to buying from a developer who owns property and offers so many options that the house is largely custom built to your specifications. Because a custom-built house can run the gamut from economical to very expensive, builder reputation is critical. See Chapter 17 on expanding and remodeling your home for additional information about monitoring the building process.

If time is of the essence, keep in mind that contracting for a new house can often turn into "hurry up and wait." It takes time to build a new house, builder standard or custom. Existing and ready-to-go may be best for you. An existing house that is fully operational without any significant maintenance needs is a ready-to-go purchase. Often, decorating tastes will need some modification, but there are happy occasions where everything is just right. This is second best to having your custom house designed and built, but with the added advantage that you are free of surprises in delays or cost overruns. This may be your best of all possible worlds. It's here now. Call the moving company.

More typical is a house that will need some work to correct one or more deficiencies identified during the home inspection. When the work is minor there may be no delay in your moving schedule. This is a reasonable expectation when purchasing an existing house that is presented as being ready for moving in. Most houses have some deficiency that the home owners have become accustomed to, or in fact, may not even be aware of. Have them fix the problem and call the moving company next week.

Fixer-Upper

Don't turn away so quickly, please. With vision, a strong dose of courage, and some knowledge the fixer-upper may just be the house for you. But a **fixer-upper** is a house that needs a lot of work. This is not for the faint of heart. Great values can be had in purchasing a lot of work, especially if the house is in a great location. If you have the interest and a modicum of construction talent—or a very talented and supportive family—this may be just the ticket to house wealth. But it's wise to understand the extent of rehabilitation needed before you commit to the purchase. Don't sign anything until you have had a comprehensive engineering inspection.

Many people have bought HUD houses or a foreclosure fixer-upper without a thorough evaluation, only to learn of significant deficiencies like leaking or underground oil tanks that have to be removed, water intrusion, mold, or structural problems. Getting good legal advice may be needed. Call your lawyer. Patience is surely needed when you're looking for a good fixer-upper. Don't even think of calling the moving company just yet.

The Department of Housing and Urban Development has houses for sale. These are generally for lower-income people. They may be in poor condition and in poor locations, but for the right buyer they can be a terrific investment. HUD houses become available through a form of foreclosure in which the defaulted mortgage was acquired by HUD and the house is sold at, or near, market value. A good place to begin research if you are interested in a HUD home is on their web site that displays frequently asked questions at *www.hud.gov/offices/hsg/sfh/reo/ reobuyfaq.cfm*. HUD houses are sold as-is, meaning that whatever needs to be done is your responsibility. This may require extensive work before local authorities will provide a **certificate of occupancy**. The main HUD site location is at *www.hud.gov/ homes/homesforsale.cfm*. A current list of HUD houses for sale can be found at *www.hud.gov/offices/hsg/sfh/reo/homes.cfm*. You will need to work with a real estate broker on HUD houses.

If you are interested in low purchase price, and who isn't, still beware of TV ads that talk about "no money down" low-cost purchases, as if anyone can become wealthy accumulating houses. For some this is true. Armed with the information in this book we hope that if you go down this path, you will succeed beyond your wildest dreams, but it can be a roller coaster ride. Just don't get seasick. Hang in, do your homework, and be prepared for surprises. Internet searches, reading newspapers, and talking with bankers are all good places to start. Again, patience is its own reward if you are looking for a foreclosure in a desirable area. Many people look at a foreclosed house as a means for investment. You will need to live in the house to get the advantages of obtaining a mortgage and tax benefits. Improve it, sell it, and try again. If this appeals to you the biggest hurdle is just to get started with the first house purchase. Hang on and enjoy the ride.

Whatever your route—HUD, foreclosure, or fixer-upper—there is risk involved. If you know what you're doing and you're gutsy, go for it. Just be careful. With fixer-upper purchases, performing a thorough risk assessment is more than important. This should not be a "blink" decision. Critical thinking is needed. Get good advice. Talk with an expert or two. Learn about construction and house equipment maintenance to refine your ability to perform preliminary condition assessments. A checklist is provided later in Chapter 11 on home inspection section. Study it so that you'll be able to make good decisions quickly when you're dealing with foreclosures or low cost, potentially high-value houses.

Specialty Homes

Historic older houses can be likened to older people. Some age well; some do not. Some are beautiful; others, not. Some provide loving comfort while others can be a royal pain in the neck. But their very age and ageless style attract so many of us to both well-weathered people and experienced houses. Charm and beauty abound in historic houses. These can be truly romantic homes.

Learning the history of prior occupants is always exciting. Sometimes you'll get lucky and find a house that has had only one or two families living in it since it was built way back a century or two ago. This is a home well-lived in and can, indeed, be romantic. As with any romance there is a level of maintenance not often realized that never ends. Whether for a loved one or a historic house, the romance has to be nurtured. When you have the desire, finances, and willingness to provide the high level of care needed, living in a historic home can be a wonderful experience.

Not too many of these houses remain as they were originally constructed, which can present maintenance problems and, sometimes, structural challenges. Floor loading was lighter in those days and there were fewer closets and storage spaces. Modifications often create poor joints between old and new sections, particularly if they were not done well. Stone foundations may not have been maintained. Keeping roof and surface water away from the foundation may not have been attended to as needed. Insulation did not exist or was very poor but, strangely, this is one of the reasons that historic buildings have weathered so well. Wet wood could dry better and faster with air flow into and around the house than it does in today's very tight "energy-efficient" houses. Most historic houses that have not been extensively rehabilitated will need a lot of work. If you are up to it and the work is done well, the result can be extremely satisfying. Keep the romance alive.

What if the historic house is listed on the national register of historic homes? Think carefully because you will be obliged to maintain the appearance of the house in character with its time period. See the web site at *www.cr.nps.gov/nr/about.htm*. What if the historic house is not listed on the national register but within a local community historic district? Then there will be local regulations that apply typically to the exterior appearance of the house. Local committees take great pride in their historic districts so be prepared to accommodate their requirements. It's best to investigate and fully understand your responsibilities when acquiring a house listed on the national register or located within a controlled historic district.

Romance isn't restricted to times gone by. It's alive and well today in locations that inspire the poet in all of us. One of today's truly romantic living experiences is to live at the water's edge—ocean, river, or lake. Water views provide living art that is continually changing. It's romantic, all right, but it has a very practical side that could be a downside. It's subject to the whims of nature. All waterfront property will be affected by wave action. Many waterfront locations have greater wind exposure that increases demands on the house for weather protection. Tidal areas where the water rises and falls have additional potential erosion concerns that require shore protection to reduce loss of property.

The **Federal Emergency Management Agency (FEMA),** in conjunction with local communities, develops flood zone designations. Flood insurance rate maps (FIRM) are created, designating an "A" zone where there is a one percent chance of a flood in any given year. Base flood elevations are determined from studies that indicate the height at which a new home must be constructed that would essentially keep it above that one percent value. This is the minimum building height standard under the National Flood Insurance Program. Flood zones are not just limited to waterfront properties but may extend well inland of water. Local flood maps can be viewed on the web at *www.fema.gov*. Go to the web map store indicating the address of the house and select "view." You do not need to log on or purchase a map in order to view a map online.

How many times do we hear people wax rapturously over the view in hilly or mountainous country? Who wouldn't want to waken with the morning sun or watch a beautiful sunset at the end of a perfect day? Who wouldn't want a room with a view? Wow! Who could turn down the drama of vistas that can be viewed from a hillside house? Like the waterfront house, an Alpine chateau may be your romance of the century, but it comes with a cost. Is it practical? Will the hill continue to hold the house or is there potential for landslides? These are important questions that need answers before committing to the purchase of a hillside house. Management of water on a hillside is extremely important to reduce the potential for erosion and land movement. Many communities with potential hillside erosion problems have special requirements for hillside construction, including necessary reviews by an engineer. A conversation with the local municipal engineering office will be helpful.

Order a house from a catalog? Blue jeans, yes, and yes to thousands of other items, but a house? As we know, early in the twentieth century you could order a house from the Sears Roebuck® catalog. Manufactured and mobile houses are still made today in factories under controlled conditions. The mobile house is equipped with wheels and generally not permanently attached to the ground. A manufactured house has a steel frame and may have had wheels attached to permit highway travel to the site. It may be permanently attached to the ground with a foundation. These houses tend to be more engineered built than frame-constructed on-site houses.

Larger houses are shipped in half sections and bolted together at the site. Fewer materials may be needed because of the controlled conditions resulting in economy, along with the benefits of factory quality control and the fact that construction materials are not exposed to weather. The factory environment can have the added benefit of a stable workforce and consistent supervision. There are many trailer-park communities with single-wide and double-wide houses that are converting over to manufactured houses. However, manufactured or trailer houses do not have to be located in a trailer community. These houses are available new and used and often can be relocated. Trailer communities will also be discussed in Chapter 8 on condominiums.

Back to the 1910 Sears Roebuck® house for a moment. It was shipped in parts as is the prefabricated modular house of today, which is constructed in factory conditions and then shipped in sections or modules to the lot where the foundation and site have been prepared. The house is assembled on-site and typically finished by a local builder. When completed, these houses look like on-site constructed houses but have the advantage of factory construction for most of the house. Site preparation, foundation design, and construction coordination are critical. Selecting a builder who is experienced in modular construction is very important. This type of house can be constructed on a lot you purchase or on a lot owned by the local builder. Some developments are constructed entirely in this manner. Transportation costs from the factory to the site are an important consideration.

Another specialty house is the A-frame. Its dramatic design makes it very resilient to snow load, so it is very popular as a winter vacation home. The triangular structure is very strong and allows snow and rain to slide off the roof, which also serves as two sides of the house. These houses are available in one-and-a-half- and two-and-a-half-story designs. Windows can be installed in the sides and, with proper orientation, part of the side can be used for solar panels to create electricity. Interior space is generally very open, usually with the upper half-story serving as a loft. Just as the A-frame is ideally suited to winter ski slopes, its openness is equally at home as a beach house.

Even more rustic is the log cabin which brings forth images of early American frontier settlers. Log cabins housed many a pioneer family well into the late 1800s. The Homestead Act of 1862, signed into law by President Abraham Lincoln after the secession of southern states, provided rights to open land with the requirement that the land be farmed and that a house, typically a log cabin of at least 12 feet × 14 feet (3.5 meters × 4 meters), be constructed. These houses were generally crafted of hewn or round logs. Honest Abe knew a thing or two about log cabins, having been born and raised in one in the wilds of then-frontier Kentucky.

If you want frontier authenticity today, log houses are available, ranging in size from small cabins to large houses of unique charm. They usually come in kits of precut and numbered logs for ease of assembly. Of course you could handcraft a log house if you're handy with a chain saw. Another way is to purchase an existing log house, dismantle it, and relocate it to your property with additional construction as needed. There are drawbacks to this approach, however. Outside of the jigsaw puzzle aspect of such a project, old existing log houses are subject to insect and water damage. Very careful inspection is necessary. For died-in-the-wool frontier buffs, extensive information is available on log-building construction. One source is the Log Home Book Store at *www.lhgic.com*.

If becoming a landlord is in your plans you may want to consider a multi-family house where you can live in one of the units. Multi-family houses may be constructed as such from the beginning or may be converted from single-family houses. If that's your cup of tea, understanding current construction requirements will help you to realize potential deficiencies in existing modified structures. Fire safety is one of the more important considerations. Zoning conditions, also, will be important to understand. Multi-family houses may require registration and conformance with certain local or state housing regulations. The two-family house is a common arrangement where the units may be side by side or over and under. Utilities may be combined or separate.

Home-Buyer's Checklist

- Have I reviewed various house features and styles?

- Have my family and I determined what size and style house we want?

- Have we studied how various house styles and special features would impact our lifestyle?

- Have we prioritized our basic needs, wishes, and specific desired property features?

- Do we have time to look at everything that's available?

- Am I familiar with how local and regional planning and zoning can create nasty surprises?

- Would we consider a fixer-upper?

Chapter 8

What Should I Know About Condo Ownership?

*T*here's more—a lot more—in condo purchase than meets the eye. This is one more reason we hammer away at "do your homework!" Ty and Mica did not do their homework. Young and newly married, they were thrilled to find a vacancy in a beautiful condo community that had just become even more desirable as a result of undergoing the glamorous face-lift of total exterior renovation. Ty and Mica happily agreed to the listed price in the innocent assumption that the dollar signs reflected the cost of improvements. What they did not know was that the new look hadn't yet been paid for. The renovations had been mortgaged by the condo association board of directors.

Ty and Mica became battle-bloodied twice over. Not only had they bought high, but they also bought their share of monies owed through higher maintenance fees than their seller had been paying. Morally, disclosure should have been the obligation of the seller, who was entitled to and furnished with the board's financial reports and meeting minutes. Had Ty and Mica been more sophisticated in home buying, they could have asked for this at the beginning and may not have fallen into the lovely—but expensive—trap they found themselves in.

Before you purchase a condo unit consider the critical information presented in this chapter. Get help from your accountant or lawyer, if needed. You are not just buying a place to live—you are investing in a business organization. In fact, the value of understanding the business organization can be far more important than an engineering inspection of the unit's structure and systems. People have purchased condo units and later learned that they needed tens of thousands of dollars to pay an assessment that could have been anticipated. People have purchased a condo unit and later learned that a pending law suit not only cost them much out-of-pocket money, but also reduced the value of their unit. People have purchased a condo unit and later learned that extensive common property remodeling was mortgaged. In this case, the new unit owner not only paid a higher price for the unit but also had to pay off the mortgage, including the additional cost of interest. In this chapter we will be discussing the information you need to know *before* completing your purchase of a condo unit. Where you may find it difficult to understand certain documents, a source of help will be identified, such as an accountant or lawyer.

Condominium and **home-owner association** living has seen enormous expansion in the last 25 or 30 years, resulting in a whole new lifestyle with all the pros and cons attendant to living in close quarters and sharing fiscal responsibility. According to a recent estimate by the Community Associations Institute: "More than 54 million Americans live in an estimated 274,000 home-owner and condominium associations, cooperatives, and other planned communities." See the Community Associations Institute's web site at *www.caionline.org*.

This is a rapidly growing segment of the housing population for a number of reasons. First, there are a large number of living units per **acre** of land. Particularly in urban areas where the cost of land is so high, condo living can be a cost plus. Condo units are particularly appealing to first-time buyers, empty-nesters who are downsizing, and retirees. Condos are also being purchased as second homes at vacation and resort areas. Typically a condo unit owner owns only the space between the walls of her unit and usually does not own the building structure or the land under the building. Condo owners own a small percentage of the entire association property, together with all of the other unit owners.

Along with condo unit ownership there are rights, obligations, and restrictions that are defined in various documents and by municipal and state regulations. There are monthly fees for maintenance and potential periodic assessments for unplanned major expenses. Living is very close to others within a community where there may be many **common elements** and areas designed to be shared with neighbors. For people who need or have experienced more personal privacy, lifestyle adjustments have to be made. One way or another, everything has its price.

Another price—or adjustment—in condo living is relinquishing your freedom to do just as you please with what is, after all, your own property. You can't just take a sledgehammer to an offending wall or divider, or turn that unused second bathroom into a home computer station. Approval from the association is often needed to modify the space within your unit, even minimally.

Many associations may offer, as part of their attraction to residents, lovely amenities at little or no extra cost, such as pools, tennis courts, and golf courses. Some even have on-site yacht clubs, right in, or almost right in, your own backyard.

Community Living

Community living is a lifestyle definitely different from living in a detached, single-family home with your own property between neighbors. You may be king of your condo castle, but much less so than when you own property independent of others. Of course, in all cases, there are local and state government regulations that will affect residential structures and uses of property and buildings. As a condo unit owner, you are typically very close to your neighbors. Balconies and patios may abut with little, if any, barriers. This can seriously cut into the privacy of the cocktail hour or peacefully watching the sun go down. Your neighbor may be enjoying his drink and watching his sun go down hardly an arm's length away.

Even in the most soundproof buildings, some sounds will pass from one unit to another. Here comes another adjustment. Unless your ears are severely insulted by blaring TVs or blasting boom boxes, you'll find that you soon get used to the sounds of others. Muted sound from next door tends to be of little consequence. In a little while you won't even hear it any more. Of course, if you draw the short straw and live beside or beneath an inconsiderate lout who is a loud-sound freak, you do have the right to bring the problem to the association board that can bring down their collective weight on the offender.

It's all a matter of adjustment on everyone's part. Everyone needs to share common areas in accordance with rules, in understanding and with consideration of the neighbors. When everyone cooperates, the world turns smoothly. That it often works is pleasingly amazing, especially since few have met their condo mates before purchasing their unit.

Learning about your future neighbors—if you can—will be an important part of your prepurchase due diligence. There is comfort in knowing that life with these new neighbors will be compatible with your desires and interests. People who spend time at home only to sleep may not be so affected as those who like to entertain outdoors or actually live in the outdoors of their homes. Find out as much as you can ahead of time.

If you contemplate having a pet, will the community permit the type and size of pet you are considering? If you are a biker, will the community tolerate motorcycles? Will you want to have a home office? Condo association rules and local zoning regulations often both affect certain activities, such as having a home business. A home office where you are doing part-time office work may be considered different from a home business where you are actually transacting business deals, even if only via the computer.

Master Deed and Bylaws

The **master deed** is the primary document that creates a condominium in accordance with state law. It includes a legal description of the property and defines ownership rights, responsibilities, and restrictions. The bylaws are a legal document that defines the corporation's operating standards and procedures. In this section, we will review typical elements of both the master deed and bylaws to provide you with an overall understanding of these documents. The master deed and bylaws are complementary documents that need to be reviewed together. Please remember that legal advice can only be given by a lawyer, but not all lawyers have a good working knowledge of condominium law and condominium governance in the state where you are planning to purchase a condo. See Chapter 6 about obtaining professional help to guide your search for legal assistance.

The master deed defines the boundaries of the units within the condominium. A unit is an individual residence. The legal definition of the property is included within the master deed. Exhibits include a site survey and unit layouts. There may be multiple buildings. The description of the units will include what is owned by the unit owner and what is owned in common with the association. Each unit owner is a "tenant-in-common," which means that the unit owner is an investor in the overall property with rights and obligations defined in the master deed. The master deed will define the common property areas that are for general use of all unit owners in accordance with defined regulations that may be generated by the **board of trustees**. There are also limited common areas, such as the previously mentioned balconies, that are property owned by the association but limited in use for a particular unit owner.

Ownership and percentages of ownership are specifically detailed in the master deed. Percentage of ownership is the basis for unit owner voting rights. It's similar to the amount of stock one owns in a corporation, which determines the voting power each unit owner has. Common expenses are detailed, outlining expenses that are to be shared by all unit owners, including expenses for maintenance and repair of limited common elements. Access rights for the association's representative to enter the property of a unit owner are also defined in the master deed.

Selling requirements and leasing restrictions are another part of the master deed. Any restrictions for unit-owner mortgaging may be detailed together with insurance requirements. There may be extensive procedures to follow when you plan to sell your unit.

Even decorating provisions may be detailed in the master deed defining restrictions about what can be done, and what can't be done, without first getting approval from the association. Window treatments do not escape the scrutiny of an eagle-eyed association. To a lot of people this seems unreasonable but there's a method to the madness. It's called uniformity-conformity. While residents may grumble, there is comfort in knowing that the regulations maintain the pleasing look of the place. Exterior alterations, if permitted at all, would certainly require prior approval of the association, especially when common or limited-use common property is involved.

All associations have a board of trustees whose functions are defined in the master deed and expanded upon in the bylaws. In the initial period of new condominium development the board is controlled by the builder. The master deed details procedures for the developer to ease out of control and eventually lose all board membership rights as units are sold. Eventually the board of trustees will be run entirely by unit owners elected in accordance with the bylaws.

Bylaws define the operation and procedures of the corporation that manages the condominium and enforces the provisions of the master deed. Bylaws define the types of meetings to be held, including regular meetings, annual meetings, and special meetings. Meeting notices and voting provisions are defined. The important distinction between meetings for unit owners and meetings of the board of trustees are detailed. The annual meeting agenda is defined. Matters that require voting upon by the entire membership or specified percentages of the entire membership are defined. For example, it may require approval from 75 percent of the entire membership to modify the bylaws or to approve projects with a cost exceeding a certain value. The powers and duties of the board of trustees must be clearly defined.

Amendments to the master deed and bylaws are necessary from time to time, perhaps necessitated by state legislation modifying condominium laws or by changes necessary for the proper operation of the condominium association. The master deed and bylaws will define the requirements for any amendments. In all cases, when proper amendments are created, they will need to be filed with county authorities where they become public records. When reviewing original documents filed in the order in which they were created, it can become cumbersome to tie original documents to subsequent amendments. Sometimes the association may publish a consolidated document, which often includes a statement indicating that it does not take the place of the original filed documents. These records are available to the public for review. They may be obtained from the condominium association or through your lawyer.

Financial Statements

Financial statements are required for all condominium associations. In this section, we will provide a very basic introduction into financial statements. The association's financial statements will probably be a compilation by a certified public accountant (CPA), limited to presentation in the form of financial statements with supplementary schedules of information that are the representations of management. Compilations are not audited or reviewed; thus the CPA does not express an opinion or any form of assurance that the statements are correct. A review, however, is a more thorough level of accountant review. A formal audit is the highest level of accounting verification that the statements fairly represent the true financial condition. Even in audits, CPA's will have qualifying statements. There are no guarantees. At least having an accountant prepare the statements is better than just management making their representations. For assistance in understanding a particular set of financial statements you should consult an accountant.

Condominium associations are subject to federal tax. Under the Internal Revenue Code, associations may be taxed as condominium management associations or as regular corporations, at their election. An association may elect either method in any year and will generally select the method that results in the lowest tax due. As a nonprofit corporation, the association may not be subject to state tax.

Financial statements show what has happened to money the association received, where it went, and where it is now. They provide a picture of past events at a certain point in time. They show money that is owed to others and the change in value of the condominium association. Financial statements can appear quite frightening. Let's try to simplify how to read the statements without the fear-provoking fine print and numbers everywhere. Many of us may have a hard time reading a food package label. There is too much information, making it difficult to understand, especially with the use of obscure terms. First of all, there are just a few basic elements to financial statements. Let's think in these basic terms and then look at some of their details. We will give you an outline to follow, starting with terms, and then providing explanations.

Statements themselves can range from simple five-page documents to volumes of mind-boggling detail. In all cases there will be only three categories of fundamental information: assets, liabilities, and equity. Then there will be a presentation of revenue and expenses. A presentation of cash flow completes the basic financial statement data. Following the numbers presentation there will be notes. These are very important as they explain all the numbers and point out unusual conditions. Many people read the notes first, before they even begin to try to interpret the numbers.

If you were to describe your own financial condition with a financial report you would start with all of the things you own. Money in the bank is certainly a starting point. You may have a pension plan or a life insurance policy with a current value, were you able to get at that money. You own things, such as a car. The car is interesting because generally there is a loan to pay off. So while you own the car you also owe money. All of what you own is "assets" and all of what you owe is "liabilities." Watch out for those two little words—*own* and *owe*—it's only the last letter that's the difference between solvency and financial chaos. When you make a thorough list of these things you begin to develop your own financial statement.

The third item in your financial report is the net difference between what you own and what you owe. This is your "equity." Assets, liabilities, and equity are the three elements of the accounting equation. Simply put: equity = assets − liabilities.

Now, of course, accountants cannot leave it so simple. They need to start with assets and thus financial statements are presented in the form: assets = liabilities + equity. Now, for everybody who is mathematically challenged, this is advanced algebra but it does not need to get any more complicated. When you think of your own financial condition it's straightforward to create two lists— one showing what you own and the second showing what you owe. After you total each list, the third element, equity, is just a subtraction of what you own less what you owe. That's simple enough. As we discussed when you were preparing to obtain a mortgage, you will have already prepared your own financial statement. Business statements are very much the same, just with some additional complicated requirements.

When reviewing the financial statements of a business or condominium association the same principles apply. However, a few additional factors become important to understand. For example, financial statements do not show current market value of properties that could be sold. Thus, there could be an understatement of the true value of what is owned. That is why, when an individual or a business obtains a mortgage, a current valuation of properties must be made to help the financing company understand that making this loan is a prudent risk.

Financial statements are a picture of the numbers at a particular point in time in the past. They also describe where money came from and where it was spent during a particular period of time. They do not predict the future. We can, however, study past financial statements to look for trends that prompt us to ask questions about events that may affect the future. Whether a condominium association is financially solvent (in the black)—they own more than they owe—is the first question to resolve. Then ask all the additional questions you want. The answers will help you decide whether this is a good investment. Remember, you are becoming an investor in the business of the condominium association, not just a home owner.

Assets

We'll discuss each of the three elements of the accounting equation and then review the additional information that is typically part of a financial statement, including each category's important subheadings. We'll start with assets. Cash is an asset. Cash is easy to understand. We all have some cash in the bank if we are about to become home owners. Cash is one of the "current assets" because it is readily available for use. There may also be investments and certificates of deposit listed among current assets. A current asset would be those assets that could be converted into cash within one year. Other current assets may include monies that are due the business. These are called "accounts receivable." For condominium associations there may be member "assessments receivable," which is money due to the association but not yet paid. For businesses that have inventory, that would be another current asset. Prepaid expenses also are in the current-asset category. They might be for services such as lawn maintenance paid in advance for a future time period beyond the date of the financial statement. In addition to current assets the asset category will list property as a category. As previously mentioned, property is not valued at market value but at original cost, less any credit taken for tax purposes. This is called **depreciation**. Depreciation in accounting is the allocation of the cost over its useful life. This can provide an income tax deduction without a cash outflow.

Liabilities

Liabilities are the obligations a business has to pay others. In the liabilities section, we have a subtotal of values due to be paid within a year that are called "current liabilities." We also have a subtotal of values for the long-term liabilities that are monies owed beyond one year. For a condominium association, any long-term liability begs questions. Here all monies due, but not yet paid, are recorded as "accounts payable." Assessments prepaid by condominium association members, but not yet due, are listed as current liabilities. Condominium associations often have escrow requirements all members must pay when they first acquire their units. The amount of those escrow deposits is listed as a current liability. Any long-term debt, less current installments, would be in the long-term liabilities section and again something that requires a full understanding.

Equity

The third and last part of the accounting equation is the equity section. This is the difference between assets and liabilities. Greater value of equity indicates a greater financial strength of the business or organization. We'll discuss more about that after we go over the income statement, cash flow, and the notes section of the overall report.

Income Statement

We have covered what determines equity or net book value of the business or condominium association. Now we will look at operations for the past year, or statement reporting period, to learn where the money came from and how it was used. This portion of the report is called the "income statement," in which there are two major categories: "revenue" and "expenses." It will show monies left over at the end of the period—or the loss of money, if that is the case. A condominium association will report this as excess revenue over or under expenses and will typically show starting fund balances and ending fund balances.

For a profit-making business the income statement shows profits or losses; thus it is also called a "profit and loss statement." The revenue portion shows major sources of revenue such as maintenance fees, interest income, late fees, special assessment, etc. The expense portion shows general and administrative expenses, ground maintenance, utilities, repair expenses, and other categories such as lawn care, etc.

Statement of Cash Flow

The last statement that is part of the overall financial statement is the statement of cash flow. This identifies the sources and uses of money used during the reporting period with the final increase or decrease in cash resulting from operating activities and investment activities. It shows net cash provided by operating activities. It will show if money had to be borrowed in order to meet expense requirements.

Notes

Following the balance sheet, income statement, and statement of cash flow, there will be notes that explain significant accounting practices and any other explanations the accountant deems necessary before signing off on the overall financial statement.

Now that we have a brief overview of the financial statement, let's discuss what we want to look for when we first get these documents. As we've mentioned, many people first read the notes to identify unusual activity or conditions. Pending law suits and other known pending liabilities may be noted in this section. A significant change in an accounting practice may give cause for questioning. What we are seeking is twofold: first we want to know that the business of the condominium association has been generating enough money to pay all of its expenses; and second, we want to learn if there are any pending potential liabilities that would cause the association to raise the maintenance dues or levy unexpected assessments. All loans should be questioned. Are there any major loans or mortgages?

One deceptive method that questionable condominium associations may use to improve the value of individual units is to mortgage major renovations, causing the unit price to increase. This requires that future maintenance payers pay for the improvement with the hope that they would never be the wiser, just poorer. This allows existing members to get away with not paying for an improvement that could result in their realizing large gains upon sale of their units. In that case, the future unit owner not only pays a higher price for the unit but also has to pay the costs of the major improvement and, adding insult to injury, interest costs charged to that mortgage.

Now here's an interesting little sidebar. Have the statements been prepared by one accounting firm or are multiple accounting firms being used? If the latter is the case, ask why. If a comparison of actual costs versus budgeted costs can be obtained—good. This will be very useful to review. Ratios of significant cost areas can be compared to identify trends or unusual increases or decreases. This can lead to more questions if financial statements for more than one year are available. Ask away—you have to be as fully informed as possible. Financial statements can, on the other hand, provide some comfort when the business of the condominium association is sound with income greater than expenses and no major problems identified.

Capital Reserve Studies

Capital reserve study funding is critical to reduce the need for large assessments. A **capital expenditure/amount** is a very large expense that does not occur regularly, such as replacing a roof. A **capital reserve** study is an analysis of the life of capital expenditures, which directs that money be saved over time so that when a capital expenditure is needed the money will be available. Thus, current owners are essentially paying a use cost for major common elements that will need to be replaced after a relatively long period of time. You need to know where you stand in that time frame. The capital reserve study should clarify this. You could be on "easy street" if major improvements have been made recently, or you could be heading for a fall if the job is scheduled for two weeks after you close with insufficient capital reserve funding.

You have now scraped together the funds to make that big condo purchase, and have adjusted your finances to pay the mortgage, insurance costs, and the monthly maintenance fees. The last thing you want is to be assessed a large chunk of money for a major condominium association expense. Except for an act of nature or misfortune, such as a tornado, flood, or garbage truck running into one of your buildings, most major expenses can be anticipated. Hopefully there is insurance to offset these events. The purpose of a capital reserve study is to set aside the money needed to build up a reserve account for major repairs and replacements of common items, such as driveways, roof coverings, exterior siding, sidewalks, irrigation systems, fencing, and other capital items.

Depending upon the age of the buildings at the time of the initial capital reserve study, basic building components such as stone foundation walls, steel plumbing piping, and so on, may also need to be part of the study. A very old or historic building that has been converted into a condominium will definitely need to include such fundamental elements of the building in the capital reserve study.

Let's step back right here to get everything in focus. The first thing you need to know about a condominium association is whether a capital reserve study and capital reserve fund exist. This is critical. The next thing you need to know is the quality and completeness of the study and funding. Because this second question is a bit more difficult to determine you may need assistance from your accountant. The quality of the study involves two major factors: (1) the completeness of the capital items considered part of the study; and (2) the reliability of the expected life assigned to each of the elements of the study. Typically, these studies are performed with engineering supervision to ensure proper judgment in creating the list of items and ascertaining the expected remaining life for each of the items.

There is another part of these studies too complicated for most people to evaluate—the assumptions that are used in the mathematics of estimating and distributing replacement costs over time to determine funding level requirements. It may be possible to learn how reserve fund charges have changed in recent years. Having a stable contribution rate helps ensure that each owner pays her own fair share of ongoing deterioration of common areas.

After satisfying yourself about the completeness and quality of the fund, the third and last thing to determine about a capital reserve fund is to what extent is it fully funded. Try to learn what percentage of the current desired funding level is actually funded. This will help you assess your risk of potential assessments after you become an owner in the condominium association.

Condominium Board

All condominium associations have a board of trustees (directors) who are elected by the membership to oversee management of the association. You will want to get a sense of the quality of this board and the extent to which it might be an "old boy" club. Transparency of board activity is probably the single most important thing you will want to learn. Copies of recent minutes will help you assess the board's attention to association matters. Remember, though, that minutes can be written by creative writers, so talking with one of the board members will provide even more information for your assessment. The association's bylaws discussed earlier will detail the size and role of the board. These are important documents you will want to review. Each state has community association laws, but you may need a lawyer who is knowledgeable in condominium law to see if the association's bylaws are currently conforming to state laws. Board involvement will depend upon the people who sit on the board and the extent to which they use their power wisely in a manner beneficial to all members of the association. After reviewing the minutes, ask some questions. How long have the current board members served on the board? Does the mix of board members reflect the mix of ownership? When the association has unique facilities such as a golf course, swimming pool, or yacht club, dig a little to find out how many of the board members are avid users of these facilities and who they are. It's amazing sometimes to discover how delicately the needs of those facilities will be treated. Of course, your conclusion will be affected by your own interests but that may be why you are considering buying into that specific condominium association in the first place.

Ask what board subcommittees exist? Do nonboard members participate in various subcommittees? Board members are just people, after all. An association can develop a "personality" in the way board members are treated or in the way board members treat the general membership. Sometimes board members are so autocratic that they ignore even reasonable requests or inquiries from residents. On the other hand, board members are sometimes treated as if they were janitors, on hand merely to attend to the whims of owners who can be tough to please. Not all board members are good at dealing with difficult people, and vice versa.

It can be a rough two-way street because it's only natural that all associations will have at least a few "difficult" people.

Some boards may divert member issues to the management company with direction to take a tough stand. Try to learn about the personality of the association. A positive indicator would be that association members are interested in joining the board because they care about the community. If you're lucky, you can be grateful to the altruism of a board that does fine work in managing member interests in a fair and equable manner.

One of the tough but necessary jobs of the board is to enforce rules and regulations to assure equal and fair treatment of all association members. It can be expected that some association members will violate rules. How the board encourages a dialogue to reduce the adversarial nature of rule enforcement is important to achieving even-handed applications of the rules. Try to learn how the board manages conflict resolution and rule enforcement and to what extent there are ongoing conflicts and disciplinary actions.

You have to recognize that some seemingly arbitrary rules have a basis of reason. What you can or cannot have on your patio or terrace is just to rein in the Mardi Gras fellow who'd install blinking lights and sound effects if he could get away with it. There are always some people who thrive on excess and that's not great for the rest of us. You can grumble about regulations but try to remember that without them, the Mardi Gras boy might throw in a flock of pink flamingos—and he lives right next door to you. There are rules because live and let live doesn't always work in a tight space.

Management

Small condominium associations may manage their affairs directly; however, most associations subcontract to a professional management company or hire staff to perform day-to-day administrative functions. The style of management will affect the quality of life in a particular condominium association. These are the people you will be dealing with on a daily basis for issues needing association attention. Management will handle financial operations of the property to ensure that membership fees are collected and association bills are paid on time. They will negotiate contracts for services and monitor the performance of companies that are awarded contracts. Depending upon the size of the association, there may be on-site management personnel or a central office that serves multiple associations. Management people may help to resolve complaints and assist the board in achieving compliance with rules and regulations.

Home-Buyer's Checklist

- Am I ready for community living?
- Do I understand condo ownership documents?
- Have I investigated the management of any condo developments I might be considering?
- Have I investigated the association's financial position?
- Have I investigated potential association liabilities?
- Am I willing to live within the association's rules?

Chapter 9

How Do I Find the Home for Me?

While our focus is on helping everyone in the house-hunting business, we cannot resist relating a short tale close to the heart of one of our authors. Peter is an engineer, Harley biker, and—perhaps closest to his heart—a blue-water sailor. When Peter began his house search he knew it had to be waterfront. He researched miles and miles of inlets, creeks, and rivers along the northern New Jersey coast before he found his dream home with its breathtaking view of one of Jersey's most beautiful rivers. His mileage should, perhaps, be reported in knots because he searched by water!

From the water Peter could compare dockage facilities, proximity to the channel, and overall suitability to his and his boat's needs. Only then did he enlist a realtor for the nuts-and-bolts knowledge he needed about cost, character of the neighborhood, public transportation, and all the other mundane things a buyer has to know. While this isn't everyone's typical approach it shows how the house search can be fun.

Wow! You got ready. You got set. And, now you are ready to go. Let's analyze all that you already know, before you actually start house shopping. You've done a lot of homework. You know your needs and what you can afford. You know that there are professionals out there who are ready, willing, and able to help, not only in your search for the perfect house, but also in evaluating sources of money. You also know whom you will need to help complete the deal. One of the most important things is that you have written everything down. Now it's time to create and execute your written plan.

You may have to broaden your horizons because houses in your price range may not be readily available in your target area. Your time schedule also may make it advisable to consider more than just one area. Whatever the case, you will need to do research and prepare a plan for each area. In some communities you might be able to conduct the search on your own; in others you may need professional help. And, you may need different professionals for each different area. In this chapter, we will help you find *The House;* later chapters will cover making the offer, getting the home inspection, and negotiating the deal. Let the journey begin.

Location, Location, Location

Location is critical to the value of a house. When you hear that old refrain, location, location, location, it starts with the community, then a specific area or street within the community, and finally the actual location on a particular street. Some towns are much more expensive for a variety of reasons. Thus, town is the first location to consider.

Even within a particular town there are areas that are more desirable and more expensive than other areas. The reasons why may or may not affect your priorities. To the extent that the more desirable areas within a town remain in demand, your selling price will be protected when the time comes for you to sell. Areas of towns do change, however, and sometimes on the downside. For example, a section of a town that has no commercial development may be very desirable until plans are approved for a large mall, practically next door. The third part of location is the actual location on a particular street. One side or the other may be more desirable because of a view, sidewalks, adjoining property, and so on. Corner lots often are more valuable and cost more in taxes because they have greater street frontage. Deciding on locations is your first step. You already know your needs and have a commuting range in mind, so let's get out the maps. Draw a circle of acceptable commuting distance that includes the communities you may reasonably consider.

Take a Sunday drive—at least one—through those areas. It's a pleasant way to get a direct feel for various locations within each of your target communities. Stop at a food or convenience store to pick up local papers and any free, local house guides. Depending upon the time you can devote to finding *The House*, you might want to subscribe to local papers. The Internet is also invaluable for researching listed houses and community information.

There comes a time to fish and stop cutting bait. You don't want to ever after sorrow about the one that got away. But you do need to know where the fish are. There may be an ideal spot where you want to live but, as in fishing, unless the fish are there your time will be wasted. Preparation doesn't have to end if there's a shortage of desirable houses where you're looking. A little bit of luck might just turn up the ideal house in the ideal location. Patience is often rewarded when you know just what you want. To carry the fishing analogy a little further, you can strike when the fish are ready to bite.

We have already discussed time constraints that may affect your options. If you have only a small window of time, you may be forced to settle for less than what you really want. The more time you have, the more research you can do in investigating neighborhoods directly. You may learn of a house just going on the market or, better yet, before the word gets out. For the right situation, this can be an excellent opportunity. It's one of the reasons to use a real estate professional who knows a lot of people in a particular neighborhood, and who may hear about someone's interest in selling before that information becomes public.

Before you explore, you need maps. Start with a map that gets you to the target community. An excellent Internet source of maps is *www.mapquest.com*. You should also have state, regional and detailed local maps of each target area. Often the local chamber of commerce can provide a local map as part of their relocation package for newcomers. Most chambers have worldwide directories, so call the chamber where you live now for addresses and phone numbers for chambers in your target areas. You may have to pay postage but you'll find that fat packet they send well worth it.

Visiting the area is more than just driving through and observing the landscape. You need to learn the personality of each part of the communities that pique your interest. You have an advantage if you already have local knowledge. While you may not have lived in the area, having friends who have lived there, or still do, is a big plus. Another option is to develop acquaintances in the area. Even if you're moving a great distance from where you now live, try to spend at least one full day in each target community to get the feel of the place before you involve real estate professionals.

Develop a business card for yourself; your name, phone number, and title of "Home Buyer" is all you need. We don't recommend including your current home address, but include a fax number and e-mail address if you have them. Use a phone number that has an answering machine. If you have more than one phone number, pick one or use them all! On the back of the card, indicate the size and type of house you are looking for, such as "three bedrooms with garage." Cards can be made on your computer or at a local print shop. Do not use your work business card as it would only confuse people. Your objective here is to find a home, not to drum up business. Every person you meet could be the contact who can lead you to your dream house. Trade cards and date them so you can remember who you met when you handed out your home-buyer card. With luck, that person just might call you with a lead.

As we have mentioned, in every town some locations are more desirable than others. You cannot know too much about your chosen community and the areas within the community where you'd like to live. This is a very important part of your homework, because when you are ready to make an offer and enter into negotiations, your knowledge will mean power. It will help you decide what is reasonable and what is unrealistic.

If it isn't possible to get to know the neighbors right away, you can at least get a feel for the neighborhood. Some of the things you need to learn go to the heart of how you live. If you have or plan to have children, how does the neighborhood stack up as child-friendly? If you have children, you might want to attend school games of the same age children. Networking with their parents will tell you a lot about the community. Neighborhoods undergo changes with differences in generations. Do you want to be one of the first in an older neighborhood that is attracting young people just starting families? Or do you want an established neighborhood for your stage of life? Getting out and meeting the locals is priceless.

Read the local papers to understand what is happening in the communities and why. You will learn about development projects under consideration and you will learn what is controversial. Learn what local people are debating. What are their concerns? Perhaps the culture of the town or neighborhood is changing. Would you consider it for better or worse? If the locals consider it worse and you consider it better, that may improve you negotiating strength. However, the opposite can be a distinct disadvantage.

If one local paper seems very biased toward certain points of view, read more than one paper. In the case of real estate ads, local papers, regardless of their politics, can clarify market pricing.

Talking with local merchants will give you a taste of the town and its various neighborhoods. Just having a cup of coffee at a local breakfast meeting place gives you a seat in the theater of local personality. Meeting with religious leaders of your persuasion might help you decide if you will be comfortable here. Anytime you meet with local people, you benefit and your fact pool grows.

Stop in at town hall during business hours to meet the public servants who make the wheels turn. They can give you information about the town and available services. Town size often determines whom you will meet. In a large community you may find yourself talking with someone just working at an information desk. In a very small town you may run into a one-person office, and that one person could turn out to be the mayor. In any event you'll pick up the flavor of the community and, who knows, you may even pick up some good leads. In the local municipal building, whatever its size, you can learn if there are any significant zoning changes in the works. If you're considering a historic district you will be able to learn about any regulations that might apply. A community bulletin board with general information can tell you a lot. Every stop on this journey adds to your store of knowledge.

Stop in at the local chamber of commerce for information about the local businesses and the more prominent businesspeople in the area, schools, park systems, and general activities. If you haven't already called or written ahead for a relocation packet, the people at the chamber will surely load you up with almost more than you can carry. The chamber is also a great source for networking. If you have time, try to attend a chamber event—you will be amazed at what you can glean. And you'll meet people you'll need to know once you move to the area.

After you have gotten a direct sense of target communities by visiting and reading, you can obtain additional information via the Internet. But keep in mind that Internet research, while fast and easy, is for facts and not feelings. At this stage, you are using the Internet for information to confirm your selection of target communities. Later, we will be using the Internet for data on specific houses in those areas. Some Internet information may be misleading, however, and can be clarified only through direct observation. Nothing can take the place of in-person direct visits for the feel of the community and potential locations within its borders. Visiting also introduces you to a slew of contacts you can follow up with because you have already met them.

Once you have visited and have a good grasp of the personality of each neighborhood and community, you may still need to confirm your initial selection of a target area. Here's where deeper Internet research can tell you if there are houses within your budget. Even in the most expensive communities there will be areas with lower-priced housing. Because you have made visits you may already have direct knowledge of varied pricing levels. You can confirm general pricing and availability levels for your target locations on the Internet. Many houses, however, may not be listed there. Certainly, houses that have yet to come onto the market aren't listed anywhere. Internet research is wisely used to qualify and finalize your target locations. Decide which specific communities you want to search and make a list.

House Search Work Sheet

Complete your house search work sheet. Here you will note your target communities and list the primary criteria for the house you are looking for. This is a working tool you will use throughout your search.

House Search Work Sheets

Name: _____

Phone Number: _____

Other (e-mail, fax, etc): _____

Target communities

_____   _____

_____   _____

Primary criteria

	Necessary (A)	Important (B)	Desired (C)	Notes
Number of Bedrooms	_____	_____	_____	_____
Number of Bathrooms	_____	_____	_____	_____
Master bath	_____	_____	_____	_____
Dining room	_____	_____	_____	_____
Family room	_____	_____	_____	_____
Fireplace	_____	_____	_____	_____
Garage	_____	_____	_____	_____
Special	_____	_____	_____	_____

Notes:

Select the Professionals

Now that you have selected specific communities and have completed your house search work sheet, you are ready for professional help. We previously talked about the general approach in seeking professional help. Here we will discuss specifics for making decisions within your target communities. In a buyer's market there are many houses in your price range. This gives you the advantage of time to be very selective and you will probably get a better overall price deal. In a seller's market, with relatively few houses in your price range, you will be more likely to face a bidding war with other buyers who are prepared to offer more money for the same house. As a seller's market slows down, lesser quality houses remain on the market longer. This makes your search even more difficult. When the inventory of houses for sale is low in a seller's market, the help of an experienced real estate professional can make a significant difference.

Whether you begin your search with a real estate agent or on your own, there are both financial and search-time ramifications. It can be argued, for and against, that working with a real estate agent can better protect your interests and may even save you money. Many people start their house search without using a real estate agent. The Internet seems to suggest that you can do it on your own. If you can find an owner who is selling without an agent, he's not paying commission. If his house is fairly priced, less the commission value, you will certainly save money. But if you don't want the hassle of do-it-yourself, you need someone to do the work for you—to search public records and private firm records, and exploit personal contacts. In this scenario, you want a real estate professional on your team.

Selecting the right person in the right firm is important. You need an agent with experience in your target neighborhoods; someone who has regularly worked with the size and value of the house you want. The better, more experienced real estate professionals who have regular ongoing personal contacts or correspondence with people in your target neighborhoods should fill the bill. They will have the pulse on who is considering a sale because of a potential job relocation or change in family status.

While it is not pleasant to ponder, the big D's, divorce and death, are often the reason for houses being sold. These events are sometimes signaled in advance and are known to the experienced local real estate professional. The more successful real estate agents are those who generate the most sale listings. They get those listing because their contacts in the neighborhood help them scout out leads. When you find an agent who has advance knowledge of potential sales, that person will be more important than their firm. A source of Realtors$^{®}$ working in specific towns can be found at *www.realtor.com*. You'll find many other Internet commercial sources but, remember, not all real estate sales agents are members of the National Association of Realtors$^{®}$. If that designation is important to you, look for the little circled letter R (registered mark) that indicates membership in the National Association.

All that walking and talking you did during visits to the neighborhoods may already have identified real estate agents with potential. You may want to flip pages back at this point to review the real estate sales section of Chapter 6. Many real estate sales people have individual web sites that include their own listings so you can compare your target house with the ones they are listing. This will give you a feel of that person's suitability.

If you cannot find that special person, look for a firm that does a lot of work in your target neighborhoods with the size of your target house. While there are many very valuable services a real estate professional can provide, the first and most important function is to find *The House* that meets your needs—within your budget. If you can find it on your own, you may not need the real estate professional, providing you have a good real estate lawyer. Finding that special house is what we are concentrating on at this stage of your journey. The more you know about your target neighborhoods, especially if you can identify sellers of acceptable houses before they are offered to the public, the less need you have for a salesperson.

When you walk into a real estate **brokerage** office you may be assigned to a salesperson who is "next in line." This could reduce your selection options, but on the other hand, a less experienced person may work especially hard in your interest. This could overcome some, or with luck, all of his lack of experience. You need to feel good about the real estate salesperson you decide to work with. Be sure that you have the best person working for you before signing any agreements. If you are not certain that a particular real estate salesperson is the right person for you, keep your options open. At the very least, keep any agreed-to exclusivity to a relatively short period of time so that you can see how the agent will work on your behalf. When it is necessary to sign an agreement, it is best to first have it reviewed by a lawyer.

Look, Look, Look

Getting Organized, Plan Your Work, Work Your Plan

As you begin looking, get organized. There is a saying about getting organized and that is to plan your work and work your plan. It's a lot like managing a business where others do some or much of the work while you are the chief executive officer who provides leadership and monitors performance to ensure results. Another analogy that may be even closer to the mark is that you are both coach of a team *and* a key player. You not only coach, but you also go out onto the field and play whatever position needs attention. The game of buying a house is a serious game, and like professional sports, you need a game book. You may be a team of just one, or you may have lots of professionals and friends helping you. The fundamentals are the same. You're going to need a portable filing and storage system to keep track of information. You're ahead of the game if you began to accumulate critical information when you determined what your needs were and outlined your financial condition. Now we will take it further so you have working tools to provide structure in decision making.

You'll need at least one three-ring binder, perhaps more. You may want a zip-top tote bag, such as the kind you can get from *www.landsend.com* or *www.llbean.com*. While the larger bag may seem excessive, you will be surprised how much information you will be accumulating during the journey of finding your dream house. The big bag *is* your portable office.

A one and a half-inch binder is probably a good start. Your best bet is the more durable reference version with clear insert covers on front and back. These are available at any office supply store. Also pick up a package of clear three-ring binder business card holders and at least one set of index tabs with 31 tabs. You'll also need three-hole punched notepaper. The idea of having 31 tabs is so you can pencil in on the index sheet at the front of the tabs the type of information you place behind each tab. Depending upon the complexity of your search, particularly in different target areas, you may want to go for a major 31-tab section for each area. This could evolve into separate books for each area. We'll describe categories of information you ought to separate. Of course, each house will warrant its own section. You may want some three-ring pockets to hold loose sheets of paper or documents until you get a chance to punch holes. Maps, news clippings, or other such documents that will never be punched may be kept in a pocket. Create a section for notepaper so when you want to jot down information on a particular house you'll have paper for your notations ready to file in that house section. For detailed maps of each target area our suggestion is to print an $8\frac{1}{2} \times 11$ inch (18 centimeters $\times$ 28 centimeters) map of the general area to be slid into the clear rear cover. You can keep your house search work sheet in the front cover.

For each target area you will want separate sections for maps, community information, contacts from real estate salespeople, other contacts, a section for notes of meetings and conversations with each real estate agent you're actively working with, and a section for each of the house listings you are considering. In each agent's section you will want to keep any and all documents associated with that agent, particularly every written agreement. As you can imagine, each section could balloon to the point where you may need subcategories for the wealth of information. Go right ahead and create subsections. It's easy to get tabs and with three-ring binders you can rearrange the information or start new binders at any time.

In the house listing sections you'll easily see where you can subdivide, but for now we suggest filing all of the information about a particular house into the appropriate target area section. Later, when you get ready to make an offer on a particular house, you may want to create a separate binder for just that house. We'll talk about that a bit later in this chapter.

Working with real estate sales professionals helps build an inventory of houses to think about. Your own Internet work will add more. You may receive Internet "listings" with key information by snail mail, but more frequently they will be sent via e-mail. As you collect information about a particular house, file it into the appropriate section in your looseleaf binder and then, as more data on that house accumulates, add that information to the same section. Here's where those blank sheets of notepaper come in handy for quick notes of thoughts you might lose if you don't write them down.

Sometimes a house is available for sale but doesn't have a listing, or it hasn't yet been put into the open market so no listing was created. In such a case, you can use our house checklist to record the features you have been told exist. As you consider houses to visit, try a drive-by curb assessment before actually scheduling an appointment to view the house. Take a photo. You can use a throwaway film camera, a regular film camera, a phone camera, or an economical point-and-shoot digital camera. You do not need a sophisticated camera for your house pictures because all you need is a visual memory jog after the drive-by. The advantage of digital is that you see the picture right away. If you have a computer, you can save the picture electronically. If you have a digital camera with no computer but just a printer, write the date and house address on the back of the print. Saving the photos on a computer is less important than having the picture in your project book in the section with all of the other house details.

When you make your first official visit you will have the opportunity to take more pictures. Right now we suggest just the drive-by photo. You can decide later whether you want to schedule an appointment to view the house. Grouping a number of houses for this cursory curb view is a quick way to prioritize those houses you'll want to follow up on.

House hunting requires a very flexible schedule for research and scheduling visits. Think carefully about the time that work and family demands of you and how you can create the needed chunks of time to find your house. In the beginning you may not need to take time off from work. Later on, though, when you enter into a contract, you may need to use vacation time or personal days for inspections, closings, and moving. Professionals in the real estate world are accustomed to working evenings and weekends, but most sellers won't have much more free time than you. When it is necessary for the seller to be present for an inspection, everybody may need to make some adjustments.

Working with Your Real Estate Agent(s)

You will need to work closely with your real estate agent. As with any group of people, real estate agents range from exceptional individuals who grasp your needs immediately and apply themselves diligently, to order-takers who do little more than coordinate the paperwork. Knowing the skill and dedication level of the agents you are working with is task one. Then you have to decide how best to manage their work. At the same time, the exceptional agent will be managing you, as well as searching for your dream house and negotiating on your behalf. The average agent will benefit from having your needs clearly defined, yet you will still need to monitor his activity. If one agent cannot provide you with enough leads, enlist a second or third agent. You may have to recruit a whole team to work on your behalf.

This is your campaign to manage—you're the coach. All of the people you work with are part of your team. They will be working with a lot of other people as well so you may need to compete for their attention. Providing clear direction to your team is the first step. Establishing what you can expect and when you can expect it comes next. Set definitive response-time targets. Set up a regular communication schedule. Even if there is nothing new to report, ongoing communication assures your agents that you are monitoring their activity. You're telling your agents that you need and appreciate their help and that they will be earning their fee. Real estate salespeople work for commissions. They don't make any money unless a sale is made and closed. Anyone in the business long enough has been burnt by people who are not seriously shopping, or who continually search for homes outside of their reach. Experienced agents, many times, will have made a sale only to lose it at closing because of some irreconcilable detail.

Think of your search for a house as if it were your second business—Moonlight & Company. Up until this point, we have been coaching you to develop your business plan. Now you need to set up shop with regular business hours. A realistic time schedule tells your staff—your agents—when you'll be available with minimum interruption. For example, you can set 6 P.M. to 8 P.M. as your regular working hours at Moonlight & Company. Only a few people are so independent that they can accept or be permitted frequent interruption throughout their real-life day-job hours. This new house hunting business of yours does not have to be only a night or weekend job, however, as you might have early morning and lunchtime hours free to monitor your "business phone." Inevitably, as you narrow down your search, interruptions to your normal routine will increase. Plan for these interruptions to the extent your income-producing job will permit. If you have regular coffee breaks during the day, put that time to work. Use designated phone numbers with answering capability—maybe a new cell phone with message capability. You can turn it on during your scheduled moonlighting business hours and have it take messages at all other times. Because cell phones don't always work in every area, have at least one backup land line, such as your current home phone. You can't run this moonlight operation alone, though. Don't even try. You need a trusted surrogate who is available to help with phone calls, someone who will know when and how to interrupt your normal routine for high-priority communication. Your wife? Your husband? Your partner? A close friend or sibling? You might want to note work hours and phone numbers on your house-search business card.

Listening to advice is not always easy and not all advice is good. At times, preconceived ideas can make us deaf, even to the best advice. Keep your ears open and listen. Write down the advice you get even it if seems inconsequential. What at first may seem "way out" could turn out to be gold. Write down advice from friends and professionals. You will be inundated, of course, and the advice may not be comfortable or in line with your initial thinking, but it might turn out to be valuable after all. When you have the time to review your notes you may find yourself reevaluating your original thinking.

Monitor the performance of all of your help. Whether they are hired professionals or generous friends you need to devote more of your energy and time with the better performers. There is a saying in business that you get what you inspect. A monitoring program will help define and refine your expectations. As we have mentioned, regular—perhaps weekly—phone conversations with your real estate agents will help to reinforce their motivation. Remember, you're the coach motivating the players on your team. Monthly face-to-face meetings are a good idea, particularly if you have had little interaction during the month. Besides, it's amazing what you can pick up from body language when you meet in person. Regular assessment and coaching of your players will help your team's performance.

We suggest setting aside a small amount of quiet time once a week to review your progress, even if it's only a half hour. Think about what is and is not happening. Write three columns of information: (1) what is happening; (2) what is not happening; and (3) what should be happening. This is your weekly business report on Moonlight & Company. It should include performance reviews of any professionals you have retained. This is the time to assess all the advice you've heard—you may want to reconsider your earlier plans. Weekly reviews are generally too short for overall revision of your basic plan, but that does not prevent you from thinking about the possibility of the need for revision. Three-month time periods would be more reasonable for rethinking your basic plan. Your three-month time budget for progress review will probably take one or two hours.

First Visit

Your first house visit is bound to elicit an emotional reaction. Meeting a new house is like meeting a new person—are you compatible? First impressions may be positive, neutral, or negative. Your gut reaction tells you whether you want to come back for a second visit. If you feel good, you're going to want to know this house better. If you don't feel good you may want to write this one off, even if the house meets your basic requirements. It's a tough spot to be in because, as in the fish analogy, you're going to be afraid this might be the one that got away. We will discuss the second visit and how you can do it almost at the same time as the first visit, if really necessary, but we want to be sure you have performed an initial review. When you find that the house is largely as advertised and meets your minimum requirements, try to reserve judgment and continue with your first-visit review. It has been said that women see what they can make of a house and that men don't see beyond existing problems. In both of those judgments there are shortcomings. Don't allow your initial impression to generate too much excitement for or against a particular purchase. Virtually all existing houses have some problems or lack some desired features. If you have plenty of houses to choose from, you can be more selective. Much of the time, however, the market can be quite limited and you may be pressed toward making decisions for fear of losing this house to someone else. Sometimes, too, what you see upon your visit is not at all like the real estate ad. What if you find a garbage dump next door? Funny how no one mentioned that.

As you drive to the house, take note of its location within the neighborhood. Take a moment to look at the whole streetscape. Look at the neighbor's houses. Ask yourself, "Do we want to live here?" Is the overall picture one you could be comfortable in? If anything at all is out of focus or jarring, remember that it probably will not change. If your first impression is positive, it's time for a photo opportunity. Take a picture of the house from the street and then take two more, one looking to the left and one looking to the right. Hopefully you have become so at ease with your camera that you can take pictures without skipping a beat. Practice will improve your photo-taking skills. Remember, you are not taking contest pictures, just note-taking. The pictures are visual notes you can review at a later time. Without photos you'll never remember everything you've seen. Try to make your camera a friend. As you approach the house from the street look at how it is located on its property. If you are with a real estate agent, he will almost surely try to hurry you right into the house. If there are no reasons not to go in, go ahead—ring the bell and let's see the inside of the castle. Even if it's love at first sight, you still need to go back outside and walk around the house to look at both sides and the rear. When you go back out, remember to take at least one photo of the backyard and another of the rear of the house.

When you first enter the house, follow your nose. Smell for any and all odors. Get a good sniff immediately because your nose adjusts to odors very quickly and you might miss something important. If there is a basement, give it the nose test first. Musty, damp-smelling basements can mean trouble. If the basement passes the nose test, you still have to be careful. Make a note of burning candles, room deodorants, food cooking, or any other odor-masking activity. Be wary if you think the owner may be trying to hide any odor problems. Try to distinguish between pet odors, people-activity odors such as cooking odors, and odors that are from moisture or other sources that may remain in the house after the current occupants move out. The last thing you need is the unpleasant surprise discovery of a mold or moisture situation you might miss if your nose isn't on full alert.

Try to get a quick sense of the layout when you first come in. Where are the different rooms? How does reality compare with information you have previously received about the house? Is the list of rooms you expected to find realistic? Ask yourself if they are what you expected. During your initial visit you will want to know that you understand the basic house. You may already have seen some documents describing the house and now you will confirm if the actual house is what you thought those documents said. For example, particularly in older houses, there may be a room listed as a bedroom that is, in reality, too small, or lacks a closet or a necessary exterior window. This is the kind of initial observation you need to make during your first visit. You'll get your emotional reaction, at the same time, confirm the features of the house and the property. If the house has been modified, the seller may have documents you can review or even have copies for you to keep in your trusty three-ring binder.

Make a rough sketch of the floor plan of the house if one is not already available from the seller. Use one sheet for each floor. Again, as we discussed with your photo-taking, do not try for any level of perfection. The rough sketch is just to jog your memory when you are considering a variety of houses and want to remember important features about each one. A rough sketch can easily be transferred later to graph paper for a scale layout of each room, which will be an invaluable tool in deciding what goes where when you're ready to call the mover.

Confirm the list of major rooms. Are they as advertised? Sometimes a seller will call a hallway a separate room when it already houses laundry equipment and functions as a mudroom. This creates a distorted picture, especially when a listed five-room house includes one room that has no regular living function. Hallways, mudrooms, breakfast-nook areas, and bathrooms are not typically classified as main rooms. Living rooms, dining rooms, kitchens, and bedrooms are main rooms.

Second Visit

Even if you take only five minutes to go out to your car to review some paperwork and then return to the house, you will experience some of the benefit of a second visit. A longer time between visits will give you the leisure to balance the pluses and minuses of a particular house. A second visit is necessary to reduce some of the emotion created by first impressions. You may be one of the very few whose gut reaction is always on the money, but if you're like most people, you need a second visit. Depending upon how many houses you're looking at, a third visit may be necessary. When you are able to space your first and second visits, you will have time to review your notes and photos. At the second visit you may want to bring your whole family—certainly the ones who will live in the house—and perhaps a trusted relative, friend, or advisor. We guarantee that all of these people will have emotional reactions on their first visit to the house. If they don't jibe with your reactions, listen anyway. You may be pleasantly surprised when the kids and Uncle Joe see things you might have missed. Write it all down.

The second or third visit is not to elicit an emotional or compatibility reaction—you've already done that. Now you have to determine what needs to be changed or where you may have to rethink your expectations to make this house your home. The second visit allows you to see the condition of the house more objectively. It's also a chance to perform a pre-inspection assessment. What are the differences, if any, between your notes and photos and what the house really offers? Budget more time for this second visit so you'll be able to meet the neighbors. You might want to come back to say "hello" during weekend or evening hours when they are out and about and have more time. Your real estate agent will almost surely be able to arrange introductions.

Prior to the vital second visit, you may want to draw up a list of questions that go beyond our suggested mini-self-inspection checklist. Have your agent present your questions to the seller in advance so the information is readily available.

Mini-Self-Inspection—A Personal Checklist

Our mini-self-inspection checklist is included in Chapter 11. A review of that chapter will help you better understand the value of the mini-checklist. This self-inspection will be particularly helpful not only for selecting the house to bid on, but also for your selection of a home inspector.

Making a Selection to Bid

For each of the houses you have studied you will have the seller's data, visit records, photos, checklists, and a mini-self-inspection. You may think you are ready to make a selection only to find that more visits or additional selections will be needed. This is not necessarily a one-shot process. Do your best not to get discouraged. Success may take much more effort than you ever imagined, but this is too important a trip to be taken without a dependable road map. All of your research and advertising in all its forms should highlight the way, but Murphy's Law can't be ignored. Things do go wrong, even when they shouldn't.

Sylvester Stallone states on his web site, *www.sylvesterstallone. com*, that before his star rose he experienced "six or seven thousand rejections." You may not aspire to become a movie star, but you deserve success in finding your dream house. House-searching can present enormous difficulty. Stallone was essentially broke when he finally sold *Rocky*, and now he is beyond rich. Think of him for inspiration if the going gets tough.

You might consider trial selections as you accumulate experience visiting potential houses. Compare your findings with your original objectives and compare house possibilities. One benefit of a trial selection is that you expect to continue the process. You can begin trial selections as early as you've made two visits to only one house. You may be very lucky. Some people always seem to get a parking space right in front of a restaurant on a very busy street. You may be one of those lucky people. They will tell you it is because they expected to get that parking space and went directly for it. Consider as your mantra: perception, persistence, and patience.

Three factors will be presented to evaluate your candidates:

1. Emotional compatibility;

2. Meeting your house needs;

3. Meeting your budget.

Emotional compatibility is your gut reaction—how you feel about a particular house that might become your home. Does the house make you feel good? You deserve to have positive feelings when thinking of your home as your castle. Sometimes a house will need changes—perhaps a new exterior look or modified layout. If that's the case, you might as well face increasing the budget for this particular house. Evaluate the house with and without the changes. Give each house an A, B, or C score, just like in school.

Meeting your house needs directly relates to the criteria you have established. If you need four bedrooms, three bedrooms will not suffice. Again, as with the first factor, if it is possible to modify a den, for example, to become a bedroom, add the conversion cost to your original budget. Is it worth it? Again, we suggest using the A B C method for evaluation.

Meeting the budget is clearly a self-limiting criterion. Without some magic, you will at least have to meet your budget. This factor should incorporate whatever additional funds are needed for the house to satisfy your basic needs and that old will o' the wisp, emotional compatibility.

Consider a Mail or Door Knob Campaign

A mail or door knob campaign might be a good idea to consider when prospects for finding your house are slim. A letter to home owners advising them of your interest in their house or a house in their neighborhood may just produce a lead. This is often done by real estate agents when they are shopping for listings or seeking out a house for a client. You can learn the house numbers just by walking the street. Phone books that include addresses may also provide this information. Here is a sample letter you can use:

> Dear Home Owner,
>
> (Identify yourself such as My wife and I) are seeking to buy a house in (note neighborhood or town). We are searching for (list your needs such as a three-bedroom house with an attached garage). If you are considering selling your home, we would appreciate the opportunity to talk with you. If you have a broker, we would be happy to talk with him or her. If you know of other homes available for sale in your area, we would appreciate learning who we can call.
> Thank you very much for your consideration.
>
> (your name, such as Mr. & Mrs. John Doe)
> (your phone number)

House-shopping Tool Kit

1. Your home-buyer business card with your name, phone number, and title: Home-Buyer. Add e-mail and fax information if you have them. Consider noting on the reverse of the card your target location and size of house you want, such as "three bedrooms, two bathrooms, with garage." Consider noting regular hours when you can be reached at your designated house search phone number.

2. Note cards or notepaper for your three-ring binder.

3. File card system for business cards for everyone you meet. For those without a business card, write the name on a blank card and file it in your system. Write the date you meet each person on their card to help your memory. Consider three-ring binder business-card polypropylene pages.

4. Maps. State, regional, and detailed maps for each target community. You will need maps to find your way around. You will also need a working map you can mark with notations about houses for sale in target neighborhoods. Consider creating a tackboard with a map where you can post colored, numbered pins referencing house-sale research. For each target area copy that map section onto an $8\frac{1}{2}$ inch × 11 inch (18 centimeters × 28 centimeters) three-hole paper to insert into your three-ring binder.

5. House-search work sheet.

6. Project three-ring binder(s). This is where you will maintain most, if not all, of your house-search paperwork.

7. Camera. Can be a one-time-use film camera, phone camera, or simple point-and-shoot digital camera. Nothing fancy is needed. In fact, an inexpensive, small easy-to-use camera will

be best. Digital cameras with a large memory card let you take a lot of photos, but a lower-memory-size camera is fine. The easiest cameras to use are those small enough to fit into a shirt pocket. You just point and shoot. Even professional photographers with sophisticated cameras often carry simple point-and-shoot cameras when speed and ease of use are important. Remember, you're not taking portraits, but you do want recognizable pictures. They may be your most important memory device in notetaking. Keep them organized by house address and date.

8. House checklist

Home-Buyer's Checklist

- Have I completed the house-search work sheet?
- Have we looked, looked, looked in all the suggested and available locations, locations, locations?
- Have we done the recommended Sunday drive-through?
- Have I found a real estate agent I trust and feel comfortable with?
- Have we made, or yet scheduled, that big first visit?
- Is a second visit yet on the agenda?
- Have we introduced ourselves to potential neighbors to get the feel of the community?

Chapter 10

Making the Offer: How Much Should I Pay?

Buying a home, especially a "used" home, is unlike any other purchase you make. Except in very strong seller's markets, the price is subject to active negotiation between the seller and buyer. "Well," you say, "how is that different from buying a used car?" The difference is that with a house, the price is only one item that can be negotiated. All the terms of the sales contract can be modified to suit the parties involved. A good agent working for a buyer can get many valuable concessions without altering the sales price. In fact, allowing the seller to believe she is getting her asking price is often a good way to get those concessions.

Still, the sales price is of utmost importance. The amount you can finance will depend on this number. You need to go into negotiations with a clear idea of what the house should sell for and how much you personally are willing to pay for it (these are not necessarily the same thing). In this chapter, we will look at some sources of information and methods for getting a good approximation of a home's value. We will also examine things to consider when setting your **reservation price**—the most you would pay for the home—and the **offering price**—the price you will use to start negotiations. We will end this chapter by reviewing contract terms you may want to negotiate in addition to the sales price.

How an Offer Is Made—The Sales Contract

Whether you are working with an agent or going on your own, you have to submit a written **offer** when you decide to buy a house. The most effective and legally accepted form of offer is a standardized **sales contract** that you make out with terms that are acceptable to you and signed by you. Realize that this contract has no binding effect as long as it is signed only by you. However, once the seller signs the offer without making any changes to the language, you have a legally binding contract to buy the house. Therefore, you should not include anything in the offer that you are not serious about doing. The seller might just sign it. More than likely, the seller will make alterations to swing the deal more toward her favor and resubmit it with her signature. This is called a **counteroffer** and still does not constitute a legal contract until you sign it. A counteroffer is the rejection of the offer and the substitution of a new offer. Counteroffers can go back and forth. The important point is that once both parties sign without changing the language, you have a contract for the sale of the house.

In many states, licensed real estate agents have to use special forms created by the state real estate commission when preparing an offer. If you are unrepresented by an agent, you can use any form, including the commission's form. The state's form will comply with all state laws and regulations affecting home sales, so that you need not hire an attorney when using that form. On the other hand, without an agent or an attorney, you will be somewhat at a disadvantage in understanding everything that is in the contract. It is never a good idea to sign a legally binding document that you don't fully understand. In most cases, you will be reasonably protected by using the promulgated form and hiring an attorney to explain any features that you don't understand. The same function can be performed by the real estate agent if that agent is serving as your buyer's agent.

Use of a "binder" is customary in several states. The buyer and seller, often assisted by a broker, sign a one-page agreement called a binder. Within a few days of the binder (the amount of time varies by state law) the parties are expected to get their attorneys to prepare a contract. The purpose of the binder is to take the property off the market, preserve the transaction, and allow time for attorneys to prepare a detailed contract that will be acceptable to buyer and seller.

Depending on the capabilities and mutual cooperation of the attorneys, this can go smoothly and satisfactorily or not. Attorneys sometimes get tied up in other matters and cannot prepare a contract within the statutory time limits. There can be miscommunications between clients and their attorneys, whereby the attorney thinks a certain problem is a deal breaker and breaks the deal, when the issue was not intended to be a deal breaker at all. If your attorney doesn't provide the timely service you need, the other side may think you are causing a problem. The attorney engaged by the other side will not talk with you directly because it would be unprofessional to avoid your attorney. But you can speak with the other principal and let him or her know your true intentions and that you really want to complete the agreement.

A sales contract should include these essential sections:

- A description of the property you want to buy. In most cases, the address will suffice.

- Identification of the buyer (you and anybody whose name will go on the deed, such as your spouse) and the seller.

- The **consideration**. This is what you are prepared to give the seller in exchange for the property. In most cases, the consideration is the sales price to be paid in cash to the seller.

In some cases, the buyer proposes that the seller provide financing for all or part of the sale. This agreement would be reflected in the consideration section of the contract.

- A **closing date**. The contract states when the sale will be consummated. Often, the buyer sets the closing date.

- **Contingencies**. These are circumstances that could terminate the transaction. Common contingencies concern the condition of the property (an inspection turns up information that could cause the buyer to back out of the deal), financing (the buyer is unable to get financing that is affordable), and sale of another property (the buyer will complete the sale only after selling her current home).

State and federal law determine how these clauses are constructed and worded. Other than that, the contract includes any provisions that are agreeable to both parties.

How Much Deposit?

It is customary to accompany your offer with a cash **deposit** (in some sections of the country, it is called **earnest money**). The deposit is recognized in the contract and shows that your offer is a serious one. The deposit counts as part of your down payment when the sale goes to closing. If you fail to complete the transaction and there is no contingency to cover your failure, you forfeit the deposit. The deposit should be large enough to show you are serious, but small enough so that you can write a good check at the time you submit the offer (the broker representing the seller will place your check in **escrow**, where it will stay unexecuted until the closing; still, you want to have sufficient funds to honor the check). Your agent can advise on how much is customary, but usually around five percent of the sales price is sufficient.

Before You Make That Offer

You may want to get pre-approved for a mortgage before you approach a seller. Pre-approval eliminates most of the uncertainty of getting financing and may make you a more attractive buyer to the seller because of the reduced risk of the sale falling through. It is especially advisable when markets favor sellers. You will want the seller to know you are pre-approved for financing but not the specific amount of the limit on your loan approval. Just let them know that you can borrow enough to support your offer.

Making an Informed Offer

The most important part of your offer is the price. In this section, we will look at some of the ways you can arrive at an offering price. Essentially, your offer should be based on the value of the property to you (your reservation price), less a discount to give you negotiating room. This discount ideally allows you to raise your offer to meet the counteroffer of the seller without exceeding your reservation price. First, we will look at how you determine your reservation price, and then at how much you should discount your offering price.

Market Benchmarks

In Chapter 3, we looked at some sources of information on **market values**. The Internet offers sites that give you an idea of what homes are worth in the neighborhood and maybe even value estimates for the specific house you want to buy. In addition, you can find published data on house sales prices averaged for metropolitan areas, counties, and some cities. The National Association of Realtors® reports median sales prices for metropolitan areas across the country. The Office of Federal Housing Enterprise Oversight (OFHEO) publishes a home price index that indicates appreciation rates for every metropolitan area in the United States. In addition, you may find articles in local newspapers showing price trends for individual neighborhoods. Search archives for the paper covering your target area.

All these information sources are good for providing you a context for framing your value opinion. These data are especially helpful if you are moving to a new area of the country. If nothing else, they might reduce some of the "sticker shock" you get when you see the sellers' prices.

At some point, you have to separate the concept of "market value"—the amount that the typical buyer is willing to pay for the property—from "your value"—the amount it is worth to you. In a well-operating market (and housing markets usually are not well-operating), buyers who value a property below its market value end up not purchasing the property. However, you might be in the right place at the right time and get the property at your price before someone else offers more. At any rate, you certainly do not want to pay more than the property is worth to *you*, no matter how the market sees it.

You are aiming at determining your value rather than market value. It is necessary to know what the market value is as well, because it might be lower than your reservation price. Market value will be close to the asking price in most cases, especially if the property has been on the market for a while and the price has been reduced.

Appraisers have an accepted procedure for estimating market value. Those techniques can be adapted to estimate a home's worth to you. The appraiser is trained to view the property from the standpoint of the typical purchaser. You, however, are uniquely suited to view the property from your personal perspective.

Comparing Sales Prices

If you wanted to buy a new camera, you probably would start by going to a store and checking the prices. If you had done some research and knew the type of camera you wanted and what features you needed, you could quickly home in on a price. The procedure appraisers call the "market comparison method" is not far off from this process of seeing prices paid in the market for properties similar to the one you want.

The procedure is straightforward. You get information from the market on how much similar homes cost. You then adjust that information to match the homes that have sold to the one you want to buy. Since you are not setting the price, only your offering price, you don't have to be highly specific in your estimate—a ballpark number will suffice.

There are a number of ways to get market data. We reviewed some of them in Chapter 3—Internet sources like *www.zillow.com* and local real estate agent sites. You can get a list of homes for sale from the National Association of Realtors' home search page at *www.realtor.com*. Zillow offers value estimates of a number of homes that are not necessarily for sale. Real estate agents' sites will provide sellers' asking prices for homes on the market. If you are working with an agent, ask the agent to run an analysis on recent sales of homes in the target area. These will be actual sales prices; the most direct indication of what similar homes should sell for. Sometimes real estate agents publish and distribute newsletters and flyers with information on recent sales. If you live in a state that requires the disclosure of prices in deeds, then you can find prices of houses that sold at the courthouse, registrar of deeds. Sometimes the local newspaper will report such data (you should already have become a regular reader of the weekly real estate or "homes" section of the paper). When you find a property that is a reasonable substitute for the one you want to buy, go and see the home and note any differences in quality, size, and location.

After you collect the data, it is time to do a little analysis. Appraisers call the homes that sold for which they have price data **comps**. That is short for **comparable properties**. They are comparable to the "subject" property they want to appraise. The appraiser has to adjust the price for the comp to reflect anything that is better or worse than the subject property. If the comp has a two-car garage and the subject only a one-car garage, the appraiser will deduct something from the comp's sales price to compensate. Likewise, if the comp is missing something the subject has, the appraiser will increase the comp price.

The difference between the appraiser and you is that the appraiser adjusts prices for things that the market values, while you are concerned only with things that you value. If the two-car garage is something you would like to have, then deduct an amount from the comp price equal to what you would be willing to pay for that feature. If you couldn't care less about a feature, then ignore it and don't adjust the comp price.

After you adjust each comp price in this manner (only do this to the comps that you would consider a reasonable substitute for the subject property), you will have a collection of adjusted prices that should hover around the value you place on the subject property.

Now is the time to ask yourself an honest question. Could you see yourself buying a home like one of the comps? How committed are you to the subject property? Some people find the perfect house when they shop and instantly fall in love with it; there is no alternative for them. If that house had not been for sale, though, they would have had to settle for another home. It is important to recognize how much you want the home. It could be the perfect choice and no other will suffice. It may be the best of a group of homes that would also be acceptable. Or, it may just be one choice among an equally serviceable collection of homes.

If you are relatively indifferent, the adjusted comp prices are useful to show whether the seller is asking too much for the property. A truly indifferent buyer can treat the homes as if they were interchangeable and pick the one with the best price. However, even within one subdivision or a condo building of almost identical units, the homes have distinctions that makes one more attractive than the others.

If you are totally committed to the home you are pricing, your bargaining room is a bit tight. You, an able and willing buyer, will likely be paying a price based more on "able" than on "willing." In other words, you may be willing to pay any price that you can afford to get the home. Being pre-approved for financing and knowing how much cash you have available to complement the loan will help you determine how much you are able to pay. The adjusted comp prices might come in handy to support an offer to the seller below the asking price.

Building Your Future

The second method used by appraisers is the "cost approach." The reasoning here is that a typical buyer would pay no more for a house than the cost of building an equally useful one. The assumption is that you could go out and buy a piece of land in a similar location and build a home that would be just as good as the subject. The new home, however, will not have the wear and tear of the subject and that could make it more valuable. So you deduct an amount from the costs for depreciation and that gives an estimate of the subject's value.

Doing a full-cost-approach estimate is a lot of work and is probably not worth it for the purpose of getting a reservation price. However, you can get information from builders who are active in the area. Often, they will have model homes that you can compare with the subject and adjust anything that is different and that matters to you.

The same question we brought up earlier applies here. Is building a new home or buying into a new subdivision a reasonable alternative for you? Since building takes time, it is probably not appropriate for someone relocating from another town. New custom construction is more suited to move-up buyers who have a better idea of the features they want. There are a large number of choices that must be made when having a new home built.

Move-up buyers might want to make a slightly different comparison if the reason they are moving has something to do with the size of the home. Assuming that the location and neighborhood are satisfactory, a reasonable alternative to moving might be enlarging or remodeling the existing home. Estimates for such work can be obtained for little or no cost from remodeling contractors.

Once you have the cost of a new custom home, or an improvement to your existing home, you need to deduct an amount to account for the age of the subject property. If you value the quaintness of the subject, you will not deduct for what appraisers call "obsolescence." But you might take something off for the fact that components of the subject will need to be replaced or repaired sooner than on a new home. Unless the subject is a "fixer-upper," this shouldn't be too much, but needs to be included to get a good estimate. Recognize that if you underestimate the amount of depreciation, the cost-based estimate of value is still useful as an upper limit for your reservation price.

Suppose the home you are looking at is a fixer-upper. Or, what if you like the location, neighborhood, and the general layout of the house, but it is missing some feature you want? You believe that feature can be added after you own the home. For example, you may want hardwood floors and know that you can install these floors in the house. It is not unusual for home buyers to make some major improvements to the home immediately after taking possession.

In this case, you will need to cost out the improvement and subtract that amount from your adjusted sales price derived from comparable sales. Your reservation price is the amount you would pay for the house with the feature, less the cost of making the improvements. There is a bit of inconvenience involved in having to remodel the house after you move in, but you also get to tailor the improvement to your exact specifications and tastes.

Buy or Rent

The final method used by appraisers is the "income approach." The property is valued for its ability to produce rental income and various methods are available to convert that income to a value estimate. For properties like homes that are occupied by their owners, "income" is the rent that the owner could have earned if she were not living in the home.

This analysis compares the cost of buying the home to the costs of renting an equally satisfactory home. Some first-time buyers have to settle for renting if their hopes of buying are frustrated for some reason. Renting might not be equally satisfactory, but it is a realistic alternative. Ask yourself if renting is an option. It would almost never be an option for anyone who currently owns a home, but probably is an alternative for those who currently rent. How much more would you have to pay in rent to get something comparable to the subject home? How much more than that would you be willing to pay per month for the benefits of home ownership?

Although appraisers go to the trouble of converting the rent into a value estimate, you might be able to avoid this step. Ask the real estate agent to estimate the monthly payment needed to buy the subject home (agents do this all the time). Then, just compare the monthly loan payment to the rent payment. There are things that are not priced into these figures, but they might not be important to you or they may cancel out when you consider both sides. To judge how comparable the rent and loan payment figures are, consider the following:

- The loan payment probably includes a little to amortize the loan, producing equity buildup, a type of forced savings that you should recover when you sell.

- There is a greater chance that your rent will go up in the future at a faster rate than would your loan payment, unless you are using an ARM, especially one with a teaser rate.

- Some of the loan payment might provide itemized tax deductions that will allow you to save some on your income taxes.

- Buying likely will require a cash down payment that is greater than the deposits required to rent. In either case, the money used for down payments and deposits could have been invested in a bank account where it would earn income.

- Buying allows you to profit from the future sale should the property increase in value. There is no assurance of this, however, and the possibility exists of the property losing value.

- There are costs involved in selling the property that make moving much more expensive than if you are renting.

- Be sure to compare rent to the total monthly payment, including escrow contributions. The costs of insuring and paying taxes on the rental property, borne by the landlord, are passed on to you in the rent amount.

- If the comparable rent includes some utilities, you will have to back out an estimate of what those costs would be if you paid them.

Once you decide on the monthly payment that equals the rent you would pay for a comparable home plus any premium you attach to ownership, you can back into a reservation price. Here you will be doing the monthly payment estimate in reverse order:

- First, take out an amount that reflects the tax and insurance escrow payment that you added to the loan payment for your comparison.

- You now have your maximum principal and interest payment.

- Based on the financing you will use to buy the house, enter the loan term (in months) into the "N" button on an appropriate calculator.

- Enter the interest rate in the "i/yr" button.

- Enter into the "PMT" button the comparable monthly payment amount you calculated in the first step.

- Push the "PV" button and you will get the loan amount (if it is a negative number, just ignore the sign).

- Add the down payment you had planned to make. The result is your reservation price for the home based on the alternative of renting a comparable property.

Work Sheets

Building Your Reservation Price

Amount you can afford to pay each month $ _____

Multiply by tax/insurance factor*   × _____

Affordable loan P&I payment   = _____

Typical loan term   _____ years

Typical loan interest rate   _____ %

Find the payment in the loan payment tables for the
appropriate loan term and interest rate

Find the loan amount from the table $ _____

Add the amount of cash available for down payment   + _____

Amount you can afford to pay for the home   = _____

*If you live in an area with high tax and insurance costs, enter .68.
If taxes and insurance are relatively inexpensive in your area, enter .85.
Otherwise, enter .75. A more exact approach is to deduct the estimated
monthly real estate taxes, insurance, and mortgage insurance if required.

Making an Offer Based on Your Reservation Price

The reservation price is the highest price you would be willing to pay for the home, though you hope to get it for less. The seller does not know your reservation price or that of any other potential buyer in the market. The seller places the home on the market with an asking price that represents the best she thinks the house will fetch. Buyers respond with offers of something less than the asking price. In a normal market, the buyer and seller will banter back and forth and settle on some figure between the asking price and the buyer's initial offer.

If you make your offer at your reservation price, you have nowhere to go in the negotiations. Therefore, it is customary for buyers to discount their offering price a bit to provide negotiating room. There is no cut-and-dried rule for how much discount to make. It depends on two basic factors: market conditions and your devotion to the house.

Over time, housing markets cycle from conditions that favor buyers (**buyer's market**) to those that favor sellers (**seller's market**). Between these two extremes are normal markets in which neither side has all the advantages though one side may be stronger than the other. In a seller's market, there are lots of buyers for each property on the market and sellers can dictate their price. In times of high housing demand, sellers may even be able to get sales at prices above their asking price because buyers are willing to bid up the price to snatch it away from competing buyers. Responding to printed ads is of little use, since the home may have already sold before the ad appears. If you are a buyer in a seller's market, you may have to offer your reservation price and hope for the best.

How to Tell a Buyer's Market from a Seller's Market

We know that market cycles exist but it is not always easy to detect what phase of the cycle the market is currently in. It is especially difficult to pick up on the change from one phase to the next. Often, the difficulty is caused by the lag in getting data about current market conditions. Cycle phases are much easier to pinpoint long after the fact. This may be interesting to historians, but is of little use to someone trying to buy or sell a home.

If you know what to look for, it is easier to figure out the state of the market through ordinary observation than to rely on statistics. You can tell a lot by looking around the town and reading local news articles and letters to the editor in the newspaper. A buyer's market has a lot of homes for sale compared to the number of willing and able buyers. Expect to see:

- More homes with For Sale signs than you normally would see.
- For Sale signs stay up for long periods of time—long enough that the name of the broker has changed at least once.
- For Sale signs tout a reduced price.
- Homes that were for sale are being advertised for rent.
- Stories of rising numbers of foreclosures.
- Announcements for large-scale auctions of repossessed homes.
- Sellers and home-builders offer concessions (free trips or televisions) to attract buyers.

You might suspect that a seller's market prevails when you see:

- Very few For Sale signs in yards (unless they are prohibited by local covenants or ordinances).
- News of lotteries being conducted to choose buyers who are allowed to bid on homes (this is more commonly used with new condominium projects).
- Stories about people making big profits by "flipping" homes—buying homes to resell at higher prices after maybe doing some cosmetic improvements.
- Frequent discussions on news and business shows about the booming housing market.
- References in the news about the housing-affordability "crisis."
- New home-building projects spread throughout the area—existing rental complexes being converted into condominiums.

When we bought our current home, we were buying into a seller's market—sales were booming, prices were rising, and there were not that many homes to choose from considering the size of the area. We really wanted to live in a particular community and found the one house there that appealed to us. However, the house had been on the market for only a few days, and it was in the middle of winter, normally a relatively dead season for home-buying. So we discounted the asking price by quite a bit. The result? The seller came back with a price well above what we offered but still a little lower than the original asking price.

When a buyer's market prevails, there are lots of homes on the market, while buyers are relatively scarce. Sellers have to market their homes more aggressively and are more receptive to all offers, even those well below their asking price. In such conditions, you might attempt a **lowball offer**—one substantially below the asking price. How successful this strategy will be depends on how motivated the seller is. Some sellers faced with such disappointing offers will retract the home from the market or simply sit and wait for a better offer to appear. Unfortunately, you have no way of knowing how motivated a seller is, but you might expect that a seller's motivation will increase as the home languishes on the market. (Interesting idea: Researchers have found that sellers who use "charm" pricing—those ads that list the property for slightly less than a round number, like $199,900—are indicating that they consider the price firm—one sign of an unmotivated seller).

Even in a buyer's market, you may not want to make a lowball offer if you really want the home. The seller might take offense and refuse to even consider your offer. If the home is not special or would need a lot of work after the purchase, you might be somewhat indifferent to whether the seller takes your offer. In that case, lowball to the extent that you dare. On the other hand, if the home is the one that you really prefer to all others, you will have to be more accommodating. In a buyer's market, you will be making an offer only slightly below your reservation price, and in a seller's market, be prepared to outbid all comers.

Other Things to Negotiate

The sales contract describes all the terms of the sale, not just the sales price. All of these items are negotiable and some of them might be more important to you than the price. The complexity of a real estate sale means that there may be something in the deal that could make it a bargain even if you pay the asking price. In this section, we will look at several of these items.

Closing Costs

Expenses incidental to the transaction can add up to as much as 10–15 percent of the sales price, and they all have to be paid in cash at closing. A cash-challenged buyer might be able to get the seller to pay most of these costs in exchange for agreeing to the seller's asking price. Assuming the appraisal supports the seller's price, the buyer can finance a larger portion of the home's costs than if she had bargained down the price and paid her own closing expenses. This is because the maximum loan amount is based on the sales price rather than the net price paid by the buyer.

Before you propose any of this, recognize that custom, not the law, dictates how closing costs are allocated between buyer and seller. In general, buyers pay:

- All expenses arising from the loan, such as discount points, fees, and all those mysterious, "junk" fees that inevitably show up on the closing statement.

- Premium for a home-owner's title insurance policy, if so desired.

Sellers commonly pay:

- All sales commissions, even for an agent contracted to serve as the buyer's agent.
- Costs of a termite inspection.
- Premium for the lender's title insurance policy.

In the sales contract, you might ask the seller to pay a certain number of discount points to the lender (these result in a lower interest rate) or to meet any other specific expense. Alternatively, you might state that the seller will pay up to an amount equaling a specific percentage of the sales price. In most cases, the seller will have cash coming at the closing (even if that cash will go directly into the purchase of another home), and it should make little difference what the sales price is as long as the net cash is the same. For example, selling the home for $250,000 and paying $3,000 in buyer's closing costs is no different from selling for $247,000 without paying any buyer costs. In either case, the seller is getting the same amount of money. To a buyer who is financing the purchase, it can make a big difference.

Closing Date

The closing date is the day when ownership passes from seller to buyer. It is also the day when the bills come due and you have to be ready to present that certified check for everything not covered by the mortgage loan. In many cases, the seller wants the closing date to be as soon as possible, because it is likely that she has already bought another home and is making two mortgage payments. That may be fine with the buyer if she is ready to move in. Often, the interests of seller and buyer do not fit so nicely. The seller may need time to find a new home. The buyer may want time to sell her current home or to move from a distant town.

The buyer initially sets the closing date in the offered sales contract. If the seller changes the date with a counteroffer, you know you have a negotiable item. An earlier closing might mean that you will have to sell your home after you take possession, thereby putting you in the position of making two mortgage payments. A later closing might mean that you will have to find temporary housing after you move. Estimate what these changes will cost you and try to get something in compensation if you agree to the seller's date.

If the closing date causes a problem of logistics, you might include a provision in the contract for taking possession of the house at a different time than the closing. If you need to move in before the closing, you might ask for a lease for the interval up to the closing (the seller might waive any rental payments if the house is unoccupied). If the seller needs to stay after the closing, you might agree to lease the property for that period. Don't agree to an open-ended lease period with no termination date. If the agreed-upon period expires and the seller still needs to occupy the home, negotiate another lease. Even if no rent is charged, there should be some type of written agreement to cover issues of liability in case an accident happens.

Repairs

Unless you are buying an acknowledged fixer-upper, you expect the home to be in reasonably decent condition. Yet a lot can be wrong that may not have been apparent when you looked through the house. That is why most buyers hire a professional inspector to check out the house. You don't want to incur the expense of an inspection until you have a claim on the house—sometime after the sales contract is finalized and before the closing date. The sales contract needs to set out what happens if the inspection turns up significant problems.

There are two common ways to handle this contingency—the **limited concession** or the **option period**. Under the limited concession, the seller agrees to cover any repairs found necessary by the inspector up to a finite dollar limit. This arrangement tends to favor the seller, since her liability is contained. She can plan on spending the maximum in the contract and incorporate that into the sales price. If the inspection uncovers a major problem, the buyer has little recourse other than to walk away from the deal.

The option approach establishes a limited period when the buyer can cancel the transaction for any reason and retrieve her deposit. The option period gives the buyer an opportunity to have the home inspected. If the problems are not curable, the buyer can exercise the option and cancel the sale (this option works in reverse: if you exercise the option, you cancel the sale; if you do nothing, the sale is on). If repairs are needed and the buyer wants to proceed, she might ask the seller to make the repairs prior to closing or adjust the sales price. In other words, the buyer makes a renegotiated contract a requirement for not exercising the option.

Whether you get an option or a concession likely will depend on the law or custom in your state. The specifics—option length and fee or the limit to the repair concession—are to be negotiated. As the buyer, you will want the length of the option period to be long enough to have an inspection done, complete with a list of required repairs and estimated costs. Ideally, you will want to get the option without a fee. The option fee is credited to you at closing but is forfeited if you do not complete the transaction. Essentially, it becomes compensation to the seller for taking the home off the market for the duration of the option.

Contingencies

With the sales contract, you are promising to buy the home under the terms stated in the contract. If you are unable to complete the transaction, you forfeit your deposit. Moreover, it is possible that you could be sued for damages or even forced to go through with the sale, although this rarely happens. There are things that can make it impractical for you to buy the home and you need to provide for these in the contract.

Almost all sales contracts have a contingency clause to cover financing. This clause protects you if you are unable to secure financing at affordable terms. The wording states that if the buyer cannot get a loan at an interest rate below a specific ceiling, the sale will be canceled and the buyer can recover her deposit.

Less frequently, the sales contract will have a contingency to cover sale or purchase of another home. The buyers may want to make the sale contingent on selling their current home, or, more rarely, the seller may hinge the sale on finding a replacement home. Since these auxiliary transactions are under the control of the buyer or seller, these contingencies amount to an unlimited option.

Contingencies can be extremely important to the buyer but present a liability to the seller, who would prefer a clean transaction without the uncertainty introduced by the contingencies. Therefore, the buyer should expect to pay some price premium for these clauses. The common financing contingency written with reasonable terms (a maximum interest rate a bit above the current market rate) should have no effect on the price except in the strongest seller's market. A sale-of-current-home clause's impact on price depends on current market conditions. If the market is active, the impact will be minimal, but if the market is slow, the seller will expect to get her asking price in exchange for agreeing to the contingency. Also, the seller probably will want to limit the time that the contingency is in effect and will want the right to accept backup offers in case you do not buy the home.

Special-Situation Extras

A really motivated seller might be able to provide assistance to the buyer in special situations. When mortgage financing is expensive and difficult to obtain, the seller might step into the role of the lender. The terms of such **seller financing** can be as important as the sales price in determining how much you pay for the home. If you like the looks of a home but are not sure it is the home for you, you might propose a **lease-option** as an alternative to an outright sale. A seller probably will not be receptive to such an arrangement unless the housing market is really dead and she must sell the house right away.

Seller financing can take several forms. The seller could finance the whole sale with a first mortgage. There would be no other lender. You would pay a cash down payment and make periodic payments to the seller over the term of the financing. This type of arrangement might be of value if you have trouble obtaining financing through normal channels—for example, if you are self-employed or the loan is very large. The seller might prefer to give you a loan at a below-market interest rate in lieu of a discount on the price.

A more common form of seller financing is similar to a second mortgage. Often the first mortgage is assumed from the seller. An example is a sale in which the $150,000 sales price is met with a first mortgage of $100,000 assumed from the seller, a $40,000 second mortgage taken back by the seller, and a $10,000 cash down payment. How much seller financing affects the true sale price is unknown at the time of the sale, because of the risk that the buyer will default on the loan payments or that the loan will be refinanced before it runs its full term.

While not truly seller financing, a similar type of seller concession is the rate **buy-down**. The seller agrees to pay additional discount points to the lender in exchange for a lower interest rate for the buyer. The lower rate may allow the buyer to qualify for a larger loan than otherwise. The cost to the seller of providing this concession is fixed by the number of points required by the lender. If you think you will have a problem qualifying for a loan large enough to buy the home, you might try to negotiate a buy-down into the contract.

With a lease-option, the buyer leases the home rather than purchasing it immediately. The lease includes an option to purchase the home sometime in the next several years. In the meantime, the buyer gets to try out the house and become familiar with all of its charms and faults. When the tenant-buyer is in a position to buy, she can exercise the option and complete the purchase. Or, the buyer can decide not to become a buyer and finish out the lease, letting the option expire.

The leasing period allows the tenant-buyer to gather her resources, repair a damaged or nonexistent credit standing, or wait until interest rates come down. In some cases, a portion of the rent is applied to the purchase price in the form of a down payment. The option price may be fixed at the commencement of the lease or based on some predetermined formula (like a fixed amount indexed to inflation). As you can see, it would be a truly desperate and patient seller who agrees to a lease-option, but there are times in the market cycle when sellers are that motivated.

Home-Buyer's Checklist

- Collect data on price trends in the city and neighborhood where you think you will buy. Look for any reports of price trends in the local area. Ask your agent for sale prices of comparable homes.

- If a brand-new home is a viable alternative for you, collect information on what it would cost to build a home like the one that is for sale. If you currently own a home and are satisfied with the location, find out what it would cost to upgrade the home to be more like the one you are contemplating.

- If renting is a realistic alternative for you, find out what the rent would be for a home like the one you plan to make an offer on. Figure out how much you could offer to pay for the house without the monthly payment being more than comparable rent.

- From the data you have collected, develop an approximate reservation price representing the most you will pay for the home.

- From your impressions about the home and what is available in the market, decide how much you want this particular home. Evaluate whether market conditions tend to favor buyers or sellers or possibly are neutral.

- Based on the information you have, decide on an offering price for the home.

- Consider the other terms of the sale and which ones are of particular value to you. Estimate how you can meet the seller's asking price and use concessions or some other term to bring the cost down to your desired offering price.

Chapter 11

Home Inspection— The Physical Exam

W e're not in the horror-story business but they do raise their ugly heads now and then, thus reinforcing our advice to always look for qualified people at every stage in your home-buying experience. One such story involves a less than qualified home inspector who neglected to inspect a crawl space even when he could see from the entrance that a brick-supporting pier was not in tip-top condition. Only after Aaron and Baylee moved into the house did the fault become apparent when, to their horror, the entire first floor settled two full inches and the local code-enforcement people told them to vacate the house. After much grief and litigation, the house needed to be reconstructed.

Paul and Jeannie were more fortunate because in their situation they hired a professional home-inspection engineer whose thoroughness revealed a structural defect that the seller was not aware of. He discovered a failing foundation wall that few would have recognized. His recommended solution saved the wall and the deal. Don't ever underestimate the value of a thorough professional inspection.

The Home and Its Bones

A house becomes a home when you live in it. It must be looked at carefully, however, before you decide that a particular house is to be your home. An overview of the entire house will increase your understanding of important conditions to be evaluated by a home-inspection engineer. This will also help you to do some of your own preliminary inspecting when considering different properties. Home inspections today are a normal part of the process of buying a house. This was not the case only a few years ago, so you may find that some people performing home inspections are new to this type of work.

A house is a structure created by a human, located within a defined land area of earth—a product of nature. Problems with what a human constructs can be corrected by humans. Problems with nature may or may not be compensated for by humans. Nature, including the weather, is outside the control of humans, so it is important for a house to be sited and designed to best accommodate the beauty and forces of nature. How the building is situated on the property will have a large bearing on its exposure and durability. Characteristics of the property also have a bearing on the design requirements of the house and the level of maintenance needed. Some locations have greater risks than others. Beautiful views from hillside or waterfront locations are not without peril. This is all part of the romance of owning a home that is *more* than just a house. A house on a hillside will have different considerations from a waterfront house or one within a development on relatively flat land with good public storm-water drainage systems. Violent weather potential will vary with locations.

A house is an organized composite of various systems and components. A basic understanding of these systems and components will help you identify potential concerns. It will also help you to better understand the information a professional inspector will provide. Equally important, this understanding will help you manage the maintenance of your new home. When a house is built or remodeled, local building codes apply to every aspect of the building and all of its systems. Once the house is built, codes generally do not apply unless property maintenance codes or local ordinances might require such things as smoke and carbon monoxide detectors. Home inspections are not code-compliance inspections. If a house had an addition constructed without the necessary building permits, a code-compliance evaluation might be required by the local code-enforcement agency before issuing a continuing certificate of occupancy.

In this chapter, we will introduce the basic components of houses with a sketch for useful reference. We'll give you a checklist so you can perform you own mini-inspections as you look at different houses. An overview of the inspection process and special inspection requirements will make you a better consumer. We'll take you by the hand with guidance on hiring a professional home inspector and how to act on his report. We will also offer suggestions on how to best utilize home inspection information in your negotiations with the seller. Life expectancy information is included in this chapter's appendix.

The sketch on the next page identifies certain terms used to describe structural, framing, and exterior cladding parts of a house.

Houses are built of materials such as wood, steel, concrete, etc. Materials from nature may be expected to have irregularities. There are also human-made materials, and combinations of human-made and natural materials. All of these materials have different physical properties that are affected by their use and the environmental conditions of moisture, temperature, and loading considerations. Wood and concrete usually shrink after initial construction. Wood shrinkage is due to drying of the wood when it loses some of

Figure 11–1: House Framing ("The Bones")

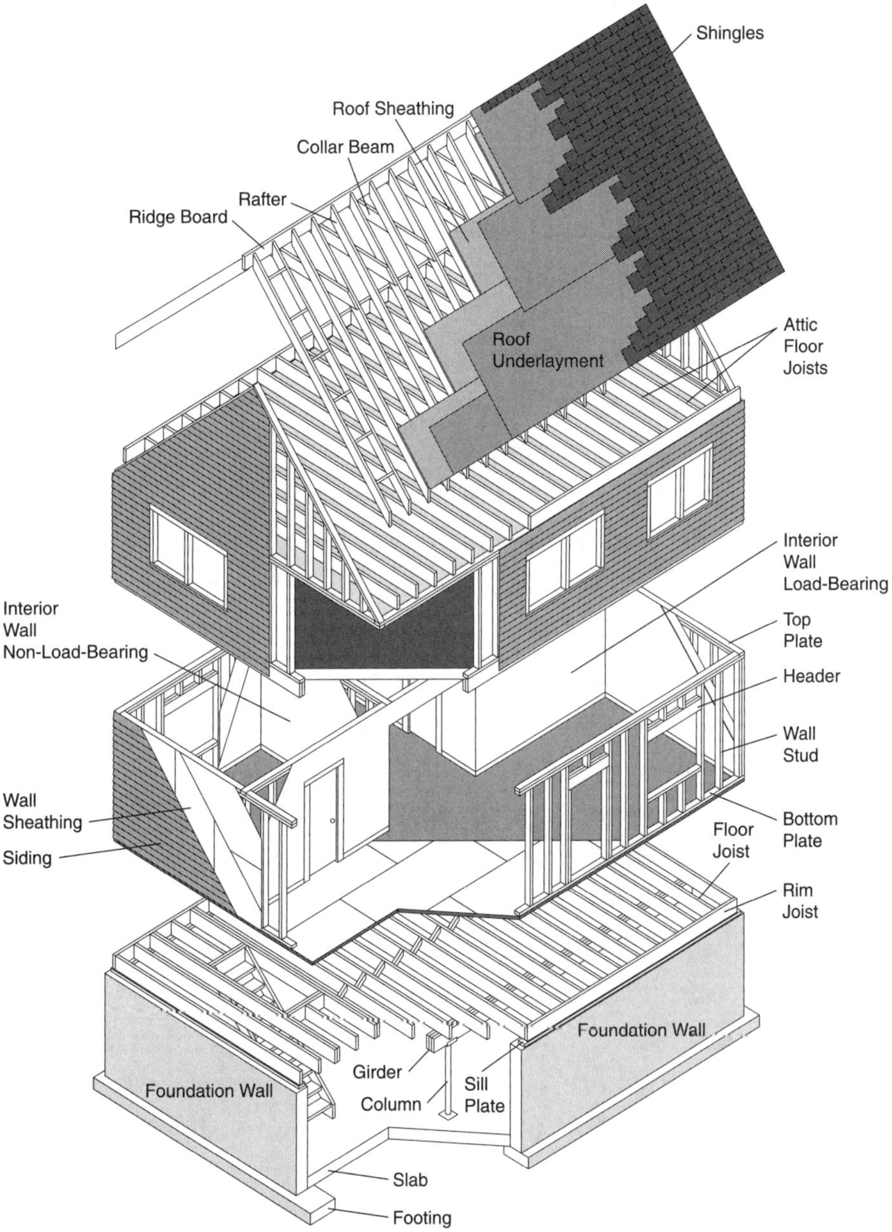

This illustration shows the skeleton of a typical home.

its moisture content. Wood regularly expands and shrinks as moisture levels increase and decrease. All materials shrink or expand with changes in temperature. Overloaded materials can bend or break. Understanding how to differentiate shrinkage from settlement or structural movement is best left to an engineer who may be needed to evaluate significant movements. A professional home inspector must understand these issues so he can explain them to you if a serious problem exists, and if further engineering evaluation is necessary.

Design considerations for a house begin with the land where the building is to be located. Characteristics of the property and its soil are important. For an existing structure, this will have already been considered by engineers and architects involved with the original design and location of the house on the property site. But over time, land may be modified by erosion or movement. A qualified home inspector should be able to detect this.

Roof-water and surface-water drainage is one of the most important property considerations. The single, biggest cause of problems to any building is water in all its various forms. When you think of the large area of the roof it becomes obvious that roof water cannot be allowed to just seep into the soil at the foundation. Hillside, waterfront, and other special considerations also require study. The property may have safety issues as well that need to be considered during an inspection.

The foundation is the primary support system for house framing. In areas where soil freezes, the foundation's bottom or "footings," located below the frost line, are not visible. Waterfront and hillside homes may have piling foundations where part of the pilings is visible and part is buried. The type of foundation will vary according to the type of soil conditions and property characteristics. Expansive soils, like clay, grow when wet and need stronger basement walls than would be needed with easy-to-drain sandy soils. In houses with basements, part of their foundation walls are visible. Houses constructed on concrete pads or "slabs" may present other problems.

The framing system rests upon and is connected to the foundation. This is the skeleton—the bones of the house that support the exterior barriers, roof and siding, and the interior floors and walls. The framing system may be a combination of steel, wood, and masonry units. Around the framing system a shell is built to protect the inside from outside weather. Above the frame is the roof. Siding and attics are insulated in modern houses and need features, such as flashing, to reduce the potential for moisture intrusion at all openings. Flashings are special barriers used between different materials, including window and wall joints and at roof transitions. Severe weather variations, such as those found in tornado- and hurricane-prone areas, call for special design considerations.

Siding is a lot more than an overcoat for a building. As with any building siding (cladding) material, windows, flashing systems, and sealants that are poorly installed can leak and allow water intrusion, which may even delaminate or decay sheathing, causing water damage to structural members and possibly contributing to mold generation. Moisture intrusion often goes unnoticed for long periods of time, as it generally does not cause obvious structural distress. If you see discoloration, ask for a professional evaluation. Certainly, any failing sealant or lack of proper flashing calls for careful evaluation. While serious structural damage does not result from loss of just a few framing members, allowing water intrusion to continue could result in structural failure.

Management of water at any building is one of the most important factors for the continued well-being of the building. Roof water, surface water, condensation water, water intrusions, and leaky plumbing are all sources of water that lead to building damage. It does not matter what type of cladding system is used. Water must be drawn away from the building, particularly away from the foundation. Wall-draining and wall-ventilation systems help and are, in fact, needed with certain types of siding, but by themselves they are not the answer to keeping water out of the building. Good design requires attention to flashing and sealant detail. Good construction requires that good design detail be properly fabricated. The prolonged health of a house requires vigilance and ongoing maintenance.

All buildings are expected to have major systems to provide electricity, water, heat, and air conditioning. Plumbing systems must bring fresh water into the home and take out wastewater. Electricity, water, and fuel may be provided by local utilities in most areas. In some rural areas, private water and private sewers are needed. Fuel may be stored in tanks on the property. Wells and septic systems require special inspections, not just when buying a house, but on a regular periodic basis.

Equipment, appliances, and building materials do not last forever. Knowing the age of your roof and heating systems will provide clues to their potential remaining life. In the appendix of this chapter there is a copy of the Life Expectancy of Housing Components from the U.S. Department of Housing and Urban Development Residential Rehabilitation Inspection Guide.

Many materials can and do last a long time. Wood, however, can rot from moisture exposure. Wood can be eaten or destroyed by insects. Steel, too, is not forever—it can rust. Wood, steel, and concrete can be overloaded and bend or break. Foundation walls can move due to poor drainage or poor soil conditions. Electrical and mechanical devices can break or wear out. Because you want to know the condition of the house you are investing your future in, it is important to have a professional inspection of all of its structural, electrical, mechanical, and plumbing systems.

It is also important to understand the management of water. As noted above, water is the greatest source of damage to buildings. Rain water, surface water, plumbing-leak water, condensation water, elevated groundwater, flood water, etc., can all cause problems. Never underestimate the possible damaging effects of any type of water.

Your Own Inspection—Mini-Checklist

Caveat Emptor—"buyer beware"—is a good maxim to follow. You don't want big surprises. Do your own mini-inspections before you consider entering into a contract. This can lead to questions that will help you evaluate potential professional home inspectors. If you are serious about purchasing a certain house and can arrange a home inspection prior to contract, it will be easier to pull out of a bad deal. Typically, however, home inspection is not performed until after a contract has been entered into. It is important to have the contract contingent upon an acceptable home inspection. Where there are attorney review periods, there may be three or more days after the contract is signed and before the time period starts, to have the home inspection. These time periods are for both sides to agree to all contract details and to prevent a buyer from making a rushed decision. Usually sellers will not want their houses inspected by a professional inspector until they know that they have a firm contract. Contracts typically allow an escape for the buyer if structural defects are found that exceed an agreed-upon value.

Understanding more about what a professional inspector does will help you perform a mini-inspection and increase your understanding of the true condition of the house.

Try to get a seller's disclosure of issues they know about. Often, significant problems are not remembered, realized, or revealed by the seller, which is another solid reason for having a professional home inspector. This is particularly important if there is any question about structural integrity or major system capacity. Sellers who have lived in a house for a long time should have greater information than owners who have lived in the house for only a short period of time.

We have prepared a simplified checklist to help you identify potential areas of concern. Regardless of the age of a house there are varying levels of condition. Even new houses have defects, though in a new house they may not be apparent to the untrained person. If you are thinking about buying a house that will need renovation or upgrading, the more value will be derived from your mini-inspection.

Mini-Self-Inspection—A Personal Checklist

A = Adequate

B = Repair/Maintenance

C = Replace/Investigate

• Take pictures
  front and rear views plus additional significant features

• Talk with neighbors

• Consider home location
  ____ flood plain or other high risk or violent weather locations
  ____ zoning problems

• Age of the home _____
  ____ are architect or engineering drawings available?

- History of additions or major alterations
  - ____ were there building permits?

- Site conditions
  - ____ drainage—does roof and surface water flow away from the foundation?
  - ____ safety—are there any trip and fall hazards (walking height changes)?

- Roof covering age _____

- Exterior _____ (type)
  - ____ siding—does the building have EIFS?
  - ____ windows
  - ____ doors

- Foundation _____ (type)
  - ____ any major cracks?
  - ____ any water entry problems?

- Interior
  - ____ doors—ease of operation
  - ____ walls—any leaning or large cracks?
  - ____ floors—are they level?
  - ____ any water entry or mold problems?
  - ____ any odors

- Insulation—does it exist and is it adequate?
  - ____ attic
  - ____ side walls
  - ____ crawl spaces

- Plumbing
    - ____ do all fixtures work?
    - ____ public water or well—need quality testing—how good is the aquifer?
    - ____ public sewer or septic (private waste-disposal system)

- Heating
    - ____ any operating problems?
    - ____ heating costs
    - ____ age of system

- Air conditioning
    - ____ any operating problems?
    - ____ age of system

- Electrical
    - ____ any visible electrical problems?
    - ____ electric costs

Home inspections are visual condition assessments so they are vulnerable to concealed conditions. Recent remodeling can cover defects. Knowing that local building permits were obtained and satisfactorily closed out is helpful. Additions and remodeling done without the necessary building permits should raise a red flag. There may be issues that demand the specialized knowledge of a qualified inspector or specific technical evaluator.

Hiring a Professional Home Inspector

Having a knowledgeable objective evaluation of your new home will give you the peace of mind that you are making a good decision. If problems are found, the professional inspector will help everyone fully understand what needs to be done to correct the problems. Experience matters. Being objective matters. It should not be left to an inexperienced friend or relative who may be available at a good price. Friends and family can help, but unless they are professional home inspectors they may incorrectly identify or overlook problems. Your needs must be properly served. A professional home inspector has credentials and experience that will give you the confidence that significant issues will be identified during the home inspection. The higher the level of licenses held by a home inspector, the better will be his required code of ethics. Many home inspectors also have building code enforcement licenses including Building, Plumbing, and Electrical. An inspector who has all three has significant, additional demonstrated experience and knowledge. Having all three code enforcement licenses will probably be found only with licensed professional engineers or architects. Experience increases the probability of correctly identifying problems.

Home inspections are visual so they will be limited to what can be seen, which makes education and experience even more important. The results of your mini-inspection may show that the services of a licensed professional engineer or architect are necessary. Certainly, you will want a licensed professional engineer or architect if you found major cracks in the foundation or significant interior wall and floor movement. It is important to learn what standards are being used by the inspector you are considering. States with home inspection licensing requirements may have standards similar to the ASHI standards referenced below. Experience and ability to go beyond the basic standards can vary. A licensed professional engineer or architect who performs building inspection engineering has a higher level of education, experience, and problem-solving expertise. The most comprehensive set of standards for residential and small commercial building inspections is provided by The National Academy of Building Inspection Engineers (NABIE) at *www.nabie.org*. NABIE is a preferred source for licensed professional engineers and architects because the experience of their members will have been evaluated and their work product peer-reviewed in order for them to obtain membership in the Academy. There are home inspectors with association membership that requires experience and demonstrated ability. The American Society of Home Inspectors at *www.ashi.org* is one such association. Additional home inspector organizations include: National Association of Home Inspectors at *www.nahi.org* and National Association of Certified Home Inspectors at *www.nachi.org*.

When investigating an inspector it is important to learn about the individual's problem-identification skills. Problem-identification and problem-solving skills vary with the professional level of the inspector. Visual inspections limit the information available to the inspector, so education and experience become critical factors in deciding which inspector to use. Does the inspector understand the problem well enough to describe it adequately? Or, does the inspector just refer all problems to others for further investigation? In the latter situation there may never be a true understanding of how significant a problem really is. This is a serious disservice to the home buyer. How well the problems are described is critical so all parties can understand what is serious in order to negotiate a fair settlement or to decide not to continue with the purchase. How good the inspector is at problem-solving communication is a question to ask of attorneys, realtors, or referring people who have had experience with the individual you are considering to perform your home inspection.

Friends and relatives in the area where you are buying who have had positive experiences with a home inspector may be good sources. It's the individual inspector who really matters. Realtors can be sources for home inspector referrals, but some people prefer not to rely on the realtor whose commission might be lost from an adverse inspection. Phone book directories and web-based directories are additional sources. Your real estate attorney is usually dependable in recommending a professional home inspector because he will have seen many different reports and will have had experience dealing with the inspector when there are issues to be resolved.

Try to have a direct conversation with the inspector whom you are considering. If you can talk only with office staff, try to get a sense of how the inspector would work with you. Choose an inspector who will answer your questions and who wants you to be present during the inspection. Be sure the inspector follows up with additional communication should it become necessary to resolve issues with the seller. Ask for background information about the home inspector and for details of his services to be e-mailed to you for review. Ask for a fee quotation. Be prepared to provide the home inspector with specific information about the house you are purchasing, such as a copy of the real estate listing so he will understand the needs of the particular inspection. Think about what you have learned and then make your decision.

The Inspection—Checking It Out

Be at the inspection if at all possible. If you cannot be there, have a spouse, relative, or friend present to report direct observations of significant findings. If you have selected an inspector who will graciously answer questions, you will glean much information— even maintenance tips. This is the time when you will really get to know the house you're buying. Enjoy the tour. If you follow the inspector around, ask about important observations so you can see for yourself. If serious problems are found, it will be helpful to see those problems firsthand to understand them and how they might be solved. If you do not follow along with the inspector, be sure he shows you the more serious problems. When you are on your own, make notes about anything questionable and be sure to ask your inspector. You are there to learn and the inspector is there to educate you. Serious problems will require corrective action. The better the home inspector, the greater the probability that good communication will result in an understanding by all parties that will lead to satisfactory conclusions. A home inspection provides an overall evaluation of structural conditions and the condition of the heating, air conditioning, electrical, and plumbing systems of the house. Many home inspectors will also evaluate appliances that are part of the sale. However, in some places, many home inspectors do not consider structural conditions. Then, you will need a structural engineer.

Generally, an inspection starts with observations of how the house is sited on the property, the shape of the property, and how roof water and surface water flows away from the foundation.

Property issues include walking areas and electrical safety concerns. All walking surfaces, including stairs, decks, and balconies, must be evaluated. All exterior electrical outlets must be checked for ground-fault circuit-interrupter outlet protection.

Exterior observations include roof, siding, windows, and doors. Surface conditions will be observed. Flashing and sealant systems are particularly important. These observations will help you understand repair maintenance needs and potential replacement needs.

Interior observations include framing and all major systems. Everything that operates should, at least, be sampled for operating condition. Not every window will be opened, but a representative number should be operated. Walls, floors, ceilings, and doors need to be evaluated. Electrical, plumbing, heating, and air conditioning systems all need to be operated and evaluated. Keep in mind, though, that weather conditions may restrict the operation of certain equipment.

Ventilation and energy efficiency must also be evaluated. Attic and crawl basement areas should be entered and evaluated. Evidence of water entry and moisture intrusion is particularly important for the home inspector to evaluate. Chimneys and fireplaces, to the extent visible, need evaluation.

Wood-Destroying Insects and Environmental Evaluations

Termites and Other Wood-Eating Insects

Termites and other wood-eating insects destroy the structural integrity of wood. There is some type of wood-destroying insect virtually everywhere, requiring inspections everywhere. Inspections are a standard requirement for mortgages. Inspections must include looking for evidence of termites, carpenter ants, carpenter bees, powder-post beetles, and other wood-destroying insects. These inspections are best done by people who perform *only* wood-destroying insect inspections and treatments. Wings and insect debris are some of the things they are looking for to identify the presence of active wood-destroying insects. Experience is critically important for the insect inspector to correctly identify these small items amongst other debris. The home inspection industry is growing and many people are trying to be a one-stop shopping experience. It is recommended that people who only perform termite inspections and provide termite treatment services should be retained to perform this inspection. A source for additional information is the U.S. Department of Housing and Urban Development at *www.hud.gov*.

Oil Tanks

Oil tanks, particularly underground oil tanks, present an environmental hazard when there are leaks. Oil tanks in use need a special evaluation, which at the very minimum, leads to obtaining oil-spill insurance in the buyer's name. It is especially important to identify the existence of underground oil tanks no longer in use because they need to be abandoned with proper building permits. Documentation of properly abandoned oil tanks must be maintained along with the property deed and passed on to the next buyer. Your home inspector may identify that a prior oil service existed, triggering the need to have further environmental evaluations.

Radon

Radon testing is one of the more common environmental tests often done by home inspectors who are qualified to perform the testing. Radon gas is an odorless, colorless gas that comes out of the earth from the natural decay of uranium, which exists almost everywhere. Radon studies have determined that high exposure causes lung cancer. Sample testing is straightforward and there are effective methods to reduce exposure depending upon the type of home construction. The recommended action level is 4 picocuries per liter. The U.S. Department of Environmental Protection states that the risk of exposure from 4 picocuries per liter of radon gas is equivalent to the risk from smoking 10 cigarettes a day or having 200 chest x-rays a year.

Lead

Lead paint, a source of lead poisoning, is common in houses built before 1940 and somewhat less so in houses built between 1940 and 1960. In 1978, it became illegal to use lead paint, so any home older than 1978 has the potential of containing lead paint. Home sellers are required to sign a disclosure, but often such disclosures state that the sellers don't know because they never tested for lead paint. Peeling or chipping lead-based paint is an obvious source of lead. Children can be exposed to lead if they bite on painted surfaces with lead-based paint or ingest chips of such paint. A less obvious source is airborne dust coming from operating windows that have thick coats of lead-based paint. Where there is a concern it's best to have a sample of the paint tested at a qualified testing laboratory.

Another source of lead can be drinking water that goes through old copper water pipes that had been soldered with lead-based solder. In 1988, the use of lead in solder was banned. As houses age, deposits built-up within the water pipes can lessen some of the lead-based solder exposure. Water testing is needed when this is a concern.

Asbestos

Asbestos has been used in construction because it is fire resistant and a good insulator. But it is a fibrous material that has been identified as a carcinogen. Asbestos had been commonly used as insulation for steam heating pipes, in roofing and siding material, flooring, and for heating and electrical insulation. It is of particular concern when it is in a "friable" state, which means that, were it squeezed, it would go into small dust particles that can be easily breathed in. Asbestos cement-siding shingles generally are not friable but sanding or drilling such shingles should not be done without appropriate personal and environmental protection. Removal, or any other approach to reducing risk of exposure to known asbestos, requires a specialist. Certain materials might be identified as typical of those containing asbestos but lab testing will probably be needed to confirm its presence.

Additional Environmental Hazards

Formaldehyde is a hazardous compound that was generally used in foam insulation before the early 1980s and can be present in other construction materials. Urea-formaldehyde foam used for insulation contains formaldehyde, which over time has reduced emissions. If this material is suspected, special air-quality testing should be performed.

Hazardous wastes may exist on certain properties, such as chemical factories or chicken farms where hazardous materials had once been used. This is typically not something considered during the purchase of a house. Large developments constructed on waste sites or where toxic materials were in use should have studies performed to determine that the site is now safe for use. The U.S. Department of Environmental Protection Agency (EPA) has identified many of these sites. Commercial building purchasers typically have environmental studies done as part of their purchase, but again, this is not usually studied with residential purchases.

Contaminated groundwater is another potential hazard. Where there is a well on the property, well-water testing is necessary. Where the property has had a prior underground oil tank, soil testing will be needed if there has not been a certified proper abandonment of the prior oil tank. Public water supplies are tested by the public utilities supplying the water.

Mold has become the current fashion in the wardrobe of environmental concerns, even though it has been with us forever. Mold needs moisture, humidity, and organic (i.e., wood, paper, etc.) material to grow. Certain types of mold are more toxic than others. Mold might be invisible. It could be behind walls or even behind vinyl wallpaper. Air-sampling testing may be necessary when mold is suspected. Different molds will affect people differently. There are *many* kinds of molds. If anyone who will be living in the house has any type of breathing problem while in the house, air-quality testing should be considered.

If there are any other environmental health hazard concerns checking with the local public health officials should be considered to learn what community action has been or is being taken to reduce risk in the area where you are buying your house. A good source for environmental information is from the EPA at *www.epa.gov*.

When Special Evaluations Are Needed

Septic systems, wells, and **exterior insulating and finish systems (EIFS)** need special evaluations beyond the scope of the typical home inspection. Violent weather potential presents additional evaluation considerations.

Septic Systems

Septic systems can be complicated because they are biological treatment facilities on your property. Septic systems are dependent upon bacteria to reduce human waste, and they need adequate soil conditions to filter the waste water. There are two components to the septic system. One part handles the human waste called "black water." The other part, called "gray water," handles the drains of the kitchen sinks and laundry. Depending on its location, a septic system may have a life span of 15 years or longer. Septic systems are expensive to repair or replace, so it is very important to have an invasive evaluation of the septic system by an expert as part of the home inspection process.

Wells

Water is so necessary for life that it cannot be taken for granted. It needs to be plentiful and pure. City water is regularly tested by public agencies for our protection. A well, however, is a local water supply that needs an adequate source with a dependable pump system. Home inspectors generally test the workings of the water supply system within the house but there are two additional questions that must be answered. One has to do with the quality of the water supply. This can be tested and needs to be done regularly. Most communities have regulations requiring such testing, particularly when there is a sale of a house. The second question is: How good is the aquifer (the source of the water)? This question might be asked of the firm that installed the well. They will know its depth and should generally know something about the quantity of water at that depth and whether there are "dry" periods. Talking with neighbors may be helpful to learn if they have any well-water quality or quantity concerns.

EIFS—Synthetic Stucco

Traditional stucco is a cement coating, often over a masonry wall, or with wire mesh over plywood. It has a long history of satisfactory performance when properly applied by a mason. Houses may contain both traditional stucco and EIFS, which has exterior insulation with a coating applied over the insulation. A properly applied and maintained exterior insulating and finish system (EIFS) has aesthetic and energy economy qualities for both new and rehabilitated buildings. EIFS is a system with many components. When properly applied in accordance with manufacturer specifications by experienced applicators, satisfactory results can be expected. EIFS must be applied to work in conjunction with other building systems including roofing, wall penetrations, and attachments.

EIFS has been widely used in Europe since the late 1960s. Large commercial buildings have achieved great benefits from utilizing EIFS. Single-family residential applications, however, have had some very bad experiences. North Carolina mold problems are the most notorious. The biggest difference between large commercial work and residential work is often attention to detail starting at the design phase. EIFS for commercial and residential buildings are basically the same. It is the lack of attention to details that causes problems, particularly with sealant at penetrations. Roof, deck, and grade-level areas all require proper flashing and distance between the EIFS and the wetted surface. As the area of the wall increases, expansion joints become necessary. Utilization of a manufacturer-approved applicator is recommended. Obtaining a manufacturer warranty is also important.

News about the North Carolina EIFS problems and recent press about mold problems undermines confidence in EIFS. Unfortunately, there is a general lack of moisture-study data for other types of siding construction. Experience and developing studies suggest moisture intrusion problems can occur in just about any building cladding system.

Inspections of EIFS can range from a cursory visual examination to a comprehensive destructive evaluation. Probably a period of five years maximum would be appropriate for maintenance inspections, unless some visual indication suggests the need for an earlier evaluation.

Third Party EIFS Inspection Certification programs began with the Exterior Design Institute (EDI) at *www.exterior-design-inst.org*, a nonprofit organization, founded for the purpose of training and certifying inspectors and moisture analysts. A specialist is needed to evaluate EIFS as part of the home inspection. EDI is one source for such a specialist.

Violent Weather Areas

Hurricanes, tornados, flooding, wildfire, and landslides are examples of violent weather problems. Parts of our country and specific locations have a greater probability of developing one or more of these violent home-destroying weather conditions.

Freezing weather and areas where there are periodic poor air-quality problems are additional weather-related problems.

For a variety of reasons it may be desirable or necessary to live in an area where violent weather becomes a part of your life. Knowledge of the potential for violent weather may be beyond the scope of a home inspection, but should be identified by your home inspector and will certainly be important for you to understand. Even new building codes do not always keep up with the latest techniques for weather-resistant construction. Older homes may have much less, if any, protection. The FEMA Coastal Construction Manual documents recent techniques for hurricane-resistant and flood-resistant construction. See *www.fema.gov*. The "Fortified...for safer living®" fortified home is one of the newest approaches to construct violent-weather-resistant homes with requirements that exceed the most stringent building codes. See *www.ibhs.org*.

The local Office of Emergency Management and local Red Cross chapters have a wealth of information for any area you are considering. Additional information can be found at various U.S. Government sites including *www.fema.gov*, *www.noaa.gov*, *www.hud.gov* and *www.earthquake.usgs.gov*.

Waterfront

Coastal and tidal waterfront will have inspection needs different from small-lake areas. The potential for flooding or other violent weather conditions is important information and will guide the special inspection requirements. Foundations and house elevations are two of the most important characteristics for the professional inspector to evaluate. Shore protections, such as bulkheads, require inspection by experienced specialists. In flood zones, a Flood Elevation Certificate is important for you to understand the vulnerability of the house to flood-water entry. Flood Elevation Certificates are prepared by a professional land surveyor and also help to ensure getting the most favorable flood insurance rates.

Hillsides

Hillside locations can vary from a gentle slope on well-draining earth to areas with high potential for landslides. Different foundations are needed depending upon the location. Some locations may have natural risks that no human-made foundation can withstand, such as a mud slide. Often, new construction in these areas will require special precautions by municipal engineers. Evaluation of these homes by an engineering specialist is recommended.

The Report

The home inspection report may range from a handwritten checklist to an extensive document with typed descriptive information about the observations and findings particular to your house, along with photos illustrating actual observations. Some reports look extensive, but in fact contain boilerplate computer-generated generic information that would be better kept in a maintenance manual or textbook.

You are looking to find existing problems and what you need to do about them. The better report will have a typed discussion of observations and clearly worded findings with photos to illustrate significant issues. Also, there should be checklists indicating the relative conditions of hundreds of items. A typical home inspection should record 300 to 400 observations and you want to know what was and was *not* observed. You will want to know what needs correction now or in the near future. A good report will identify corrective actions and maintenance issues that will need future action.

Home inspections can have expectations exceeding what is possible because these are only visual inspections. Not all home inspectors have the experience to go into depth in all areas of the home and its systems. Some will recommend obtaining extensive outside contractor opinions for unknowns. This can be a problem for the buyer who is relying upon the home inspection to reasonably understand the overall condition of the house. It is critically important to know what limitations are cited in your report. Consider if additional evaluations are needed. This inspection work is expensive, but it is needed to help you make one of the most expensive decisions of your life. You want to reduce surprises of potential problems that were not evaluated.

Read your entire report very carefully. If you do not understand any part of it, ask your home inspector for more information. If there are recommendations for additional evaluations, don't be shy. Ask your home inspector how thorough he was in inspecting these issues so you can determine if additional inspections are necessary, and whether *you* should have these additional inspections done or if they should be done by the seller. For example, if evidence of a prior underground oil tank is cited in the report, it will be necessary for the seller to confirm that a proper abandonment was performed with building permits or soil testing. Property scanning will be required to give you the peace of mind that you will not have an environmental clean-up problem to deal with. Consider what other inspections may be needed for serious problems identified by your home inspector that you were not aware of prior to your purchase.

Evaluating the Problems

The primary reason for home inspection is to have an objective evaluation of the true condition of the house. The marketplace has a way of creating appropriate value based on supply and demand. When there are problems that may not have been known to the buyer, careful consideration of what needs to be done is important. Certain problems, such as a failed termite inspection, must be corrected to obtain a mortgage. Other problems, such as requirements for a continuing certificate of occupancy that may be required by the local community, also have to be addressed. After that, it is generally up to negotiations between the buyer and seller. If agreement cannot be reached concerning serious problems, the deal may need to be abandoned. Often the home inspection report brings about an awareness of generally understood conditions now being seen in a new light. An old roof with less than five years of predictable life, or an old heating system that will need to be replaced within five years, are examples of vital information you will want to know from your home inspection. But, these are not typical examples of conditions for which the home seller might be willing to make any price adjustments. The seller will probably feel the selling price already took these facts into consideration.

However, a faulty heat exchanger in a furnace, of any age, is something that must be repaired because it is a life-safety issue. A faulty heat exchanger can allow carbon monoxide to enter the heated air-distribution system. Another example of a serious problem that may not be known to a home seller, is a failed (broken) girder (main beam) in a crawl basement because that is a building structural failure. Such a finding may not be known by the seller even if there have been settlement indications with cracks in floors and walls. All houses will get some settling cracks and framing movement over time. An extensive number of significant necessary repairs may also cause the need for adjustment consideration. Unless the problem is due to nature, such as a failing hillside, structures and systems created by humans can be repaired or replaced by humans. Almost every home will need some improvement. The important thing is to differentiate between the necessary, immediate corrective actions and those that could be done over a period of time. If you are planning to remodel the kitchen, any findings about the kitchen appliances really should not matter.

The following priority guide will help you select which problems need immediate attention, either by the seller or when you move into the house. Life-safety, health, and sanitary issues head the list. No one wants himself or a family member to get hurt or sick. When purchasing a historic building that has original painted surfaces, it can be assumed that lead paint will be present. While lead paint is listed with the life-safety priority issues, you may make a decision to accept the house in that condition and not use the lead paint as a reason for rejection, or to necessitate immediate, corrective action. Building structural issues are next in importance, followed by necessary building functions, such as heat. This list is a guide to help you determine which problem issues are acceptable, need further evaluation or negotiation, or are a cause for looking elsewhere.

Priority for Problem Repair

- Life-Safety, Health, and Sanitary issues
  Electrical, physical, chemical, and fire hazards. Causes of carbon monoxide. Kitchen and bathroom health and sanitary issues. Lead paint or asbestos. Contaminated water supply. Rodent problems. Mold problems.

- Building structural failures
  Foundation and framing failures. Wood-destroying insect (termite) problems.

- Necessary building functions
  Proper functioning plumbing, electrical, and heating systems.

- Water-intrusion issues
  Roof, window, basement, exterior cladding, and condensation water problems.

- Building maintenance issues
  Refinishing of surfaces.

- Comfort Issues
  Air conditioning, better heating distribution, newer appliances, better working fixtures.

Negotiating with the Seller

Depending upon the home inspection findings, you may be so happy with the overall condition and value of the house that further negotiations may not be needed. When there are significant problems that affect the value of the house, or would cost so much that you cannot go forward without a price adjustment, you have the option to withdraw from the purchase, or negotiate. Unless you are skilled at negotiations, assistance from a real estate professional is advisable. Even if you are a great negotiator, your effectiveness can be increased by having an intermediary acting on your behalf. When both sides have attorneys, they generally handle most of the negotiations. Realtors may handle negotiations. In some cases, particularly when you have a good relationship with the seller, it can best be done directly between you and the seller. While you may never feel comfortable negotiating directly, it is important to know that you are entitled to get fair consideration for what you are purchasing.

One of the values of having a professional home inspector is that an objective opinion about the true condition of the house is rendered to the fullest extent visually possible. Armed with this information, you are equipped to make decisions about the value you are getting for the price you are going to pay. Remember that this house will be your home. You deserve to feel good about it, considering the marketplace realities of what value one can get where you wish to live.

Home-Buyer's Checklist

- Have I performed my mini-inspection?
- Have I retained the most reliable and knowledgeable home inspector?
- Do I honestly feel comfortable putting my trust in my home inspector?
- Have I thoroughly studied my home inspector's report?
- Are unearthed problems feasibly correctible?
- Are there too many problems to be financially within my budget?

Appendix: Life Expectancy of Housing Components

The following material was developed for the National Association of Home Builders (NAHB) Economics Department based on a survey of manufacturers, trade associations, and product researchers. Many factors affect the life expectancy of housing components and need to be considered when making replacement decisions, including the quality of the components, the quality of their installation, their level of maintenance, weather and climatic conditions, and intensity of their use. Some components remain functional but become obsolete because of changing styles and tastes or because of product improvements. Note that the following life expectancy estimates are provided largely by the industries or manufacturers that make and sell the components listed.

Appliances

Appliances	Life in Years
Compactors	10
Dishwashers	10
Dryers	14
Disposal	10
Freezers, compact	12
Freezers, standard	16
Microwave ovens	11
Electric ranges	17
Gas ranges	19
Gas ovens	14
Refrigerators, compact	14
Refrigerators, standard	17
Washers, automatic and compact	13
Exhaust fans	20

Source: Appliance Statistical Review, April 1990

Bathrooms

Bathrooms	Life in Years
Cast iron bathtubs	50
Fiberglass bathtub and showers	10–15
Shower doors, average quality	25
Toilets	50

Sources: Neil Kelly Designers, Thompson House of Kitchens and Bath

Cabinetry

Cabinetry	
Kitchen cabinets	15–20
Medicine cabinets and bath vanities	20

Sources: Kitchen Cabinet Manufacturers Association, Neil Kelly Designers

Closet Systems

Closet Systems	
Closet shelves	Lifetime

Countertops

Countertops	
Laminate	10–15
Ceramic tile, high-grade installation	Lifetime
Wood/butcher block	20+
Granite	20+

Sources: AFP Associates of Western Plastics, Ceramic Tile Institute of America

Doors

Doors	Life in Years
Screen	25–50
Interior, hollow core	Less than 30
Interior, solid core	30-lifetime
Exterior, protected overhang	80–100
Exterior, unprotected and exposed	25–30
Folding	30-lifetime
Garage doors	20–50
Garage door opener	10

Sources: Wayne Dalton Corporation, National Wood Window and Door Association, Raynor Garage Doors

Electrical	Life in Years
Copper wiring, copper plated, copper clad aluminum, and bare copper	100+
Armored cable (BX)	Lifetime
Conduit	Lifetime

Source: Jesse Aronstein, Engineering Consultant

Finishes Used for Waterproofing

Paint, plaster, and stucco	3–5
Sealer, silicone, and waxes	1–5

Source: Brick Institute of America

Floors

Oak or pine	Lifetime
Slate flagstone	Lifetime
Vinyl sheet or tile	20–30
Terrazzo	Lifetime
Carpeting (depends on installation, amount of traffic, and quality of carpet)	11
Marble (depends on installation, thickness of marble, and amount of traffic)	Lifetime+

Sources: Carpet and Rug Institute, Congoleum Corporation, Hardwood Plywood Manufacturers Association, Marble Institute, National Terrazzo and Mosaic Association, National Wood Flooring Association, Resilient Floor Covering Institute

Footings and Foundation

Poured footings and foundations	200
Concrete block	100
Cement	50
Waterproofing, bituminous coating	10
Termite proofing (may have shorter life in damp climates)	5

Source: WR Grace and Company

Heating Ventilation and Air Conditioning	Life in Years
Central air conditioning unit (newer units should last longer)	15
Window unit	10
Air conditioner compressor	15
Humidifier	8
Electric water heater	14
Gas water heater (depends on type of water heater lining and quality of water)	11–13
Forced air furnaces, heat pump	15
Rooftop air conditioners	15
Boilers, hot water or steam (depends on quality of water)	30
Furnaces, gas- or oil-fired	18
Unit heaters, gas or electric	13
Radiant heaters, electric	10
Radiant heaters, hot water or steam	25
Baseboard systems	20
Diffusers, grilles, and registers	27
Induction and fan coil units	20
Dampers	20
Centrifugal fans	25
Axial fans	20
Ventilating roof-mounted fans	20
DX, water, and steam coils	20
Electric coils	15
Heat Exchangers, shell-and-tube	24
Molded insulation	20
Pumps, sump and well	10
Burners	21

Sources: Air Conditioning and Refrigeration Institute, Air Conditioning, Heating, and Refrigeration News, Air Movement and Control Association, American Gas Association, American Society of Gas Engineers, American Society of Heating, Refrigeration and Air-Conditioning Engineers, Inc., Safe Aire Incorporated

Home Security

Appliances	Life in Years
Intrusion systems	14
Smoke detectors	12
Smoke/fire/intrusion systems	10

Insulation

For foundations, roofs, ceilings, walls, and floors	Lifetime

Sources: Insulation Contractors Association of America, North American Insulation Manufacturers Association

Landscaping

Wooden decks	15
Brick and concrete patios	24
Tennis courts	10
Concrete walks	24
Gravel walks	4
Asphalt driveways	10
Swimming pools	18
Sprinkler systems	12
Fences	12

Sources: Associated Landscape Contractors of America, Irrigation Association

Masonry

Chimney, fireplace, and brick veneer	Lifetime
Brick and stone walls	100+
Stucco	Lifetime

Sources: Brick Institute of America, Architectural Components, National Association of Brick Distributors, National Stone Association

Millwork

Stairs, trim	50–100
Disappearing stairs	30–40

Paints and Stains

	Life in Years
Exterior paint on wood, brick, and aluminum	7–10
Interior wall paint (depends on the acrylic content)	5–10
Interior trim and door paint	5–10
Wallpaper	7

Sources: Finnaren and Haley, Glidden Company, The Wall Paper

Plumbing

Waste piping, cast iron	75–100
Sinks, enamel steel	5–10
Sinks, enamel cast iron	25–30
Sinks, china	25–30
Faucets, low quality	13–15
Faucets, high quality	15–20

Sources: American Concrete Pipe Association, Cast Iron Soil and Pipe Institute, Neil Kelly Designers, Thompson House of Kitchens and Baths

Roofing

Asphalt and wood shingles and shakes	15–30
Tile (depends on quality of tile and climate)	50
Slate (depends on grade)	50–100
Sheet metal (depends on gauge of metal and quality of fastening and application)	20–50+
Built-up roofing, asphalt	12–25
Built-up roofing, coal and tar	12–30
Asphalt composition shingle	15–30
Asphalt overlag	25–35

Source: National Roofing Contractors Association

Rough Structure	*Life in Years*
Basement floor systems	Lifetime
Framing, exterior and interior walls	Lifetime

Source: NAHB Research Foundation

Shutters

Wood, interior	Lifetime
Wood, exterior (depends on weather conditions)	4–5
Vinyl plastic, exterior	7–8
Aluminum, interior	35–50
Aluminum, exterior	3–5

Sources: A.C. Shutters, Inc., Alcoa Building Products, American Heritage Shutters

Siding

Gutters and downspouts	30
Siding, wood (depends on maintenance)	10–100
Siding, steel	50–Lifetime
Siding, aluminum	20–50
Siding, vinyl	50

Source: Alcoa Building Products, Alside, Inc., Vinyl Siding Institute

Walls and Wall Treatments

Drywall and plaster	30–70
Ceramic tile, high grade installation	Lifetime

Sources: Association of Wall and Ceiling Industries International, Ceramic Tile Institute of America

Windows

Window glazing	20
Wood casement	20–50
Aluminum and vinyl casement	20–30
Screen	25–50

Sources: Best Built Products, Optimum Window Manufacturing, Safety Glazing Certification Council, Screen Manufacturers Association

Chapter 12

How Do I Negotiate?

S ue and Gerry lucked out when they arrived at negotiating. Each had been through the expensive mill of divorce and had picked up some valuable pointers in the process. They could, in fact, have written this chapter. They had experienced, firsthand, the fine art of negotiating and had developed considerable skill.

What they didn't have was piles of money. Both Sue and Gerry had high paying jobs but very little cash as a result of their divorces. Most of the houses they fell in love with were out of their price range or needed too much work for which they did not have the money.

Good things come to those who wait, it's said, and that's just what happened when they found a house that needed a lot of work but in all other respects was a dream house. The owner was in a hurry to sell because she was downsizing and had already purchased her next house. Their negotiating skills, together with the seller's motivation, brought about a happy ending for all parties. Sue and Gerry persuaded the seller to lend them the funds for renovations. With this agreement, they proceeded forward to settlement and were all happy. It doesn't get much better than that.

Homework, Homework, Homework

Good things often come in threes. In negotiating, the three key factors are homework, homework, and more homework. Homework will increase your confidence and prepare you to make decisions under pressure. Even if you have a lot of experience buying houses, every deal is different. People and legal documents all play a role in shaping negotiations. The only factor you can really control is the thoroughness of your own preparation, which will put you in a better position to keep cool under pressure and maintain a positive state of mind.

Part of your preparation will be to expect the unexpected. You may not be able to anticipate all the surprises but you can be sure that there will, indeed, be surprises. If you know that certain areas may be iffy, develop contingency plans. Being on top of things will increase your confidence and do wonders for your negotiating power. Remember, power is what others perceive, so maintaining a positive presence in spite of adversity puts you in the driver's seat. Think of negotiating as a game where you have to continually try to seek an advantage or leverage. To some, negotiation is the art of compromise where everyone loses to a certain degree because seldom does an initial position survive intact to the very end. Fortunately, negotiating doesn't have to be a win-or-lose proposition. The better prepared you are in knowing your needs and the better job you did in searching for a home, the better off you'll be at resolving details. You win by achieving your overall goal regardless of whether you pay a bit more or less, and regardless of any concessions you may need to make as long as your objective is met. If you find that your end goal is not realistic, get out that thinking cap and modify your objectives. By doing your homework, you can make it a winning proposition or decide to move on to something that may be even better. Sometimes you simply have to cut your losses if continuing would be adverse to your needs and goals. Suppose, for example, that your home inspection reveals a catastrophic problem. You'll have to withdraw from the deal unless it can be resolved. Some of the toughest negotiation takes place after the contract is signed because that is when you are most restricted.

While we may relate negotiating to a game and refer to game plans and use terms like "coach" and "captain," negotiating is *not* a game. In games there are specific rules for each side with intermission periods and points for scoring. Negotiation is a give-and-take process and life is a series of negotiations. Sometimes negotiating can feel like piloting a fighter jet or driving a roller coaster. Relax. Take a drive out to the country in your favorite car and try to enjoy the view. Eleanor Roosevelt said, "No one can make you feel bad without your own consent." Right on, Eleanor. She knew that during negotiations, a strong personality will use assertive behavior to weaken an antagonist's position for her own gain. Keep in mind, though, that negotiating in house buying can be delegated, at least in part, to professionals such as real estate agents and lawyers. You may have fine professional support, but be careful of assumptions. Don't assume anything and don't let anyone push your emotional buttons. Listen and ask questions. Set aside stumbling blocks. It's easier to go around a large boulder than try to break it up to continue straight on your course. By the time you pulverize a boulder, you may forget where you're going.

Home-buying negotiating actually begins long before the contract is signed. In fact, the very first impression you make on the professionals and sellers you encounter will affect their dealings with you. If they see you as strong and confident, then you are. People who know what they want have a better chance of getting it. We have already covered the information you need to gather and the decisions you needed to make before starting your search. We have presented ideas for finding the perfect house. You have determined what to offer for a particular house. Keep in mind that much of what most people communicate is nonverbal, so how you approach everyone with whom you have dealings will affect their perception of your strength. Subtleties of body language, how we dress, and how we talk can make a difference.

Understand the Contract

Rule number one is to get legal advice for all legal documents. Once you sign a contract, you limit your options. You will be bound by the terms and conditions of the contract. Different states have different laws and many local areas have standard contracts that have been developed over time by experienced people. However, standard contracts may not fit your specific needs and may not be suitable for a specific property. There are even contracts available for purchase on the Internet. At the risk of sounding repetitive, only a lawyer can give you a legal opinion.

To many of us, contracts have too many obscure words, frequently written in too-small type, where even English majors may need not only a magnifying glass, but an unabridged dictionary to understand many of the terms. Nonetheless, it is incumbent upon you to have a general understanding of the contract. What happens if you want out of the contract? Even a lawyer-prepared contract may not be perfect. Special attention should be paid to the provisions that would allow you to opt out if terrible problems are discovered or develop. The contract protects everyone's interests.

Time periods and deadlines are critical, so you will need to know if you have adequate time to do what is needed. Understand all time-sensitive provisions of your contract so you don't miss a deadline and find yourself committed to something you don't want. You must be sure you have enough time to get done what needs to be done.

As contracts are customized to include provisions for more contingencies, they become larger and can be very cumbersome. Typically, before a contract is written, there will be an agreement about price. Some of the more common contract clauses will be discussed. When using contracts prepared by a real estate broker for the seller, you want to be sure that your rights as a buyer are protected.

Full names of buyers and sellers are used in the contract. Their marital status may also be necessary. The required, clear definition of the property may include a common mailing address along with a tax map location, including block and lot designation. The size of the property may also be noted. There should be a listing of equipment to be included in the sale and any other special features that are included with, or excluded from, the sale.

An attorney review clause provides a defined time period for the parties to consult with their respective lawyers who may well disagree with provisions of the contract. If not resolved by lawyers for both parties, this clause should provide the right of either party to terminate the contract. In some states—New Jersey, for example—there is a required attorney review period during which no contract can become binding until that period has elapsed. This allows each party's lawyer to resolve contract language concerns. Be sure to monitor that time period so you do not lose your rights and your deposit, or even be at risk for greater liability.

This is not the time for anyone to act as her own lawyer unless she is a member of the bar, and even then, lawyers do not always act for themselves. Attorneys often choose a fellow attorney to represent them. If you elect not to have a lawyer you could be asking for trouble. You may not be able to change the contract under the attorney review provision without the seller's agreement.

Purchase price and method of payment must be defined, along with provisions for deposits and return of any deposits, should the deal not be completed. Generally, the purchase price or deposit provision spells out who holds the buyer's money and when money is transferred to the seller. The options include your attorney, the broker, or the seller's attorney. These are negotiable terms. You will probably have more control when your attorney holds the deposit money.

The deposit usually includes an initial deposit and a subsequent payment that will be defined in the contract. The initial deposit may be hundreds to thousands of dollars depending upon the price of the house. The additional deposit may be up to ten percent of the purchase price. The additional deposit will generally be due in the same number of days allotted for inspection contingencies; typically ten days following attorney review. Contingencies for mortgage approval and sale of an existing house will be discussed later and there needs to be clear language about what happens to the deposits should those contingencies not be satisfied.

A provision in the contract is needed to ensure that there will be a clear **title** and that **title insurance** can be obtained. A clear title is free of any **liens** or any legal questions about ownership of the property. Any restrictions concerning the use of the property, or the rights of others to use part of the property, must be spelled out. The **deed** will need to be transferred and recorded. Certain specialty clauses may be needed if there are known restrictions on the property, such as utility easements and wetlands building restrictions, or if tideland instruments, such as a riparian grant, are needed. Title insurance provides financial protection should there be problems with the title, such as liens. Sometimes title insurance excludes certain property features, such as waterfront tideland instruments. If you expect to be buying a property with a waterfront grant, you will want title insurance to include that feature. This should be identified by your lawyer in case a different title insurance company may be needed.

Contingency provisions are a very important part of the contract. Typically, a financing or mortgage contingency is included to allow the buyer a specified time to obtain a mortgage commitment. You might also need a provision for meeting the necessary appraisal. Appraisals are performed by independent contractors—typically for the mortgage company—to provide confidence that the value of the house is adequate to support the mortgage requested. The mortgage commitment contingency may have maximum mortgage loan interest values stipulated. These are all negotiable issues.

There may also be a contingency for the sale of the buyer's house. Some types of mortgages may not be acceptable to a seller. If the seller will not accept a contingency of mortgage approval or the sale of the buyer's house, these issues may need to be addressed prior to obtaining a contract. While almost any provision is negotiable, there may be limited time to reach a compromise once the contract has been drawn. It is important to determine beforehand which contingencies are important to you. Another important provision is for home inspection. In each of these contingency provisions there will need to be wording that allows the contract to be terminated should certain defined conditions not be met. Defining those conditions requires good legal advice. Here we go again. Only a lawyer can give you . . .

Many sellers would like to sell their house **as is** with no liability for any undisclosed condition. Frequently, this term is included in the contract, even when there are contingency provisions. You must have your lawyer's assurance that if you accept an "as is" provision, there will be adequate protection should the title search or home inspection reveal undesirable problems. It may be necessary for your attorney to obtain and include in the contract stipulations from the seller, any conditions that could present difficulties. Your seller may swear that there has never been an underground oil tank or any basement flooding. Your lawyer may advise you that certain stipulations will give you legal recourse should the seller's statement not be true.

A financing provision may limit how the house is to be financed. For example, a conventional mortgage may be stipulated in the contract because FHA financing or a GI mortgage may be not acceptable to the seller. The lack of such a provision may allow you to arrange any type of financing you wish. Real estate commissions must be defined in the contract with stipulations of who is responsible and when the commissions will be paid.

If you have an existing house that must be sold before you buy your dream house, then you will want a contingency for that sale. Not all sellers will agree to such a provision, particularly during periods when house sales are slow. This may require some clever negotiating. Your homework is to find an advantage the seller will agree to. You will need to learn what the seller's needs are so that you can best present your own position.

Closing and possession dates must be defined. If the buyer moves in before the closing or if the seller remains after the closing, both parties have to be flexible. Specific contract language will be necessary to ensure that everyone's interests are protected. If closing and possession dates are different, adequate insurance and other protective provisions must be clearly written into the contract.

In Chapter 11 we talked about the home inspection, which is a critical third-party assessment of the condition of the house. The home inspection contingency must be detailed in the contract. Suppose you have a seller who will not allow an inspection contingency because she wants to sell the house "as is." It may still be possible to have inspections prior to completion of the contract, so the benefit of a third-party assessment will be available to you before you continue with the purchase. The time period is negotiable and may range from 5 days to 30 days after completion of attorney review. Typically the period is 10 days. This may depend on features that may require special inspections, such as septic systems, water potability, and/or swimming pool inspections, among others. After the inspections are completed, a reasonable period of time must be established for the seller to respond and agree to correct any deficiencies. Otherwise, you would be justified in trying to negotiate an adjustment to the selling price. If the seller does not agree, she will, no doubt, give up the contract and return all deposits to you, the buyer.

The contract may include a listing of personal property and/or specific features of the house to be included as part of the sale, such as expensive lamp fixtures and appliances that are to be removed or replaced. Typically, a preclosing walk-through is provided in the contract to allow the buyer to inspect the house just prior to closing. The contract needs to define what is to be done if there are defects or damage to the property that had not existed previously or were not known at the time of the home inspection. What if there were storm damage from a tree falling on the house? If major systems, such as heating or air conditioning, do not work, how does the contract provide for adjustment and corrective action? A specific preclosing damage clause may exist in the contract to detail how damage is to be corrected and at what point the contract can be voided without penalty.

In the case of a new house, there will be extensive lists of features that may not have existed at the time of the initial contract but are to be included in the sale. Detailing these features is very important to be sure that the quality level of each feature is specified. There will be guarantees, warranties, and punch-list periods in which the builder/seller will be responsible for corrective action. You have to know and agree to how these guarantees, warranties, or punch-list agreements will be enforced. It is best to have clearly written statements defining terms and conditions and the quality level of corrective work. Contract language for all contingencies is very important because you want to be able to get out of the deal if there are unacceptable contingency conditions.

When you have a complete understanding of the contractual provisions before you sign the contract, you're really ready to roll. The bulk of the negotiations should be virtually completed when you're ready to sign. This is all to your advantage for greatest protection and the greatest value. Negotiating, however, is not fully complete until the title is transferred and the monies are paid out.

Who Are the Players?

A player is anyone who has some influence or involvement in the buying and selling process. When you think about it, there are a lot of people who will play some role in your house-buying adventure. Make a list of all those with whom you will be dealing directly and another list of those who will be in the background. They are the second team. The influence of family members of buyer or seller cannot be overestimated. Try to get a handle on who influences whom, and how. Certainly, brokers, financial agents, lawyers, inspectors, and other professionals will play direct roles that can help or hinder. A good start is to assume that all of the players will be looking to protect their own interests and to avoid any problems that could possibly prompt a law suit against them. Unfortunately, this natural self-interest can limit their effectiveness in looking after your concerns. Whatever you hear from others, you are the most important person in looking after your own interests and in filtering advice. Look out for "Number One."

Hopefully the people you will be dealing with on the other side will have a modicum of trustworthiness and not be hostile. Are you dealing with an individual seller or with a group, such as an estate or corporation? Sometimes buyers and sellers never meet until the final closing if, indeed, they ever meet. Learning about the seller can start with any information that describes the house. When you tour the house, you're bound to pick up lifestyle information about the seller, or at least about the people who live there. They are not necessarily the same. Observe what is happening within the house; is it consistent with what you have been told?

Even owners listed on the deed may be influenced to such an extent by others that they represent only part of the ownership equation. For example, a young couple may have used family money to buy the house they are now selling and will again be using family money to buy their next house. It's a safe bet that these young owners are heavily influenced by one or more key family members, such as a father, mother, or whoever the money person is. You can be sure that Mr. or Mrs. Deep Pockets will have plenty to say. Remember, money doesn't talk—it screams. Everything you can learn about the sellers, even if they are not in the clutches of a family financier, will be helpful information during critical negotiations. It will behoove you to find out about their personalities and lifestyle that are key to their motivations. You may learn, at the very least, what you might have to anticipate. What you are told may be true but it may not be the entire truth. Be on the lookout for additional clues as to what is motivating the sellers. And, be sure to find out how critical their time constraints are.

When you are dealing with a For Sale by Owner house you may be up against a lack of experience, a very shrewd operator, or anything in between. FSBO suggests a desire to avoid paying a real estate commission, which may well be a large part of the reason for FSBO. So much is done on the Internet today that it is easy for sellers to think they can pay a reduced fee to a FSBO Internet site or firm, but chances are they will not have the good, dependable, professional support a responsible realtor could provide during negotiations to closing. Here is where you will need to dig around to make sure that not only do you have a good house, but that all aspects of the sale are done in a professional manner.

Learn the expressed reason for the sale and then consider whether there may be any additional motivation. Sellers may volunteer why it is necessary for them to move on. If they don't volunteer, just ask them. Moving up to a larger house in a more desirable neighborhood or job transfer are two very common reasons for sale. Divorce and health problems are two more reasons. There is a great difference in negotiating with people moving up in the world with company-supported job transfers as opposed to dealing with people who have to sell due to divorce or health disasters.

When you are dealing with a divorce, anticipate communication complications. You're dealing with a man and woman who may not be communicating that well with each other. On top of a conspiracy of silence, you may run into adversarial lawyers: his versus hers. The potential for anger in a divorce situation is bound to influence at least some aspects of the transaction, if not many. Sales due to divorce are difficult at best. There will be additional lawyers, so more players are involved that you will need to learn about. Agreements may be difficult to obtain. Information is often not forthcoming. When dealing with a divorce, having a sense of how difficult it is going to be may help you gauge your own timing. Anticipate delays and conflict. Remember Murphy's Law—whatever can, will go wrong. But you can use the leverage of the divorce conflict to your advantage. Patience is needed, but you are not part of their battle. You have to keep whatever empathy you may have for the battling parties from affecting your needs, but don't back off reasonable demands. You have to obtain a fair price and you have to know that you are making a sound investment.

In the case of death as a reason for sale there can be a different element of communication difficulty, particularly if there is a "committee" that has to be pleased as part of the estate settlement. Greedy heirs get itchy palms when they can't agree with each other. Try to find out as much as you can about the survivors. You never know when this information will come in handy. It may give you leverage and, at least, might be important in shaping your negotiating style.

Even if you are not faced with squabbling relatives, death makes achieving a middle-ground settlement more difficult. Often the estate or surviving parties may have excessive expectations beyond money and feel some entitlement benefit for their loss. On the other hand, a quick sale may be possible with great advantage to the buyer. Early on, make an assessment of the speed in which you want to proceed. Try to understand the motivations of the seller or selling representative. A house with a lot of family history is not always easy to part with. Showing respect for what was important to the lost loved ones helps build rapport with bereaved relatives. People will often give some benefit to others who love what they love. The fact that you plan to remove grandpa's favorite sunroom is something you can keep to yourself. You don't have to tell the grandchildren.

A job transfer may be stressful for the family who has to move, but it can be a boon for the buyer if the seller's transfer to a distant location is within the same company. Often an employer will pay relocation costs and possibly guarantee sale-price protection. This can be a bonanza for you. It's a whole lot easier to have problems corrected when the cost is born by the employer and not the seller. A job transfer because the seller has lost a job or is going to a different company is another kettle of fish, with implications affecting your negotiations. It can be both positive and negative. Losing a job puts pressure on the seller and creates financial stress that can make her more vulnerable, and possibly willing to accept less as the pressure builds. On the other hand, it can very understandably make the seller more difficult to deal with. Patience—yours—can indeed be a virtue. Since patience is its own reward, you could benefit very nicely.

Without the complications of divorce, death, or a cross-country relocation, there are also the considerations of health or aging. How old are your sellers? How long have they lived in the house? Is the house too big or too much for them now? Are they selling because of ill health? Knowing why they are selling is a plus to you. When you are looking for any kind of concession during negotiations, it may be helpful to show understanding of the difficulties of the other party. Sincere empathy is not only admirable; it can ease negotiations considerably and make it easier for the other party to agree to your requests. You'll never know if you don't try.

Whatever category your seller fits, try to learn the status of the existing mortgage and home equity loans so you'll know ahead of time what pressure may exist upon the sellers. At the final closing you will learn how much the sellers paid to settle their mortgage, but it could be interesting and helpful to know if they had very little to pay off, or if the mortgage was so large that they were having a hard time making payments. There have been times when the seller has had to pay more to close out the mortgage than what she receives in payment for the house. Perhaps you can't get blood from a stone, but you may discover previously unknown, unfavorable conditions to which the other party will agree. The more information you have, the better you can estimate how much maneuvering room you have left. It can be counterproductive to squeeze too hard.

Talking with the neighbors can bring information about your sellers and, certainly, about the neighborhood, but this can be dicey. If you find yourself listening to the neighborhood Chatty Cathy, look around for the warning flag. If Chatty says your sellers are cheapskates who did very little to maintain their house until they put it up for sale, file that away for investigation. But if Chatty tells you more than you ever needed to know about your sellers, she's not going to be shy about telling everyone else within earshot everything she learns about you when you become her neighbor. Just a word to the wise.

On the other hand, you may meet a sincerely nice neighbor who can assure you that the sellers have been meticulous in maintaining their house. You may learn that the sellers are very nice people to be fully trusted. If there is a hint of somewhat the contrary, put that aside for the moment too. You can look into it later. Listen, and file away what you need. Every little bit of information helps load the data base in your mental computer.

Remember that you, as the buyer, are one of many parties in the negotiations. Your own personality can't help but influence others' reactions to your requests and affect the outcome. Sometimes it is helpful to have a third party advance certain requests because they can do it in a more gentle, accepting way. To the extent your family influences your actions, you may or may not want to involve them at critical stages prior to making commitments. The personalities of a husband-and-wife team or a partner team may determine who should take turns in leading the different stages of negotiating. Understanding the personalities and styles of the other parties will help you decide when someone else should try a different approach. Some personalities are simply more difficult to deal with. When faced with difficult people, try to use the member of your team who can best work with that type of personality.

Brokers and sales agents are players too, and they range from very experienced to wet-behind-the-ears order-takers. A very experienced sales broker will guide you through every stage of the buying process, and help identify characteristics of the people involved to strengthen your decision-making and negotiating skills. As you work with sales agents or brokers you'll soon learn about them personally and professionally. They are team members, but remember that you are coach, captain, and star pitcher of the team. How much freedom your salesperson has is within your control. When you have star players who follow the game plan, you'll want to give them as much freedom to maneuver as possible. When you have weak players you will need to coach them closely and carefully. If they don't perform, send them to the bullpen and play first base yourself.

Lawyers too are players, not only on your team, but also on the seller's team. The more you know about their personalities and how they interact with their clients and the other side's lawyer, the better. Complications of relationships are greatly intensified by the different styles lawyers employ. Experienced real estate lawyers facilitate the process. But people do not always select attorneys experienced specifically in real estate or lawyers who will work effectively with the other side. Remember that your lawyer is on your team, working for you, or darned well should be! Most attorneys deserve a great deal of respect, but just because they are lawyers does not relieve you as captain and coach. It's *your* life. It's *your* money. It will be *your* home. Don't abdicate *your* job as boss.

As with any service for hire, home inspectors range from very competent and knowledgeable to immature and inexperienced. Check your inspector's qualities and professionalism extensively before you hire her. When you do meet, size this person up, so you'll know how personality may influence professionalism and to what extent you can rely on assistance during the negotiations. Inspectors can be authority figures providing credible justification for certain negotiating positions that are hard to refute by the other side. But if a home inspector just refers all potential problems to follow-up consultations with contractors, you may get little assistance. How well they write their reports makes a difference in whether the other side will be willing to negotiate on real problems.

All of the professional people you work with throughout your home-buying experience will have some effect on the negotiations, including the home inspector and mortgage people. The more experienced they are, the better they will support your game plan. Try to learn about these people before you hire them. Don't be afraid to ask for references. A true professional will be happy to provide them.

Urgencies

Urgencies can sometimes cause bad decisions but they can also create great opportunities. The more urgent you are, the more vulnerable you will be to making mistakes, unless you have your game plan well thought out. Developing contingency plans will be your best defense when urgencies raise their inconvenient heads. Think about the bad things that might happen and determine in advance how you might deal with those events when you have to make rapid decisions. Later in this chapter, we will discuss decision making under stress. Here we want to look at urgencies that may affect you and the seller. Seller urgencies can often be turned around to your advantage. Some urgencies exist prior to contract stage; others may develop as things go along.

As a buyer you may have an urgency to move because your lease is about to expire. This might put you in the unenviable position of agreeing to less than you deserve. During a buyer's market when there are many more houses for sale than available buyers, there may be an urgency to know that a deal may be completed within a reasonable time. If not, you may want to move on to another house while the market still favors the buyer. Think about your urgencies but keep that information to yourself. What you know about the seller can be beneficial to you, but what the seller knows about you could tip the scale. It works both ways. You shouldn't tell lies but you also do not need to tell others every little thing they may ask. Some things are simply none of their business.

If your sellers have already purchased their next house, that extra mortgage may create enough pressure for them to want to compete the deal as quickly as possible. On the other hand, your sellers may have another place to go, such as a second home where they can wait until the cows come home before accepting a deal that offers less than what they want. The seller may have a new job to go to that requires her immediate move, but will it require the entire family to move right away? The seller may have debts that add financial value to a speedier closing.

Third-party urgencies—not always known—may interfere with your negotiations. Vacations, family problems, and job priorities can all impact both team; yours and the seller's. Understanding the urgencies of third-party players during negotiations will help you be prepared for unpleasant interruptions. Negotiations take on a rhythm. Whatever the rhythm, let the beat go on! Depending on your taste and generation, a classical music piece can be very pleasant compared to hard rock. Don't knock hard rock, all you dancers; it has its own rhythm. Problems develop when the rhythm is interrupted due to urgency by one of the key parties. It can be hard to regain. If you run into a problem you can't, or don't feel comfortable in orchestrating, pass the baton. Here is where you might want to send in a substitute, such as your lawyer or broker, who can pick up the beat and keep negotiations moving along without much, if any, interruption.

Power Is Perception

Power in negotiations is relative and may change as the process unfolds. It is not like weight lifting where the laurels go to the strongest person. Power gives you the advantage in that the other side may bend more to your original position than hold tight to their own. Keep in mind that to conclude any negotiation it may be necessary for each side to give a little. Leverage is what you are seeking to offset any shortage of real strength. A lightweight child can balance a heavy adult on a seesaw by leverage when the adult sits relatively close to the center. Almost no one can pick up a car, but if you use a jack, you can lift the car to replace a tire. In negotiating, we are looking for the sweet spot on the seesaw, or tools like a jack, to give us leverage. Your objective is to develop as much leverage as you can to influence the seller to accept your position or a reasonable compromise.

When the other party thinks you have leverage, you will have the advantage. It is not absolute, but relative. How the other party thinks is the key. Stubborn street bullies are impossible to negotiate with because they almost never concede power to the other party. If you are dealing with this kind of unpleasantness, try to use leverage with a more reasonable member of the bully's team—her lawyer, for example. Don't take negotiating positions personally because your own emotional reactions will diminish the other side's perception of your power.

If the word "power" makes you uncomfortable, think "advantage." Power may be too strong a word for some people. Power may elicit visions of a bully. What you are really after is *strength*. In direct face-to-face negotiations, nonverbal communication can reinforce, or erode, a position of strength. Think about this when you are watching TV. Political debates and movies where negotiating is taking place can be real eye-openers. Watch and listen for nonverbal communication indications. Tone of voice, body language, clothing; all have a definite impact on how people respond. Tone of voice and body language can be even more important than what is actually spoken. What you're wearing can reassure an opponent of your respect, or be taken as an insult. There's a time and place for shorts and a tank top, and it's *not* the bargaining table.

When you know you are dealing with a person who makes you uncomfortable, or whom you may make feel uneasy, send in your best substitute. Know your strengths and weaknesses in face-to-face confrontation and put yourself forward only when you can use your strengths. Use a stronger team member when you are uncomfortable. That's not weakness; its good management. Maybe you can't put on the "poker face" that James Bond bravely wore, even when he was staring death in the eye. That's not necessary for our house-buying negotiating. It's okay to be human. The role playing we'll discuss later in this chapter will help you play your part like a star. Unless you are a professional negotiator, this advice is only to help you be better prepared.

You want to convey clearly to the seller and her team that you are serious. This will help you create power leverage. Remember, you are the buyer. You can go elsewhere with your money. Of course, you do not need to jam that into the face of the seller. Just knowing in your heart and mind that you have control puts you in a position of strength. Grant yourself the gift of power. Do not allow others to reduce your self-worth. You don't want to provoke or anger the seller, just reach a reasonable conclusion. Power, or strength, is not just your personality, however. The fewer contingencies that must be met, the stronger will be your position. Understanding and accommodating the special needs of the seller add to your strength. Being liked by the seller is a plus that can only enhance your position of leverage.

Do not confuse dominance and aggression with power or strength. Dominant and aggressive loudmouths are difficult to deal with. Build your team with professionals who can achieve your objectives without putting anyone on the hot seat. Because you are in the position of buying a house, you have more ability and more power than you realize. The other team's members don't have to agree with you. You don't have to agree with them. Your self-confidence will give you the edge.

Role Play

Practice negotiating with your partner or a friend. Role playing is a fascinating technique that can strengthen your "poker face" and reaction to new challenges. Practice reacting to positions that are not logical. The dumber the better—it makes you think. Brainstorm for ideas that might be challenging to your goals and anticipated positions. Work on your nonverbal skills and learn more about your emotional buttons. Plan to have another team player handle the face-to-face negotiating when one of those buttons starts sending out danger signals. Rehearse your reaction to positions that may be unfavorable to both sides where no satisfactory compromise could be reached. This helps you to develop a walk-away position. Advance knowledge may help you accept a little less than what you really wanted, but not so much as to throw you into walk-away mode.

One team tactic is the "good guy, bad guy" technique, where one team member takes a position almost favorable to the other side while another team member takes the opposite tack. The idea is to get the other side to be happy in acquiescing to a lesser position than they expected. There are many tactics used in negotiating. We will discuss a few of the more common ones that buyers and sellers use so you won't be surprised. These tactics are not encouraged, but mentioned simply because they exist. We encourage you to use professional help; a pro has been there before and can recognize a ploy.

Let's start with two buyer tactics that can cause trouble during negotiations. They can be the kiss of death for the whole deal. In "Low Ball" the buyer may offer a ridiculously low price. This can be risky if the price is too low, but may be successful if the seller is forced by urgency, or any other reason, to accept. If a buyer is hostile, the seller will probably also turn hostile, and there go the negotiations. Another sneaky buyer tactic is to agree to a sale price when you have already planned to hire a friend as a deal-killer home inspector so that you can then demand great reductions. These two tactics are nasty and often result in bad feelings and failed deals. Reasonable people with reasonable goals create the best deals for everyone involved.

An equally bad seller tactic is the "Know Nothing" approach where, even though the sellers have lived in the house for many years, they claim to know nothing about any issues affecting the house. Know Nothings will claim that the knowledgeable party is out of town and unavailable. Often, Know Nothings may have merely refinished parts of the house cosmetically, to hide problems from even the best of inspection engineers. This type of seller is begging for a law suit if serious problems are uncovered after the deal is closed. If you feel that the seller is a Know Nothing, get a legally binding disclosure statement or affidavit so you'll be prepared for any potential law suit.

Time is a significant constraint during negotiations. Be very careful not to violate time deadlines. Issues that arise from contingency inspections always add drama to the negotiations and may set the stage for "Big D" tactics: Deny and Delay. If you think you're facing Deny, be patient and clear-headed because even with known problems, if reports are not complete and clear, a purchase may still be concluded leaving you with no further recourse. Often, only a few of the inspection defects are addressed. Unaddressed problems may create a Denial powder keg. You don't want to buy a house with a built-in law suit. If you do know about a problem, such as a wet basement in a flood zone, and do nothing to resolve the problem during your negotiating, you may not have a leg to stand on later when flood waters are lapping at your cellar stairs. In such a situation, the seller will probably agree to solve some small problems, but leave out big ones that may have been clearly identified. This affects the seller's potential litigation liability. The buyer may need to be prepared to walk out and kiss the deal good-bye.

Delay is a tactic used in negotiations to frustrate the other party into concessions. If you find yourself maddeningly frustrated, take a break. You may want to scream, but a little time out can help to separate your emotional feelings from the facts. Write down what *is* and what is *not* happening. Put that writing away and do something pleasant as a diversion to clear your mind. Then retrieve the writing and decide what should be happening. Write that down. The process of writing and deferring judgment can be an effective catharsis. So can a nap. Don't revisit the writing until after you've had a snooze. Remember, it's not what happens that bothers you, but your interpretation of what happens. Try to separate your frustration from your objective, which is to buy this house. Talk with your team. Can you find a way around the obstacles or do you need to get out of this one and look elsewhere? Be careful if you are thinking you can bluff your way out of the situation. That can backfire. You can get up and walk out as a bluff, but you may lose the deal. Sometimes just thinking that you have the power to walk out is the stimulus you need to carry on. Keep your options open and remember, if you think you're being handed a lemon, you can always make lemonade.

Setbacks

Rejection of offers is a normal part of the buying and selling process. Try not to react emotionally. You want to make a deal that gives you fair value for your money. The seller, naturally, wants to get as high a price as possible. A rejection might be telling you that you are getting close. Often, you can refine your offer to complete the deal satisfactorily. If you anticipate rejections, you will be better prepared to counteroffer. Preparing for rejection may have to be part of your buying strategy. Keep in mind that it is just as emotionally draining to the seller to have to reject a reasonable offer. Selling the house is her goal.

Reasons for rejection may not be clear to you at first, but it is important to learn the why of it. Sometimes reasons are clearly stated when an offer is rejected. At other times there are subtleties that will need to be thought out. A higher offer, or one with more favorable terms from another party, is obviously a valid reason for rejection. If you are prepared for a bidding war, then go forward. If not, pull out and look elsewhere. When the house you have found is your dream of dreams, a rejection becomes most challenging. You already know what financial maneuvering room you have to raise your offer. Perhaps there are terms that can be made more favorable to the seller. Seek advice from your professional real estate sales agent.

Pricing, terms, and financing are the three major elements of an offer. It does not always have to be just a price adjustment to make a counteroffer. Fewer contingencies or a faster closing may be just the catalyst to complete the deal. Dale Carnegie always encouraged salespeople not to accept "no" until they had heard it seven times. You may not have the patience or stamina to survive seven rejections but a couple of rejections, might inspire you to greater effort.

Additional examples of setbacks include inspections that turn out bad, a house that does not appraise at the selling price, or a loan that falls through. Depending upon the severity of the problems, these may turn out to be opportunities to negotiate revisions in the sale price or terms and conditions of the purchase. Negotiations are never complete until the final money changes hands with the transfer of the deed.

Decisions Under Duress

When you are tired and stressed it's all too easy to make mistakes. You need a game plan for making good decisions. This is where your homework will pay dividends. The more organized your research, the easier it will be for you to respond quickly and with confidence, even when you are stressed. Understanding and prioritizing your house needs and your financial capabilities is key to making decisions under duress. Before actual negotiations even get underway, you can anticipate various offers and counteroffers. Like any team sport, the larger your playbook, the more options you will have when the push is on.

Make sure your emotional safety net is in place and in good repair. The most difficult decisions are those made in anger or when you are emotionally upset. You have to learn to recognize the danger signals of emotional pressure. Know when you need to take a break, even if it's only for five minutes. Keep calm. If you have a partner, set up a contingency plan in advance that you agree to follow. You may not even be aware that you are becoming angry, but to your partner it can be as clear as day when you tighten your jaw. A simple "John, we need to take a break," may be all that's needed. It's too easy to trip yourself up when you're in a tight spot. Buying houses can be very stressful. If you don't have a partner, try to line up a friend or someone you can call on to provide an emotional check when you think you are over-stressed.

Your tolerance for risk will influence your decision making under pressure. Become comfortable with your level of acceptable risk. It's okay to be a high-risk player as long as you know that the higher the risk, the greater the chance of high loss. There always needs to be some level of risk or else nothing will get done. Some element of risk is inherent in house buying. There can be greater reward with higher risk, but going out on a limb should not be necessary if you have thoroughly done your homework. Through your early research and due-diligence inspections prior to closing, you can manage the risk elements. The more comfortable you are that you did your homework, the less stress the normal level of risk will add to the buying process.

Trust and Ethics

In negotiations, truth and trust are always important, but unfortunately, are not always present. Negotiating for a favorable position is honorable. Deceit and lying are not and will only backfire. Sometimes people flirt with untruth as if, by not telling a complete lie, it is okay. Innocent failure to remember important information such as a basement flood is, at best, flirting with untruth. Convenient, total failure to remember is deceptive and may constitute fraud. There is great risk in dealing with deceitful people. Some people may never overcome a first impression that they cannot be trusted—because they can't. Building a relationship based on trust is the best approach to lessen any potential for deception during negotiations.

Sometimes you find yourself dealing with a hostile person who is uncooperative, at best. This could be due to a bad divorce. Maybe it's indigestion or tight shoes. While this person may not intend to be deceptive, anger or any other reason for hostility may create the same atmosphere as dealing with someone you really can't trust. When you must deal with a hostile or untrustworthy person it becomes even more important to work with ethical professionals who can be trusted. Good legal assistance and a very thorough building engineering inspection reduce your risks of not finding the truth.

Home-Buyer's Checklist

- Do I understand all the players?
- Am I comfortable with my realtor and my lawyer?
- Do I fully understand the terms of the contract?
- Have I developed contingency plans?
- Do I have the talent and the cool to keep control in negotiating?
- Am I able to let go in favor of another team member when necessary?

Chapter 13

The Close, Settlement, and Escrow

*T*he culmination of a real estate transaction is called either a closing or a **settlement**, depending on where you live. These terms are interchangeable. Settlement is when money and property are exchanged.

Ideally, the buyer(s) and their attorney sit on one side of a table and the seller(s) and their attorney on the other. An independent third party, often a person employed by a real estate title insurance company, is the closing agent, who is at the head of the table.

Why Is Closing a Necessity?

Once a transaction is closed, sellers go away. Unless all the financial and legal matters are completed satisfactorily, the buyer may never see the seller or the other party or parties again. Think of the transaction as your only opportunity to pay for the property and other costs and to get good title to the property. Perhaps there will be a second chance to correct things, but don't count on it. That would probably require hiring a lawyer, litigation might be involved, and the results would be uncertain. So, closing is the time to get it right.

At closing, no one wants to be promised performance later. Don't feel mistreated if your personal check is deemed unacceptable; this is normal. You'll need to bring a certified check or cashier's check. Your lender will probably wire money. The seller will likely pay out a significant amount of cash from the funds provided by the buyer. Sometimes, when the seller has little or no equity in the property, the seller must pay to close. Consequently, the seller needs cash, or its equivalent, from the buyer.

The seller must provide the deed. A deed will be prepared using a preprinted form with the names of the buyer(s) and seller(s) and the property's identifying characteristics filled in. Soon after closing, the closing agent will take the deed to the county courthouse to be recorded. The mortgage (which may be called a "security deed" or "deed to secure debt," depending on where you live) will also be recorded at the courthouse. Recording gives "notice to the world" of ownership, obligations that are secured by the property, and certain other instruments.

Though potentially various parties can close a transaction, most often a title company employee acts as the closing agent. Closing is most likely to be held at the title company or at a bank. The title company's closing agent prepares the deed for the seller's signature, records it, and receives money from the buyer and the lender. The closing agent figures out how much money is from each source, who gets what, and will promptly record the deed.

The title company closes only when everything is in order. Certified checks and/or money wires must have previously been received for the amount needed by the buyer. You, the buyer, must bring cash or equivalent (certified check) for the equity and closing costs. At the end of the transaction, the seller receives a check for his equity less expenses, and money is wired to the seller's lender to pay off the seller's loan if there is one.

Also at the end, buyer and seller will be provided with a **closing statement**. This will show a description and the amount of each cost and which party pays and which party receives each amount. The bottom line will be a total of the amount to be paid or received at the end of the transaction.

What Day Is Closing?

Most of the time the buyer(s) will set or identify the date of closing in the contract of sale (or whatever other name is used for the form that provides an agreement of sale; in Texas it is called an "earnest money contract"). Usually the buyer(s) will need to be present at the closing. Often the seller wants to be there as well, and both parties often want their attorneys present.

It is often difficult to schedule the closing date and time so that at least five people can be present at the same time and place. Even when they agree in advance, illness or death in the family or another more urgent commitment by one party may cause rescheduling.

In addition, many things must occur before closing. The new lender must be satisfied as to the buyer/borrower's creditworthiness, the property's value, and the property's good title. This requires that the buyer's credit be acceptable, that the house be appraised (typically for at least the amount of the purchase price), and that investigation of the title not disclose any insurmountable problems. This research and reporting will take at least two weeks for a house. Four weeks is not uncommon.

Who Is Present?

In some states, notably California, closing is done "in escrow." The closer, often called an "escrow agent," puts together all the paperwork that has been signed and money that has been arranged, without the need for the parties to be present. If all the papers and funds do not come together, the agent will not close.

Perhaps this California style will become more widely embraced. California requires more paperwork than most other states, so maybe it is more suitable for them. For now, though, if you're the buyer, expect to be there with any co-owner, such as your spouse.

Your Signature

Expect to sign many documents. You can take a stab at reading each one, especially to see if it sets off any alarm bells. If there is disclosure that the house you are buying was built on a site previously used for hazardous materials, for example, it should not be acceptable.

In many situations, the buyer will just lean over to ask his attorney if it is okay to sign each form. An experienced real estate attorney has probably seen most or all of the forms previously and will respond accordingly. Still, don't take your signature lightly. There are reasons why someone wants your signature on each piece of paper, so make sure you have at least a general idea of what it is you're signing.

If you sign something and then immediately discover it is something you didn't intend to sign, scratch out your name, tear up the paper, and walk out. If you sign at closing and pass the papers along, your signature indicates that you agree to whatever is written on that paper. It will be tough, and often impossible, to back out later.

The package of things to sign will seem to be endless. It will include:

- Mortgage: pledge of property as collateral
- Note: amount borrowed, repayment terms
- Truth-in-Lending statements
- Escrow requirements
- Closing cost estimate
- Acknowledgment of property condition

- Tax certificates
- Closing statements
- Disclosure forms

Power of Attorney

If you must be elsewhere on the day of closing, you can give someone else power of attorney. Make sure that person is trusted and knows what he is doing. The real estate broker often wants to attend the closing to be certain that (1) the transaction closes and (2) he gets the brokerage commission that is due. Although the broker or agent may be in a fiduciary capacity, don't count on that person to close for you. The broker has his own interest at stake in addition to yours.

Unpleasant Surprises

It may happen that the seller is not present at closing. This can pose a problem for you. The seller may have visited the closing agent a day or two earlier, signed all the papers, and then gone off on a fishing trip out of reach of a cell phone or fax machine. You are then presented with a closing statement that requires you to pay a $1,000 fee that was supposed to be the seller's obligation. What can you do?

Possibly you're relocating. You just drove 1,000 miles from your old house, which you sold. You stayed in a motel last night, and the mover's truck, with all your worldly goods, has arrived and is ready to unload. The baby is whining in the closing room and your two other children are hungry and restless in the office area. You're expected to report to your new job assignment the next day. Do you sign and pay the extra $1,000, or do you walk away and wait for the seller to return next week?

Most people would bite the bullet and pay the $1,000 with the expectation that an honest seller will pay it back when he returns; it would cost that much to stay in a motel for a week. But at what amount do you say, "No! I'm not closing"?

To try to avoid this type of surprise, consider a provision under **RESPA**, described below. It gives you an opportunity to inspect the closing statement one business day before closing if you request it. Though this may be a nuisance for the closing agent, we strongly encourage you to exercise this right.

Real Estate Settlement Procedures Act (RESPA)

At the start of every professional boxing match, the referee offers this warning to both fighters: "Protect yourself at all times." This is good advice for home buyers as well.

In an effort to protect the public before a real estate closing, or at least make the public aware of what to expect, the government passed a law known as the **Real Estate Settlement Procedures Act**. Most people in the business refer to it by its acronym, RESPA. RESPA covers most residential mortgage loans used to finance the purchase of one- to four-family properties. Such property could be a house, a condominium or cooperative apartment unit, a lot with a mobile home, or a lot on which a house will be built or a mobile home placed using the proceeds of a loan.

Purpose of RESPA

The purpose of RESPA is to provide potential borrowers with information concerning the settlement (closing) process so that they can shop intelligently for settlement services and make informed decisions. RESPA does not set the prices for services; its purpose is merely to provide information about settlement (closing) and costs.

Materials to Be Received Under RESPA

Under RESPA, a person who files a loan application for property covered must receive from the lending agency a pamphlet titled *Settlement Costs and You,* and a good-faith estimate of the costs of settlement services. The lender has three business days after receiving a loan application to mail these materials. From that time until settlement, the loan applicant has an opportunity to shop for loan-settlement services. One business day before settlement, if the loan applicant requests, he has the right to inspect a Uniform Settlement Statement, which shows whatever figures are available at the time for settlement charges. At settlement, the completed Uniform Settlement Statement is given to the borrower or his agent. When there is no actual settlement meeting, the Uniform Settlement Statement is mailed.

Uniform Settlement Statement (HUD-1 Form)

As discussed, the Uniform Settlement Statement (usually called the HUD-1 Form) is used in all RESPA-affected transactions (which include most residential transactions).

Settlement Costs and You

The pamphlet *Settlement Costs and You* contains information concerning shopping for services, home-buyer's rights, and home-buyer's obligations. It also includes a sample Uniform Settlement Statement (HUD-1 form) and describes specific settlement services. In addition, it provides information concerning a comparison of lender costs and describes reserve accounts and adjustments between buyer and seller.

Read RESPA and Shop

Most home buyers, especially first-time home buyers, will be first-time borrowers. It will be helpful to read *Settlement Costs and You.*

There are so many variations of loans to choose from that home buyers may wish to read the latest edition of Barron's *Keys to Mortgage Financing and Refinancing* to decide which type of loan is best for them.

The good-faith estimate provided under RESPA by one lender may be shopped around to other lenders. The purpose would be to seek lower expenses, a lower interest rate, a longer or more secure lock-in, or a more suitable type of payment schedule or interest rate (i.e., fixed versus adjustable rate).

Often, you can shop for mortgage rates over the Internet or by telephone, decide where you want to apply, and go there in person. Most lenders won't take you seriously unless you have a house under contract, and most purchase contracts require you to apply for financing within a few days. Some lenders will help you pre-qualify (i.e., estimate the maximum loan you will qualify for), and others will pre-approve you for a certain maximum amount. When your loan is pre-approved, the seller (and real estate broker) will rest assured that that part of the transaction is almost risk-free.

Lenders include commercial banks, savings and loans, credit unions, and mortgage brokers. Although they are in the same market for money, variations in their costs and the rates they offer can be significant. That is, a difference of a one-point fee up front is a significant amount of money. A one-quarter percent difference in the interest rate will mean about $250 per year per $100,000 you borrow. Over 30 years, the extra cost will add up.

Demystifying Closing Statements

A closing or **settlement statement** is a list of who pays what money and who receives what money. The price of the house, the amount financed by the buyer (or loan payoff by the seller), and expenses of the buyer and seller are all brought together. As the buyer, you will likely gasp at all the fees you must pay.

Seller's Closing Costs

We won't focus on the seller here except to make you aware that he or she will also gasp. In most transactions, the seller will pay a brokerage commission, a title insurance policy (for the buyer or lender), prorated **ad valorem taxes**, legal fees, and various other expenses that are in the contract. It is likely that the seller has a substantial remaining balance on a mortgage, perhaps a second mortgage, and/or an outstanding home equity line of credit. To retire the loan(s), the seller must pay all of the principal plus accrued interest.

Buyer's Closing Costs

The more you learn about the fees and expenses that will be charged at closing, the better equipped you will become to negotiate the contract to buy the house. That knowledge will arm you to request in the contract that the seller pay many of the fees. In some transactions, the seller may receive a great deal of cash from the sale and may be in a position to help you purchase the house.

Buyer's Likely Costs

The items that you, the buyer, will probably need to pay for at closing are shown below, followed by the general estimated cost.

1. *House:* Price in contract, agreed through negotiation.

2. *Lender's points.* The lender will likely charge discount points, closing fees, or both. The typical range is 1–3 percent of the loan amount.

3. *Loan application fee.* This will vary from $0 to $500 or more.

4. *Credit report.* $50–$100.

5. *Appraisal.* $250–$500.

6. *House inspection fee, if unpaid.* $300–$750.

7. *Termite bond, if unpaid.* $50–$200.

8. *Loan processing fee.* $0–$250.

9. *Document preparation fee.* $0–$250.

10. *Hazard insurance escrow.* Some lenders seek 14 months of insurance, representing a full year's payment plus two months, into escrow account.

11. *Tax escrow.* Accrued taxes plus at least two months of taxes paid ahead, into escrow account.

12. *Prepaid loan interest.* Interest from date of closing to end of month. Loan payments will begin one month later.

13. *Title insurance.* Most sellers pay an amount that covers most or all of the lender's requirements. The mortgagor (buyer) may desire title insurance to cover the equity.

14. *Mortgage insurance (if applicable).* Application and first year's cost.

15. *Attorney fees.* $500–$1,000.

16. *Deed and mortgage recording fees.* $50–$100.

17. *Local transfer taxes.*

18. *Flood insurance certificate.* To determine whether the house is in a flood plain.

19. *Condominium or cooperative association fees, if applicable.*

Sources of Funds

Typical sources of a buyer's funds at closing include:

1. Down payment, paid with contract.

2. First mortgage.

3. Second mortgage.

4. Ad valorem tax proration paid by seller, credited to buyer.

Of course, the buyer must come to closing prepared to pay the balance due. A certified check is customary.

The HUD-1 Form

The settlement statement will most likely be prepared on a form called HUD-1.

The left side of the first page of HUD-1 shows the borrower's transaction. The top portion, lines 100–120, is called "Due from Borrower." It includes what the buyer must pay: house, personal property, and settlement charges, which are detailed on page 12. Line 120 is the sum of what the borrower must pay at closing.

Lines 200–220 detail the borrower's source(s) of funds: the deposit, new mortgage loans, and any other mortgage loans, such as an assumed mortgage loan or seller financing. Adjustments for items unpaid by the seller, which may include prorated taxes or insurance, are included there. Line 220 is the sum of sources of the buyer's money.

The difference between the amount due from the borrower (line 120) and the sum of the borrower's sources of funds (line 220) is the amount the borrower must pay at closing.

The right side of page 1 is an accounting of the seller's side of the transaction. The sales price of the house and other property is shown in line 420. Reductions in seller receipts, such as to pay off the mortgage and for accrued but unpaid interest and taxes, are written in lines 500–520. The seller will receive a check for the difference between lines 420 and 520.

Prorations

Taxes are the item most likely to need to be prorated between buyer and seller. Suppose the local tax districts assessed your house for $10,000 in property taxes for the entire year. For simplicity, let's say this includes school taxes and assessments by city, county, and other tax districts. The tax covers the entire calendar year—say 2008—but is due and payable on December 1, 2008.

You close on the house on July 1, 2008. The seller is held responsible for taxes for the portion of the tax year during which he owned the house: January 1, 2008, through June 30, 2008. This is 182 days (2008 is a leap year). Therefore you, the buyer, must collect 182/366 of $10,000, or $4,972.68, from the seller at closing. These funds will go toward paying $10,000 in taxes on December 1, 2008.

Notice that if the closing were to occur after December 1, 2008, and the seller had paid the taxes on schedule, you, the buyer, would have to pay the seller for the taxes from the date of closing through the end of the tax year.

Possession at Closing

Often, a seller is reluctant to give possession at closing. This is because sellers have been known to be "stood up" at closing. Their possessions have been put on the moving truck en route to another city, but the buyer doesn't appear at closing. The seller needs the cash to close on his new house, so he has a huge problem.

To allay a seller's concern, the contract may allow the seller to provide possession within a certain number of days following closing, typically three to five days. Optimally, one of the parties has some flexibility. If this provision is used, the buyer's transition may be more relaxed, but the buyer must be vigilant to be assured that the seller doesn't remove some items that were included in the sale and that the seller is careful to avoid property damage during the move-out period.

Home-Buyer's Checklist

- Make certain your moving schedule allows you (and your spouse or co-buyer) to be present on the date set for closing; if not, provide a power of attorney to a trusted person.

- Read *Settlement Costs and You* to learn your rights under RESPA.

- Make sure you have enough cash to cover the down payment and closing costs, and bring a certified check to closing.

- Perform a walk-through inspection (before closing).

- Get keys from the seller, *change the locks,* put utilities in your name, and get them turned on.

Real-World Example

A high school math teacher and his sister inherited a house. The teacher paid all the taxes and other expenses for two years while they held it, so his sister owed him half of what he had paid. Here's what he wrote about their closing:

> If you've never been to a closing, basically all the work is done beforehand by the lawyers, and you go and sit at a table and sign papers that they put in front of you. Then they give you a check and you leave. It's a pretty passive endeavor for both the buyer and the seller. I know it's my fault for assuming the two lawyers were capable of doing math, and I actually had a feeling that they had done it incorrectly and I didn't say anything because I hadn't actually looked at the numbers until I walked out. I'm really just enormously disappointed

in America, as a whole, after this botched turn of events. Now I have to rely on my sister to send me a check for the difference (a significant amount of money) and explain to her that the two lawyers just did the math incorrectly.

Here's what they did (with the numbers changed). Let's say that after all the fees and everything my sister and I grossed $20,000 for the house, which would leave $10,000 for each of us. Let's say that my sister owed me $3,000. The lawyer then said, "Okay, I'll write the smaller check so that it's $3,000 less than the larger check," and so wrote one check for $8,500 and the other for $11,500.

All he did was split the amount he owed me in half because the lawyer couldn't see the two different pieces separately. What needed to happen was that he should have said, "Okay, the sister has $10,000 and she owes $3,000, so she'll get $7,000. The brother has $10,000 and is owed $3,000 more, so he'll get $13,000." The checks should differ by twice the amount owed, once for the plus and once for the minus.

My point is that, two days before I have to go back to work teaching abstract math to 14 year olds, I have to deal with not one but two professionals who are both not only lawyers—so presumably intelligent—but real estate lawyers, and presumably deal with money and figures on a regular basis, who can't solve a real-life problem involving division by two and then subtraction.

Work Sheets

Uses of Money

House cost _____

Discount points paid by buyer _____

Loan application fee _____

Credit report _____

Appraisal _____

House inspection _____

Termite bond _____

Loan processing _____

Document preparation _____

Hazard insurance escrow _____

Tax escrow _____

Prepaid interest _____

Title interest _____

Mortgage insurance _____

Attorney fee _____

Deed and recording fee _____

Transfer taxes _____

Flood insurance _____

Condo or co-op fee _____

Total _____

Sources of Money

Down payment _____

First mortgage _____

Second mortgage _____

Ad valorem tax proration _____

Total _____

Chapter 14

Insurance

*T*here is a bewildering array of insurance policies available to home owners, with varying levels of coverage. The home owner needs to select the ones that are most critically needed at an affordable cost. This chapter will provide some suggestions to guide you through the maze. The first issue is to remind you of the purpose of insurance.

Purpose of Insurance

The purpose of insurance is to protect you from major consequences of an event. There may be a one-in-a-thousand chance that your house will experience a fire or flood with major destruction in a given year, or that you will have a serious illness or die in a given year. You and/or others potentially affected by this disaster would endure great hardship if such an event occurred.

Though chances are remote that such an event will happen to you, it will likely strike someone in a given year. Insurance companies are formed to spread that risk among policyholders. If a thousand home owners each pay $500 a year, then potentially the insurance company has $500,000 (plus investment earnings, minus administrative and sales expenses) to pay for damage from a fire or other insured catastrophe that occurs to one of these home owners. Were it not for insurance, that one home owner in a thousand each year would suffer the disaster without money to rebuild.

As a general rule, insurance is intended as protection against a disaster or major event. In recent years, people have extended insurance to cover relatively minor and foreseeable events. People now buy insurance (or maintenance agreements) to protect their household appliances, automobile tires, and dental hygiene expenses.

While the cost to repair or replace a refrigerator, washer, or dryer is not trivial, do they really warrant insurance? Is the premium you pay to purchase an extended warranty worthwhile? Probably not. The retail store where you bought the appliance and the insurance company must build sales and administrative costs into their premiums, and these are high in comparison to the total annual payout. Some dental insurance policies cover routine checkups and cleaning twice a year, which are built into policy costs. Do people really need insurance for small, routine events? Probably not, though some would argue that many people would otherwise avoid going to the dentist for preventative care, in effect increasing the likelihood and costs of a major dental problem. Also, uninsured patients are often charged much more than the aggregate of what they and their insurance company would pay if they were insured; many doctors and dentists "take **assignment**," that is, accept whatever the insurance company is willing to pay, even though the nominal charge is higher. Although this may not be relevant to home buying, it is noted to reinforce the message that there are many factors to consider in selecting insurance. The essential point is that you need insurance to protect against a calamity but not for small, routine items.

Buying a House

Most home buyers are also borrowers, which brings a lender into the picture, typically for 80–95 percent of the price. At a minimum, there will be two types of insurance required: title insurance and home owner's insurance. If the house is in a flood plain, most lenders will require flood insurance. Loans for more than 80 percent of the home's value will require mortgage insurance. At least three additional types of insurance may be suggested to you: home-owner's warranty, disability, and credit life.

Title Insurance

The lender will require you to purchase title insurance to the extent of the amount borrowed. This protects the lender in the event of a past title problem that becomes known after your purchase. For a small, additional amount you can purchase a policy to protect your equity, called a **mortgagor** policy. The good thing about this type of insurance is that you pay the premium only once.

Despite the fact that lawyers and other qualified professionals provide a title search to be certain of the seller's ownership, errors and omissions can occur. Someone, perhaps an undisclosed heir or former spouse, may pop up with a valid claim to ownership or to partial ownership. Though it doesn't happen often, the lender wants protection, so you must buy a policy to provide that protection. For a small, additional amount, you can buy a policy to protect your equity. We recommend that you do so unless your attorney tells you that it is a waste of money.

Home-owner's Insurance

Home-owner's insurance, sometimes called hazard insurance, comes in different levels of protection, and can vary by state. Often there are two or three levels of standard policies offered in a state. An insurance agent can provide a list or picture book of events that are insured by each level of policy. Generally, home-owner's insurance protects against fire, theft, and damage from water caused by a ruptured pipe or water that falls from the sky into your roof, but not from water rising from a nearby body of water. Hail can ruin a roof, which is a costly repair that is often covered. Damage from hurricane or tornado winds is often covered, but water damage from storms may be difficult to collect on when there is a possibility that flooding was involved. Typically, termite damage is not covered. Damage from mold may also be excluded these days.

The mortgage lender will insist that you bring to closing an insurance **binder** that is sufficient to indicate that the property is covered to the extent of the mortgage amount. Later, an official policy will be written.

Amount

The lender will insist that the policy's minimum amount be the mortgage amount. The lender won't allow you to insure for less, though you may insure for more, so as to cover your equity.

In the event of fire, your house may be totaled, but the land will still be there. So if the mortgage is 80 percent of value, and if the improvements are new and are also 80 percent of value, there may be no need to buy more insurance. If the house burns to the ground, you can collect enough to pay off the mortgage and have the land free and clear with value equal to your equity.

If the house is not new, you will probably want to insure it for replacement cost. For example, suppose your house is 50 years old. You bought the house and the lot it is on for $250,000. The lot, if vacant, is worth $50,000. But the improvements, which are worth $200,000 (by difference), would cost $400,000 to replace. Most likely, you will want $400,000 of insurance. If your house burns to the ground and you must rebuild, you'll need to spend the replacement cost new, which is $400,000.

In a new house, replacement costs may increase over time with inflation. Meanwhile, the mortgage debt is reduced through amortization. The lender may require less insurance because the debt is reduced, but you may actually need more. It is prudent to review the amount of insurance at each policy anniversary date. Your agent may be helpful and may have replacement cost estimates on a per-square-foot basis.

Co-insurance Clauses

A **co-insurance clause** in an insurance policy that requires the insured to carry a minimum percentage of the amount at risk. To the extent that less insurance is carried, the insured is considered a co-insurer of the property.

The background is that some home owners (or business owners) recognize that a total loss is unlikely. They expect the fire department to put out the blaze before the property burns to the ground. Therefore, instead of insuring for replacement cost new, say $400,000, they insure for half of that amount as their expected maximum loss and reduce the premiums accordingly. An 80 percent co-insurance clause requires that 80 percent of $400,000, or $320,000, be covered. If only $200,000 of insurance is carried on a property worth $400,000, the company will pay only 50 percent of the loss ($200,000 ÷ $400,000 = 50%). So if a loss of the expected maximum of $200,000 is suffered, the company will pay only $100,000.

If the property is insured for $320,000 or more, the 80 percent requirement is met, and the company will pay the full loss, up to the policy limit of $320,000.

Contents

Most home-owner's insurance includes contents such as furniture, up to a set amount or percentage of the insured amount. For example, a $200,000 policy may allow up to 40 percent for contents, which is $80,000. Consider whether you want full replacement value or market value; there could be a big difference in the cost and amount of reimbursement.

Valuable jewelry, china, silver, furs, paintings, a stamp or coin collection, or specialized equipment, such as a computer, are not covered unless separately listed on a schedule ("scheduled"), with an increased premium applied. You may need an appraisal to justify the coverage.

Deductible

The deductible amount is what you must pay in the event of an otherwise fully insured loss. It is subtracted from the total loss to derive the insurance proceeds you will receive. Policies with smaller deductibles have higher premiums. We suggest high deductibles to reduce premiums—unless your finances could not afford a relatively small loss (under $1,000).

Flood Insurance

A national flood insurance program was started around 1970. It is a federal government program because no company wanted to accept all the risk from local areas where they operate. If a house is within a 100-year flood plain, as defined by the Army Corps of Engineers, the lender will require flood insurance.

You should not expect the Corps of Engineers boundaries or the incidence to be perfectly accurate. Some places thought to be in 100-year flood plains could flood several times in only ten years. Some low-lying areas that are not within the delineated flood plain can flood. As urban development continues to replace absorbent natural soil with asphalt or concrete, rainwater runoff accelerates. It may be years before the Corps revisits the creek and redraws the maps to extend flood plain boundaries.

Although New Orleans is below sea level, the levees were supposed to protect it from flooding, so flood insurance was not required. When Hurricane Katrina hit, it was a disaster of mammoth proportions. Not only were tens of thousands of homes washed away, but few of the home owners had flood insurance.

Few home owners realize that they can buy flood insurance even when they are not in a flood-prone area. The cost may be minimal. If your house is in a low-lying area, adjacent to a body of water, or on the edge of a flood plain, it is prudent to get flood insurance.

Mortgage Insurance

Loans over 80 percent of value will require mortgage insurance. This protects the lender in case you default on the loan. The cost is often applied annually at .20 to .80 percent of the principal. FHA loans require a mortgage insurance premium that may be calculated up front (that is, about two percent of the debt) or an increase in annual interest rate of half a percentage point. Veterans Administration (VA) loans have a guarantee for part of the amount borrowed, up to a specified limit.

Private mortgage insurance (PMI) may require both a premium and an increase in the rate. For example, a 90 percent **loan-to-value ratio** may require two discount points up front, plus one-quarter percent added to the annual interest rate; a 95 percent loan may require two and one-half points, plus one-quarter percent added to the rate. The effective rate on the extra amount borrowed is high. The one-quarter percent added to the rate applies to the full amount borrowed (not just the 10 percent increment over the 80 percent standard loan-to-value ratio). Also, the 10 percent increment borrowed (90 percent versus 80 percent) is reduced by two discount points, so you are borrowing 8 percent more, not 10 percent. Consequently, the borrower is paying a high effective interest rate for the additional 8 percent of principal borrowed.

The private mortgage insurance premium should be eliminated when the loan is paid down to what would have been an 80 percent loan-to-value ratio; sometimes an appraisal will be adequate. With normal amortization, reducing the loan from 90 percent of value to 80 percent takes about seven years at today's 6 percent interest rate and 30-year term. It will take longer at higher interest rates.

This type of mortgage insurance protects the lender, but is very costly to the buyer in an insidious manner. If possible, the buyer should raise the down payment to 20 percent by some other means of borrowing to avoid this high cost of money.

Credit Life Insurance

Credit life insurance may be offered when you buy a house and obtain a loan. If you or your spouse dies, the mortgage will be retired. This may be reassuring, but it is just an expensive form of life insurance.

Credit life insurance is really term life insurance with coverage to the extent of debt. Most home buyers will find that they can get the same amount of term life insurance elsewhere at a much lower cost. There is typically no reason to have insurance exactly to the extent of the debt. Most people, especially those with young children, need much more insurance.

Disability Insurance

It is possible to arrange disability insurance to the extent of the mortgage payment. If you cannot work, disability insurance kicks in the payment after a waiting period of 30–180 days and continues to pay until you are able to return to work. Many people will find that their need for disability payments exceeds the mortgage payment and that disability insurance is available at a lower rate through their employer or a separate policy.

Home-owner's Warranty

A **home-owner's warranty (HOW)** policy may be offered either for a new home or for an existing one. Some builders provide a one-year warranty, with ten more years through a written insurance policy for the sale (i.e., at no additional charge). This will protect the new home owner, especially in the event that the builder files for bankruptcy or leaves the community.

Some policies may provide strong protection, while others offer only minimal protection. Suppose a crack develops in the house's concrete foundation. One policy may require the builder to merely put $5 worth of caulk in the crack while another may provide for a rebuild of the foundation. While it is difficult to read the fine print on the policy, the Internet may provide a source for research of that policy and possibly for comments by those who had claims against the insurer.

Many "pre-owned" homes are sold with a home-owner's warranty. Most often these policies don't cover structural problems or termite damage. They merely cover electrical, mechanical, and plumbing systems. Often the choice of service providers is limited, and the responsiveness of service may be uneven.

This type of insurance may be worthwhile when the house is older and has two or more of each type of covered appliance, such as the furnace, central air conditioning unit, water heater, and so on. If you're new to an area and don't know who to call for a repair, this may be useful. However, you'll need to phone in the problem to the insurance company, wait for a service technician, pay a $50 fee for each visit, and then accept their diagnosis. The company may supply the lowest-cost replacement—with a greatly increased fee for an upgrade. Suppose your trash compactor goes on the blink. The company will install a basic model for the $50 fee, but if the color of the basic model clashes with your kitchen's décor, you'll need to an additional $150 ($200 total) for an upgrade. You could have bought the new model for $200, installed, so what's the point of warranty insurance?

If you're buying a house that's more than ten years that has two water heaters, central air conditioning units, and furnaces, you will appreciate this type of insurance coverage. If you are insured and they say that you need an expensive new part, pay the $50. You won't need to call for a second opinion. But if they say that the problem was not insured because of the previous owner's neglect, you may need to call for a second opinion as to the cause of the malfunction.

Conclusion

Some types of insurance are required in the home-buying process: title insurance, home-owner's hazard insurance, mortgage insurance when the down payment is less than 20 percent of value, and flood insurance if the property is in a flood plain. You must insure for at least the amount of exposed debt. Additional amounts to cover your equity are optional.

Other types of insurance are optional. These include credit life, disability, and home-owner's warranty insurance. Often, these types of coverage are unnecessary or available elsewhere at a lower cost.

Keep in mind that the purpose of insurance is to protect against extensive damage from unpredictable events, not from routine, predictable occurrences. It is best to be protected against a major disaster, yet not to be nickel-and-dimed by insurance premiums for regular events.

Home-Buyer's Checklist

- Do you need a mortgagor title insurance policy?

- Do you need to "schedule" valuables such as jewelry, furs, and collectibles?

- What deductible amount is appropriate for your home-owner's policy?

- Do you need a home-owner's warranty to cover electrical, mechanical, and plumbing repairs?

- What is your worst nightmare? Does the insurance policy you are considering provide coverage to protect against it?

Real-World Example

Even when you are insured, collecting on a claim may be quite a struggle. Norman and Genevieve Broussard owned a home in Biloxi, Mississippi, until Hurricane Katrina devastated the Mississippi Gulf Coast on August 29, 2005, and left the Broussards with nothing but the slab foundation. The Broussards had home-owners' insurance with State Farm and assumed that they would be covered. They were stunned when their claim was denied.

The Broussards claimed that their house had been destroyed by hurricane winds or a tornado spawned by the storm, a type of damage covered by their insurance. State Farm blamed all the damage on Katrina's storm surge. This is a common problem in hurricane insurance claims: State Farm and other insurers say their home-owners' policies cover damage from wind but not from water, and that the policies exclude damage that could have been caused by a combination of both, even if hurricane-force winds preceded a storm's rising water.

The Broussards sued State Farm for the full insured value of their home, plus $5 million in damages. In January 2007, a U.S. District Judge awarded the Broussards $223,292 in actual damages, and a jury awarded a further $2.5 million in punitive damages. The Broussards are not yet out of the woods, though: more than a year after their home was destroyed, they still have not received the insurance settlement, and a State Farm spokesman announced that the company will probably appeal the decision of the Gulfport judge and jury.

Work Sheets

Title Insurance

Company name _____ Phone number _____

Representative name _____ Phone number _____

Address _____

Coverage description _____

Hazard Insurance

Company name _____ Phone number _____

Representative name _____ Phone number _____

Address _____

Coverage description _____

Flood Insurance

Company name _____ Phone number _____

Representative name _____ Phone number _____

Address _____

Coverage description _____

Home Warranty

Company name _____ Phone number _____

Representative name _____ Phone number _____

Address _____

Coverage description _____

Chapter 15

Utilities, Setting Up the Home, Maintenance Planning

This is a February fairy tale with Glenda the Good Witch, Dudley Doright, and a dedicated realtor—plus a prince and princess who lived happily ever after.

Lisa and Burak, the royal couple, through four years of cramped apartment living, dreamt of elbow room, space for a houseful of kids, and room for family and friends to visit—in short, a sprawling, old Victorian with a wraparound porch. This prince and princess were on the ball, and were prepared to compromise if it became necessary. It wasn't.

As they pulled into the tree-lined street of gracious 100-year-old homes they couldn't help but notice the one still wearing last week's snow on the roof. Dudley's car was in the driveway. Glenda, the owner, greeted them at her thermo-pane door and ushered them into her snug home's warmth.

The house had been fully insulated—attic, walls, even the basement when Glenda had had a new furnace installed. All the windows were state-of-art. Not one draft could find its way inside. Lisa and Burak lucked out, all right. The only drawback was constant company who didn't seem to want to go home. Now it's your turn to come home.

Initial Transfer of Services

Congratulations—you've come a long way in this home-coming journey. Closing is getting closer. In this chapter we will discuss the initial transfer of services but, before we offer one word on that subject there is one enormous word thaat cannot be put aside—insurance. Insurance must be in place at the moment of title transfer. Read Chapter 14 on insurance. It's vital.

Having said that, we return to utilities with three magic words: plan, plan, and plan. By now you know we often think in threes. Even with planning to the third power, it will probably take more time than you ever expected to get your utilities connected. Before you can live in your new home, basic utility services have to be activated in your name. Sometimes a utility service, such as natural gas, is actually shut off and needs to be re-activated, requiring a utility service person to physically enter the house. This can add to any already existing delay. The seller will have to close out his or her service before yours can be established. Hopefully this can be coordinated with starting up your service. Some service transfers are easy and can be done simply through a meter reading for billing, but others require time available at the house, long waits, and "press this, press that" on the telephone, or even visits to the local utility office. If you have a professional real estate sales agent, she can handle much of the initial transfer of services work. You can also go to web sites to find a firm to perform the transfers; at least for those companies with which they have a relationship. One source is *www.connectutilities.com*. Internet transfer services limit your options but as is often the case with utilities, you have very few, if any, options anyway.

An Internet transfer service may not have any relationship with a service provider that serves your area. Be careful not to get involved with a third-party provider who will try to resell you a service you could have gotten cheaper by going directly to the utility company. Each utility probably has an Internet site that may allow you to sign up for their service online. Otherwise, expect to make a significant number of phone calls with infuriating lengthy wait times. Contact the appropriate service providers well in advance of your closing to learn how much time is needed to activate their services and whether there is the potential for direct transfers without any service interruption.

Here is a list of basic services you may need at the time you move in:

- Electricity
- Water
- Sewer
- Fuel (gas, propane, oil)
- Telephone
- TV (cable, satellite)
- Security
- Garbage

Just as you kept a house-search book, you should keep a house-maintenance book. This is a long-term reference record of services, sources, and costs of any and all work done for as long as you own the house. A good idea is to add brief notes on quality and reliability of service. Otherwise, you may not remember that that Ms. So-and-So left a mess behind when she finished a job. No one will come after you if you aren't meticulous, but you'll be mighty glad when you have been. Such a book is easy to maintain. It's easy to use as well because everything you'll ever need to find is right there at your fingertips: names and numbers of contractors, instructions for use, service manuals for appliances, and what to do if . . . . You'll be glad you have all of this handy if an emergency arises. Emergencies are very fond of surprising us without warning, and often in the dark hours of night.

The first step in building your house book is to list each utility service you will need and the service provider's name. Not all of the listed utilities in our work sheets will apply to your house. If you have a septic system, you generally will not also have a public sewer connection. If yours is an all-electric house, you obviously will not need a fuel service provider. For those who need a fuel provider, sources vary. Natural gas is typically piped directly to the house, while propane and oil require regularly scheduled deliveries to avoid running dry. These deliveries will probably be based on the former owner's history and can be adjusted, if need be, to your usage.

Do not assume that the service providers will know that you are moving in. You have to inform them. And your seller has to inform them she is moving out. They all have business payment formalities that have to be addressed before starting or continuing their service. For your planning purposes, the current owner will have most of the information you need. At the very minimum, she should have copies of paid bills. Ask for copies of the home-owner's bills that will give you provider connect information and phone numbers. The bills will also give you some historical cost information.

Some of the services you want may not be the same as the seller. For example, if the seller had cable TV and you prefer satellite service, you will need not only the new service provider, but also installation of special equipment. Sometimes there are phone company choices, particularly if you use one of the Internet phone services. If you elect to use one of the Internet services, consider also having basic traditional phone company service with a simple, nonbattery, nonelectric, traditional phone that uses copper wire so you are not dependent upon electrical power for emergency phone communication. Maintain your cell phone coverage, but again, for safety and emergency communication, conventional phone service is most dependable.

Plan ahead for all of your utility connections. Utilities work on tight schedules and do not look upon new connects as emergency situations. Electrical service may take two to three days to get turned on. Telephone and cable connections may also take a number of days. Where water and sewer service are provided by a local community public authority, you may need to register at the authority office. And, don't be surprised or shocked if you are asked for a deposit. With first-time home buyers, utility companies will generally require a deposit that may require a visit to their local office.

There may be additional services or maintenance chores you may want to learn, or take on, to avoid the cost of contractors. During the growing season, grass cutting needs constant attention. If you don't have the time or inclination, there are landscaping services available—at a price. If you're cost-conscious—and lucky—there may be an eager and enterprising teenager down the block. If there is a lawn irrigation system in place, hopefully it will be operative when you take possession.

Contracts will be needed for any service you decide to hire out—lawn maintenance, if you use a professional, and maintenance of the sprinkler system, shrubbery, trees, swimming pool, if there is one, and pest control. You may want to consider firms that had previously served this house unless there had been some past problems. When you consider other contractors, start with those who serve your neighborhood so you will have some leverage from your neighbors.

Pre-Move Maintenance, Repair, Replacement

Take advantage of any time you have between your closing and when you move in to make any changes or corrective actions.

Most repairs and replacements, along with refinishing or redecorating, can be much more easily done before you, the family, and the furniture take up residence. First, review your home inspection report for lists of all maintenance repairs or servicing recommended. Often, you will have only negotiated for the most urgent repairs. Get with it! You paid handsomely for your professional home inspection. It only makes sense—dollars and cents—to pay attention to all of your inspector's recommendations.

Then list all of the optional work you would like to have completed pre-move or shortly after you move in. Think about how you want this house to become your home and plan, plan, plan the necessary work. Here we go again. Some of your merely "desired" projects may take some time especially if they tax your budget. Keep this list current, even if it takes a year or two.

Making your new house your home is a journey, but you've known that now for quite a while. Enjoy the trip as you look forward to the destination that rearranges itself all the time as new ideas present themselves. Whether it is a major renovation or just some new decorations, you change the atmosphere of the house you just bought into the home you love living in. It takes on your identity. Sometimes you may have to make temporary changes to suit your lifestyle for a while before you make a more major change. You can live with the computer in a corner until you have the cash for an office room over the garage. Simple decorating changes are easy and work wonders. A touch of paint, new curtains, a toss pillow—it's amazing what a difference little touches can make. Just arranging and rearranging your furniture or hanging some family pictures can change this house into a home—your home. A home is much more than a shelter. A home creates special feelings with warmth that enriches your life.

As you advance your plan of converting your house into your home, you have to consider the maintenance and repair needs identified in your home inspection report. Often, unfortunately, many of the items do not get resolved before you own the house. Problems that have not been taken care of will not go away by themselves. You may have a rude awakening when you come back down to Earth and have to face corrective action that cannot be avoided. Money is often the biggest factor as to when you will, or can, plan for the work to be done. Some items can wait. For example, if the air conditioner unit is not working properly, you can wait until the next cooling season to repair or replace the unit. But if winter is just around the corner and the heating system is not working properly you will not have the option of waiting.

Balancing your budget between desired improvements or modifications and necessary repair is difficult but very important. As much as you may want to redecorate some rooms, if there are priority maintenance repairs, you may be forced to do the repair first. Repair says, "Right Away." Redo may say, "Next Month or Next Year." Dreams say, "Someday." But if "Right Away" gets done and out of the way, then "Next Year" can become "Next Week" and all of a sudden it's almost "Someday." The sun may not shine everyday, but surer than death or taxes, the sun always comes back.

Deferred maintenance exists in almost every house, in different forms. Here's an example: painting the woodwork that has had the life scrubbed out of it, but isn't a life-threatening situation. Some work cannot be deferred. For example, regrading the property because the soil right at the foundation wall has settled, and water, seeking its level, is seeping into the foundation wall. Guess which project gets done first? Some things just insidiously creep up on us without forewarning, like an air conditioner that calls it quits in the middle of a heat wave. Nondeferrable maintenance items are often big budget items and can shoulder "Someday" right out of the picture.

Balancing between desired improvements for lifestyle quality, and work that is indispensable to prolonging the life and well-being of the building itself, is not easy. Delaying too long in doing preservation painting and wood refinishing may allow decay or rot to develop, or cause deterioration that will be more expensive to repair than if you had done the painting maintenance on schedule. It's easy to forget painting needs when a house has largely maintenance-free vinyl siding, but you cannot afford to overlook any wood trim. You have to keep up with the upkeep. If wood trim is ignored, it is particularly vulnerable to damage, such as decay or rot that may allow water entry into the house, causing hidden damage that can run riot quietly and unnoticed till it is too late.

So, we have determined that maintenance is essential. Remodeling is another story altogether. Remodeling is *Major* with a capital *M*, particularly remodeling of a kitchen or bathroom. These are high-ticket projects. If you have any money left after you've taken care of necessary, corrective-action repairs, and deferred maintenance needs are provided for, maybe it's time to think about the big jobs, the "Someday" projects. Thinking is free and you may find that you can modify your heart's desire to keep within a reasonable budget. Major make-overs are usually beyond the capabilities of an amateur. Unless you are willing to live in a construction site as you get work done piecemeal, call a professional. You may find that good guidance from an interior designer or architect, when you are contemplating significant remodeling projects, might actually save you money in the long run. The input of a design professional goes beyond just the actual work to be done. Professionals are specialists in creating good feelings. They also help keep the remodeling work consistent with the overall feel of the house. For more major projects, think of the big picture. If you plan ahead for future expansion, you can make sure that intermediate steps are in style with the desired end result. All too often do-it-yourself can turn a house into a hodgepodge of improvements that do not blend well.

It goes without saying that when remodeling or even minor modifications can be performed before you move in, there will be less disruption. Anyone who has survived a major kitchen make over can tell you horror story after horror story. If the lady of the house is also queen of the kitchen, life can be a nightmare because, as everyone knows, "If Mama ain't happy, ain't nobody happy."

Maintenance Planning

You can reduce potential problems by regular maintenance. No matter how great the condition of the house is when you first buy it, all materials wear and every operating device will need some level of maintenance or periodic replacement. You probably can do much of this work yourself. You may think you are all thumbs, but it's amazing how even a major klutz can become quite competent. If you simply cannot or choose not to learn how to maintain and repair your new home, prearrange for professional help if you can afford it. If you go the do-it-yourself route, however, always remember the carpenter's rule: measure twice, cut once. We know a fellow who did that with crown molding he was installing in his living room. He carefully measured twice, then cut—an inch too short. So he did it again, literally. Measured twice, cut once—two inches too short. There's a lesson here somewhere.

If you decide to use professionals, line up your specialists at the beginning and keep their information in your house book. Primary is a list of professionals you can call upon in an emergency, such as a plumber, electrician, and heating and air conditioning technician. A handyperson can be a savior! As a starting reference, make a list of all professionals who have worked at the house before you took ownership. Also, ask your seller for any and all installation and operation manuals for equipment and appliances within the house. Put them in your book. You may want to consider maintenance service contracts for key appliances, such as heating and air conditioning. Checklists are provided at the end of this chapter to assist with maintenance planning, whether you do it yourself or have a contractor do the work.

There are many web sites that can be very helpful, but you still need your trusty, basic home-maintenance book right at hand. Always keep it in the same place. Large home supply firms such as Home Depot® and Lowe's® are good starting sources for current information about almost every aspect of home maintenance. Their staff people are often professionals in their own right and are usually more than willing to answer even the wildest questions. If you are really lucky and have an old-fashioned local hardware store in your area, consider yourself in clover. A real neighborhood hardware store can be a fantastic resource for professional references and technical assistance. A real, old-fashioned hardware dealer usually knows more than one way to skin a cat. This person is a treasure.

When it comes to equipment, manufacturer's web sites often offer very good maintenance and operational information about their products. The more specialized the device, of course, the more important will be the manufacturer information. Download from the Internet all installation and operating literature for every appliance and file the information in your house book.

Just as important as dependable heat and water is maintenance of the house's weatherproof condition. At the very minimum, a thorough weatherproofing assessment will be needed every five years with specific repair or replacement work planned for the interim. For example, if upon your five-year inspection you determine that the roof needs to be replaced in just two years, put that on your maintenance calendar and budget for the work accordingly. Unless Mother Nature pulls a violent fast one by dropping a tree onto your house, most weatherproofing maintenance can be planned within your five-year inspections. Certainly local conditions like flood exposure and a potential for violent weather will have a direct bearing on how frequently you assess the weatherproof characteristics of your new home.

Roof, siding, windows, and doors are right there for easy inspection to make sure that they will keep rain and other weather elements outside where they belong. Likewise, visible sealant systems can regularly be inspected easily and repaired, if necessary, in a timely manner. Unfortunately, when sealing systems fail at windows, doors, and other penetrations, there can be moisture intrusion damage. Conditions like mold, that are not obvious, can develop into serious problems. In addition to the obvious barriers, flashing systems can become damaged or wear out. Some sidings, like EIFS (exterior insulating and finish system), need regular sealant replacement to ensure a weathertight barrier. Sealants at brick-to-window and brick-to-door openings also need periodic evaluation and may need replacement.

Maintaining clean roof-water gutters is important in weatherproofing maintenance. You may want to look into gutter protection systems now available to keep gutters clear of leaf buildup that can cause clogging. Also, make sure to keep clearance between the house and trees and shrubbery to keep moisture and insects away from the siding. Roof-water run-off control and property-drainage grading needs assessment during the five-year inspection to ensure that all roof water and surface water is flowing away and downhill from the foundation wall. Plan any needed corrective action during the interim between these inspections. When you have a very heavy rain, do not climb into your favorite old chair for a snooze. Climb, instead, into your rain gear and go outside to face the elements. This is the perfect time to study exterior conditions— while it is actually raining. Look for places where water is overflowing the gutters and where water does not flow away from the foundation wall. Then you'll know where to look for indications of water problems when you go back inside. This little exercise will also show you where you'll need to take corrective action to fix your roof-water control system and property grading.

Owners of houses located in areas subject to floods and violent weather need to take precautions to reduce potential damage. *Before* the flood or violent weather event is the time to review your preparations. A great web site is the FEMA site at *www.fema.gov/plan/index.shtm*. It features an "Are You Ready?" guide with specific guides for each type of major, natural hazard, along with information about technological and even terrorism hazards. FEMA also has a site with "how to" guides at *www.fema.gov/plan/prevent/howto/index.shtm*. Both FEMA sites are excellent guides for specific hazards, such as flooding. They outline precautions you can take to make your house more resistant and suffer less damage in the event of a disaster. Natural hazards listed in the "Are Your Ready?" guide include: floods, tornadoes, hurricanes, thunderstorms and lightning, winter storms and extreme cold, extreme heat, earthquakes, volcanoes, landslide and debris flow (mudslides), tsunamis, fires, and wildfires. Technological hazards listed in the guide include: hazardous materials incidents, household chemical emergencies, and problems at nuclear power plants. As a sign of the times, even terrorism information is now included, alongside a basic family communications plan.

As the seasons change, so do the needs of your house to resist normal seasonal conditions, such as freezing. Mark on your maintenance calendar seasonal checks for conditions expected in your area. For example, to prevent water pipe breakage when you have ice potential, you will need to stop water flow to all unheated areas that are subject to freezing. As you probably know, when water freezes, it expands with tremendous force that can break virtually any household pipe or plumbing fixture. You may need to blow out irrigation or lawn sprinkler pipes with air. Vacation homes located in areas that freeze need to be winterized by draining water and/or installing adequate amounts of antifreeze in fixtures, such as toilets, to prevent water from freezing. The same applies to any unheated out buildings. Docks and piers in water that freezes will need de-icing systems installed and maintained. These "bubbler" systems have thermostatic controls to agitate the water to reduce potential for icing. When such a system is not practical, the docks will have to be taken out of the water.

Other than the natural hazards discussed above, which vary in intensity according to location, there are additional special location maintenance considerations. If you are in an area where there are tornadoes or other potential natural disasters, you should definitely review the FEMA information for specific guidance on how to best prepare your house and family for these potentially disastrous conditions.

Electrical

Since 1752, when Benjamin Franklin went kite flying during a thunderstorm in his electrical experiments with lightning, scientists have had great respect for the power of electricity. In our homes, electricity powers small and large appliances. It brings instant light, sight, and sound into our lives but its power can be dangerous. Electrical work is not to be undertaken by amateurs. We'll help you learn how things work and how to recognize problems, but don't think of doing electrical work yourself unless you are a trained and licensed electrician. Safety is paramount.

Electrical systems do not require regular maintenance, but it is essential that the safety features of the electrical system are maintained. Unsafe electrical wiring can cause fires and personal injury. Electricity can kill. Comprehensive free guides to checking for interior and exterior electrical safety are available for download at *www.hud.gov/owning/index.cfm*. You'll also find a list of government publications under "Related Links" near the bottom of the page. Just as houses come in all sizes, their electrical systems have different capacities.

The total electrical power available to a house is a function of two factors: current or amperes (amps) and voltage. Think of electric current in terms of water flow where a larger pipe allows greater flow than a smaller pipe. Thus, a pipe that would allow a certain amount of water to flow at a low pressure will allow more water to flow at a higher pressure. Voltage is like pressure. A typical three-bedroom house has an electrical service with 100 amps and 240 volts. The product of these two factors is wattage, which is a measure of total power. Lightbulbs have watt ratings that tell you the amount of electrical power they consume when lit.

Electrical power is distributed by a local utility with overhead or underground wiring to a meter, usually located on the side of the house. Power is wired from this meter to a house disconnect that may be located in the main service panel. The service panel is used to distribute the electrical power in 120-volt branch circuits. Typical branch circuits have 15-amp and 20-amp circuit breakers. Certain electrical appliances, such as air conditioners and clothes dryers, have a 240-volt electrical cable with higher than 20-amp circuit breakers. This wiring goes to a special outlet that will not accept an ordinary electrical plug.

Old electrical panels may have fuses, but the modern electrical panel has circuit breakers which are switches designed to trip automatically when the wiring heats up. A short in an electrical device or wiring causing too much electricity to flow will make the circuit breaker heat up and trip. Overloading a branch circuit with too many appliances will also cause tripping of the circuit breaker. If the circuit breaker does not trip, there may be a fire hazard.

When the electrical power is turned off, there will, of course, be no current flow. For safety's sake it is good to have the electrical power switched off, even when changing light bulbs. This becomes supremely important when working with the electrical wiring. Absolute confirmation that there is no electrical flow is essential before working with open electrical wiring. If you are not fully qualified to work with the wiring directly, don't consider doing it. Hire a licensed electrician. Electricity can kill.

All electrical connections require a suitable housing to prevent the wiring from connecting with another wire or with other materials. There should never be any loose electrical wiring or unboxed electrical connections. Thus, one of the initial maintenance priorities is to ensure that all electrical terminations are properly protected. Your preclosing home inspection should confirm this.

To illustrate how electrical power is distributed, and for ease of discussion ,we are going to use 120-watt light bulbs. A 120-volt branch circuit will need one amp for each 120-watt light bulb, so a 15-amp circuit could light 15 bulbs. When more than that amount of electricity is in demand, the circuit breaker will heat up and at a certain point, shut off or trip to avoid a potential fire hazard. When this happens, it is a signal that something is wrong and you need to understand what happened before resetting the circuit breaker. Kitchen circuits are typically 20 amps so if too many appliances, such as a mixer and toaster, were operated on the same circuit at the same time, there may be an overload and a tripping of the circuit breaker.

This brings to mind a famous story that grew out of the great November 1965 northeastern blackout, at that time the largest blackout in history. Within four seconds of an electrical failure in upstate New York, thirty million people in eight states and part of Canada were plunged into a darkness that lasted up to thirteen hours. Seconds earlier, at quarter after five that afternoon, a certain accident-prone New York City woman had begun dinner preparation to the accompaniment of her countertop radio and kiddy TV in the next room. She fired up her oven to preheat, dropped two slices of bread into her toaster to brown, and switched on her mixer to blend the sauce for a new casserole recipe she'd found in a magazine. Everything blew. All our lady could think of was, "Oh, I've done it again! I guess I really am Calamity Jane." Right then, she looked out the window where all of New York City lay in darkness as far as the eye could not see. Quietly, in awe, she whispered, "Oh, what have I done this time?"

Happily, the northeast grid is in much better shape today. Wherever you live, if you trip a circuit breaker, you can generally reset it. However, be careful not to use too many appliances at the same time. If you do trip, take a look at the kitchen outlets and at the circuit breaker to check for any smoke or indications of burning before resetting the circuit breaker. If there are indications of smoke or burning, get an electrician to investigate before re-setting the breaker. Whenever you reset a circuit breaker you will need to fully shut it off and then turn it on. If it goes right back off, keep it off and call a licensed electrician.

Sometimes an electrical switch will feel hot to the touch. This often happens with dimmer switches and means that there is something wrong. The situation should be evaluated by a knowledgeable person or a licensed electrical contractor. If you have dimming of lights when a major appliance like an air conditioner or electric clothes dryer is turned on, there is probably an imbalance in the distribution of electrical power. Overheated electrical devices and significant dimming of lights suggest overloading in part of, or possibly, in the entire system. Sometimes when power supply from the utility is overloaded, an excessive voltage drop will cause this condition. Overuse of air conditioners during a heat spell may cause voltage drops and even interruptions of electrical power. During these periods when voltage is affected it's a good idea to disconnect sensitive appliances, such as computers and TV. A call to the utility company will tell you if there is a voltage problem. For the more technical-minded home owner, a volt meter could confirm the situation.

Lightning storms can also cause interruptions to electrical power. In addition to voltage drops there may be spikes in the voltage that can cause damage to sensitive appliances. Power interruptions can be accommodated by using uninterrupted power supply (UPS) devices, particularly for computers. These are batteries that will maintain power for a short period of time. If you don't have these, you should have a surge protector to guard against start-up damage to equipment that was running when the power went off. Short-term back-up battery power can be used for other devices such as sump pumps. For longer power interruptions an engine-generator system would be needed. This requires a special electrical installation by a licensed electrical contractor in addition to provisions for fuel supply.

Low-voltage electrical devices are increasing in popularity. Low voltage—lower than 24 volts—reduces physical hazards and is often used for landscape lighting, as well as some indoor lighting. Doorbells have long been low voltage through a transformer connected to house power. Ground fault circuit interrupters (GFCI) are a relatively recent major advance in electrical devices for personal safety. They are literally life-savers. These devices shut off electrical current faster than a traditional circuit breaker in a way that reduces any chance for injury or death. Of course, the device needs to be properly installed and working. Just because you see it on the wall does not mean it is working properly. Many existing houses do not have GFCI's installed in all necessary areas. All exterior outlets and all areas where there is water, such as bathrooms and kitchens, should have GFCI protection. There are low-cost testers you can use to check that these GFCI devices are working. Only one circuit interrupter is needed for each branch circuit. It may be installed in the electrical panel or at the first outlet in that branch circuit. These devices protect only those outlets that are downstream of their location and can fail from exposure to weather and general use, so it is important to check regularly that they are operational. The push-button at the outlet or disconnect is the first means of testing, but the above-mentioned electrical testers that create a ground fault are more reliable.

Most people haven't the foggiest idea of how much electricity their lights and appliances draw, so just for the fun of it, we offer the following not-so-useless information. It may, in fact, be very useful in monitoring power usage. Electrical bills are expressed in 1,000-watt hours or kilowatt hours. The use of one watt for one hour would equal one watt hour. A 120-watt light bulb left on for one hour would consume one watt hour of electricity. A kilowatt hour would require 1,000 120-watt light bulbs operating for one hour. Even with every lamp or overhead in the house on high alert, you won't come close. But, a high-wattage appliance such as an electrical hot-water heater may consume 5,000 or more watts per hour! Now your eyes pop open. Reviewing electrical bills over a long period of time—two years or more—will allow you to monitor normal seasonal electrical usage. Should there be a significant change, learn why or get help from an electrical contractor.

Water Supply and Plumbing

Water supplied by a public utility is generally safe to drink because the water is monitored by the utility and the government. Government-monitored water systems will usually provide published water-testing results, if you are interested in reviewing them. There is no harm in asking. Well water needs regular testing, at least yearly, to ensure that there is no contamination. With well water some undesirable ingredients can be filtered out. During periods when there is questionable water quality, keep a supply of bottled water on hand. Of course, you'll have to be aware of the "use by" dates on the bottles. Replacing bottled water regularly is insurance against going dry.

Just as necessary as a water supply is the necessity for a waste-water disposal system. This can be a public sewer system or a private sewer system. Public systems are generally maintenance-free, especially when they are gravity systems with no pumps. You may run into problems like clogged pipes. If you cannot claim some skill in using a "snake" to remove the source of the clog, call a plumber. If waste pipes are very old, more than 50 years, there could also be breaks that can stop the flow of waste water. These need urgent, corrective action. Call a plumber. Septic systems need inspections and potential clean-out on a three-year cycle.

Fuel supply is a consideration, whether your house is heated by natural gas, propane, or oil. Natural gas is supplied through underground piping from a local utility to a meter usually located at the outside of the house and needs no home-owner maintenance. Natural gas has a very pungent added odor ingredient to alert home owners of any leak. Sometimes this odor can be detected just by turning on the stove. If that odor is smelled, get everyone out of the house immediately, and do not operate any electrical device, not even light switches. Immediately call the gas company or police to report a gas leak. Propane and fuel oil require storage tanks and regular refilling before the tanks are empty. If you have a history of usage from the former owner, you are one step ahead of the game. Having tank insurance is also advantageous in the event of a tank leak.

Plumbing systems include piping to distribute domestic water, piping to remove waste water, appliances to heat water, appliances that use water, and fixtures in bathrooms and kitchens. Pipes can clog and corrode. Appliances and fixtures wear out and break. See the appendix in Chapter 11 for estimated life of appliances to guide your replacement budget. Maintenance for plumbing fixtures starts with being prepared for leaks. Know where the house shut-off valve is located and know where shut-off valves are for sink fixtures and appliances. Valves and faucets have seals that need periodic replacement when the valve fails to shut off fully. Toilets have seals that also will need periodic replacement if there is a leak or if the toilet fixture is loose.

We have a friend whose mission in life, for a while, was asking everyone she ran into if they knew where their major shut-off valve was. She found out the hard way when she woke in the wee hours to the not-so-gentle sound of running water—galloping water. When she got out of bed to investigate she was ankle deep. A little two-dollar valve on the toilet had broken and the water was rushing with the speed and strength of a fire hose. Of course the plumbers she called weren't about to venture forth at 2:00 A.M., but one kind soul did tell her where to look for the shut-off valve. She found it, but not until a few hundred dollars worth of water damage had ruined a good night's sleep. If a little old lady accosts you and asks if you are on friendly terms with your pipes, hear her out.

Most plumbing maintenance consists simply of looking for leaks. Plumbing leaks can be very small and not easily detected until significant damage is done. When an upper-floor bathroom or laundry room leaks to the room below, make a hole in the ceiling below to allow water to drain before further ceiling damage results. One shouldn't have to be reminded that water filtration systems require regular replacement of filters. The same diligence applies to water-softening systems that require regular replacement of the salt supply.

Heating and Air Conditioning Systems

Heat may be provided by a central system or unit heaters. Central heating systems that provide heat to the entire house or large parts of the house are served by one heating unit. These systems can be fuel-fired or electric. Typical heating systems fuel-fired by natural gas, propane, or oil include warm-air furnace, hot-water-boiler hydronic heating, and steam boiler. Steam boilers use gravity to distribute the heat, and thus do not need the pump required for hydronic heating or the blower fan needed for warm-air heating. Each of these systems has different maintenance needs. Oil-fired furnaces and boilers require some maintenance different from gas-fired.

Forced warm-air heating systems often can accommodate a central air conditioning system using the same air-handler. A heat pump, however, runs both an electrical central heating and air conditioning system. Electric and fuel-fired unit heaters that are stand-alone systems are typically used to heat a single room. A garage is a perfect example of where a unit heater might be used to maintain some heat but at a lower heat level than the house.

Wood-burning heating systems also include unit heaters such as a fireplace or stove and central warm-air-ducted systems. There are some combination systems but these are not typical. All warm-air systems have filters that need regular changing depending upon their service life. Filter life can range from less than one month to more than six months, depending upon the quality of the filter and the degree of particulate matter in the air.

Air conditioning systems may be stand-alone units or central systems that are interconnected with the heating system, as in the case of warm-air systems. Or, they may have independent distribution ducts. Typically, air conditioning systems use a refrigerant, but there are systems that use water evaporation or even a heat source, such as gas or steam. All air conditioning systems have filters that need regular replacement and mechanical equipment that will need servicing. Generally, air conditioning inspections are recommended yearly when spring temperatures reach 60°F (15°C).

Kitchen Appliances

Kitchen appliances need regular cleaning and some maintenance. Checking operational conditions and looking for water leaks or smelling for gas leaks need to be done routinely. Fortunately, natural gas has that added pungent odor we spoke of earlier. This can help to identify a gas leak. If the odor is only momentary after igniting a stove burner there may not be a leak. But, as we have mentioned, when the odor is not associated with lighting the stove, or lingers, shut off the gas supply, do not operate any electrical device, get out of the house, and immediately call your local police/fire department/gas utility.

Property

Landscaping adds beauty to a property but it brings with it the need for maintenance and care of the shrubbery, plants, trees, and lawn. Here again, you have a choice of paying a lot of money to have others maintain your property or learning how to keep it up yourself. Some people find great peace and satisfaction in gardening—it can be fun to play in the dirt, to plant things, and watch them flourish. And there is a wealth of "how-to" literature for tillers of any size property. In addition to books that you can buy at home centers and advice from local nurseries, there will probably be at least one university in your state that has an agricultural extension service for additional expert assistance. These can be invaluable sources of information. If you are not a back-to-the-soil home owner, you can be glad that landscaping services have become big business.

Driveway and walking surfaces include dirt, loose slate, gravel, asphalt, pavers and mortared slate, and stamped or plain concrete. Depending upon location each has its own advantages and disadvantages. When mortared joints are used, mortar repair will be needed as cracks develop. Pavers will require replenishment of dry sand. Repaired cracks and holes will, unfortunately, be obvious. Maintenance for the sake of appearance will require a bit more work depending upon the quality of the original surface. Sealers on asphalt help if the surface has not been too damaged. Concrete driveways generally need little maintenance if they have not settled and cracked. Tree roots, however, may cause heaving damage to sidewalks and driveways. They worm their way under the pavement and can actually lift heavy slabs or segments. Short of cutting down the offending tree and extracting the intrusive roots, you can make repairs by filling in cracks or gaps with concrete for an even, unbroken path. But trip-and-fall safety hazards call for serious priority maintenance repair. You may have to lift up heaved segments to level off the ground surface and start anew with repaving.

Home Expense Budgeting

Oh, boy, here come more pocketbook considerations. You have to be able to budget for both short- and long-term repairs. As we have suggested, start with all the information you can obtain from the seller. Hopefully she will have saved paid utility bills for water, fuel, and electricity. These vary according to season so you may want to consider going on a plan that averages your costs over the year. Fuel and electricity suppliers can set up a payment plan to cover these heaviest costs of heating and cooling. And remember, some uses of electricity, such as an electrically heated spa, can send the power bill soaring. Historical information from the seller or the utility is very useful in creating your initial budget. This historical information is also useful to point out a potential maintenance problem if you see any sudden, significant cost increase. For example, if the water bill increases disproportionately, there may be hidden water leaks such as within a toilet or a lawn irrigation system. Electrical costs that increase disproportionately to cooling high-degree days may indicate service or age issues with your air conditioner. Energy efficiency can be improved in almost any home. See *www.energystar.gov* for information about government programs.

The easy part of this budget planning is the ongoing utilities. What is more difficult is planning for major repair and replacement costs, such as a new roof or new heating system. A difficult to do, but useful concept is to establish a savings account to accumulate money before it becomes necessary to handle the major expense of large improvement projects. Our work sheets will help you get a handle on how to budget these savings. Our suggested five-year plan is a basis for major expense budgeting. If you are not able to create a fund, you will have to find the money during the year in which the expense must be made. You may need a home-owner equity loan for major items, such as a new roof or new siding.

However you finance repairs, keep records of contracts, paid bills, and receipts. File them in your house book. It's easy to forget when a certain job was done or replacement made, who did it, and how much it cost. This applies to small jobs, but keep in mind that the cost of major repairs and replacements can play a large part in ascertaining house value when you decide to sell. Don't throw out any house bills—file them! You will never regret creating and maintaining that good old house book.

Home-Buyer's Checklist

- Have I made a list of services to transfer?
- Have I assigned my real estate professional to complete the transfer or will I need to make it happen?
- Have I begun my home-maintenance book?
- Have I created a prioritized maintenance schedule and budget?

Appendix: Budget and Maintenance

Service Providers
For all: Company name

             Address

             Service phone number

             Billing phone number

Boat dock de-icing

Cable

Electrical utility

Fuel (oil, natural gas, propane, wood)

Garbage

House cleaning

Security

Snow plowing

Swimming pool

Telephone

Water softener salt supply

Water utility

Emergency
For all: Phone number

Fire

First Aid

Local Clinic (include address)

Local Hospital (include address)

Police

Maintenance and Service People

Creating your own approved supplier list will have you ready when an emergency occurs or when you need confirmation of a major repair or replacement. You will want to qualify each of these service providers as discussed in our text.

For all: Key person
             Company
             Address
             Phone number

Air conditioning
Appliance repair
Audio-visual-entertainment service
Blinds and curtain service
Carpenter
Carpet cleaning
Chimney sweep
Driveway repair service
Electrician
Floor sanding and refinishing
Garage door service
Gutter cleaning
Heating
Lawn service
Mason
Painter
Plumber
Roofer
Septic cleaning
Termite and pest control
Tile installation/repair

Tree trimming
Wallpaper/wall coverings service
Well

Material Providers
For all: Company Name
             Address
             Phone Number

Garden supply
Hardware and home supply
Lumber yard

Equipment List and Service Capacity
(Much of this information should be within your home inspection report.)

For all: Date of installation
             Manufacturer
             Date of manufacture
             Model #
             Serial #
             Capacity
             Installer (company)
             Energy source (natural gas, oil, propane, electricity)
             Owners manual

Air conditioning system
Clothes dryer
Clothes washing machine
Heating system
Hot water heater
Range
Refrigerator

Maintenance Plan

Fall

Attic/roof ventilation
Flues: check for sealed flowing condition
Gutter and downspout cleaning: ensure good drainage
Lawn: re-seed and fertilize, remove leaves
Weather-stripping windows and doors
Winterize unheated exterior water fixtures
  Exterior faucets
  Lawn irrigation system
  Pool
  Boat dock/pier
  Unheated out-building plumbing

Winter

Confirm attic ventilation and no condensation
Gutter and downspout cleaning: ensure good drainage
Install storm sash

Spring

Check chimney and chimney flashing
Check for driveway and sidewalk trip-and-fall hazards
Check roof covering condition and roof flashing
Check sump pump operation
Conduct your annual five-year plan inspection
De-winterize exterior water fixtures
Gutter and downspout cleaning: ensure good drainage
House cleaning
Remove storm sash and install screens
Stucco and brick to window/door sealants

Summer

Confirm crawl space ventilation and no mildew
Gutter and downspout cleaning: ensure good drainage

Monthly Maintenance Checks

Filters for HVAC and any water filters
Fire extinguishers
Plumbing leaks
Shower and tub tile wall grout
Smoke and carbon monoxide alarms

Five-Year Plan

Identify major repair or replacement needs over the next five years based on an annual inspection. Include in the plan major improvements, such as modification or additions including kitchens, bathrooms, added rooms, etc. Include the estimated value of these projects in your budget. Update this plan annually every spring. The following list of major items is only for brainstorming. Most of these items may not need replacement or planned major repair in the next five years. Your home inspection report should be a basis for the initial plan.

Air conditioning system
Basement dewatering
Bathroom fixtures
Deck
Doors
Exterior painting
Fireplace
Foundation
Garage/carport
Heating system
Hot tub/spa
Interior painting
Kitchen appliances
Landscaping
Pool

Roof
Shed
Siding: sealants/repair/replacement
Wall coverings
Windows

Five-Year Weatherproofing Inspection Checklist

Conduct a thorough inspection every five years using technical assistance as needed from your approved supplier list and add the major repair/replacement items to your next five-year plan. See the typical life expectancies in Chapter 11 on home inspection for guidance on replacement timing. For example, a shingled high-slope roof covering typically lasts 20 to 30 years depending upon the quality of shingle used, quality of its initial application, and ventilation. Every element in the "skin" of the house needs to be weatherproofed to prevent interior damage due to wind-driven rain. Where complete waterproofing cannot be had, then diversions are the next best thing. Roof overhangs are one form of diversions. Flashing systems with drip edges are another form of diversions.

Basement waterproofing
Brick mortar joints
Deck
Doors including flashing, weather-stripping, and seals
Driveway
Porch and steps
Property drainage grading
Roof covering and flashings
Roof water run-off control
Sidewalks
Siding (EIFS needs inspection by an EIFS expert)
Windows including flashing, weather-stripping, and seals

Chapter 16

Refinancing

*R*efinancing is arranging a new loan to replace the loan or loans that are presently on the house. Refinancing (or "refi," as it is called in the trade) can be costly. The new lender likely wants an application fee, a title insurance policy, appraisal, credit check, survey, attorney fees, recording fees, and discount points, especially if the loan is being offered at a below-market interest rate. Private mortgage insurance or FHA insurance premiums may be required. There may be an increase in the amount of escrow required for taxes and insurance. The old loan may have prepayment penalties.

Fees are likely to be 1–2 percent of the full amount of the debt, plus discount points, additional escrow amounts, and prepayment penalties on your old mortgage. Because of this high cost, refinancing is not to be taken lightly.

Reasons to Refinance

The three principal reasons for refinancing a mortgage loan are:

1. To reduce the interest rate.

2. To extract cash to use for another purpose.

3. To improve the financing terms.

Reduce Interest Rate

A great reason to refinance a loan is to take advantage of lower interest rates. For example, suppose you have a fixed-rate loan that you obtained when interest rates were high. You may find that you can get a new loan at a lower rate of interest. A home owner can significantly reduce monthly payments with this tactic. If you can refinance at lower interest rates but don't, your lender will enjoy it and think of you as foolish.

Aside from the transaction costs of refinancing, there is no downside to simply reducing your interest rate. You will need to compare the reduction in interest rates to the transaction costs to determine whether it is worthwhile. Suppose transaction costs are two percent of the loan. If the interest rate is reduced by two percent, you will recoup the cost in a year and continue to save significantly on interest for as long as you own the house, or the remaining mortgage term. If the interest rate is reduced by one percent, it will take two years to recoup the transactions costs— still worth it.

But if the interest rate is reduced by only one-half percent, you'll need to put on your thinking cap. It will take four years to recoup your transaction costs, and you'll get no interest on that money. Will you stay in the house that long? Should you wait for interest rates to decline further before refinancing? Will the lender allow you to refinance again in a year without duplicating all those fees?

If you are comfortable with financial calculations, you can use an Excel® spreadsheet or a financial calculator to assist with a refinancing decision. For the rest of us, consider this approximation: At interest rates of 6–8 percent, each one percent of transaction costs require an interest rate reduction of at least one-eighth percent to break even, assuming you'll keep the new mortgage for ten or more years. So, if you must pay two percent for transaction costs, you'll need to reduce the interest rate by at least one-quarter percent ($2 \times \frac{1}{8}\% = \frac{1}{4}\%$). This is the *minimum*. It is just break even. You will really need a deeper interest rate cut to make it worthwhile for you.

Extract Cash

Another good reason for refinancing is to extract cash to use for another purpose. The most likely uses are to:

- Make home improvements, such as adding a room or remodeling the kitchen or bathroom.

- Pay for a child's education.

- Retire high-interest debt.

- Pay emergency medical bills.

- Raise money to start a business.

Since the added debt will take a long time to pay down, it is considered unwise to use the cash for a short-term purpose such as a vacation. Perhaps buying a car should be considered valid because a car has longevity (though not as long as most loan terms) and refinancing is much cheaper than car payments.

Refinancing to extract cash requires the same transaction costs as noted earlier. The difficult issue is that the transaction costs apply to the full amount borrowed, not just the bit that you need.

Consider this simplified, though exaggerated, example. You presently owe $88,000 at eight percent interest, with 25 years remaining on your mortgage. You need $10,000 cash to pay an overdue medical bill arising from an emergency uninsured operation. You'll need to borrow $100,000 to get the $10,000 cash. Why? Because transaction costs will be two percent of the *full amount* that you borrow, that is, of the whole $100,000. This is $2,000. So you'll need to borrow $100,000 to pay off the

$88,000 existing loan and the $2,000 in transaction costs to be left with $10,000 in cash.

Paying $2,000 in transaction costs is a steep price just to get $10,000 cash. It's 20 percent. Fortunately, the loan will remain in place for many years, so you can amortize its cost over the years, though with interest.

The reason this is an exaggerated example is that the amount extracted is relatively small. Had you extracted a larger amount, the transaction costs would still be two percent of the total principal borrowed, but would be a smaller percentage of the cash you received. For example, if your present loan were $68,000, you could extract $30,000 cash with the same $2,000 in transaction costs.

When the amount you need is relatively small, consider a home equity loan or line of credit (described later). Typically, any fees are based on the amount of new money that you borrow.

Improve the Financing Terms

Innovative mortgage loans with seemingly attractive terms have been available for more than a decade. Between 2000 and 2004, many adjustable-rate mortgages (ARMs) were offered bearing unusually low initial interest rates—some at far less than four percent. ARMs were generally tied to short-term interest rates plus 2–3 percent. These were initially offered when short-term rates were at historic lows and were well below long-term interest rates.

In 2006, short-term interest rates rose far more than long-term rates. In economists' parlance, the yield curve flattened. With a flat yield curve, ARM rates at 2–3 percent above Treasury bill rates put them well above the interest rate available for long-term fixed-rate mortgages.

When long-term fixed-rate mortgage rates are at or below rates for adjustable-rate mortgages, it makes sense to convert an

ARM to a fixed-rate mortgage. The same is true for other types of loans, including hybrid ARMs, graduated-payment mortgages, and others that have potential interest rate or payment changes. Refinancing with a long-term fixed-rate mortgage will eliminate the risk brought by rising interest rates.

Other Possible Benefits

Loan Assumption

In some situations, refinancing may be helpful before you sell your home. When rates are low, you may obtain a loan that can be assumed by the buyer. If rates increase before you sell, or if mortgage loans become hard to get, an assumable loan can add to the resale value of your home.

Many loans have a "due on sale" clause that prevents a loan assumption or gives the lender the right to raise the interest rate upon an assumption. There may still be a benefit for a buyer in assuming a loan even if the interest rate is increased. The down payment and transaction costs may be lower than for a new loan.

In a loan assumption, the initial borrower and the recent home buyer are both liable for the loan. If the recent home buyer defaults, the lender can look to either party to cure the default. When selling a home where the buyer assumes your mortgage debt, it is a good plan to get a release. The document used for this purpose is a **novation**. In this agreement, the lender releases the original buyer from further liability.

"Subject to" Mortgage

Upon the sale of mortgaged real estate, a new buyer would prefer to purchase "subject to" the loan. The buyer becomes liable only for payments. If that buyer defaults, the lender can look only to the original borrower. So, for a home seller, it is preferable to have the buyer assume the loan because that causes the buyer to be personally liable.

Tax-Free Proceeds

Borrowing is not normally a taxable event. So when a home owner refinances and extracts cash, the cash received, which adds to debt, is not taxable. This is likely to save income tax money, especially when compared to selling an appreciated asset to raise cash.

Further, the interest expense on a personal residence may be tax-deductible by those who itemize their income tax deductions. The increased debt may generate increased tax deductions, but there are limits. Generally, a loan up to $100,000 above the cost of the original purchase and improvements will qualify. Check with your tax advisor.

Refinance Loans Available

Most of the loans available to a purchaser are also available to one who refinances. (An exception is when a state offers low-rate loans to first-time home buyers.) Generally, the same rules apply, except that the value of the house is measured by an appraisal instead of a sale contract. Some lenders are willing to accept an automated valuation model (AVM) instead of an appraisal. The AVM cost is much less—perhaps under $100, whereas a professional appraisal that typically includes a personal inspection and detailed comparison, is $300–$400.

Refer to Chapters 5 and 6 for what you should know about mortgages and how to select the right one.

Home Equity Line of Credit

Many banks will offer a home equity line of credit. They will estimate the amount of equity you have in your home and offer to lend a portion of that. They may provide a checkbook so that you can write checks as you need to pay money, and then you can pay off the loan as you see fit. Often the interest rate is favorable, fees may be relatively small, and you pay interest only on the amount you borrow.

However, sometimes fees can become excessive, so be watchful. If you don't pay the interest on your home equity loan each month, the bank may be allowed to zap your checking account. If there isn't enough money in your checking account but you have overdraft protection, you will find they charge large fees in each place—the loan and your checking account—for a relatively small amount of interest. Never mind that you have a significant balance in a savings account at the same bank—they love to add a $30 fee to your home equity loan (plus interest) and another $30 fee to your checking account with overdraft protection. Further, if you *don't* have overdraft protection, you may get that $30 charge for every check that bounces as a result of the account being overdrawn. That can quickly amount to more than the $200 check you should have written to cover interest. This is why you need to be watchful!

Reverse Mortgage

The reverse mortgage is a relatively new type of loan, intended for home owners who are house rich but cash poor. Program availability and specific terms change periodically, and the borrower's age is an important element in the loan terms.

Here's how it works: There is no existing mortgage, or the balance is small. The lender provides an initial lump sum in cash to pay off an existing loan or gives cash to a home owner who has no existing loan. The lender then makes monthly payments to the borrower for a period of years, or until the borrower dies or leaves the house. The loan balance, which begins with the initial funding, is increased with each payment, plus interest calculated on all of the lender's payments. The lender expects that the home's value will exceed the loan balance at all times, so that the house can always sell for more than the debt.

Personal Liability

Some people are under the erroneous impression that they can walk away from their home and let the lender keep it. They apply for the largest refinancing loan available, with a plan to receive maximum cash and ship out. They are not aware that when they accept a loan, they provide their personal assurance of repayment in addition to giving the property as collateral. Lenders will foreclose on the property, sell it at a loss through foreclosure, and then get a judgment against the former owner for their loss plus expenses. This is called a deficiency judgment. Some courts allow that to be enforced; others are not too keen on enforcement. The borrower should always be aware that he is personally liable. Even if the deficiency cannot be repaid, it will serve as a stain on the borrower's reputation.

Early Loan Retirement

You can save a significant amount of interest on your loan by reducing the time to pay it off. The reason that mortgage loans have long terms (often 25 or 30 years) is to stretch out the cost so as to reduce the monthly payment. However, a main drawback of a long-term loan is that the interest paid over the life of the loan may be three or more times the amount actually borrowed.

There are a number of types of loans that provide rapid amortization. The easiest to arrange is a 15-year mortgage. This will significantly increase each and every **principal and interest (P&I) payment**, typically by 20 percent, to pay off a loan in 15 years instead of 30. **A biweekly mortgage** is another approach. The payment required is one-half of a monthly payment for a standard mortgage. This amount is paid every two weeks. Because there are 26 two-week periods in a year, it is similar to making 13 monthly payments in a year. Such payments will significantly shorten the amortization period, although this arrangement may adversely affect affordability, especially if you are stretching the budget to buy the home. It is especially useful for people who are paid every week or every two weeks, and less suitable for those paid monthly or even twice a month (which is not quite the same as every two weeks).

An alternative is to arrange a 30-year loan to keep the payments at an affordable level. Then you can pay more each month in a lump sum when you have some extra cash. Keep this important caveat in mind: If you encounter hardship after making extra payments, your lender many not be amenable to reducing or skipping your future payments. You must still pay regularly.

Before prepaying part of a loan, be certain that your lender will cooperate by applying the extra payment to the current principal balance. Some lenders apply prepayments to the escrow amount or to the last required payments—unfavorable procedures for a borrower. Fortunately, some lenders make it easy to apply advance payments to the principal by providing a space on the coupon book so you can indicate the application of an extra payment.

Prepayment works like this: The principal and interest (P&I) portion of your payment (don't count taxes and interest) has been financially engineered to pay off (or *amortize,* a fancy word for loan reduction) the loan over a certain period, with interest due on the unpaid balance. In a long-term mortgage loan, most of each payment in the early years is for interest, with a small amount for principal reduction (amortization). As the loan is reduced, less of the P&I payment goes for interest and more is used to reduce the debt. Suppose you make an extra payment to reduce the principal. Thereafter interest will be less, because it is applied to the reduced principal, so more of each future payment will reduce the principal and hasten the reduction of the debt. Any advance payment effectively earns compound interest at the same rate as the mortgage bears. The advance payment, plus earnings based on it, will shorten the loan term.

Refinancing Under Financial Distress

Suppose you were able to qualify for a home mortgage only because you and your spouse both work. You need both paychecks to afford the loan payments, but one of you loses your job, and suddenly you are left with only one income. Your shrunken budget is not enough for the payment and other necessities. You may try to sell the home, but the market is soft and you can't get enough money to cover the mortgage amount. Do you abandon the home and default on the loan?

This may not be your only option. You may be able to restructure the loan so that you can afford it. At least you may be able to buy time until your income is reinstated. Here are a few considerations:

- **Extend the maturity.** You may be able to negotiate an extension to the maturity of the loan. If the loan is relatively new, this has very limited effect. Most lenders can't extend the maturity beyond 30 years. In addition, the extension of a few years will have only a small effect on payments. For example, the monthly payment on a 25-year, seven percent interest loan of $150,000 is $1,060.17. If the loan were extended to 30 years, the payment would be reduced to $997.95, a difference of less than $65 per month.

- **Pay only interest.** A more promising option is to temporarily pay interest only. You pay only the interest due on the principal balance and do not retire any of the balance.

When you start making principal payments again, the monthly payment will be higher than before unless the maturity of the loan is also extended. In the example above, payment of interest only would reduce payments to $875 per month, a difference approaching $185 per month.

- **Arrange for negative amortization.** If the interest payment alone is too high, you might be able to restructure the loan to require some payment below interest due. This would be set at the maximum amount you could afford and would be for some limited period. During the time of reduced payments, the balance of the loan will be increasing, because the difference between your payment and interest due is added to the principal. In our example loan, if you pay $800 a month, $75 would be added to principal in the first month. This amount would gradually increase since the principal balance and interest due increases.

- **Refinance at a lower rate of interest.** If interest rates have declined since you took out the loan, you can refinance at the lower rate, possibly for a longer term.

When it becomes apparent that you cannot make the loan payments, contact the lender. You will want to avoid having the lender start foreclosure proceedings against you. Once the lender forecloses, the entire loan becomes due, not just the lapsed monthly payments. The lender would like to avoid foreclosure and forced sale of the house and may be willing to work out a loan restructuring. If you can get a cosigner on the loan, it may help the negotiation.

Some loans, going by various names such as "flexible," "smart," or "option" mortgages, allow you to alter the amount you pay each month. At any time during the life of the loan, you may convert the loan to interest-only, make a minimum payment (somewhat like a credit card), or even skip a payment. Of course, any time you fail to pay at least enough to cover the interest accrued, you create negative amortization and your debt actually becomes larger with each payment. This type of loan can be helpful for someone with variable income, but you need the discipline to make up for missed interest payments when the cash becomes available.

Refinancing Short-Term Loans

Sometimes refinancing is not by choice but by necessity. You must arrange new financing because your existing financing is expiring and there is a balance due. There are several situations where you may have temporary financing.

Construction Loan

You had the home newly built and still have a construction loan or a bridge loan extending beyond the term of the construction. These types of loans carry higher interest rates than regular home loans. You will want to find "permanent" financing as soon as possible (a **permanent loan** is the long-term financing for the period you own the home).

Seller Financing

When you bought the home, the seller provided the financing as an inducement to make a sale. Often loans of this type are set up with monthly payments based on a long-term schedule. After a few years, however, the entire outstanding balance becomes due as a balloon payment. For example, a loan might be for $150,000 at seven percent interest with payments according to a 30-year schedule. Monthly payments are $997.95. After the third year, the balance of $145,090.44 becomes due.

The reason a seller sets up the loan this way is to limit his exposure to the risks of a lender. A buyer might be attracted to the arrangement because the loan is made at a rate of interest lower than the prevailing rate, or the buyer can't quality for a loan from a lending institution. If you have one of these loans, you should consider the term of the loan as an opportunity to arrange permanent financing.

Suppose the balloon payment is coming due and you can't find permanent financing. You may be able to negotiate with the seller to extend the loan. If not, you may have to sell the home.

Other Financing Types

There are other types of loans used to attract buyers that may present refinancing opportunities. When interest rates are high, builders sometimes offer buy-down loans. These loans provide a below-market interest rate for the first several years of the loan term. The rate may even be graduated. For example, the interest rate may start at three percent the first year and rise to five percent the second and so on until it reaches the market rate. These are not adjustable-rate mortgages; the schedule of rate increases is fixed. If interest rates decline, however, you may find that you can refinance with a fixed-rate loan at a lower rate.

Another type of loan that is similar to the buy-down is a **graduated-payment mortgage**. In this loan, the interest rate is fixed, but the payments are reduced for the first few years. This means that the principal balance actually increases during those years. You may still refinance (base your decision on whether there is a lower interest rate available on new financing), but the amount of the new loan may need to be more than the original one.

Home-Buyer's Checklist

In deciding whether it will be beneficial to refinance your home, ask yourself these questions:

- Is the interest rate on your current mortgage higher than the prevailing market rate of interest?

- How much cash can you extract?

- How much must you pay in fees?

- Do your circumstances justify a reverse mortgage?

- Is refinancing less expensive than other forms of debt? Is a home equity line of credit more suitable than all-new financing?

Real-World Example

Since 1990, the Smiths had endured financial problems caused by recurring health issues and periods of unemployment. All those years they had struggled and somehow managed to meet their mortgage payments. They knew that their current level of income and their creditworthiness were far inferior to the time when they had originally applied for their loan. The loan carried a ten percent interest rate. They were aware that everyone around them had refinanced at six percent interest, give or take one-half percent, but they were certain that their income was not sufficient or steady enough to qualify for a new loan.

Meanwhile, employees at the mortgage company had informally tagged the Smiths' file: "The Smiths haven't refinanced and are still paying ten percent. They must be fools."

Work Sheets

Reasons for refinancing	Amount
1. Extract cash	_____
2. Reduce interest rate	_____
3. Change loan term	_____

Difference in loan principal

Principal of new loan(s)   _____

Principal of old loan(s)   _____

Difference   _____

Difference in loan payment

Payment on new loan(s)   _____

Payment on old loan(s)   _____

Difference   _____

Difference in loan term

Term of new loan(s)   _____

Term of old loan(s)   _____

Difference   _____

Compare:

Difference in principal   _____

Difference in payment   _____

Difference in term   _____

Do the differences make financial sense?

Are they favorable for you?

Chapter 17

Remodeling:
Adding to Your Home

We'll walk you through all the angles of remodeling the right way. But first we have to share the sad tale of what *not* to do.

Paul and Jeannie had a nice house but it was too small for Paul's aging mother. The mother needed wheelchair access and an accessible bathroom, so they decided to expand. At a family wedding, George, a distant cousin in the home building and renovation business, offered them a deal they couldn't refuse. They gave George $75,000 to start the project but neglected to obtain any legal review or **due diligence**. All seemed on the up-and-up at first. George hired an architect and got the required demolition permits to remove part of the roof and siding and pour footings for the expanded structure. Even after Paul and Jeannie paid George the additional funds he requested, everything came to a screeching halt. George quit their job, leaving Paul and Jeannie high but not quite dry—open to the elements. Water and mold moved in.

While George used their money for other jobs, Paul and Jeannie sued and won a judgment—an empty victory, because George couldn't pay. This is as bad as it gets but it illustrates how you have to protect yourself. Let's review some good practices to help you avoid problems.

Creating the Design

You love your house—you've made it your home. You love the neighborhood—it's your home place. But since you bought the house, you've had two sets of twins and one batch of quadruplets and there isn't enough room for all of their things, much less the kids themselves.

That's a pretty wild scenario, we agree, but there are as many reasons for expansion or remodeling of houses as there are people living in those houses. Perhaps you find that the kitchen you agreed to live with ten years ago has reached the drive-you-crazy point. You can add miles to your pedometer walking back and forth and back again in a poorly designed kitchen. Maybe you're tired of staring at a cabinet door over the sink. A window there would be lovely.

Whether you are considering an interior improvement such as a remodeled kitchen, or you are thinking of a very major addition, we offer ideas in this chapter that can make it all a little easier. We want you to have an enjoyable experience with the improvement project itself. We know you are planning to make your life more enjoyable with expanded or renovated space. What you need to recognize is that there is potential for defective construction work due to lack of properly defined work and poorly trained, poorly supervised workers, along with a shortage of skilled craftspeople. To reduce the chances of problems with construction work we need to look again at another one of our famous threes: plan, plan, and plan.

Begin with what you already have and follow up with what you'd like to have. Determine if you need to have shoddy work undone and replaced. If you truly have defects, no amount of cosmetic treatment is going to change them. Be brutally realistic. If you have to rip out to get rid of the bad before you can bask in the wonderful, plan to do that first. Plan each step of your project, step by step. A lot of people want to jump right into the work thinking that the sooner they start, the sooner they'll finish. Something learned by people who get work done right the first time, is that while planning may take what seems like an inordinate amount of time, it's worth it. In some cases, more than 50 percent of the calendar time for a project might go just into the planning phase. The better the quality and detail of planning, and especially contingency planning, the more likely the project will progress smoothly, on time, within budget, and with the desired results.

Plan for your needs. How much would you expect to get out of this house if you were to sell? Just as when you were looking for your home, you want to consider all of your potential needs when it comes time to investing in improvements. Try to think of the overall picture. Develop a plan for near and long-term improvements and renovations. Of course your budget will be restrictive, but by planning for the eventual, you will be better prepared to know that your interim steps will fit. Every property is limited in how much expansion can be done. The overall condition of the basic house may also limit the point at which replacement or major renovation may be more effective, and even more economical than expansion.

Keep your home's location in mind when you plan improvements or additions. Include zoning considerations in your planning. Does the area justify the expense of major remodeling? Understand the marketability of your improved or expanded home. Will a buyer want your beautiful, big house if it is surrounded by smaller, unimproved houses? Some locations, such as ocean front property, have almost limitless potential for resale and do justify the expense. Other areas of starter homes, perhaps, are limited by the entire neighborhood and cannot repay heavy investment in expansion. You may find that the cost of improvements for additional space may not seem to be economically sound in your present location. But it does make sense if you are simply not able to move, or if you plan to remain at this location for a very long time.

Later in this chapter, we discuss local zoning requirements and how you may be able to expand your house, even if the standard zoning rules do not permit an expansion. Understanding potential land use changes is very important because you do not want to increase your investment in an area that may become negatively affected by new zoning. Before you invest your time and money considering design approaches, get a full understanding of what you can do in your specific location. Know what your local real estate market will bear so that your investment will at least retain its value.

Whatever you are doing or plan to do, plan some more for interruptions to your daily routine. Interruptions invariably result from any improvement project. From the smallest bathroom improvement to complete renovation of your entire house, you can expect glitches. Even when you think you are fully in control of a manageable project, be ready for surprises. Contingency planning is not only important; it's essential. You may become the best fixer-upper on the block with all of the equipment and parts needed to tackle a project. Then something breaks when stores are not open or no longer have a supply of that one item you must have.

When you are using contractors, delays normally happen, but every so often a significant interruption could leave you without a kitchen or bathroom for an extended period of time. For more major projects, moving out of the house may be necessary. However, when you live in your home during a renovation you can monitor work more effectively. Just be ready for problems to occur so you won't be unpleasantly surprised.

Create a budget early on, before you even begin to map out the project planning. Know that you will need to adjust your budget often—upward. Somehow costs never seem to go down, so be ready for higher numbers. When you work with design professionals, their initial assessment of budget requirements will not include new ideas that inevitably develop as the project unfolds. Their estimates are based on what you originally said you want. Happily, your design professional may be able to suggest less costly alternative methods or materials that still meet your needs. It is important to encourage developing alternatives right from the start. Consider bracketing a target budget below your absolute not-to-exceed budget. By bracketing, you create three possible approaches at different cost levels, so when "must haves" sneak in, you may be able to adjust your final plan to meet your budget. Remember, as the job progresses, things will undoubtedly come up that will affect your budget. Staying within budget requires regular monitoring and some flexibility. Sometimes, certain items can be taken out of the project before the budget reaches the breaking point and put aside to be done in the future. Identify these items in your early planning stage so you know the lesser result will still work. For example, in a kitchen remodeling project a center island might be postponed for a later time—provided, of course, that the center island does not contain the only stove in the kitchen.

Whether you are using an architect, a contractor, a supplier, or public resource material, plan for alternative design approaches. This will give you peace of mind in that your final design selection is the best choice for you. It can give you budget choices. Some design approaches allow a greater choice of contractors, which could be a distinct benefit at those times when contractors are particularly busy. The differences may be in the look or in the functional aspects of your project. Of course, there are many levels of component costs that could be considered. Sometimes, for example, a kitchen is designed to accommodate that highly desired, but very expensive refrigerator. If you install a smaller, less expensive fridge, you may find you have space for an impressive side-of-refrigerator wine rack. Now you have two design alternatives and a contingency plan should the budget threaten to explode.

You can find stock designs on the Internet, as well as in catalogs and books, with workable approaches to just about everything. Sometimes even design professionals use stock designs as the basis for their creations. Studying these different approaches to design can be an enjoyable rainy-day activity. In the case of any design approach, it is the attention to detail of your actual conditions that determines how likely the selected design will achieve the result you want. Don't leave anything to guesswork or assume that all will be perfect. Assumptions almost always lead to surprises, and sometimes nasty ones.

Local home improvement centers offer excellent design details for kitchen and bathroom projects when you buy the materials from them. These may be particularly attractive for the do-it-yourself, budget-limited home owner. An advantage is that the home improvement center can offer packaged approaches. They may not be the highest quality that custom cabinetmakers can create but they often save money. Since the home improvement center will sell you the specific items needed for the work, you will know exactly what you are getting. Keep in mind that home improvement centers will limit you to buy only what they sell.

Contractor-generated designs offer another route to creating your improvements. However, these often tend to be the least detailed and you may not always know exactly what you are getting. When the project work is not very detailed, the contractor may have to adjust quality levels to maintain the budget as the project progresses.

Architects

Architects are creative design professionals who know how to utilize space in a way that provides aesthetic and functional satisfaction for different lifestyles. They keep current in knowledge of the latest ideas and products so you can be assured of the best combination of materials and technologies. They are also well informed on building codes so you know that your work will meet approval.

An architect will see your space through the filter of how you want to live and can show you exciting ways to utilize or expand your existing house. Some interior renovation projects can benefit enormously from the architect's creativity. Interior designers and interior decorators can bring varying skills to interior improvement projects. There are architects who specialize in interior design and there are those who specialize in exterior landscape design.

When considering different architects, ask about similar projects they have done. The artist in the architect will be revealed as you study her work. Distinct approaches by some architects may or may not appeal to you. You need to be comfortable with your professional's artistic approach and your personal relationship with her. Creative work often involves stretching the boundaries of what you would have previously accepted, so your personal/professional relationship can be as important as artistic compatibility.

It is always helpful for the architect to have direct experience with the local planning board and local building department. The more she knows about how your community works, the better chance that plans will be acceptable to the local officials. This is particularly true when you need variances from the zoning official or variations from the local building department. We'll tackle this later in the chapter.

Prior clients of the architect you are considering can provide a wealth of information, particularly those who had similar projects done within the last three to five years. Look at the work. Learn what surprises the prior clients experienced. Learn how the architect expanded the client's thinking and what the architect provided that was beyond their expectations. Ask about their relationship as the project progressed. Learn about the willingness of the architect to inspect work-in-progress and modify her design as problems developed. Learn about the relationship of the architect with the builder. Ask prior clients what they would have done differently.

A valuable service is to have your architect also be inspector of the work. This ensures that the architect will learn about problems that may need design modifications as the project develops. This will also increase the responsibility of the architect to ensure that the project is completed satisfactorily.

Engineers and Land Surveyors

Engineers are very good at applying science, mathematics, and technology to solving problems and achieving a design objective. On home improvement projects, engineers are often retained or coordinated by the design architect. They may be needed for site work or the design of specific structures or systems. Sometimes the home owner will contract directly with the needed engineers, even when they are coordinated by the architect. For example, a design project may require special structural designs for building elements, such as the roof structure or floor support for which an engineer is retained. Someone needs to coordinate the design professionals to avoid any design conflict. On some projects the engineer is the overall design professional, and on other projects the architect has that honor. In residential work, the architect is usually the overall design professional. Typically, state registration laws provide for an architect to design a home in its entirety and for engineers to design structural and system elements within the home.

Site plans are needed for both new projects and home expansion projects to show how much of the property is to be affected by the expansion and to detail the boundaries of the new or expanded home. These documents are drawn to scale and must incorporate information needed to meet local zoning requirements. This is necessary for the local zoning function to confirm that the work will meet local requirements. A site plan will require information from a property survey that is prepared by a licensed, professional land surveyor. Some professional engineers are also land surveyors.

Soil evaluation may be needed where there is any concern about the strength of soil. Yes, soil has strength characteristics that determine the footprint size of a foundation or if soil reinforcement will be needed. Certain locations, such as hillside and ocean front, require special foundations and may need soil evaluation prior to the engineering design. Engineers who specialize in soil evaluation work are often needed for this analysis. "Soil logs" are borings into the ground that determine the type of soil present at different depths and what groundwater conditions are present. Groundwater elevations vary due to weather conditions and location. It is important to be sure that basement floors are sufficiently above seasonally high groundwater to prevent flooding. Soil logs are also used when septic systems are installed to get the necessary information for the design of the septic system.

Septic systems are designed by engineers and are needed in areas where public sanitary sewers are not available to remove plumbing wastewater. Soil conditions and size of the property will determine which of the various types of septic systems is needed on your property. As the house size changes, particularly with more bedrooms and more bathrooms, the size requirements of a septic system will also change. You may have heard the terms "grey water" and "black water." Grey water is what comes from a washing machine and does not contain human waste. Black water contains human waste products that will need biological treatment in a septic system before the wastewater is filtered back into the earth.

Drainage system design may be needed on certain properties to ensure that roof water and surface water flows away from the foundation. Sometimes a landscaper creates the drainage system. Hillsides and very flat or depressed properties present special challenges in drainage system design. Water of various sources is the largest cause of damage to houses and property. Preventing foundation damage and property erosion are important aspects of the drainage system design. Particularly difficult drainage challenges require engineering attention. Sometimes one or more dry wells are needed. "Dry wells" are large holes or containers in the ground, usually filled with stone, to collect piped drainage water or grey water and dissipate it into the earth at a measured rate similar to the way septic systems dissipate the sewage water.

Foundation work and structural design are jobs commonly done by engineers. An architect may be qualified to do this work as part of residential design, but in more challenging situations you will probably want an engineer to perform the analysis and design.

Other systems often designed by engineers are electrical systems, plumbing systems, fire-suppression systems, and heating, ventilating, and air conditioning systems (HVAC). Licensed contractors are often qualified to perform these designs but engineers are called upon to provide the design in more challenging situations, or when technical issues exist, or assurance is needed that a thorough analysis had been done. Larger contractors usually have engineers on staff.

General Contractors

The **general contractor** is the concert leader of all of the work that needs to be done to complete a project. Estimating, planning, purchasing, coordinating, supervising, and problem solving are just some of the jobs done by a general contractor or through direct employees. General contractors usually have core skills developed through education and experience. General contractors range in size from single-person firms to large organizations that have construction planning, estimating, and project-management staff. Individual and larger firms often have architectural or engineering expertise.

Keeping their direct employees working is a business demand so that contractors can meet their payroll. Depending upon the workload of the general contractor, keeping employees fully employed may mean that they are working in areas outside of their strengths. For the additional workers needed, general contractors subcontract or hire temporary people. Often, specific skills are subcontracted to firms specializing in those skills. We will outline a few of these specific skill contractors in this chapter. Pick-up labor is very common in the construction industry and sometimes poorly trained people are used above their skill level. As you evaluate general contractors, consider their organization and unique core skills. Ask how they do things.

Project experience is very important for general contractors because they are the super-coordinators of a wide variety of details. Your specific project may need a general contractor with specialized experience. For example, when house-lifting is needed, it is good to have a general contractor who has managed projects that included house-lifting. Pile foundations present another situation where you need specific experience. When architectural design details are minimal or when no architect is being used, be sure that the contractor has the design experience and expertise necessary for your project.

Favorable interaction between the architect and general contractor is a key factor in achieving good results. If they have worked well together in the past, so much the better. Architects are artistic people who may not dot every "i" and cross every "t," while contractors have their preferred way of doing things. Herein lays the potential for conflict. When contractors and architects have prior experience working together, learn how they work out their differences. Be sure to interview prior joint clients.

Specific Skill Contractors

You may be surprised at the number of different skills involved in building, whether it is in new building or renovation. General contractors often hire specific-skill **subcontractors** in various fields, many of which do not require licensed skilled workers. Even when licensed people are used they may be supervising many lesser-skilled and unlicensed workers. However, electrical and plumbing work is another story. In the old days, apprentices had to serve long periods of time—perhaps up to four years or more—in learning their trades to qualify as full electricians or plumbers. Today, electricians and plumbers qualify in much less time but still must undergo intensive training and testing before they are licensed. Typically, licensed electrical contractors perform only electrical work. Similarly, licensed plumbing contractors do only plumbing and hydronic heating work.

Masons are skilled craftspeople who work with concrete, concrete block, stone, brick, and mortar. Foundations are frequently constructed using concrete for footings and hollow-block concrete masonry walls. Some building components are crafted with concrete and block masonry. Brick may be used as structural building components or as cladding for the building envelope.

Mortar is a cementitious material that is used to bind the block masonry, whether concrete or brick. The quality of concrete and masonry components will vary, as will the quality of the work itself, in creating and applying the mortar. Some block walls require steel reinforcement and grouting to fill the cavities with a mortar-like cementitious material. The masonry contractor will be one of the first contractors on the job because everything starts with a foundation. Some masonry contractors are also general contractors.

Framers and carpenters do the actual construction or erecting of wood framing. If much steel is used, ironworkers may be needed, but most houses today are largely constructed of wood. Framers also erect engineered wood and factory-made structural wood components, such as trusses. Like masons, many framing contractors also become general contractors.

Wallboard installation and taping of the joints is anther specialty. Taping may even be done by a separate contractor, as this is a particular skill that makes a difference in how well the wall looks after the joints are covered. Gypsum wall board, often called by the brand name Sheetrock®, is meant to look like plaster with no visible seams. Taping hides these seams. The small amount of real plastering that is done today requires a special masonry skill. Some framing contractors will try to do some or all of this work.

Floor installation is another job that is typically subcontracted to firms that specialize in wood or firms that specialize in tile, depending on the flooring to be installed. Tile firms usually do walls also, such as in the bathroom.

Additional subcontractor categories include heating and air conditioning, kitchen design, audio-visual entertainment, painting, wallpapering, landscape design and installation, driveway and pavement, and garage doors.

Handypersons

Handyperson firms are increasing in popularity, particularly for two-income families and those who are home-repair challenged. These firms do all sorts of home repair and small jobs, from changing light bulbs to repairing damaged walls, replacing components such as toilets and electrical outlets, and performing small improvement projects. They do ordinary maintenance as well as minor work. Ordinary maintenance does not need a building permit, as will be discussed in the building permit section of this chapter. Handypersons may be individuals or firms with employees of widely diverse backgrounds. The individuals will have a core skill and be generally knowledgeable about a lot of specialties. Some of these individuals learned their skills as part of a maintenance operation in a large business. Others came from the construction trades. In some states there is a requirement for all home improvement and repair people to have a license in order to obtain building permits. These licenses are more for control of the business than a license for technical expertise, as is the case with an electrician or plumber. Some handypersons also have specific skill licenses, such as electrician or plumber, that expand the value they can bring to solving your problems and implementing your improvement projects.

Contracts

Often, home owners sign off on a contractor's proposal that may be perfectly adequate. More likely than not, however, such an agreement may be sorely lacking in sufficient detail to ensure that everyone knows what to expect. The primary purpose of a contract is to protect your investment. You have to know what duties the contractor agrees to and what she is purchasing for the job. Contracts provide a basis for legal help if the job done is less than what you were promised. While you could have an oral contractual agreement, it is best to have a written contract prepared by, or at least reviewed by, an attorney. The better job you do in creating a solid contract, even when you know you are dealing with an honest contractor, the greater chance you will have of satisfactory results without any need for legal recourse. Contracts can range from a one-page document to the size of a book. We will outline important features of home improvement contracts for you to consider. Not every job will require all of these provisions, of course.

Start and end dates are essential in every contract. You will want to know the time period for performance of the work. Your agreement may provide incentives for improved performance and penalties for delayed performance.

Communication provisions are important to determine how and where buyer and seller can communicate formal announcements about provisions of the contract. E-mail is being used more often and effectively because it provides a record trail. Some contracts may also require regular mail communication, certainly in the case of termination notice, which would require Certified Mail.

Insurance on the part of the contractor for liability and workers' compensation is absolutely necessary and on some jobs, bonding may also be required. Be sure that there is a requirement for any subcontractor to also have adequate insurance. You may want to specify that certificates of insurance be provided before any work is started. Many contractors today utilize pick-up laborers who may not be paid through the contractor's regular payroll, and not subject to workers' compensation insurance premiums. In such cases, be sure that all—and we mean *all*—of the contractor's workers are protected by the contractor's insurance. You do not need a lawsuit because someone is injured on your job. You may need to consult with your home-owner's insurance company to know that the contractor has adequate protection for problems not covered by your own insurance.

Building permits are necessary for almost any work beyond ordinary maintenance. If you have any doubts, consult with your local building department. Remember that you, as the home owner, have final responsibility for obtaining any necessary building permits. Failure to obtain permits can result in substantial fines. Your contract should clearly define who will be responsible for obtaining and paying for the necessary building permits. We suggest that you designate the contractor responsible for obtaining the permit, but at your expense.

Site access restrictions may be necessary for the contractor and even for the home owner under certain circumstances. Safety and security are often the two main reasons why any site access restrictions may be needed. If you are living in your home during the renovations, you may want to define acceptable work hours. Some communities have restrictions about working hours. Check with your local building department.

Defining the work to be done is critical. The more completely the work is defined, the more likely you will get what you're paying for. Design details may require extensive drawings created by an architect, engineer, or designer, depending upon the type of work. It's like cooking. Only when the recipe lists all of the ingredients along with the sequence and methods of preparation, can you expect to create a good dish. Specifications detail a sequence and or method of work necessary to get consistent results. For example, a design detail may call for a concrete slab where the specifications detail a specific quality of concrete, with strength expressed in pounds per square inch that meets the national standard for its preparation. Standards of work quality should be included in the work definition. For example, the American Society for Testing and Materials (ASTM) is now an international organization that creates standards for materials, products, systems, and services. ASTM has a Standard Practice for Installation of Exterior Windows, Door, and Skylights E2112-01. This rather lengthy document may be specified by reference in your design documents. Incorporation of this level of detail, when fully understood by all parties, helps to ensure a superior job that can be independently evaluated by third-party inspection.

Building code and local ordinance requirements may be specifically referenced, or just the requirement noted that the contractor agrees to comply with all such requirements. This includes obtaining all necessary code enforcement inspections.

Owners who want someone other than the architect to inspect various aspects of the work may schedule third-party inspections in addition to whatever inspections the local building department requires. This provision is common with specialty work, such as steel erection and exterior insulating and finish system (EIFS) siding applications.

A stop-work provision should be included if your job warrants granting your architect or a third-party inspector the right to stop work when certain defects are observed. This requires careful agreements and commitments among all affected parties so as to not impose undue interruption hardship on the contractor.

A schedule or sequence of major activity is very important on larger jobs to help everyone know what is expected, and when. It provides a closer level of detail than just a finish date. Project delays that become evident early on may warrant the need for creative thinking to keep the overall job on schedule. Project review milestones should be included if you, as the owner, want project status updates or reviews at specified work completion points in time.

A specific provision in the contract may be required to ensure the level of on-site supervision. Only the largest of jobs will have a supervisor always present. But various trades may need the contract to specify that an experienced supervisor be present while that particular work is being done. Remember that most work defects result from using poorly supervised, poorly trained workers.

Coordination of owner-provided or owner-managed work must be detailed to avoid finger pointing when you, as the owner, have taken on some work responsibilities during the project. It goes without saying—we guarantee—that if your involvement can delay the job, it will. You'll become an excuse for job delay. Corrective action plans should be considered in case there is work interruption. While unusual circumstances, such as violent weather, are easily understood as a cause of work interruption, additional acceptable causes should be thought through and clearly defined to avoid misunderstandings about time schedule performance.

Change orders are typical on larger and more complex jobs. How are they to be handled? The more you define in advance, the easier it will be to have agreement and avoid disputes. Erasers exist on pencils for good reason. And, boy oh boy, they are often needed because of errors or due to an urgent desire by you or your architect for a previously unforeseen change. One potential problem with creative people is that they never stop creating. As your job progresses you and your design team are bound to come up with some really good ideas. Will you accept some potential job interruption and higher costs by adopting the new idea through a change order or will you stick to your original plan? Unless your pockets are very deep, you may have to stick to the original plan.

Possible damage to the existing house and property, or damage to items within the house, should be covered by a contractual provision so that you'll have a mechanism for insurance or other recovery. Photo documentation of the existing house and property will be helpful to document that the damage had not previously existed.

A payment schedule with a hold-back is important, particularly a significant hold-back that will not be paid until *all* work is complete and *all* building permits have been satisfactorily closed out by the local code enforcement authorities. Hold-backs of 10–20 percent are common.

Guaranties and warranties, as applicable, are additional contractual provisions. Manufacturer warranties usually require that a manufacturer's representative reviews the work definition and inspects the work. This is particularly important with roofing and any weatherization protection warranties. Often a contractor will show you the literature that states there is a warranty, but until you read the manufacturer's fine print, you will not know what requirements must be met for the warranty to be applicable. Try to obtain a manufacturer's certified warranty for materials used and equipment installed on your specific project. You may want to consider paying the additional cost for labor and material warranties. You may need a special inspection to ensure that the manufacturer's installation instructions were followed.

Residential Construction Performance Guidelines for Professional Builders & Remodelers, published by the National Association of Home Builders, is a peer-reviewed publication that will give you a reasonable set of performance guidelines. You may want to make this part of your contract. Better builders and contractors will have already incorporated these performance guidelines into their standard contract. This publication can be obtained at *www.BuilderBooks.com*.

Violations of the contract may require stipulating a disputes-resolution provision. Get legal advice as to what approach is best for you should there be a dispute. Here again, we go back to our old refrain: Only a lawyer can give you legal advice. If anything is iffy, call your legal eagle.

Project Management

Just as you assembled a team of people to help find your home, project management applies to any improvement or expansion of your house. However, even if you have a project manager, you will need to exercise some oversight functions yourself to make sure you get what you want and are paying for. Sometimes an architect is commissioned to create the design and manage the entire project. In other situations the architect and the general contractor will jointly manage most, if not all, of the skilled workers. The larger the project, the greater number of different skilled people will be necessary. When specialists are used you may see both an improvement in work quality and performance. For example, a framing contractor may construct a staircase, or you may retain a stair specialist. If you have been careful and are satisfied that your project manager is the best you can afford, follow her advice. There are times when you have to go with your feelings of trust.

Avoid the bad and find the good. Easy to say, but again, it has to be a trust issue. As you build your trusted project team you will want to have mechanisms in place that help everyone reduce chances for error. The best problem solution is to avoid the problem in the first place. Spending more time in quality planning and problem avoidance will pay great dividends. So will recognition of good work. As work progresses, a word from you about good work will go a long way. It helps motivate your workers and facilitates progress documentation. As President John F. Kennedy said, "Management is getting better than average results from average people." As owner, you are the ultimate manager of all work done at your house.

Team leadership starts with setting sound goals and building relationships. Be aware that even relatives and friends can take advantage of each other. It is wonderful when you have established a good relationship with the people who are doing your work. As always, we encourage you to do your homework whenever you hire different types of talent. Your cousin Louie may be the perfect choice. But, then again, a total stranger may also be the perfect choice. Because nothing is sure but death and taxes, the quality of your selection homework will not be known until the job is completed. Problems will occur. Even the most perfect team may not always produce a perfect product. Your management challenge is to be sure to monitor activity, anticipate problems, and make adjustments before accidents happen. It's like driving a car. You want to keep within the lane lines and away from other vehicles and obstructions. If the car veers off the road, you have to steer it back into a good path. A strong interpersonal relationship with your team helps everyone remain alert, keep to the plan, and avoid failure. You do not need to be best friends, but a positive rapport will get you attention when needed.

When an owner decides not to retain a general contractor and to hire all the individual contractors herself, that owner takes on all of the project management duties and responsibilities of a general contractor. And, as we also discussed, there is potential for conflict when there is owner-provided or owner-managed work in addition to what is being managed by the general contractor. Coordination of owner-provided or owner-managed work is particularly tricky. Unless the design documents are unusually detailed, judgment by one trade may not be what another trade needs. The framer's approach to stud and joist location may not be what the plumber would like. For example, if you are making an addition to your home using one contractor, but you are going to do the bathrooms yourself, you are setting the stage for conflict. You are bound to run into scheduling and misalignment problems. When you are coordinating different contractors, you need to fully understand the work and needs of each contractor so that you can be sure all interfaces are acceptable to both. There is also the timing of work by each contractor. For example, electrical and plumbing work gets roughed in before the walls are completed, but isn't finished until after the walls are completed.

A project looseleaf book similar to your house-search book that we previously described can save the day. Section titles may include Design, Agreements, Project Plans, Budget and Payments, Building Permits, Work Log, Photo Log, Quotations, Installation Documents, and Reference Materials. Whew! Not all of this material will fit into one looseleaf book. Some of it may not fit into any book. These sections are starting topics. You may want to have subcategories or add additional topics, particularly if you are coordinating some or all of the work yourself. If you cannot organize your material into one book, at least create an index of all items with notations as to where you are keeping materials not held in your project book.

Maintaining a work log may just be your most valuable project management tool after you have established a good plan with detailed design documents. It provides a discipline for monitoring work progress. Hopefully, you will have selected competent design professionals and contractors. Maintaining a good log will help you to evaluate progress against your plan and provide documentation, should any dispute arise at a later date. A hardbound or spiral-bound book of blank, lined pages is best as it ensures maintenance of sequential order in your notetaking. Every important event should be recorded. How much you write will determine if you want to start a new page for every day's notes. Date all of your entries. When more than one entry is expected on a single day, note the times of each entry. You may not need daily entries but you will want to ensure that all reasonable progress is recorded. Record the positive and the negative.

Keep records of the weather. Whenever you have a discussion with your team, make notes.

Photo documentation is a very valuable tool for a complete record of your project as it progresses. It is one of the best means for evaluating problems at a later date. It's a good idea to have a complete photo documentation of the existing house and any particular features that will be changed prior to starting the project. Try to have some order with your photo-taking. Exterior shots should include one photo for each side of the house and close-ups of important new details. For example, exterior shots may include foundation, framing, siding and roof sheathing, flashing systems, roof covering, window and door installation, building paper, siding, and trim work. Interior shots should also be done in a consistent order, such as basement level, first floor, etc., starting at the entrance side of the house and working around in the same way. Be sure that all photos are date-stamped.

Modern digital cameras make this work very easy. If you use a digital camera, however, try not to take too many pictures at once or you'll be asking for trouble in maintaining your files. When you use digital, create a file folder on your computer for this project's photos. Each day that you take photos, file those pictures in a file folder within your project folder. Consider naming each day's photo files with that date. Remember to have your camera date and time function operating so the photos themselves will be dated. For each day's photo work print out a proof sheet with the file number and date listed on the proof sheet. Keep these proof sheets in your project looseleaf book. A daily index for photos taken with notes about any unique observation can become invaluable for future reference. Videos can be helpful too if you want to get a series of views at one point in time. With videos, try to maintain gentle and smooth motion as you create your documentary.

There is an old saying: You get what you inspect. This is very important in any line of work. Once you have crafted a plan for doing work, you will need a plan for inspecting that work. Even more important, you will need a plan to ensure quality. This is more than just inspecting. Quality assurance starts with the idea for your project and includes all activities from design through completion of the work and setting up maintenance programs. Quality assurance means making sure all communication is complete and documented to ensure crisp definition of what is to be done by whom, as well as confirmation that the work was completed satisfactorily. Furthermore, quality assurance requires that you have provisions in place in case you have to deviate from your original plan. Auditing the activity of every player on your project is integral to a quality plan. Your work log will help you maintain records. You will be the quality assurance manager for your project even if you have architects and general contractors. No one has a more vested interest in quality than you. Giving quality prime attention, right from the start, sets the tone for quality throughout your project. Inspections are just a part of quality. Planning for quality is your most important work. You may have the architect perform inspections, and certainly the local building department will perform inspections, but that will not be enough. Documenting what is to be done, monitoring the work, and having corrective action contingency plans in place if work deviates from the plan, are all part of your quality assurance program.

Building Permits

Local ordinance or state law determines when building permits are required and what codes and regulations apply to the work being done. It is best to assume that a building permit may be required. Check with your local building department before starting any work project. Typically, a national model code is adopted with some modifications for use by local code enforcement agencies. These model codes are organized by areas of work such as building, electrical, plumbing, mechanical, fire, energy, etc. The International Code Council at *www.iccsafe.org* is one of the model code organizations. Ordinary maintenance items included in this discussion are based on New Jersey requirements. Ordinary maintenance generally does not require a building permit. Painting or wall papering is ordinary maintenance, but paneling the walls generally requires a building permit. Why do we single out paneling? Because material used to make the paneling may be a fire hazard.

To expand upon what may be included in "ordinary maintenance" we will outline each job for each category of codes.

- Building ordinary maintenance typically includes exterior and interior painting, vinyl wall covering, wall papering, repair or replacement of interior finishes that are less than 25 percent of the wall area, replacement of glass in windows or doors, installation or entire replacement of windows and doors with some limitations, repair or replacement of non-structural members including kitchen cabinets, repair or replacement of flooring, repair or replacement of roofing not exceeding 25 percent within any 12-month period, repair or replacement of existing siding with like material not exceeding 25 percent within any 12-month period, repair or replacement of any part of a porch that does not structurally support a roof, replacement or installation of screens, installation of insulation adjacent to an exterior finish, and replacement of rain water gutters and leaders.

- Plumbing ordinary maintenance typically includes replacement of hose bib valves, refinishing of existing fixtures, replacement of ball cocks, repair of leaks involving the replacement of piping between two adjacent joints only, clearance of stoppages, replacement of faucets or working parts of faucets, replacement of valves and working parts of valves, replacement of traps, replacement of a water closet, lavatory, bathtub, shower, kitchen sink, and replacement of clothes washers and dryers.

- Electrical ordinary maintenance typically includes replacement with a like or similar item of any receptacle, switch, or lighting fixture rated at 20 amps or less and operating at less than 150 volts. Repairs to installed, electrically operated equipment are considered ordinary maintenance, as are installation of communications wiring and replacement of dishwashers and kitchen range hoods.

- Fire protection ordinary maintenance typically includes replacement of any sprinkler, smoke detector, or heat detector with a similar device, repair or replacement of any component of fire alarm or smoke and heat detection equipment, installation of battery-powered smoke detectors, and installation of battery-powered or plug-in carbon monoxide alarms.

- Heating, ventilating, and air conditioning ordinary maintenance typically includes replacement of motors, pumps, and fans of same capacity, repair and replacement of heating supply and return piping and radiation elements, repair and replacement of duct work, repair of air conditioning equipment and systems, repair or replacement of control devices for heating and air conditioning equipment, and replacement of kitchen range hoods and replacement of clothes dryers, providing that no change is required in fuel type, location, or electrical characteristics.

It is the ultimate responsibility of the home owner to ensure that building permits are obtained because local enforcement people have the ability to issue violations to local residents. As we discussed in our section on contracts in this chapter, you will want to make obtaining the necessary building permits a contractual responsibility of your contractor(s).

Sometimes, particularly with older homes, it is not practical to have to adhere strictly to the current code. Fortunately, there are provisions in the model codes to permit **variations**. Any variations need to be documented in local building department records. Typically, an alternative approach is worked out between the architect or contractor and the local construction official.

Inspections are key components of building permits. Some work necessitates that code officials perform a prejob inspection. When permits are obtained, it is important to provide correct information. For example, after there have been two roof coverings, all covering must be completely removed to permit inspection of the sheathing. It is important that the roofing contractor stipulate on her building permit application that there are two roof coverings and not just one. If you have any questions about what is needed for the permit, go to your local building department and talk with the appropriate subcode official. There are subcode officials for each category of building permit: building, electrical, plumbing, mechanical, and fire.

Violations may be issued by code officials if they find work that does not conform to code requirements. It is important that your contractor corrects any problem in a timely manner. Fines can be imposed, and as the home owner, you will be responsible. There is an appeal process but most of the time this can be avoided by good, positive, ongoing communication with your local code officials.

Evidence of completion of the building permit is essential before you make a final payment to your contractor. A certificate of occupancy or similar certificate is issued after all inspections have been satisfactorily completed. You must have this prior to making your final payment. Keep this document with your ownership papers to verify compliance with construction regulations.

Zoning

Zoning or land-use ordinances are local regulations governing the use of land within a municipality or county. Typically, a zoning authority will map a community to designate areas where residential, commercial, and industrial types of use are permitted. Zoning can be used to encourage the type of development desired by the local community. The minimum amount of property needed for certain uses and specific restrictions, such as property line setbacks, are included within the regulations. Even fully residential areas may have varying restrictions on the type and size of houses permitted. Multi-family housing or condo-style developments may or may not be allowed in certain locations. Approved sites for affordable housing are also defined in the regulations. Types of uses permitted are also defined. For example, an in-home professional office may or may not be permitted.

Zoning regulations vary from municipality to municipality and may not even exist in certain communities. Sometimes there are larger areas of planning regulations to which local municipalities must conform in the development of local regulations. Older existing uses will generally be grandfathered, but may be restricted when modifications are sought. Because these regulations are subject to local control, changes in local political structure and in the attitudes of voters may bring changes. Zoning can be restrictive and can be abused. It is helpful to have a general understanding of your existing local zoning regulations and what changes are being considered.

It is also important to learn if there are master plans in existence or contemplated that will affect your community and your personal interests. Master plans guide future development of regulations concerning the use of land. Fully developed communities have little to change unless there are massive eminent domain condemnations where the local government takes over property for a "better use." In areas where there has been relatively little development, there will be greater chances for the changes in zoning regulations.

Try to get a feel for local preferences and biases. Read the local newspaper. Local papers often have a reporter assigned to monitor the planning or zoning board. This is the body that oversees implementation of local land-use ordinances. A copy of their regulations should be available at your municipal building, usually for a charge. You may want only those pages that apply to your property. Whether you plan to purchase property or to expand your existing property, it's wise to become informed about local preferences and biases.

Variances are approved deviations from the local regulations. For example, if your property requires a 25-foot side (8 meters) yard setback, you cannot build closer than 25 feet (8 meters) to the side property line without a variance. When you live in a neighborhood where most people are only 15 feet (5 meters) from their side property line, the chances may be good that you will be awarded a variance so that you may then expand the size of your house. Before anything gets off the ground—literally and figuratively—your application will be reviewed at a public hearing. Generally, all people within, say, 250 feet (76 meters) of your property line must be notified about your application so they have the opportunity to object at the public hearing. It would be a good idea to investigate the ease of obtaining variances before submitting your application. You may need a lawyer at your side. You may also need documents prepared by a professional land surveyor, engineer, or architect as part of your application.

Home-Buyer's Checklist

- Will the marketplace accommodate the higher value of remodeling or creating an addition? Have I sought and received the best advice from a design professional?

- Have I performed reference checks?

- Do I have complete and detailed design documents?

- Have contracts and building permits been completed?

- Do I need a general contractor or am I willing and able to take on the management of the project?

Chapter 18

Vacation Home

No more horror stories. The tale of Theresa and Myles is a happy story. They loved city life, but they also loved skiing, and golf, hiking, and swimming. When they felt ready for a getaway retreat they did everything right.

Armed with a preview of our book, they went about developing a plan. They joined investment clubs and subscribed to local papers in the areas that most appealed to them. They lined up real estate professionals. They went on virtual tours via the Internet without leaving their city living room. When they visited prospective sites it was as if they had already been there. In the words of the immortal Yogi Berra: "deja vu all over again."

Theresa and Myles were able to narrow down the possibilities to those that offered the most, and then finally to one that boasted mountain trails, a four-star golf course, Olympic pool, and shopping! They found they could buy everything right in one lovely getaway village and even dine out.

Theresa and Myles had already done the do-it-yourself route when they did their homework. Now they hired professionals to facilitate due diligence and closing details. Everything went as smoothly as silk. They love their Shangri-la and don't even need a car because they can train from the city to heaven-on-earth when the calendar says "TGIF."

Workaday problems and stresses make us all wish for that magic carpet to take us to our private Shangri-la. A second house may be more in the realm of probability than you might think, if you consider renting it out part-time. It might not be a handy little money machine, but part-time rental can offset some of the expense of your getaway hideaway. Of course, it may also create a drain on the budget. Whatever your purpose in expanding your real estate holdings, we'll try to give you guidance on what you have to know and do.

Welcome to the good life. If you live in the city, do you want to retreat to a country home? Do you want to escape to the shore, to the ski slopes, or to a golfer's paradise? Or are you looking for an investment property? Many of the considerations we discussed in buying your primary residence also apply to buying a second home or investment property. But there are major tax differences you'll want to make sure your accountant has reviewed thoroughly. Obtaining mortgage money, for instance, is different from financing a primary residence. There may well be other considerations to think about depending on the type of house you buy and how it is to be used. Of particular importance is maintenance. Who will take care of things, big or small, when you aren't around? This becomes more complicated when you rent out the property.

We will not repeat information from earlier chapters so you may wish to review those chapters that apply to a second home. If you are considering a condo purchase as a second home, for instance, then certainly review Chapter 8.

Type of Home

Let's first discuss a second home that only you and your family will be using. The second home provides a permanent vacation location without having to rent hotel space. You can maintain clothing and recreational equipment at your second home, lessening the load when traveling from your main residence to your hideaway.

Later, we will discuss the house you may rent, either part-time or full-time. Chapter 19 will focus on investment property, which is a horse of a different color. An investment property is a business that should make money for you. Often people make money with the eventual sale of their primary home, but second homes may be more of a lifestyle expense rather than an investment. While the second-home lifestyle is not available to everyone because of the expenses involved, don't give up trying to make it succeed as an investment. Study the market and buy smart, following the advice we rendered earlier in this book.

Will your second home be a year-round house or just seasonal? A summer cottage may lack heat and have only an outdoor shower. A ski hut or log cabin may have only a fireplace for heat. Out buildings may be used for toilets, with a hand pump for well water in more rugged areas. Rooms may be organized for group living with little individual privacy. There are tent homes where a platform is used to erect the tent, with a small structure for plumbing facilities and kitchen appliances. Other vacation homes can be fully appointed and fully insulated primary residences, with individual rooms having heat and air conditioning for year-round use.

Condos and mobile or manufactured homes as a second home are growing in popularity. Resorts often have condo-type residences in the area or within the resort itself. All forms of recreation and lifestyle invite potential owners to second-home living. Opportunities for fun and relaxation are endless—golf, boating, hunting, skiing, ocean front, lake front, mountain side, or open-range living. Any one or all may lure you to invest in a second home. Some resort areas have even developed all-year activities. Whatever your primary interests are, a second home can provide an escape from daily life or a retreat for creative rejuvenation.

Renting out your second home, part of the time, is one way to offset the expenses. Of course when you rent, you expose your home to increased wear and potential damage. But if you plan ahead and know what you're doing, you can have it both ways. We will discuss how to handle and manage rental property but first we'll talk about how to buy that property.

Investment Clubs

Local real estate investment clubs provide marvelous opportunities to network with investors, and vendors of services to investors, in the areas you are considering. This can be a good way to learn about market conditions and benefit from the experience of others in the areas where you want to invest. Even if there is no other direct benefit from your participation, time spent at club functions may help crystallize your thinking. While these groups are generally more geared to investment owners, as contrasted to owners of nonrenting vacation or second homes, they may provide you with some added insight into market conditions and opportunities. Sometimes, just the networking alone can be invaluable in your search for property.

One source for locating a real estate investment club in your area is *www.REIClub.com*. At the time of this writing, there were more than 250 clubs listed plus additional resources linked from the REI Club site. Many of the listed clubs have their own web sites for additional information. Surfing these club sites can be time well spent, and the surf is always up on the Web! Some of the groups have subgroups that meet to discuss specific topics, such as property management or creative financing. While you have to accept the fact that many of the people participating in these clubs are there to sell their products, you might actually find that beneficial. It can, in fact, be a big plus. After you have accumulated investment property you may want to research tax deferral, utilizing the 1031 Exchange provision of the tax codes.

Partner Purchases

Unlike a marriage for life, business partnerships should begin with a clear understanding of the provisions for separation. If ever there were a screaming demand for a prenuptial agreement, this is it. Legal advice is a wise investment when you are considering creating a partnership for purchase of real estate. Here we go again—only a lawyer can give you dependable legal advice. While it may be easy to say you want to dissolve a partnership, getting someone to buy the property may be more difficult. Your partnership agreement may need to address other options besides just selling the property. Keep in mind that when relationships sour, interest in performing necessary maintenance and other functions diminishes, and this can seriously affect the value of your investment. Of course, life could be altered by an accident or natural causes that can impact on the health or life of one of the partners. Insurance for such unforeseen situations may be a necessary business expense to permit the remaining partner(s) or heirs to carry on without interruption.

Such possibilities notwithstanding, partnership purchases can be a great way to combine financial strength. Sometimes one or more of the partners will have particular skills in managing and maintaining the investment. Partnership purchases need a "marriage" agreement with provisions for the "divorce" clearly spelled out. Back to that prenup! Investments are not made for life, so having an exit strategy is one of the first and most important provisions of any agreement. Do not go forward with only a handshake. You will need a lawyer. Exit strategies involve not only how to dissolve the partnership, but also what decision criteria will apply to managing the property, investing more into the property, and determining when to sell it.

Location

Even if you think you are sufficiently knowledgeable about any area, there's nothing like on-the-spot experience. Try a vacation in the location you are considering. You'll never know until you have actually been there, even for a short time. It's amazing what you can pick up in just a few days. Get to know your potential neighbors. And read the local paper, just as you did when you researched your primary residence. Not only will you learn what's going on politically and commercially, but you'll also glean the flavor of the local life. Review the ideas in Chapter 9 on how to obtain local knowledge. It's well worth a second read.

For investment and rental property, especially when you will be directly handling the leasing and maintenance, it's a good idea to keep to property close to your primary home or in areas to which you have easy access.

Special evaluation needs will depend upon the unique nature of the property, especially when it is ocean front, hillside, or a building that had been modified or converted from a different use. Here again, local papers can be invaluable.

Pre-purchase Inspections

Part-time vacation homes have not always been constructed to modern standards or they may be located where there were few building codes or little building-code enforcement. A country house that stood the test of time may in fact be more durable than modern construction, but without the pedigree of having been constructed to modern building codes. Energy efficiency is a major difference with newer homes.

Just as you did when purchasing your main home, arrange for a pre-purchase inspection. This is more than very important because you won't always be there. Review Chapter 11 on home inspections. Remember to follow your own inspection checklist as you learn what you need to know about the house. But keep in mind that one main difference in an inspection of a second home or investment property—you won't always be on hand. Establish a prioritized maintenance program as part of your inspection. We cannot emphasize enough that you will not be at this house for much of the time. Awareness of maintenance issues may not become apparent until damage has already been done due to delay in correcting a problem. Because of this, it is definitely in your best interest to have your inspection performed by a professional engineer or architect who specializes in home inspections. They are educated and experienced problem solvers with a critical eye focused to observe subtle issues. Their experience is your best investment. A good source for this help is the National Academy of Building Inspection Engineers at *www.nabie.org*.

When you contract for your home inspection, be sure to include the requirement that you have a preventative-maintenance priority program. Ideally, you would like to purchase a low-maintenance house versus a high-maintenance house. But just as with any romance, low maintenance is not always what people get, even when that is what they want. Houses more vulnerable to moisture intrusion are higher maintenance than houses less vulnerable. For example, houses in a flood zone or on property with poor drainage need close monitoring after flood or heavy rain conditions. Your home-inspection engineer can identify actions you can take to reduce your vulnerability. Also, your inspector has to understand your use of the house so he can advise you on appropriate preventative maintenance. Houses exposed to unusual adverse conditions, such as periodic flooding, may have hidden damage or damage that has been covered up. Just because the already or frequently wetted house structure is still standing does not mean that it has a predictable remaining life span. An experienced critical eye is necessary to evaluate your additional investment. This is especially important when you will not be present much of the time to discover any subtle conditions.

In-Season Care

In-season care assumes that you will be using the home and will be there to perform most, if not all, of your maintenance checks. This is also the time to have any contractor work done as long as it will not prevent your comfortable use of the house. Different maintenance needs depend upon the location of the house. Start by developing a list of basic contractors whom you can call upon for routine or emergency maintenance. Electrician, plumber, and a heating and air conditioning technician are your starting contractor team. These people may not be needed until there is an emergency, but if you have not prearranged for their services, you may have difficulty getting help. Have that first team ready to take the field so that they'll be there when you need them.

Your home inspector or real estate salesperson are excellent sources for recommendations. Your local hardware store is another source for referrals. Your repair people are their customers. It can help to review Chapter 15 on setting up the home and maintenance planning. Consider having each of your selected contractors perform a paid inspection and create their recommended list of regular maintenance checks. This way, there will be no unpleasant surprises when the contractor is needed. Their understanding of the projected life of fixtures and appliances will help to determine specific maintenance needs. That old adage, "An ounce of prevention is worth a pound of cure," says a mouthful about maintaining a house that is not always occupied. Chances are you will probably not have a clue that anything is going wrong until there is failure. The extra investment for obtaining professional advice about your maintenance needs is part of that ounce of prevention. Preventative maintenance is the best policy for minimizing serious problems.

Off-Season Care

Off-season care includes essential maintenance during the long periods when you will not be using the house. This is especially important if you do not fully shut down all utilities and preserve the house for long-term storage. The need for scheduled checking and storm-related inspections never lets up, even when you put the house in mothballs for long-term storage with all utilities shut off. There is still potential for moisture intrusion due to material failure or storm damage from rain or flooding. That's easy to see. The insidious damage caused by condensation is another thing entirely. Condensation is like a fog that develops when warm air comes upon a cold surface that has a temperature below the dew point. Think of what happens when you breathe onto glass—the moisture that momentarily forms on the glass is condensation. Condensation problems most often occur in poorly ventilated spaces such as attics and crawl spaces, and can lead to mold formation. It can happen any time of the year in all climates, but is most prevalent when there are significant temperature differentials between inside and outside temperature and where there is inadequate ventilation.

When you preserve the house for long-term storage you will shut off all utilities including water, gas, and electricity. For the greatest protection, these shut-offs should be done by the utility companies. However, this can be a great inconvenience as it requires coordinating with the utility company, not only the shut-off, but also the start-up. Problems can arise because it is often easier to get the utility shut off than it is to get it restarted when you need it. The next best procedure is to shut off the service within your house, but in some cases this may not be adequate.

For example, it won't be adequate for water lines in an area where it freezes. You need the water line to be shut off at a location where it does not freeze. This means a shut-off below grade that may be three feet or deeper depending upon the local frost depth below which the ground does not freeze. Even if you have a basement, it could freeze when the heat is turned off. What you have to think about is what happens if there were to be a failure of the service up to the point where you shut it off. What would be the potential damage? If the potential damage is small, then it may not be a big concern.

Shutting off all electricity at the main disconnect—generally within five feet of where the electrical power enters the house—probably presents a low potential for concern. Keep in mind, though, that when you shut off your electricity, you have no power to operate any appliances, alarms, etc. Gas line shut-offs are generally located outside but may be in a basement at the side of the house.

In shutting off any service there is a detailed procedure for you to follow that is specific to your location. If you don't know the steps, you will need to hire competent professionals. For example, when shutting off water lines, you have to know that all water has been drained out of the lines and that all valves are left open. There is a sequence to opening valves during the shut-off procedure and there are techniques to ensure you have drained the lines. Remember, water expands when it freezes so great damage can occur when any water is left in the system. Sometimes antifreeze is used, such as within toilets, but that may not be enough.

The need to preserve a house for long periods of time varies with location. In cold areas it is called "winterizing," wherein you protect the house from likely damage during periods of very cold temperature. Jack Frost can wreak havoc if you are not ready for him. If you're not sure what needs to be done, check with long-term neighbors who have experience. In winter climates some people prefer to keep the heating system operating at a lower temperature, such as 50°F (10°C), not only to reduce the chance for freezing, but also to reduce the temperature range to which materials within the house are exposed. But even when the heat is kept on some, if not all, of the water pipes will need to be shut off. In deep-freeze climates shutting off the water is not enough. You will either have to place antifreeze in the water system or blow it out with compressed air. In this text we won't get into the fine details, but want you to understand that there is a lot needed when you partially or fully shut down a house during off-season. The local knowledge we spoke about is only the start.

The first time you prepare to shut down your home, make lists of what you plan to do. Do your homework. Remember that whatever you shut down will need to be restarted, and this can be more involved than shutting down, particularly so if damage has occurred. For example, water pipes can break during the off-season. When you turn on the water, you will want to do it slowly and with full checking to ensure that there are no leaks. Hot-water heaters can be particularly finicky after having been shut off and drained. Do not just rely on hiring a service. You have to understand what you want them to do and, by all means, inspect their work.

Obtaining local knowledge of what other people do is one of the most important first steps to determining what you should do. That is why we recommend that your home inspector also prepare a maintenance program. He can be a valuable source for guidance. Local contractors can also be a valuable source of information. When you have learned what has to be done, and have done it, you still can't just walk away until next season.

Having a good maintenance person to look after your house when you are away is very important. We believe this to be *essential*. This might be a year-round neighbor or a person who specializes in checking and maintaining houses. Whoever your caretaker is, he should make regularly scheduled visits, determined by how much of the house you shut down and what you left operating. He must be someone you can count on to also check the house following any significant storm.

Renting

Welcome to the landed gentry. The first thing you have to know as a landlord is that it isn't always smooth sailing. Getting a regular check from a tenant to help maintain your investment is a fiscally admirable goal, but may only be a dream. Along with that check comes responsibilities. They may be just nuisance status, but sometimes they are more problematic. Being a landlord is not an easy ticket to wealth or even just sustenance, in some cases. It is easy for people who do not own something to provide less care than if they were the owners. They may not treat this house of yours as gently as they should. And they may drive you batty with constant demands for service or repairs they could easily do themselves. Tenant mentality says that you, as the owner, are responsible for everything.

It is also easy for renters to have higher expectations than the condition of your property can provide. Think of when you have rented automobiles. Sure, you put gas in when needed, but have you performed any maintenance checks? Maybe you rented a smaller vehicle than you regularly drive to cut costs, and then felt a bit disappointed when the rental lacked your normal performance expectations. Your tenant may be of a similar mindset in expecting more of you than you had bargained for. In becoming a landlord you may open a Pandora's box of responsibility and compliance. You will be a lot better off if you know the roadblock possibilities ahead of time.

When you consider renting your house you must understand that tenants have rights that vary from state to state, so you have to become familiar with fair housing laws and the multitude of other regulations. Whether you rent on a part-time or full time basis, a good start is to research tenant rights and fully understand your responsibilities as a landlord. A link to each state source for this information can be obtained from the U.S. Department of Housing and Urban Development (HUD) at *www.hud.gov/renting/tenantrights.cfm*.

For your own protection you also need to investigate any tenant associations that help their members understand the law, promote political actions, and help members obtain assistance for actions against their landlord, who could very well be you. Individual state sites obtainable from the HUD site will probably have links to tenant association web sites for additional research. The local community in which your house is located undoubtedly has ordinances affecting the renting of property. So you will also want to check with local municipal officials for information you need to know. You don't want to find yourself in the unenviable position of not knowing. Again, check the HUD state link for further links or references to your local sources.

While you may refuse to rent to people whose income is not sufficient to pay the rent, people with Section 8 vouchers may be protected from such refusal. This is where your lawyer comes in. The time to be careful in accepting tenants is before agreements are signed, because once you have a tenant, it may not be easy to collect their rent and may be even harder to evict them.

Security deposits may be limited by laws that vary from state to state. You may be required to maintain these funds in a separate bank account that pays interest on the money. There are detailed requirements for your state.

Your ability to select renters will be limited by how you seek tenants and the restrictions placed upon you by the regulations you have just researched. Some people only use word-of-mouth to attract their tenants. Others use real estate agencies. Advertising for renters may be necessary, but where? Remember that local papers generally attract only local people. Depending upon the type of property you own, you may need to advertise to a large audience. If your house is in or near a specific-interest resort area, you will want to reach the people who ski, swim, sail, golf, hunt, parasail, or delight in whatever your location offers. You may want to advertise in a publication devoted to that activity. You can often find such magazines in a good book store or in a regional public library. Or, you can get the word out to the greatest number of people on the Internet. Response should be very good, especially if you include photos.

Unfortunately, the more you advertise, the greater are chances for undesirable tenants who may want your house. Create a personal policy of background and financial checks. Be consistent in the application of any policy. Expect to be challenged and you will be better prepared.

Maintenance and cleaning never cease so you will need to either take on those responsibilities yourself or pay people to do the work for you. Depending upon the changeover of your tenants, you may need to have a cleaning service available to perform their magic between tenants. Maintenance to main house services, including heating, air conditioning, plumbing, electrical, and appliances calls for those specifically skilled. Here's where you dig out that first-team contractor list you made earlier.

You may want to consider photo-documenting conditions at the start and end of each new tenant rental period. This can be a do-it-yourself effort or you may have someone else take the photos. Whoever is the key maintenance person for the house is probably the best person because he can perform an inspection at the same time. A video camera is all right, but still photos are easier to manage. They will provide an interesting reference of condition over time. A simple digital camera would work just fine. A camera that takes wide-angle photos is helpful but not necessary. Take a picture at each exterior side of the house. Depending upon what is on the property, you may want selected property photos as well. High-wear areas such as doors, halls, kitchen, and bathroom deserve photos. You may want a photo of each wall in each room. Try to follow the same sequence each time you take photos. Have a checklist for what photos to take to ensure consistency.

Renting out-of-town property requires extra planning, such as arranging for a local person or firm who will have a key and be able to coordinate any emergency requirements. When you use a local real estate firm to handle the renting, you may have them also handle emergency coordination. You might want to have a separate maintenance person. Knowing where to turn off the water and other services should be known by all of your service people, but there will need to be one person whom you trust to look out for your interests and protect your property. Even when you are renting property close to your primary residence, it is helpful to have at least one other person who has a key and is knowledgeable about your house so if you are not available, that person can fill in. Securing the house for safety is a basic requirement of any key maintenance person. Another basic requirement is knowing where to shut off water, gas, and electricity. Knowing where to obtain emergency medical help and police help is also essential.

Rental Agreements

For legal advice you will need to consult a lawyer. Here we go again, and here we are going to discuss some of the key provisions of many rental agreements. There are standard forms available at your local bookstore, library, or on the Internet. When you are in the position to invest in property and have tenants, it is best to have a lawyer available for potential legal issues. Right from the outset, consult with your lawyer about all aspects of your purchase and any legal agreements that will be needed. This is a business and you are the business manager.

A **rental agreement**, or **lease**, is a contract between the landlord and tenant. Even where an oral lease is allowed you will have a clearer agreement when you have a written signed document, a document written in simple, clear, easy-to-read words in plain language. You may have a standard agreement that will need to be adjusted for individual tenants, such as the date payments are due to you that follow the date the tenant's payroll check is received.

Common lease provisions include the term or length of time you agree to rent the property. It may be a month, a set number of months or another period of time, a year, or on a month-to-month basis. To be sure you are happy with the definition of the terms, you must have knowledge of the laws in your state that govern how to end or break a lease. Rent payment and the amount of security deposit need to be specified in the lease. A provision for late charges and payment of attorney's fees, should legal action be needed, may be included within your lease agreement.

Rules and regulations are important elements of a lease. Care of the property may be a separate provision. Prompt reporting of problems needs to be made clear so you can reduce any potential serious damage by repairing the defect in a timely fashion. Orderly conduct and the extent to which pets are allowed are additional provisions of typical leases.

Landlord access to the property will need to be included in your lease in accordance with your state laws, together with provisions for renewal and changing the lease.

Home-Buyer's Checklist

- Did I do my homework by thoroughly investigating local conditions?

- Does the house selected meet most of our needs?

- Have I made a plan for in- and/or off-season care?

- Am I interested in being a part-time landlord?

Chapter 19

Investment Property: Understanding Market Value

Large Investment

A home is the largest investment that most single individuals or families will ever make. Not only can a home provide a comfortable place to live; it can also be the cornerstone of an investment program or retirement plan.

If a home appreciates by five percent per year, compounded, it will increase in value to four times its original cost well within the 30 years it typically takes to pay off a mortgage. Amortization, the process of liquidating a mortgage loan over time, will mean that the 30-year mortgage will have been fully retired. A small cash down payment followed by regular mortgage payments will eventually turn into a debt-free house. That house may then be sold to purchase a retirement home and leave some extra cash—or perhaps it will be time to take out a reverse mortgage, whereby the bank makes monthly payments to the home owner.

Millions of people are ignorant or afraid of the stock-and-bond market; they feel their home is the best investment they can make, and they are right more often than not.

The Good, the Bad, and the Ugly

Not all houses will provide such positive investment results. Investment aspects can be grouped as the good, the bad, and the ugly.

- **The good:** appreciation, inflation hedge, leverage, tax savings, security

- **The bad:** high transaction costs, illiquidity, lack of diversification, being a prisoner of surroundings, high operating costs, unexpected major repairs

- **The ugly:** Hurricane Katrina

Let's deal with these investment aspects in order.

The Good

APPRECIATION AND INFLATION

The good is that almost all houses in positive economic areas will appreciate in value. The National Association of Realtors® maintains a database of average home prices for most major cities. In general, average prices rise almost everywhere in almost every year. But there are notable exceptions. The recent historical rate of appreciation in your area is not a definite predictor of the future. Also, keep in mind that your house is not the "average" house in an area. Indeed, the average house keeps getting either newer or older depending on the number of new houses built in the area. The average house also keeps getting larger because new homes are larger than the previous average size. Your house will remain the same size unless you spend extensively to expand, and your house constantly grows older.

You may be wondering: What is appreciation? How does inflation affect the value of a house? How can I benefit from appreciation?

Appreciation is the rate at which, or amount by which, the value of property increases over time. A portion of appreciation may be due to inflation. As general prices rise, so should the value of real property, just as a ship stays afloat no matter how high the water level. However, properties may rise in value even in the absence of inflation. A desirable location, a well-conceived project, population growth in excess of new construction activity, and good property maintenance contribute to appreciation in property value.

Inflation is the decline in the purchasing power of the dollar over time. Investors are concerned about the effects of inflation because an investment's real value can be eroded substantially by high or persistent inflation. When inflation rates are high, investors acquire inflation hedges, such as gold and other tangible assets. Most real estate is considered a good inflation hedge. This means the value of tangible real property tends to rise with inflation and minimizes losses due to deteriorating dollar value.

Once bought, the price of your home has been fixed. Your cost is not affected by future price increases for land, labor, lumber, copper, or concrete. If those prices rise, it will cost more to buy a new house, and existing houses will tag along, perhaps not far behind new home prices.

Today's dollar buys only about one-tenth of the goods and services that it bought after World War II. Many houses that sold for $10 per square foot before 1950 are now selling for $100 per square foot. To do so, however, they must have been well-maintained (perhaps even remodeled) and must be in an economic area that continues to be good. Of course, many homes sell for less. Some have been torn down because the neighborhood has changed. In some cases, the neighborhood changed for the worse, so that houses were poorly maintained and became unlivable, or at least undesirable. In other cases, the neighborhood changed for the better, becoming attractive to upwardly mobile buyers who would buy an old house for its lot, then tear it down to build a "McMansion." So there is no guarantee that the value of your house will increase tenfold in the next 60 years, but in general, inflation is an ally of the home owner.

Like any other investment asset, appreciation is greatest when favorable, but unanticipated, events occur after the property is purchased. If you are looking for appreciation potential, consider properties offered at bargain prices. Bargains may exist because of a temporary downturn in the market, a location that is currently out of favor, or an owner who is motivated to sell. Some properties in unattractive physical condition may offer opportunities for improving value through prudent renovation. In addition, foreclosed or unoccupied properties may offer higher appreciation potential than do completed, fully occupied properties. But watch for structural soundness and a desirable neighborhood.

Appreciation may also occur in mature, conservative properties. As long as the property remains competitive in the market, its value can increase. Therefore, returns from appreciation can be expected in many sound houses without risky speculation or property turnaround strategies. In these cases, appreciation will provide a hedge against inflation.

Brand-new homes may also enjoy appreciation, but it is often limited by new construction in the area. Builders must sell, and they can often offer incentives or amenity packages that recent home buyers cannot. This tempers appreciation potential until the area becomes built out.

LEVERAGE

For people with a decent credit rating, it is not difficult to borrow 80 percent of the house purchase price (or 80 percent of the appraised value, if less than the purchase price). Indeed, as noted earlier, loans are available for 95 percent (sometimes 97 percent) of the purchase price. This can mean that you can control a large asset with an investment from your own funds of only five percent of the cost. A $200,000 house can be purchased with only $10,000 down, plus closing costs. Disregarding closing costs for the moment, if the house value rises by ten percent in a year, your investment appreciates by $20,000. This is a 200 percent gain on your $10,000 investment (your down payment)!

Getting back to reality, you must pay interest on the loan (likely more costly than rent you'd pay on a rental unit), insurance, ad valorem taxes, and costs for repairs and maintenance. So before you think you have doubled or tripled your $10,000 investment in one year, at least consider the cost of interest. If the house appreciates faster than the interest rate or provides other benefits, leverage (i.e., borrowing money) is worthwhile. Borrowing is especially beneficial when it permits a purchase that would otherwise not be possible.

TAX SAVINGS

A tax deduction for home mortgage interest and ad valorem taxes is available to those who itemize deductions. Itemizing deductions provides benefits to the extent that deductions exceed the standard deduction. In 2005, the standard deduction for a married couple filing a joint return was $10,000. If that couple owns a home with a $200,000 mortgage at six percent, their interest is $12,000. Further, suppose ad valorem taxes are $6,000. These deductions total $18,000. The excess (compared to the $10,000 standard deduction) is $8,000. If they are in the 30 percent marginal tax bracket, their annual tax savings from home ownership is $2,400. Any other deductions—charitable contributions, for example—would also be effective. While a $2,400 tax savings is valuable, it is not sufficient reason to borrow $200,000. Over time, the interest deduction will decrease with loan amortization and the standard deduction is likely to increase, reducing the tax benefit. With future rising income levels causing a phase-out of deductions, and a growing presence of the alternative minimum tax, for many individuals and families the income tax savings will likely decline over time.

A home resale at a gain will go untaxed provided certain criteria are met. These include occupancy and ownership of two or more years and apply to a maximum gain of $250,000 for singles or $500,000 for married couples filing jointly.

SECURITY
The house will be there (barring a major physical catastrophe) to provide security. In contrast to other items of value, such as a precious stamp or coin collection, it cannot be stolen; unlike stock prices suffering the effect of back-dated stock options, its value cannot be affected by cheating. Mother Nature, however, can do extensive harm, so be sure to get ample insurance.

The Bad
There are lots of bad investment characteristics of a house. For most owners, however, a long holding period and decent maintenance will overcome most of them.

HIGH TRANSACTION COSTS
The transaction costs of buying—including closing costs, move-in, and immediate repairs—can easily exceed five percent of the total house cost. Upon a resale, transaction costs paid by a seller often grow to ten percent, with the notable inclusion of a broker commission (6 percent), title policy, and legal expenses. These costs do not include the aggravation of buying and selling, not to mention the financial strain of overlap—owning two houses at the same time. In contrast, renting avoids most of the cost and often times, the aggravation.

If you're not going to own a house for at least two years, transaction costs alone (five percent when buying *plus* ten percent when selling) will likely cause a financial loss.

ILLIQUIDITY

Whether the down payment is considered small (under ten percent or large (over 20 percent), your money will be tied up in a house. The transaction costs of extracting the money through a sale are high (as noted earlier). If you need cash for emergencies to go into business, to pay college tuition, etc., a **home equity loan** or **home equity line of credit** may allow you to gain access to some of your original investment and appreciation. These new names disguise what the loans really are—**second mortgages**—because second mortgages have a negative connotation whereas borrowing your own equity sounds just fine.

In contrast, most financial investments—stocks, bonds, and bank CDs—can be cashed in with minimal transaction costs, although 401(k)s and other retirement plan assets have bad—sometimes horrific—tax consequences for early withdrawal.

LACK OF DIVERSIFICATION

It is best not to put all your eggs in one basket, but this is inevitable with a house. You own your home—the whole thing. You cannot own a one-tenth interest in ten different houses spread across the United States. While complete ownership is fine while things are good, negative events may strike your house by chance, including events that are outside your control.

CAPTIVE LOCATION

Because you can't move your house, it is a prisoner of its surroundings. This includes both its economic and physical area. Real estate values are generally subject to surrounding economic influences. Area job growth or decline drives local housing demand. If the agriculture industry becomes depressed, the Midwest will suffer. If the oil patch becomes depressed, it will be felt by Texas, Louisiana, and Oklahoma. If the high-tech industry suffers, Silicon Valley and related areas will suffer. The demand for real estate is local—largely dependent on the economics of the region.

In addition, physical characteristics of a neighborhood affect housing prices. Much of this is often driven by the school system. If local taxpayers vote against having new libraries, school buildings, and other facilities, the neighborhoods may fall into decline.

Perhaps the residents are already strapped for cash, so they don't want a tax increase, or they see no present or future personal benefit. No matter that *you* voted for that bond issue to help preserve your home's value; others didn't.

The vacant tract of land behind your home—which you thought would always be vacant—surprisingly becomes developed as a shopping center or, worse yet, an industrial facility. Your house loses value because of the added traffic, noise, litter, or perceived dangers. After it has occurred, there is virtually nothing you can do about such a development.

HIGH OPERATING COSTS

You may not have expected your house-operating costs to be so expensive to operate. Property taxes are often 2–3 percent of value; insurance can be more than one percent in an area susceptible to major storms and utilities include oil or gas, electricity, and water. You also have a number of costs that are mostly absent for renters: tree and lawn maintenance, pest extermination, repainting, replacement (of carpets, appliances, windows, and fixtures), and remodeling.

UNEXPECTED REPAIRS

A house of any age may require unexpected foundation repairs, a new roof, or any other unexpected and expensive replacement.

The older house may have charm, but it will be costly to install new windows and doors and modernize the wiring and plumbing. Is this place an "investment" or a "money pit"?

The Ugly

The 2005 Atlantic hurricane season, with 27 named storms, 15 of which reached hurricane strength, was the most active in recorded history, shattering previous records on repeated occasions. The impact of the season was widespread and ruinous, with at least 2,280 deaths and record damages of over $100 billion. Of the storms that made landfall, five of the seven major hurricanes—Dennis, Emily, Katrina, Rita, and Wilma—were responsible for most of the destruction. Large portions of Florida, many of which were still recovering from the damage suffered in Ivan the previous year, were battered repeatedly by Arlene, Dennis, Katrina, Tammy, and Wilma (Rita also lightly brushed the Florida Keys). Many home owners were left with extensive repairs, often far in excess of insurance.

Hurricane Katrina devastated broad swaths of the Gulf Coast from Louisiana into Alabama, but its effect on New Orleans was unique. Besides losing their homes and personal property, most residents were uninsured. The levees were expected to protect against floods, so even though many homes were below sea level, flood insurance was not required. Ordinary home owner's insurance does not protect against rising (flood) waters. How ugly.

Market Value—Resale Considerations

When the time comes to resell your home, how do you know what price to ask? How much should you sell it for?

Do you start with your original cost, then add capital improvements such as the added porch, sprinkler system, fence, and also add brokerage fees, other transaction costs, and a profit margin? Does your cost set a minimum that you want to get out without a loss?

Chances are the answer is "no." You must price your house at market value if you want to sell it. General market conditions may have changed since you bought. The major employer in town has closed its factory. Or many of your improvements will have little or no value to prospective buyers. The $25,000 you spent to convert your basement to a rec room, or to convert the master bath to a Roman bath, or to install granite countertops may reflect the value of these improvements to you, but not to most prospective buyers. The $15,000 you paid last year for a new roof may impress a buyer, but she thinks of that like a transmission on a used car: if it needed to be replaced, she would subtract the cost or more from an offer, but won't pay much for the new one that is already in the car.

Market Value

The well-known concept of **market value** is applied to many types of property, including real estate. In brief, it is what a willing buyer would pay a willing seller, both of whom are knowledgeable and acting in their own best interest. In real estate appraisal, the definition is wordier and more technical, something like this:

> The most probable price that a property should bring in a competitive and open market under all conditions requisite to a fair sale, the buyer and seller each acting prudently and knowledgeably, and assuming the price is not affected by undue stimulus. Implicit in this definition is the consummation of a sale as of a specified date and the passing of title from seller to buyer under conditions whereby:
>
> • Buyer and seller are typically motivated;

- Both parties are well informed or well advised, and acting in what they consider their best interests;

- A reasonable time is allowed for exposure in the open market;

- Payment is made in terms of cash in U.S. dollars or in terms of financial arrangements comparable thereto; and

- The price represents the normal consideration for the property sold unaffected by special or creative financing or sales concessions granted by anyone associated with the sale.

You will note that there is nothing said about your purchase price or the cost of improvements you made. The question is, what would a buyer and seller agree upon under these conditions?

Real Estate Brokers

You may invite one or more real estate brokers for an interview and ask their opinion of the house's value or to suggest a list price. They can provide a **broker's opinion of value** or a **comparative market analysis**.

To provide a professional appraisal of the market value of real estate, however, one must be licensed or certified by the state. Most states provide at least two types of certification or licensure: "general" and "residential." The general certification or licensure allows the appraisal of any type of property; residential certification or licensure limits appraisers to one- to four-family houses and vacant lots.

State certification or licensing requires education and experience. It is considered a minimum. Many appraisers go beyond that and are designated by professional associations. The best recognized designations in real estate appraisal are SRA and MAI. Other well-known designations include ASA, IFA, IFAS, CRA, and CAE.

Appraisal Approaches

There are three "approaches" to real estate appraisal:

1. Market (direct sales comparison)

2. Cost (summation)

3. Income (capitalization)

Generally, the *market approach* is preferable, especially when ample data is available. The *cost approach* is considered valid for most new and recently built homes; it is difficult to apply to older houses because it requires an estimate of depreciation. The *income approach* is generally used for income-producing properties (apartments, shopping centers, or office buildings)—seldom for homes.

Market Approach

To provide a market-approach estimate, the appraiser collects information on recent sales of properties similar to the subject property (your house). These sales are called comparables, or **comps**, in trade language. The more comps, the better the analysis; most appraisal reports include at least three. The sales price of the comparable properties are adjusted to account for any differences between them and the subject property. Adjustments are commonly made for such features as size, age, condition and quality, date of sale, and location. If special financing was used in the sale, some of the sales price may reflect the benefits of the favorable loan to the buyer. The price increase due to financing must be separated from the price for the property alone.

Each adjustment is based on a judgment of how much the market is paying for a feature. Adjustments are added or subtracted to make the price of the comparable what it would have been if the comp had the same salient features as the subject property. If the comp is better than the subject in some regard, its sales price is adjusted down to equate it to the subject. If a feature is inferior, the comparable's price is adjusted upward. After all the comparables are adjusted, the appraiser estimates market value based on the adjusted sales prices, applying judgment and expertise.

The market approach is often the most useful indicator of what a house will likely sell for in the current market. By looking at the way comparables are adjusted, you may learn how certain features are valued in the market. The selection of comparables may indicate how active the market is for properties like yours. If the market is very active, the comparables will be very recent. If not, some of the sales may have occurred more than a year ago. The comparables may also indicate what features are standard in the market.

The market approach is most reliable when the market is active and there are many close substitutes for the property in the market. When activity is slow, it is difficult to get enough comparable sales to provide a reliable indication of value. When activity is extremely high, prices may be driven upward to a level that can't be sustained, leading to overstated value. If the subject property is unusual, there may not be close substitute properties in the market.

Cost Approach

The cost approach is based on the cost to replace the subject property. It starts with an estimate of the cost to reproduce the subject house with up-to-date materials and methods at current costs. This amount is reduced by the estimated depreciation in the appraised property, an adjustment required whenever the house is not brand-new. (Because new buildings have little depreciation, the cost method is often used to appraise new construction.) Depreciation comes in three forms:

1. Physical, or wear and tear from normal use. This may range from faded paint and worn-out carpet to major deterioration in the basic structure of a building.

2. Functional, or a loss in the utility of the property. This may be due to changing tastes or preferences, such as the introduction of more modern kitchen or bathroom fixtures.

3. External, or a loss in value due to changes outside the property. The opening of a nearby hospital, shopping center, or factory, or the widening of a street can raise or lower the value of a home.

When the estimated depreciation is subtracted from the reproduction cost, the result is an indication of the value of the house alone. The site (i.e., land, lot) is valued by comparing it to sites where the most likely use is similar to the subject property. The value of the site is added to the building value to get an indication of the property value.

The cost approach also gives an indication of the value of the building and site separately. It may be useful to know how much value is added by the building when a change in use is contemplated. When renovation or modernization is considered, the cost approach may indicate how much value would be added by curing various types of depreciation. Depreciation is considered *curable* when more value will be added to the property than the cost of correction; it is *incurable* when the cost of correction exceeds the value added. The analysis may also indicate building features that contribute less to market value than they cost. In appraisal terms, these are called *deficiencies* when they are inadequate or obsolete; if too good or expensive for the purpose, they are overimprovements or *superadequacies*.

The cost approach assumes that the buyer is considering the option of new construction when viewing the subject property.

The cost approach is generally used to support the conclusion of the market approach, but it may be the primary indication when the property is proposed or new construction, is unique, or when market conditions are abnormal.

Appraisals Are Opinions

Appraisals are professionally derived opinions of value. However, there is no assurance that a house will sell for its appraised value.

Generally, an appraisal by a state-certified or state-licensed appraiser is required for a federally chartered lender to make a sizable loan. Not all lenders accept all appraisers.

If you are a seller and your proposed buyer gets an appraisal that is less than the contract price that you agreed on, several responses are possible:

1. Reduce the price accordingly, or

2. Let the buyer pay the difference in cash because the lender won't cover that part, or

3. Show the appraiser some comps you know of that counter her appraisal, or

4. Find another appraiser who is accepted by that lender.

If you are a buyer and the appraisal is less than your offer, consider renegotiating the price or looking at other homes. If this house has particular features that are especially attractive for your needs and tastes, it may be okay to pay more than market value. But don't expect to resell it for more than market value.

The cost of an appraisal of a single-family home is usually $300–$400, and there's no assurance that the second opinion will provide a higher value estimate. You should consider a secondary appraisal, especially when it is justified by a large differential between the selling price and appraised value, and when other opinions (particularly the broker's or agent's) don't agree with the appraiser's opinion.

Home-Buyer's Checklist

- Is the house in an area that can be expected to grow in value or at least to maintain its value?

- Is the house structurally sound? Is it in a flood plain, on an earthquake fault, or subject to another natural hazard?

- Do you feel a need for inflation protection of your investment? Can you use greater tax deductions?

- Have you considered prices of comparable sales and replacement costs? Do you need to get an appraisal before making an offer?

Real-World Example

Arthur had a well-paying job that left him with time and energy at the end of the day. He was the frugal sort, fairly handy with tools, and had a nose for bargains. His first rental-property purchase was a fixer-upper to which he made some cosmetic repairs before renting it out. It paid off monthly like a slot machine, he proudly stated. The next year he bought two more properties and did the same; the following year, he purchased four more.

Each year Arthur added more rental units than in previous years. He spent his lunch hours fixing leaky faucets and literally, mending fences. He and his wife spent their evening hours keeping up with paperwork—leases, government regulations, rent deposits—and inspecting units for damage, preparing them for new tenants, and paying bills. Weekends were devoted to efforts that were especially time-consuming: replacing water heaters or ovens, laying new carpet or flooring, and seeking new investment opportunities. After 15 years, Arthur had three full-time employees to help care for 200 units.

Some of his daytime co-workers wondered why he went to so much trouble when his day job paid quite well. By the time his full-time job ended, however, Arthur's equity exceeded $3 million. Roger, one of his coworkers, had maxed out his 401(k) contributions. Without any personal effort, Roger's 401(k) grew to nearly $1 million, which was quite adequate for retirement, though not what Arthur had.

Roger then appreciated what Arthur had accomplished. And Arthur learned that when you own more than four toilets, you have a job with your investment.

Work Sheets

Benefits of ownership   Check if applicable

   Appreciation   _____

   Inflation hedge   _____

   Leverage   _____

   Tax shelter   _____

   Security   _____

Drawbacks of ownership

   Transaction costs   _____

   Illiquidity   _____

   Lack of diversification   _____

   Fixed location   _____

   Operating costs   _____

   Major repairs   _____

Do the benefits outweigh the drawbacks?

Is your purchase price at or below the appraised value?

Chapter 20

Selling Your Home

Major Reasons for Selling

*T*he average home owner will sell and move every 10–12 years. Major reasons for selling are:

1. Relocation: Especially for employment or economic opportunity or for retirement.

2. Size: You want a larger or smaller home or different amenities.

3. Economics: Changed economic circumstances.

4. Neighborhood:. Changed neighborhood, school system.

Relocation

Relocation for employment reasons is a frequent cause of selling a house. Some corporations will offer opportunities that require a move for advancement up the corporate ladder (at one time IBM® managers joked that the initials stood for "I've Been Moved"). Larger corporations will have standard policies and procedures as to what expenses they will pay. Some will appraise your house and offer to pay that amount, or allow you to sell it for more, if you can. The company stands ready as a buyer or a safety net.

Physicians completing their residency often move for employment opportunities, as do many other professionals—professors, teachers, attorneys, engineers, computer programmers, accountants, and so on. Countless others must move because of a changing employment situation. The factory in which they have been working is shuttered, or the workforce is significantly downsized.

Often, the local economy is depressed (causing the need to leave), and the local economy of new employment is strong. The depressed economy will generally cause difficulty in selling a house in terms of time and price, whereas the new location will have higher housing prices and less housing available on the market, so choice is reduced. There is nothing that one person can do to exert much influence on the market. In this situation, you are a price-taker, not a price-maker. Relocating is very expensive, especially when local economic conditions are unfavorable and a move is rushed.

Another reason to relocate is retirement. Perhaps the purpose is to find a milder climate or a slower pace, or to be closer to children and grandchildren who moved away to take advantage of economic opportunities. In this situation, the schedule for moving may be more relaxed—you can wait for a better offer on your house and look for a more suitable purchase.

Size

That two-bedroom, one-bath starter home that a couple bought soon after marriage just doesn't fit the present family of three children five years later. And twenty years down the road, the four-bedroom, three-bath house they bought to replace it is now too big and too difficult to maintain for an empty-nester couple. They may want to downsize to an urban condo where they can walk to nice restaurants and the theater. Fifteen years later, a retirement community will be sought.

And so, in your life cycle, housing size and amenities need to be adjusted according to your situation.

Economics

While some people think of a house partly as a status symbol, most people feel comfortable when surrounded by others of the same socioeconomic level. As economics change, so do housing preferences. Housing costs typically account for 25–50 percent of your budget. As income increases or declines, your housing situation is likely to warrant adjustment for affordability (or lack thereof).

Neighborhood

It is well known that discrimination in housing sales and rentals is prohibited, with minor exceptions. Still, there is nothing wrong with moving because of the ethnic composition of your neighborhood. Many people feel more comfortable in a neighborhood where the majority, or at least a large minority, of residents share their ethnicity. Large cities have their Chinatowns, Little Mexicos, and Scottish, Irish, Italian, Polish, or Jewish neighborhoods. The local shops cater to the dominant ethnic population. Local elementary school students can include many of a certain ethnicity.

Over time, the population mix can change. Those left behind often want to move to rejoin their ethnic affiliations. They may sell their house so as to move and retain a sense of belonging with ethnic comrades.

Major Considerations of a Sale

Costs of a housing sale are as much as ten percent of the price and with the added inconvenience of moving, a sale should never be taken lightly. Major considerations of a sale include:

- Pricing your home for sale
- Whether to use a broker
- Advertising and market appeal
- Seasonal timing

- Contract provisions, especially contingencies
- Closing and moving
- Proceeds from sale
- Tax considerations (income taxes and tax deduction for moving expenses)

Pricing and Negotiating

When you sell a house, carefully check market conditions. If you're in a seller's market, typified by rising prices and few homes on the market, you can deal from strength. Get an estimate of your home's market value, and then add a substantial margin to leave room for further appreciation or bargaining. Sometimes an out-of-town buyer may fall right into your lap and pay your asking price.

A buyer's market, on the other hand, is characterized by many houses for sale with little activity and prices headed downward. You may have to undercut the competition if you really want to sell, possibly by a significant amount if you want to sell quickly—although a quick sale of real estate does occur infrequently. No matter how low you set the price, you still need a buyer to make an offer. See Chapter 19 for approaches to estimating market value.

There are two sources available for help in estimating your home's value. An appraisal by a professional appraiser represents an impartial and expert opinion of the property's value. Many experts in the field are members of a professional organization. Some of the leadings organizations (with designations in parentheses) are:

- Appraisal Institute (MAI, SRA)
- American Society of Appraisers (ASA, FASA)
- National Association of Independent Fee Appraisers (IFA)
- National Society of Real Estate Appraisers (RA, CRA, MREA)

A real estate broker can help you by performing a comparative market analysis or broker's opinion of value, which is based on the broker's experience and knowledge of the local market. This estimate may be less objective than a professional appraisal, because of the broker's lesser appraisal qualifications and lack of independence from the transaction.

Your individual situation has much to do with pricing and negotiating. Are you desperate to sell? If you've lost your job or moved away, you may be in this position. Or you might be just eager; although you must sell, you can hold on for a lengthy period. Some sellers are proud; they don't really need to sell and can wait for the right offer. They put their house on the market to show, hoping for a high price.

Although pricing isn't everything, the more competitive your price, the more likely you are to sell quickly. The bottom line is that you must be flexible and prepared to compromise if you really want to sell.

Although everything is negotiable, monetary items most likely to be negotiated are:

- Loan discount points
- Loan origination fees
- Other closing costs
- Amount of earnest money
- Repairs or improvements
- Seller financing terms
- Brokerage fee

Nonmonetary items include:

- Closing date
- Moving date

- Conditions (subject to financing, sale of other house)

- Required inspections

- Warranties

Using a Broker

If you're considering selling your home, you need to decide whether to sell the house yourself or to list it with a **broker**. Listing does not necessarily mean that you will end up with less money for your house because of the broker's commission. Skilled agents can often negotiate a higher price. Before you decide to sell by yourself, consider these points:

- Are you in a hurry? If you are, you may become frustrated by your inability to attract prospective buyers quickly.

- Are homes in your area in demand? If so, you are more likely to do well by handling the sale yourself.

- Do you know where mortgage money is available? If not, you'll need to find out.

- Do you know what features buyers in your area are seeking? Does your home contain such features? It will be easier to sell if it does. You should weigh all the factors before deciding whether to sell your home yourself.

A broker's level of activity in your neighborhood is a good sign of interest, especially if he has sold many houses. Ask friends who have recently sold to tell you about their transaction. Which broker did they use? Did your friends receive fair treatment and good results, or are they bitter about some aspect of the transaction? What about pricing and time on the market, selling efforts, showing procedures, and just plain courtesy?

You may interview several brokers or salespersons before selecting one who you feel will best do the job. Don't make the selection on the basis of who estimates the highest value: it's not uncommon for a broker or salesperson to give an unrealistic figure just to get the listing and then recommend reducing the price in order to sell quickly.

Here are some important points to check out:

- Ask brokers what is happening in your neighborhood. What has sold and what hasn't? Ask why.

- Find out about time on the market and other market conditions.

- Ask brokers how they will advertise your house. What media will be used? Will they periodically hold an open house?

- Do they sell houses in your price range? Do they belong to the multiple listing service?

- What size is their firm? More important, is the firm a member of a national relocation service or franchise? (This may be a clue as to whether out-of-town buyers will use their services.) On the other hand, a small firm may be able to offset this advantage by offering more individualized service.

- Ask how long a listing the broker or salesperson feels is needed and what commission rate will be charged. If you are vacating the house before selling it, find out about maintenance. Will the broker see that it is properly maintained while you're away? Is there a charge for this?

Give yourself time to evaluate the services offered by all brokers. Feel free to discuss matters with friends and neighbors who have used them before selecting one.

Discount Brokers

Some brokers are not full-service. They provide reduced services for a reduced fee. Some charge a one percent commission and claim that they will do everything except show the house. That is, they will help you prepare signs, ads, and contracts. Others charge a flat fee and promise that your house will be in the multiple listing service (MLS) computer. Others may offer a cafeteria-style menu of services, with a price on each service you request.

Figure out what type of help you need to sell on your own. When you are in a seller's market, there may be no need to pay a broker $18,000 to sell your $300,000 house. But you may need help in some aspects of the sales process. In a buyer's market, you may need a broker to drive potential buyers to see your house and select it from among the many that are for sale. If you and your spouse or housemate are employed full time, you may need someone else to be available during your work hours to show it to potential buyers.

Distinctions of Licensing

Brokers and salespersons must have a state license. To become a broker, one must hold a salesperson's license for some time (usually 2–3 years depending on the state) and pass a more difficult exam.

A salesperson must have a license that is held (sponsored) by a broker. Often, a person with a broker's license will open an office with several salespersons working under him. The broker often provides office space and pays for overhead, advertising, and other expenses. Typically, the broker collects a commission from the salesperson's efforts and they share the income.

A broker or salesperson is not the same as a Realtor®. A broker or salesperson is licensed by the state; a Realtor®, in addition to being state-licensed, has joined a private association. Often, that membership can be helpful and result in better client service.

Discount brokers are licensed, but they may or may not be members of the multiple listing service (MLS). If they aren't in the MLS, your listing won't get into that book or computer database and may not be seen by as many potential buyers.

Listing Contracts

A listing is a written agreement between an owner and a broker. Under this agreement, if the broker presents you with a contract to buy your house offered by a ready, willing, and able buyer at the terms in the listing, you are obligated to pay that broker a commission. You can change your mind about selling by not signing the contract of sale, but you may still owe the broker the full commission.

The main types of listings are:

- Open: The listing can be given to another broker.

- Exclusive: No other brokers can sell. The owner himself can sell without paying a commission.

- Exclusive right to sell: Your broker gets a commission no matter who sells, even if you sell by yourself without the broker's help.

- Net: The broker's commission is whatever the buyer pays above a set amount.

- MLS: Multiple listing service: Typically an exclusive right to sell is given to one broker, who has agreed to share the listing with all other members of the local MLS.
Items to be negotiated in a listing are:

- Term. Most brokers want listings for a minimum of 90 days, though anything from 30 to 180 might be acceptable.

- Commission. Some brokers will not accept less than six percent. Others want even more for homes that may be difficult to sell and some will accept less if the home is expected to sell quickly.

- Reservation list: If you tried to sell before you listed and have some prospects, some brokers will respect your list by agreeing not to charge a commission if you sell to someone already on your list.

- Lock box: Brokers like to place a lock box on your door to make sure your key is readily accessible to other brokers when you're not at home. Some homeowners are concerned about theft by anyone who has access to the lock box. If this is a concern, don't allow the lock box.

- For Sale sign: Some brokers want to have a For Sale sign on display in your yard. If you don't want such a public advertisement of your house, you need not give sign permission to anyone. (Some neighborhood covenants and local jurisdictions prohibit such signs.)

- Subsequent contact with prospect: If someone to whom your broker showed the house buys it after the listing expires, do you owe a commission? This may depend on the intent of the parties, how much time has elapsed, state law, and what's written in the listing contract. In general, it's not a good idea to get involved in such an arrangement, either as a buyer or as a seller.

Seasonal Timing

Studies have shown that real estate activity and prices are higher in the spring and summer than in the fall and winter. Many buyers, especially those with school-age children, want to get into a home before the school year begins. The school year begins in mid-August in some places and early September in others.

Allowing four weeks to close means that most buyers want a contract on or before July 1. This gives them up to four weeks to find a house, apply for financing, and go through the due diligence process of various inspections (i.e., structural, electrical, mechanical and plumbing, termites, environmental).

Careful buyers don't wait till the last minute and they take some time to shop. So it is a good policy to put your house on the market in May or June. Perhaps you can use good weather in late March and April to repaint, plant flowers and groom shrubs, and straighten out closets so your home is looking its best in May and June.

Few people will be looking between Thanksgiving and New Year's, so don't be disappointed if you can't sell then.

Advertising and Market Appeal

Whether you are selling your home yourself or working with an agent, here are some suggestions to help you sell your house more quickly:

- Curb appeal is important. The lawn should be mowed and edged, the flower beds weeded, and the lot kept free of debris. Scrub or paint the front door so that the home looks neat, clean, and inviting.

- Windows should be washed and draperies opened to create an impression of airiness and light. If prospects are looking at night, be sure plenty of lights are turned on.

- Rooms should not be crowded with furniture. Give potential buyers the opportunity to imagine how their furnishings would fit in. But don't leave rooms totally bare, either, even if you've already moved.

- Buyers are distracted by television, stereos, and noisy children. Give the would-be purchaser a quiet atmosphere in which to view your home.

Providing Information

Any information that may be helpful should be available to prospective buyers. Make information accessible that will answer these commonly asked questions:

1. What date are you planning to move?

2. Why are you selling?

3. How old is the home, and who built it?

4. Have you maintained records of utility expenses, maintenance costs, and annual taxes?

5. Is the home completely insulated, and with what type of material?

6. Do you plan to include draperies, appliances, and other items in the sale?

7. Have you made recent improvements or additions, such as a new appliance or a ceiling fan?

Being able to answer these questions promptly is an important step toward promoting the sale of your home.

Running an Ad

Running a newspaper ad is important. The ad must convey the most vital information in as few words as possible. Including the proper information helps an ad achieve its major purpose of getting telephone inquiries. If callers have a better idea of whether your house suits their needs, neither they nor you will waste time. Take time to design an effective ad.

If you use a broker who will place an ad, try to determine that the ad is appropriate and tasteful.

Contract Provisions, Especially Contingencies

The standard contract used in your state for the sale of a home will include many items of a legal nature. If you are fortunate enough to have a helpful attorney, he may explain many of them—at least the ones you don't understand. Don't agree to a provision that is unfavorable to you just because you think the event that triggers it is unlikely to occur. Some items need your thoughtful consideration and understanding. Many of these provisions are called contingencies.

Contingencies for the Buyer

A good contract for the buyer will specify that certain requirements must be met or the transaction is canceled. If the requirements are not met, the buyer should get a full refund of any **earnest money**, also called good faith deposit money.

Common contingencies include good title, financing, and condition. If the seller can't provide good title, the buyer doesn't have to buy. If the buyer can't get the financing specified in the contract, he doesn't have to buy. If the house is found to be structurally defective, or if repair costs exceed a certain dollar amount that the seller won't pay, the buyer can get out of the contract. Other contingencies include making the purchase subject to the sale of the buyer's old house, or to the approval of other family members, such as parents, spouse, or children.

Contingencies for the Seller

If the buyer offers a contract subject to the sale of his old house, you might check into it to see whether it is marketable. You can accept the contract but include another provision giving you the right to accept another contract, in which case the first buyer has, say, 48 hours to delete the contingency and set a closing date.

Always try to think through the contingency and see whether it is acceptable as offered or what change would make it acceptable.

Closing and Moving

Issues related to closing are addressed in Chapter 13. In the contract, be sure that the terms required to close are clear and that the buyer does not get possession until closing or a few days later. Hold fast to this requirement even when the house is vacant. The buyer may move in and then be unable to close, and then you'll have to cope with a real mess.

Once a professional bowler was asked the best technique to "pick up" a 7–10 split. He replied, "Never get in that situation."

Proceeds of Sale

Your proceeds from the sale of your house are generally the check you receive when you leave the closing. There will probably be no tax to pay on the gain regardless of what you do with the money.

It is important to estimate the proceeds from the sale in order to evaluate offers on your property. The highest offer will not bring you the most money if it obligates you to pay many fees and charges. Estimating the proceeds is also important after you have agreed to sell. By carefully estimating what you should receive, you'll be able to notice any possible error on the closing statement and get it corrected before the closing. If you wait until the closing, under the stress of the moment, you may not be able to detect errors on the closing statement.

To estimate the amount of proceeds, start with the selling price. Subtract the existing mortgage(s) and other liens on the property. Subtract expenses of sale, including brokerage commissions, legal and title costs, discount points you agreed to pay on the buyer's loan, and so on. A detailed list follows:

SELLER'S ESTIMATED RECEIPTS

ALL FIGURES ARE APPROXIMATE   Date _____

PROPERTY DESCRIPTION	**SELLER'S NAME**	

		Seller Receives
SELLING PRICE		$

OUTSTANDING MORTGAGES

	Seller Receives
First mortgage .... $	
Second mortgage	
Other encumbrances	
Subtract total mortgages ....➔	$
Gross equity ....➔	$

LESS SELLER'S ESTIMATED EXPENSES   Seller Pays

	Seller Pays
Title insurance policy	$
Attorney fees	
Release of lien	
Survey of property	
Escrow fees	

Termite inspection		
Recording fees		
Broker's professional service fee		
Prepayment penalty on loan		
Photographs		
Loan discount fee		
Home warranty		

Total estimated expenses ➔ $

ESTIMATED RECEIPTS ➔ $

Note: 1. These figures are only estimated and are subject to verification by the Seller.

2. Prorations of taxes, interest, and insurance are not included in this statement.

3. Our insurance estimates are based on minimum coverage since types and amounts of coverage vary so much from individual to individual.

Tax Considerations
Income Tax on Sale
The Taxpayer Relief Act of 1997 brought relief to those who sell homes after May 7, 1997. Specifically, anyone can exclude $250,000 of **capital gain** from a sale, and a married couple can exclude $500,000.

This exclusion can be used no more than once every two years. To be eligible, the seller must have used the property as a principal residence for at least two years within the most recent five years.

This provision replaces both the "rollover" requirement (buying another home within two years) and the $125,000 one-time exclusion for home sellers older than age 55.

IRS Form 2119, once used to report the gain on sale, is no longer used. Sellers who have more than $250,000 profit on a house ($500,000 for married couples) report their gain on Schedule D of IRS Form 1040.

Tax Deduction for Moving Expenses
Most of the expenses incurred in home sales and purchases are deductible from gross income as "indirect" moving expenses when the move is related to employment and when distance and employment length requirements are met.

DISTANCE TEST
To meet the "distance" test, the new principal job must be at least 50 miles farther from the former residence than the old principal job. For example, if the former home was five miles from work, the new job must be at least 55 miles away. In the case of someone returning to full-time work or taking a first job, the principal job location must be at least 50 miles from the former residence.

TIME TEST

For an employee to meet the "time" test, he must work at least 39 weeks during the 12 months that follow the move. The work can involve more than one employer. A self-employed individual must work at least 39 weeks during the first 12 months and 78 weeks during the two-year period following the move.

Moving expenses are deductible even though the tax return is due before the time requirement is met. If the time test is not met, the taxpayer must amend the tax return for the year claimed, or declare the moving expense deducted in one year as other income in the year when the time test was not met.

EXEMPTIONS

Military personnel are exempt from both time and distance requirements when they move because of a permanent change of station. The time test is waived for any employee who:

- Moves to the United States because of retirement;

- Becomes disabled or dies;

- Is transferred for the employer's benefit; or

- Is laid off, but not for willful misconduct.

DEDUCTIBLE EXPENSES

Deductible moving expenses are:

- Transportation costs for household goods and effects, and

- Cost of travel to the new residence, not including meals en route.

Tax form 3903 is used to report moving expenses and form 3903F for foreign moves. Both are available from the Internal Revenue Service (IRS).

Home-Buyer's Checklist

- Do you have a valid reason for wanting to sell your home?

- Do you know how much you should ask as a selling price?

- Do you need a broker's help, or are you capable of selling on your own?

- Will you make your house physically attractive for buyers? Are you prepared to provide the information they need to consider a purchase?

- Do you understand contracts and contingencies?

Real-World Example

Martha and Alan were fortunate. They bought a house for $300,000 only two years earlier. After they bought, prices in the area continued to appreciate by nearly 20 percent per year. They decided to sell. They put their home on the market for $500,000, knowing it was worth only about $420,000. They refused a contract at $430,000, figuring the market would come up to their $500,000 price within a year.

It didn't. Instead, their broker said, the market "took a tumble." In the end, it took more than a year to realize a price of $390,000.

Martha and Alan don't know whether to be pleased at making a $90,000 profit in less than three years or chagrined that they refused a sale at $430,000 and had to wait an additional year.

Things could have gotten better…or worse. When the market turns south, some sellers are "stood up" at the closing.

Work Sheets

	Check if applicable
Reasons to resell	
Relocation	_____
Size	_____
Economics	_____
Neighborhood	_____
Do you need an appraisal?	_____
Do you need a broker?	_____
What is your schedule?	_____
What do you most wish to avoid?	
Owning two houses	_____
Owing on two mortgages	_____
No place to live	_____

How can you avoid potential major problems?

Glossary

Many of the following terms were adapted from the *Real Estate Handbook,* the *Dictionary of Real Estate Terms*, or the *Dictionary of Business Terms*, Barron's Educational Series, Inc.

acceleration (loan) process by which, under the terms of a MORTGAGE or similar obligation, an entire debt is to be regarded as due upon the borrower's failure to pay a single installment or to fulfill some other duty.

acceptance agreeing to take an offer.

accessibility features of a property that make it easier for use by a physically handicapped person. Examples include wheelchair ramps, wide doors, and bathroom railings.

acre a measure of land containing 43,560 square feet (4,047 square meters).

ad valorem tax a tax based on the ASSESSED VALUE of the property.

adjustable-rate mortgage (ARM) one where the INTEREST rate fluctuates according to another rate. Commonly, the MORTGAGE rate is indexed (adjusted) annually based on the one-year Treasury bill rate, plus a two percent MARGIN.

adjustment cap a limit on the amount of adjustment in the INTEREST rate on a ADJUSTABLE-RATE MORTGAGE over a 12-month period. *See* CAP.

adjustment interval period of time between the dates when the interest rate on an ADJUSTABLE-RATE MORTGAGE can be changed. This period is uniform and established in the ARM LOAN CONTRACT. For example, an annually adjusted ARM has an adjustment interval of one year. An INTERVAL ADJUSTMENT CAP sets a maximum on the interest rate change, for an adjustable interest rate mortgage, from one period to the next. A common cap limits the change in interest rates to 2 percentage points from one period to the next.

agency the legal relationship between a principal and agent arising from a contract in which the principal engages the agent to perform certain acts on the principal's behalf.

agent one who undertakes some business transaction or manages some affair for another, with the authority of the latter.

agreement of sale a written agreement between buyer and seller to transfer REAL ESTATE at a future date. Includes all the conditions required for a sale.

amortization a gradual process of reducing a debt in a systematic manner.

annual percentage rate (APR) an estimate of the actual interest rate paid on a loan based on the lender's yield. The calculation takes into account any DISCOUNT POINTS charged by the lender for originating the loan. The estimate is based on the borrower repaying the loan over the entire loan term.

appraisal an expert's opinion of the value of property derived with careful consideration of available and relevant data. States require certification or licensing of real estate appraisers for most appraisals.

appreciation Increase in the market value of a property caused by market forces, such as inflation, increased demand, or scarcity of a type of REAL ESTATE. The amount of appreciation is measured by its value or selling price, less the sum of its original cost and the cost of any capital improvements.

APR *See* ANNUAL PERCENTAGE RATE.

ARM *See* ADJUSTABLE-RATE MORTGAGE.

as is the present condition of property. The "sold as is" clause is likely to warn of a defect.

asking price the list price that an owner would like to receive. *See* LISTING PRICE.

assessed value the value against which a property tax is imposed. The assessed value is often lower than the MARKET VALUE due to state law, conservative tax district appraisals, and infrequent reassessments.

assignment the method by which a right or contract is transferred from one person to another.

assumable mortgage one that can be transferred to another party. The transferee assumes the debt but the original borrower is not released from the debt without a NOVATION.

attached housing dwelling units that are attached to each other on at least one side, possibly divided from one another by firewalls or other physical partitions. Contrast with DETACHED HOUSE.

balloon mortgage a loan having a large final payment.

balloon payment a large final payment on a debt.

bill of sale the document used to transfer personal property. Often used in conjunction with a REAL ESTATE transaction where appliances or furniture are also sold.

binder a brief agreement showing intent to follow with a formal sales CONTRACT.

biweekly mortgage a mortgage that requires principal and interest payments at two-week intervals. The payment is exactly half of what a monthly payment would be. Over a year's time, the 26 payments are equivalent to 13 monthly payments on a comparable monthly payment mortgage. As a result, the loan will amortize much faster than loans with monthly payments.

board of trustees or directors officers of a HOME-OWNERS' ASSOCIATION authorized to make decisions for the association and charged with managing the affairs of the association. Among the board's duties is enforcement of the association's BYLAWS.

bridge loan MORTGAGE FINANCING between the termination of one loan and the beginning of another.

broker one who is licensed by a state to act for property owners in REAL ESTATE transactions, within the scope of state law.

brokerage the business of being a BROKER.

broker's opinion of value BROKER's opinion, often considered by buyers and sellers; similar to COMPARATIVE MARKET ANALYSIS. Note that a broker or salesperson is not a qualified appraiser.

builder standard the lowest level of functional performance for a construction feature or appliance that will be installed in a new or remodeled house. Everything above "builder standard" may be an upgrade depending on the quality level of a particular builder. All categories of house construction features can have a minimum level, including framing sizes, insulation, roof coverings, siding, windows, doors, floor coverings, wall treatments, heating and air conditioning systems, plumbing fixtures, kitchen appliances, and so on.

building codes regulations established by local governments describing the minimum structural requirements for buildings; includes foundation, roofing, plumbing, electrical, and other specifications for safety and sanitation.

building permit permission granted by a local government to build a specific structure or reconfigure an existing building at a particular site.

buy-down pay additional DISCOUNT POINTS to a lender in exchange for a reduced rate of INTEREST on a loan. The reduced rate may apply for all or a portion of the loan term.

buyer's agent REAL ESTATE BROKER who is contracted by the buyer to act in his or her behalf. Unlike an agent representing the seller, a buyer's agent can negotiate CONTRACT terms for the buyer and provide the buyer any information available on the seller's situation. The agent's relationship with the buyer is established by contract and does not depend on the buyer paying a fee or commission.

buyer's market a situation where buyers have a wide choice of properties and may negotiate lower prices. Often caused by overbuilding, local population decreases, or economic slump.

bylaws a set of rules that govern the affairs of a CONDOMINIUM or neighborhood HOME-OWNERS' ASSOCIATION. In the case of condominiums, these rules determine much of what a home owner can do with his or her unit, as well as the common property in the complex.

cap the maximum change of the INTEREST rate of an ADJUSTABLE-RATE MORTGAGE. The mortgage may have both an annual and a life-of-loan ceiling.

capital expenditure an improvement that will have a life of more than one year. Capital expenditures are generally depreciated over their useful life, as distinguished from *repairs,* which are subtracted from income of the current year.

capital gain gain on the sale of a capital asset. If long-term (generally over six months), capital gains are sometimes favorably taxed. A principal personal residence is a capital asset, and gains on one's principal personal residence are tax-free up to a limit.

capital reserve an account maintained by a HOME-OWNERS' ASSOCIATION for the purpose of replacing building components and property improvements as needed.

caveat emptor "Let the buyer beware." An expression once used in REAL ESTATE to put the burden of an undisclosed defect on the buyer. This concept has been eroded in most states.

certificate of occupancy (C/O) a document issued by a local government to a developer or builder permitting the structure to be occupied by members of the public. Issuance of the certificate generally indicates that the building is in compliance with public health and BUILDING CODES.

chattels personal property.

closing the meeting at which buyer and seller exchange money for property.

closing costs various fees and expenses payable by the seller and buyer at the time of a REAL ESTATE CLOSING (also termed *transaction costs*). Included are brokerage commissions, DISCOUNT POINTS, TITLE INSURANCE and examination, DEED recording fees, and APPRAISAL fees.

closing date the date on which the seller delivers the DEED and the buyer pays for the property.

closing statement an accounting of funds from a REAL ESTATE sale, made separately to both the seller and the buyer. Often provided by a TITLE company. Most states require that accurate closing statements be furnished to all parties to the transaction.

cloud on title an outstanding claim or encumbrance that, if valid, would affect or impair the owner's TITLE.

co-insurance clause a clause in an insurance policy stating the minimum percentage of value to be insured in order to collect the full amount of loss.

commission
1. an amount earned by a REAL ESTATE BROKER for his or her services.
2. the official state agency that enforces REAL ESTATE licensing laws.

commitment letter a written pledge or promise; a firm agreement, often used to describe the terms of a MORTGAGE LOAN that is being offered.

common elements in a CONDOMINIUM, those portions of the property not owned individually by unit owners but in which an indivisible interest is held by all unit owners. Generally includes the grounds, parking areas, recreational facilities, and external structure of the building.

community property property accumulated through joint efforts of husband and wife and owned by them in equal shares. This doctrine of ownership now exists in Arizona, California, Idaho, Louisiana, Nevada, New Mexico, Texas, and Washington State.

comparables (comps) properties that are similar to the one being sold or appraised. Used in the market approach to APPRAISAL.

comparative or competitive market analysis an estimate of what a property might bring based on the sale or offering of similar properties, usually provided by a REAL ESTATE BROKER or salesperson. *Contrast* APPRAISAL.

concession reduction in price, rent, or other benefit provided to a tenant or buyer as an inducement to buy or lease.

conditional offer purchase CONTRACT tendered to the seller that stipulates one or more requirements to be satisfied before the purchaser is obligated to buy.

conditional sales contract a CONTRACT for the sale of property stating that the seller retains TITLE until the conditions of the contract have been fulfilled. *See* CONTRACT FOR DEED.

condo shortened form of CONDOMINIUM.

condominium a system of ownership of individual units in a multi-unit structure, combined with joint ownership of commonly used property (e.g., sidewalks, hallways, stairs, etc.). *See* COMMON ELEMENTS.

conforming loan a MORTGAGE LOAN that is eligible for purchase by FNMA or FHLMC.

consideration anything of value given to induce entering into a CONTRACT; it may be money, personal services, or love and affection.

conslidation loan new loan that pays off more than one existing loan, generally providing easier repayment terms.

contingency a condition that must be satisfied before the party to a CONTRACT must purchase or sell.

contract an agreement between competent parties to do or not to do certain things for a CONSIDERATION. Common REAL ESTATE contracts are contract of sale, CONTRACT FOR DEED, MORTGAGE, LEASE, LISTING.

contract for deed a REAL ESTATE installment sales arrangement whereby the buyer may use, occupy, and enjoy land, but no DEED is given by the seller (so no TITLE passes) until all or a specified part of the sale price has been paid. *Same as* CONDITIONAL SALES CONTRACT, and LAND CONTRACT.

contract interest rate the stated or face interest rate. Does not include the effect of DISCOUNT POINTS, fees, and PREPAYMENT PENALTIES. *Contrast* EFFECTIVE INTEREST RATE.

contract of sale *same as* AGREEMENT OF SALE.

conventional loan, mortgage

1. a MORTGAGE LOAN other than one guaranteed by the VETERANS ADMINISTRATION (VA) or insured by the FEDERAL HOUSING ADMINISTRATION (FHA). *See* VA LOAN, FHA LOAN.

2. A fixed-rate, fixed-term mortgage loan.

cooperative a type of corporate ownership of real property whereby stockholders of the corporation are entitled to use a certain dwelling unit or other units of space. Special income tax laws allow the tenant stockholders to deduct their share of INTEREST and PROPERTY TAXES paid by the corporation.

counteroffer rejection of an OFFER to buy or sell, with a simultaneous substitute offer.

credit report a compilation of information about the use of financial credit by a specific individual. The report contains the credit history of the individual and is used to calculate a CREDIT SCORE. These reports are produced by credit agencies and used by lenders to evaluate the risk of making a loan to a prospective borrower.

credit score a number that purports to predict the probability of a person DEFAULTING on a loan. Generally, the higher the number, the better risk the individual is considered to be. The score may determine whether the person gets the loan and how favorable will be the terms. The score is estimated from information contained in the individual's CREDIT REPORT. *See* FICO.

curtesy the right of a husband to all or part of his deceased wife's realty regardless of the provisions of her will. Exists in only a few states. *Compare* dower.

deed a written document, properly signed and delivered, that conveys TITLE to real property. *See* GENERAL WARRANTY DEED, QUITCLAIM DEED, SPECIAL WARRANTY DEED.

deed of trust an instrument used in many states in lieu of a MORTGAGE. Legal TITLE to the property is vested in one or more trustees to secure the repayment of the loan.

deed restriction a clause in a DEED, often imposed by a seller, that limits the use of land.

default failure to fulfill an obligation or promise, or to perform specified acts.

deficiency judgment a court order stating that the borrower still owes money when the sale of the security for a loan does not entirely satisfy a DEFAULTED debt.

Department of Housing and Urban Development (HUD) a United States government agency established to implement certain federal housing and community development programs.

Department of Veterans Affairs *See* VA.

deposit *See* EARNEST MONEY.

depreciation
1. in accounting or income taxation, allocating the cost of an asset over its estimated useful life.

2. in APPRAISAL, a charge against the reproduction cost (new) of an asset for the estimated wear and obsolescence.

Depreciation may be physical, functional, or economic.

detached house residential unit surrounded by freestanding walls and generally on a separate LOT from other nearby units.

discount broker a licensed broker who provides BROKERAGE services for a lower COMMISSION than that typical in the market. Generally, the services provided are less extensive than those of a full-service BROKER or may be unbundled, so that a client may contract for specific services. Many discount brokers charge a flat fee rather than a percentage of the selling price.

discount points amounts paid to the lender (often by the seller) at the time of origination of a loan, to account for the difference between the market INTEREST rate and the face rate of the note (which is lower).

dower under common law, the legal right of a wife or child to part of a deceased husband or father's property. *Compare* CURTESY.

down payment the amount one pays for property in addition to the debt incurred.

due diligence
1. making a reasonable effort to perform under a contract.
2. making a reasonable effort to provide accurate, complete information. A study that often precedes the purchase of property, which considers the physical, financial, legal, and social characteristics of the property and expected investment performance; the underwriting of a loan or investment.

due-on-sale clause a provision in a MORTGAGE that states that the full amount of a loan is due upon the sale of the property.

duplex a form of housing having two residential units under one roof, whether side by side or one above the other on separate floors.

earnest money a deposit made before CLOSING by a purchaser of REAL ESTATE to evidence good faith.

easement the right, privilege, or interest that one party has in the land of another. The most common easements are for utility lines.

effective interest rate the true rate of return considering all relevant FINANCING expenses. *See* ANNUAL PERCENTAGE RATE.

EIFS (exterior insulating and finish system) a synthetic alternative to natural stucco, a cement-based material used for finishing the exterior of houses and other buildings. Moisture penetration into EIFS may be problematic.

eminent domain the right of the government or a public utility to acquire property for necessary public use by condemnation; the owner must be fairly compensated.

encroachment a building, a part of a building, or an obstruction that physically intrudes upon, overlaps, or trespasses upon the property of another.

encumbrance any right to or interest in land that affects its use or value. Includes outstanding MORTGAGE LOANS, unpaid taxes, EASEMENTS, and DEED RESTRICTIONS.

equity the INTEREST or value that the owner has in REAL ESTATE over and above the LIENS against it.

equity loan usually a SECOND MORTGAGE whereby the property owner borrows against the house, based on the value of EQUITY built up by APPRECIATION.

escrow an agreement between two or more parties providing that certain instruments or property be placed with a third party for safekeeping, pending the fulfillment or performance of some act or condition.

et ux. abbreviation of the Latin *et uxor,* which means "and wife."

exclusive agency listing employment CONTRACT giving only one BROKER, for a specified time, the right to sell the property and also allowing the owner acting alone to sell the property without paying a COMMISSION.

exclusive right to sell listing employment CONTRACT giving the BROKER the right to collect COMMISSION if the property is sold by anyone, including the owner, during the term of the AGREEMENT OF SALE. *See* MULTIPLE LISTING SERVICE.

execute to sign a CONTRACT; sometimes, to perform a contract fully.

fair market value a term, generally used in property tax and condemnation legislation, meaning the MARKET VALUE of a property.

Fannie Mae nickname for the Federal National Mortgage Association (FNMA), one of two companies that purchase in the secondary market a large share of the residential MORTGAGE LOANS originated each year. Most of these loans are used to support special bond-type securities sold to investors. Fannie Mae, now a semi-private corporation, was once an agency of the federal government. FNMA is owned by its stockholders, who elect ten to its board of directors. The U.S. president appoints the other five directors.

Federal Emergency Management Agency (FEMA) more information at *www.fema.gov*.

federal fair housing law a federal law that forbids discrimination on the basis of race, color, sex, religion, handicap, familial status, or national origin in the selling or renting of homes and apartments.

Federal Housing Administration (FHA) an agency within the U.S. DEPARTMENT OF HOUSING AND URBAN DEVELOPMENT that administers many loan programs, loan guarantee programs, and loan insurance programs designed to make more housing available.

fee simple or fee absolute absolute ownership of real property; owner is entitled to the entire property with unconditional power of disposition during his or her life, and it descends to his or her heirs and legal representatives upon his or her death intestate.

FEMA *See* FEDERAL EMERGENCY MANAGEMENT AGENCY.

FHA *See* FEDERAL HOUSING ADMINISTRATION.

FHA loan a mortgage loan insured by the FHA.

FHLMC *See* FREDDIE MAC.

FICO (Fair Isaac Company) score a measure of borrower credit risk commonly used by MORTGAGE underwriters when originating loans on owner-occupied homes. The score is based on the applicants' credit history and the frequency with which they use credit. Expressed as a number between 300 and 850, the score determines not only whether the loan is approved but also what type of TERMS the lender will offer.

financing borrowing money to buy property.

first mortgage a MORTGAGE that has priority as a LIEN over all other mortgages. In cases of FORECLOSURE, the first mortgage will be satisfied before other mortgages.

first-timers people who are in the market to buy a home for the first time. They are either setting up a household for the first time (possibly after leaving college or their parents' home) or currently rent their residences. Someone who has owned a home in the past but has spent the last several years renting can also be considered a first-timer.

fixed-rate mortgage one on which the INTEREST rate does not change over the entire term of the loan.

fixer-upper a house on the market that needs extensive repairs. Generally, the price is lowered to reflect the condition of the home. Such homes may appeal to buyers who are looking for a bargain and feel confident in their ability to make the necessary repairs.

fixtures personal property attached to the land or improvements so as to become part of the REAL ESTATE.

FNMA *See* FANNIE MAE.

foreclosure a termination of all rights of a MORTGAGOR or the GRANTEE in the property covered by the MORTGAGE.

Freddie Mac nickname for Federal Home Loan Mortgage Corporation (FHLMC), counterpart to FANNIE MAE as a major purchaser of residential MORTGAGE LOANS in the secondary market. This company was originally created to buy loans from federally chartered savings and loan associations. Today, there is little difference in the operations of Fannie Mae and Freddie Mac. Together, these companies have significant influence on the standards required of mortgage borrowers and types of loans offered.

FSBO or **For Sale by Owner** A term referring to properties on the market that are not listed with a REAL ESTATE BROKER. Pronounced "fizzbo."

fully indexed rate in conjunction with ADJUSTABLE-RATE MORTGAGES, the INTEREST rate indicated by the sum of the current value of the INDEX and MARGIN applied to the loan. This rate is used to calculate monthly payments in the absence of constraints imposed by the initial rate or caps. *See* TEASER RATE.

general contractor one who constructs a building or other improvement for the owner or developer. May retain a construction labor force or use SUBCONTRACTORS.

general warranty deed a DEED in which the GRANTOR agrees to protect the GRANTEE against any other claim to TITLE to the property and provides other promises.

GI loan *see* VA LOAN.

Ginnie Mae nickname for Government National Mortgage Association, a government organization to assist in housing finance. It has two main programs:

1. to guarantee payments to investors in mortgage-backed securities.
2. to absorb the write-down of low-interest-rate loans that are used to finance low-income housing.

Graduate Realtors® Institute (GRI) a designation earned by those who complete an educational program sponsored by the National Association of Realtors® or State Realtor Boards.

graduated-payment mortgage (GPM) a MORTGAGE requiring lower payments in early years than in later years. Payments increase in steps each year, typically for five years, until the installments are sufficient to AMORTIZE the loan.

grantee the party to whom the TITLE to real property is conveyed; the buyer.

grantor anyone who gives a DEED.

Green Acres program to preserve natural open space areas to serve public recreation and conservation purposes with tax incentives.

gross rent multiplier (GRM) the sales price divided by the contract rental rate.

hazard insurance a form of insurance that protects against certain risks, such as fires and storms.

home equity line of credit a type of HOME EQUITY LOAN that establishes an account that the borrower can draw on as desired. A maximum amount is typically placed on the outstanding debt, similar to the credit limit on a credit card. Interest accrues based on the amount of money actually borrowed, not the amount of the credit line. The product is intended for people who may need to access cash in the future but have no immediate need for a loan.

home equity loan a loan secured by a SECOND MORTGAGE on one's principal residence, generally to be used for some nonhousing expenditure. Generally, two types are available. A line-of-credit home equity loan establishes a credit line that can be drawn upon as needed. A traditional second mortgage provides lump-sum proceeds at the time the loan is closed.

home inspector a professional who evaluates the structural and mechanical condition of a home prior to its being sold. Some states require home inspectors to be bonded or licensed.

home-owners' association an organization of the home owners in a particular subdivision, planned unit development, or CONDOMINIUM; generally for the purpose of enforcing DEED restrictions or managing the COMMON ELEMENTS of the development.

home-owner's insurance an insurance policy designed especially for home owners. Usually protects the owner from losses caused by most common disasters, theft, and liability. Coverage and costs vary widely.

home-owner's warranty (HOW) a private insurance program that protects purchasers of newly constructed homes, when the builder participates in the program, against structural and mechanical faults.

home ownership the state of living in a structure that one owns. Contrasted with being a renter or tenant in one's home.

homestead exemption in some jurisdictions, a reduction in the ASSESSED VALUE allowed for one's principal residence. Some states provide other exemptions for certain qualifications, such as disability or age older than 65.

HUD *See* DEPARTMENT OF HOUSING AND URBAN DEVELOPMENT.

HUD-1 form (Uniform Settlemet Statement) a standardized accounting of all the costs required to close a residential sale. The form clearly delineates the costs (COMMISSIONS, fees, and other charges) that accrue to each party in the transaction. These completed forms can be obtained prior to the CLOSING so that each party can provide a certified check for their portion of the expenses.

hybrid ARM a loan that features a fixed INTEREST rate for the first 5 to 15 years of the loan term, after which the interest rate is adjusted. Some hybrids experience only one adjustment; for others, interest is adjusted annually in the manner of an ADJUSTABLE-RATE MORTGAGE. Hybrids usually have an initial interest rate higher than straight ARMs and lower than long-term fixed-rate loans.

illiquid asset one that is not readily convertible to cash.

index

1. (*n.*) a statistic that indicates some current economic or financial condition. Indexes are often used to make adjustments in wage rates, rental rates, loan INTEREST rates, and pension benefits set by long-term CONTRACTS.

2. (*v.*) adjust contract terms according to an index.

inflation a loss in the purchasing power of money; an increase in the general price level. Generally measured by the Consumer Price Index, published by the Bureau of Labor Statistics.

inside lot in a subdivision, a lot surrounded on each side by other lots, as opposed to a corner lot, which has road frontage on at least two sides.

interest cost of the use of money. Lenders require payment of interest at a specified rate to compensate for risk, deferment of benefits, INFLATION, and administrative burdens.

interest-only loan a loan in which INTEREST is payable at regular intervals until loan maturity, when the full loan balance is due. Does not require AMORTIZATION. *Contrast* SELF-AMORTIZING MORTGAGE.

interval adjustment cap *see* ADJUSTMENT INTERVAL.

itemized deductions expenses that can be deducted from taxable income for purposes of paying federal income tax. Housing-related expenses, such as mortgage INTEREST, property taxes, and casualty losses, are among the items that can be deducted. A taxpayer who itemizes cannot take the standard deduction.

joint tenancy ownership of realty by two or more persons, each of whom has an undivided interest with the right of survivorship.

jumbo mortgage a loan for an amount exceeding the statutory limit placed on the size of loans that FREDDIE MAC and FANNIE MAE can purchase. Such loans must be maintained in the lender's portfolio or sold to private investors. These loans are typically required for purchase of luxury homes.

junior mortgage a mortgage whose claim against the property will be satisfied only after prior mortgages have been repaid. *See* FIRST MORTGAGE, SECOND MORTGAGE.

land contract *same as* CONTRACT FOR DEED.

lease *See* RENTAL AGREEMENT.

lease (with) option (to buy) a lease that includes the right, but not the obligation, to buy at a later date, at a price that is usually established with the LEASE.

leverage use of borrowed funds to increase purchasing power and, ideally, to increase the profitability of an investment.

liability insurance protection for a property owner from claims arising from injuries or damage to other people or property.

lien a charge against property making it security for the payment of a debt, judgment, mortgage, or taxes; it is a type of ENCUMBRANCE. A *specific* lien is against certain property only. A *general* lien is against all the property owned by the debtor.

life-of-loan cap a contractual limitation on the maximum INTEREST rate that can be applied to an ADJUSTABLE-RATE MORTGAGE during the term of the loan. *Contrast* ADJUSTMENT CAP.

liquidity ease of converting assets to cash.

list to give or obtain a listing.

listing

1. a written engagement CONTRACT between a principal and an agent, authorizing the agent to perform services for the principal involving the latter's property.
2. a record of property for sale by a BROKER who has been authorized by the owner to sell.
3. the property so listed.

listing agreement, listing contract *same as* LISTING (1).

listing price the price that a seller puts on a home when it is placed on the market. Listing price, or ASKING PRICE, is generally considered a starting place for negotiations between the seller and a prospective buyer.

loan application document required by a lender prior to issuing a LOAN COMMITMENT. The application generally includes the following information:

1. name of the borrower
2. amount and terms of the loan
3. description of the subject property to be mortgaged
4. borrower's financial and employment data

loan commitment an agreement to lend money, generally of a specified amount, at specified terms at some time in the future. A LOCK (RATE) may be included in the loan commitment.

loan contract document that acknowledges the debt of the borrower and establishes the terms by which that debt is to be discharged. The loan contract has all the clauses that determine how loan payments will be made, the conditions under which the borrower can prepay the loan, and what constitutes default by the borrower. A mortgage loan requires, in addition to the loan contract, a mortgage that pledges real property against the risk of default by the borrower.

loan officer the person who manages the LOAN APPLICATION process. The officer may be an employee of a bank, a MORTGAGE

BANKER, or a MORTGAGE BROKER. The loan officer works with the borrower to complete the loan application and supply supporting information, as well as oversee the processing necessary to approve the application.

loan-to-value ratio (LTV) the portion of the amount borrowed compared to the cost or value of the property purchased.

lock (rate) promise by a mortgage lender to hold the INTEREST rate constant for a specific period during the loan approval process. The lock allows the borrower to proceed with the home purchase with certainty of how much the loan will cost.

lot and block number a method of locating a parcel of land. The description refers to a map of a SUBDIVISION that numbers each lot and block.

lowball offer an offer from a prospective property buyer that is much lower than the LISTING PRICE. Such an offer may indicate the buyer's belief that the property will not attract many good offers and that the ASKING PRICE is unrealistic. Also, it probably means the buyer is interested in the property only if it can be purchased at a bargain price.

LTV *See* LOAN-TO-VALUE RATIO.

manufactured housing a term used to describe a factory-built house transported to a LOT. In contrast to structures referred to as *mobile homes,* modern units must pass a federal inspection at the factory. Also includes *modular housing.*

margin a constant amount added to the value of the INDEX for the purpose of adjusting the INTEREST rate on an ADJUSTABLE-RATE MORTGAGE.

market value
1. in economics, the theoretical highest price a buyer, willing but not compelled to buy, would pay, and the lowest price a seller, willing but not compelled to sell, would accept.

2. in APPRAISAL, the most probable price, as of a specified date, in cash, or terms equivalent to cash, or in other precisely revealed terms, for which the specified property rights should sell after reasonable exposure in a competitive market under all conditions requisite to a fair sale, with the buyer and seller each acting prudently, knowledgeably, and for self-interest, and assuming that neither is under undue duress.

master deed DEED used by a condominium developer or converter for recording a CONDOMINIUM development. It divides a single property into individually owned units, includes restrictions on their use, and provides for ownership of common areas.

mechanic's lien a LIEN given by law upon a building or other improvement upon land, and upon the land itself, as security for the payment for labor done and materials furnished for improvement.

MLS *See* MULTIPLE LISTING SERVICE.

mortgage (loan) a written instrument that creates a **lien** upon REAL ESTATE as security for the payment of a specified debt.

mortgage banker one who originates, sells, and services MORTGAGE LOANS.

mortgage broker one who, for a fee, places loans with investors but does not service such loans.

mortgage insurance protection for the lender in the event of DEFAULT, usually covering 10 to 20 percent of the amount borrowed.

mortgage note a CONTRACT that legally pledges the mortgaged property to the lender as collateral for the MORTGAGE LOAN. The note goes hand in hand with the loan contract and is executed at the same time. The note describes the property, acknowledges the borrower's obligation to repay the loan and details conditions under which the lender can FORECLOSE the mortgage loan.

mortgagee one who holds a LIEN on property of TITLE to property, as security for a debt; the lender.

mortgagor one who pledges property as security for a loan; the borrower.

multiple listing service (MLS) an association of REAL ESTATE BROKERS that agrees to share listings with one another. The listing broker and the selling broker share the commission. The MLS usually posts listings online, updating them frequently. Prospective buyers benefit from the ability to select from among many homes listed by any member broker.

NABIE National Association of Building Inspection Engineers (*www.nabie.org*), a charter affinity group of the National Association of Professional Engineers (NSPE; *www.nspe.org*). Membership in NABIE requires that a person be a licensed Professional Engineer or Architect with membership in NSPE having documented experience performing building inspections, in addition to passing an evaluation of actual building inspection work products, and approval of professional references. The three membership levels require increased years of experience and review requirements: Professional, Executive, and Diplomat.

National Association of Real Estate Brokers (NAREB) an organization of minority REAL ESTATE salespersons and BROKERS who are called REALTISTS®.

National Association of Realtors® (NAR) an organization of Realtors®, devoted to encouraging professionalism in REAL ESTATE activities. There are more than a million members of NAR, 50 state associations, and several affiliates.

negative amortization an increase in the outstanding balance of a loan resulting from the deficiency of periodic debt service payments to cover required INTEREST charged on the loan.

net listing a LISTING in which the BROKER'S COMMISSION is the excess of the sales price over an agreed-upon (net) price to the seller; illegal in some states because it creates a conflict of interest for the broker.

net worth the sum of an individual's assets less the sum of current obligations. To calculate, an individual lists the value of all possessions that can be sold in the market and nets out the amount of outstanding debt. The result is a measure of personal wealth.

notary public an officer who is authorized to make acknowledgment to certain types of documents, such as DEEDS, CONTRACTS, and MORTGAGES, and before whom affidavits may be sworn.

novation
1. a three-party agreement whereby one party is released from a contract and another party is substituted.
2. substitution of one contract for another, with acceptance by all parties.

offer an expression of willingness to purchase a property at a specified price.

offering price the amount a prospective buyer offers for a property on the market. This offer is submitted via a sales CONTRACT which constitutes a bona fide offer for the property.

open house a method of showing a home for sale whereby the home is left open for inspection by interested parties.

open housing a condition under which housing units may be purchased or LEASED without regard for racial, ethnic, color, or religious characteristics of the buyers or tenants.

open listing a LISTING given to any number of BROKERS without liability to compensate any except the one who first secures a buyer who is ready, willing, and able to meet the terms of the listing or secures the seller's acceptance of another OFFER. Often used for commercial property. The sale of the property automatically terminates all open listings.

opportunity cost the cost of choosing one course of action or investment over another. The theoretical loss may be the difference between the return on a selected investment and another investment, or it may be some nonmonetary benefit that would have been obtained by the alternative decision.

option ARM a loan that allows the borrower to choose among several alternative methods to make monthly payments. Within limits, the method can change with each payment. A common example allows the borrower to choose between a fully AMORTIZING payment, an INTEREST-ONLY payment, and a minimum payment that produces NEGATIVE AMORTIZATION. These loans are tailored to borrowers whose income or expenses are unpredictable.

option period the period within which an option may be exercised. *See* OPTION ARM.

oral contract an unwritten agreement. With few exceptions, oral agreements for the sale or use of REAL ESTATE are unenforceable. In most states, contracts for the sale or rental of real estate, unless they are in writing, are unenforceable under the Statute of Frauds. Oral LEASES for a year or less are often acceptable.

P&I *See* PRINCIPAL AND INTEREST PAYMENT.

permanent loan a MORTGAGE that is initially written for a long period of time (over ten years).

piggyback loan a combination of MORTGAGE LOANS designed to cover a high percentage of the property's cost without the necessity of MORTGAGE INSURANCE. A typical arrangement combines a first mortgage covering 80 percent of the value with a second mortgage loan supplying an additional 15 percent. The borrower makes a cash down payment of five percent of the cost.

plat a plan or map of a specific land area. An official plat of a SUB-DIVISION provides boundaries of each LOT and the location of utility EASEMENTS.

PMI *See* PRIVATE MORTGAGE INSURANCE, MORTGAGE INSURANCE.

points *Short for* DISCOUNT POINTS.

pre-approval preliminary processing of a loan for a potential borrower by a lender before a sale has been contracted. A lender's pre-approval indicates that the individual is sufficiently creditworthy to get a loan up to a stated maximum assuming a suitable property is pledged as security.

prepayment penalty a penalty imposed on a borrower when a loan is retired before maturity.

prepayment privilege the right of a borrower to retire a loan before maturity.

prequalify estimate of how much MORTGAGE LOAN a specific individual is likely to be able to get based on current income and debts. The exercise, which can be performed by anyone familiar with the formulas and current loan terms, is helpful in setting the limit on what a prospective buyer can afford.

pride of ownership a sense of well-being and pleasure that some people derive from owning a home or other real property. This feeling relates to the social status conveyed to property owners, a feeling of financial accomplishment and commitment to the local community, as well as pride in the property's appearance.

primary (mortgage) market that portion of the credit market that originates mortgage loans, including institutional lenders, such as savings and loan associations and banks, and mortgage bankers and brokers.

principal

1. one who owns or will use property.
2. one who contracts for the services of an AGENT or BROKER, the broker's or agent's client.
3. the amount of money raised by a MORTGAGE or other loan, as distinct from the INTEREST paid on it.

principal and interest payment (P&I) a periodic payment, usually made monthly, that includes the INTEREST charges for the period plus an amount applied to AMORTIZATION of the principal balance. Commonly used with SELF-AMORTIZING loans. *See* AMORTIZATION.

principal, interest, taxes, and insurance (PITI) the monthly MORTGAGE payment (P&I), with the addition of an amount deposited in ESCROW for future payment of taxes and insurance.

private mortgage insurance (PMI) *See* MORTGAGE INSURANCE.

property taxes taxes levied by local government units on the ASSESSED VALUE of real property. *Also called* AD VALOREM TAXES.

prorate to allocate between seller and buyer their proportionate share of an obligation paid or due; for example, to prorate REAL ESTATE taxes.

purchase-money mortgage a MORTGAGE given by a GRANTEE (buyer) to a GRANTOR (seller) in part payment of the purchase price of REAL ESTATE.

quitclaim deed a DEED that conveys only the GRANTOR's rights or interest in REAL ESTATE, without stating the nature of the rights and with no warranties of ownership. Often used to remove a possible CLOUD ON THE TITLE. *Contrast with* GENERAL WARRANTY DEED.

real estate

1. in law, land and everything more or less attached to it. Ownership below to the center of the earth and above to the heavens. Distinguished from personal property. *Same as* realty.

2. in business, the activities concerned with ownership and use transfers of the physical property.

real estate appraiser one who is qualified to provide a professional opinion on the value of property. All states in the United States offer two certifications for real estate appraisers: Certified General Appraiser, awarded to one who is qualified to appraise any property, and Certified Residential Appraiser, awarded to one who is qualified to appraise residences with up to 4 units and vacant lots. State certification requires education, experience, and passing a written examination. Some states offer additional categories for licensees and trainees. Several appraisal organizations offer professional designations. The Appraisal Institute is the best known in real estate; it offers the MAI (income property) and SRA (residential) designations. Others include American Society of Appraisers, International Association of Assessing Officers, International Right of Way Association, National Society of Real Estate Appraisers, National Association of Master Appraisers, and American Society of Farm Managers and Rural Appraisers.

real estate broker/agent a professional who sells real property owned by those who CONTRACT for their services. Sellers engage BROKERAGE AGENTS through a LISTING contract. Buyers often work with agents representing the seller and can hire their own agent through a buyer's representative contract. All brokerage agents must be licensed by the state in which they operate. Most states recognize two types of licensees: brokers and salespersons; anyone active with a salesperson's license must be affiliated with a licensed broker.

Real Estate Settlement Procedures Act (RESPA) a law that states how MORTGAGE lenders must treat those who apply for federally related REAL ESTATE loans on property with one to four dwelling units. Intended to provide borrowers with more knowledge when they comparison shop for mortgage money.

Realtist® a member of the NATIONAL ASSOCIATION OF REAL ESTATE BROKERS, a group composed primarily of minority BROKERS, who are professionals in REAL ESTATE and subscribe to a strict code of ethics.

Realtor® a professional in REAL ESTATE who subscribes to a strict Code of Ethics as a member of the local and state boards and of the NATIONAL ASSOCIATION OF REALTORS®.

redlining the illegal practice of refusing to originate MORTGAGE loans in certain neighborhoods on the basis of race or ethnic composition.

refinance to substitute a new loan for an old one, often in order to borrow more money or reduce the INTEREST rate.

relocatee people who are moving because they need or want to locate in a different place.

rental agreeement *Same as* LEASE.

reservation price the highest price a buyer can pay for a property and still achieve his or her primary objectives, such as keeping the monthly payments affordable or paying no more than MARKET VALUE for the property. A buyer will negotiate in hopes of keeping the sales price at or below his or her reservation price.

RESPA *See* REAL ESTATEMENT SETTLEMENT PROCEDURES ACT.

reverse mortgage a special loan designed to provide older home owners with additional income. The lender agrees to pay the borrower a lump sum amount, a monthly payment, or a line of credit. In exchange, the borrower pledges the home, which will be sold to pay off the loan at some date in the future, corresponding to the death of the borrower or such time as the borrower no longer wishes to live in the home.

sales contract *See* CONTRACT.

secondary (mortgage) market the mechanisms available to buy and sell mortgages, mainly residential FIRST MORTGAGES. There is no set meeting place for the secondary mortgage market. FANNIE MAE and FREDDIE MAC hold auctions weekly to buy those mortgages offered at the highest effective rate. Bids are collected from all over the country.

second mortgage a subordinated lien, created by a mortgage loan, over the amount of a first mortgage. Second mortgages are used at purchase to reduce the amount of a cash down payment or in refinancing to raise cash for any purpose.

self-amortizing mortgage one that will retire itself through regular PRINCIPAL and INTEREST payments. *Contrast with* BALLOON MORTGAGE, INTEREST-ONLY LOAN.

seller financing one or more loans provided by the seller to facilitate the sale of a property. Such loans may be secured by a first MORTGAGE on the property (if no other mortgage loan is assumed or originated upon the transfer in TITLE) or a SECOND MORTGAGE. Terms of these loans can be arranged to further the interests of the parties. *See* PURCHASE-MONEY MORTGAGE.

seller's market economic conditions that favor sellers, reflecting rising prices and market activity. *Contrast with* BUYER'S MARKET.

settlement *See* CLOSING.

settlement statement document that lists and sums up the amounts that must be paid by each party to a sale. It also indicates how these monies are to be distributed. Also called a CLOSING STATEMENT or a HUD-1.

single-family home a housing unit that contains accommodations for sleeping, bathing, and preparing food with access directly to the outside of the structure without having to pass through a common lobby or other housing units. The unit need not be detached, but can be included with other units in a DUPLEX or a TOWNHOUSE.

special assessment an assessment made against a property to pay for a public improvement by which the assessed property is supposed to be especially benefited.

special warranty deed a DEED in which the GRANTOR limits the TITLE warranty given to the grantee to anyone claiming by, from, through, or under him or her, the grantor. The grantor does not warrant against title defects arising from conditions that existed before he or she owned the property.

specific performance a legal action in which the court requires a party to a CONTRACT to perform the terms of the contract when he or she has refused to fulfill his or her obligations. Used in REAL ESTATE, because each parcel of land is unique.

subcontractor one who performs services under contract to a GENERAL CONTRACTOR.

subdivision a tract of land divided into LOTS or plots suitable for home-building purposes. Most states and localities require that a SUBDIVISION plat be recorded.

subject to mortgage describes a buyer who takes TITLE to mortgaged real property but does not personally accept responsibility for the PRINCIPAL. The buyer must make payments in order to keep the property; however, if he or she fails to do so, only his or her EQUITY in that property is lost.

subprime loan a MORTGAGE LOAN taken out by someone with poor credit or no established credit history. Loan terms are less favorable than those on comparable loans made to creditworthy borrowers. These loans allow many to buy homes who would not be able to qualify for standard FINANCING.

survey the process by which a parcel of land is measured and its area ascertained; also, the blueprint showing the measurements, boundaries, and area.

sweat equity value added to a property due to improvements as a result of work performed personally by the owner.

teaser rate initial rate applied to an ARM that is significantly below the FULLY INDEXED INTEREST RATE applicable to the loan. These introductory rates are used to induce borrowers to choose an ARM as an alternative to a FIXED-RATE loan. Following the introductory period, the rate applied to the loan will revert to the fully indexed rate unless an adjustment CAP limits the change.

term, amortization for a loan, the period of time during which PRINCIPAL and INTEREST payments must be made; generally, the time needed to fully AMORTIZE the loan.

title evidence that the owner of land is in lawful possession thereof; evidence of ownership.

title insurance a policy that ensures that good TITLE is transferred in the course of a sales transaction. The insurance company will handle any successful claims against the title to the property that might arise in the future. There are two common types of policies: a MORTGAGEE's policy that protects the lender and a MORTGAGOR's policy that protects the buyer.

title search an examination of the public records to determine the ownership and ENCUMBRANCES affecting real property.

townhouse a single-family housing unit that is attached to other similar units but features direct access to the outside from the front of the structure. Most often, there is more than one story in each unit. Individual units are attached to other units with a party wall that is shared between the units.

uniform settlement statement *See* HUD-1 FORM.

upgraders people who currently own a home but are seeking to buy what they consider a better home; also called "move-up" buyers. The "upgrade" may involve getting a larger home, a more conveniently located home, or one with special amenities. In almost all cases, the upgrader is looking to spend more for the new home than the amount derived from selling the old home.

VA Department of Veterans Affairs (former Veterans Administration), a government agency that provides certain services to discharged servicemen.

VA loan, mortgage a loan that is guaranteed by the U.S. Department of Veterans Affairs. Discharged servicemen with more than 120 days of active duty are generally eligible for a VA loan, which typically does not require a down payment.

variable-rate loan *See* ADJUSTABLE-RATE MORTGAGE.

variance a special grant of relief from the requirements of a ZONING ORDINANCE to an individual property owner. The criterion applied is one of hardship, in that a property might be considered unusable for the purposes allowed by the zoning ordinance if the rules were strictly applied. An example is an odd-shaped lot that is zoned residential but for which the required setbacks would preclude building any reasonable residential structure.

variation relief from the requirements of a BUILDING CODE when strict compliance would result in practical difficulty provided the exception, if granted, would not jeopardize the health, safety, and welfare of the occupants or the public.

vendee the buyer.

vendor the seller.

warranty deed TITLE to REAL ESTATE in which the GRANTOR guarantees title. Usually protects against other claimants, LIENS, or ENCUMBRANCES and offers good title.

yield curve a graph of current interest rates of similar obligations, except for the maturity term.

zoning a legal mechanism whereby local governments regulate the use of privately owned real property by specific application of police power to prevent conflicting land uses and promote orderly development. All privately owned land within the jurisdiction is placed within designated zones that limit the type and intensity of development permitted.

zoning ordinance act of city or county or other authorities specifying the type of use to which property may be put in specific areas. Example: residential, commercial, industrial.

Monthly Mortgage Payment Per $1,000 Initial Principal

Interest Rate Percent	Term in Years			
	15	20	25	30
4.00	7.3969	6.0598	5.2784	4.7742
4.25	7.5228	6.1923	5.4174	4.9194
4.50	7.6499	6.3265	5.5583	5.0669
4.75	7.7783	6.4622	5.7012	5.2165
5.00	7.9079	6.5996	5.8459	5.3682
5.25	8.0388	6.7384	5.9925	5.5220
5.50	8.1708	6.8789	6.1409	5.6779
5.75	8.3041	7.0208	6.2911	5.8357
6.00	8.4386	7.1643	6.4430	5.9955
6.25	8.5742	7.3093	6.5967	6.1572
6.50	8.7111	7.4557	6.7521	6.3207
6.75	8.8491	7.6036	6.9091	6.4860
7.00	8.9883	7.7530	7.0678	6.6530
7.25	9.1286	7.9038	7.2281	6.8218
7.50	9.2701	8.0559	7.3899	6.9921
7.75	9.4128	8.2095	7.5533	7.1641
8.00	9.5565	8.3644	7.7182	7.3376
8.25	9.7014	8.5207	7.8845	7.5127
8.50	9.8474	8.6782	8.0523	7.6891
8.75	9.9945	8.8371	8.2214	7.8670
9.00	10.1427	8.9973	8.3920	8.0462
9.25	10.2919	9.1587	8.5638	8.2268
9.50	10.4422	9.3213	8.7370	8.4085
9.75	10.5936	9.4852	8.9114	8.5915
10.00	10.7461	9.6502	9.0870	8.7757
10.25	10.8995	9.8164	9.2638	8.9610
10.50	11.0540	9.9838	9.4418	9.1474
10.75	11.2095	10.1523	9.6209	9.3348
11.00	11.3660	10.3219	9.8011	9.5232
11.25	11.5234	10.4926	9.9824	9.7126
11.50	11.6819	10.6643	10.1647	9.9029
11.75	11.8413	10.8371	10.3480	10.0941
12.00	12.0017	11.0109	10.5322	10.2861

This table offers the monthly principal and interest payment required to amortize a $1,000 loan.

To use:

1. Find the intersection of the Interest Rate Percent with Term in Years
2. Multiply the amount at the intersection with the loan amount in thousands.

For example, a $150,000 self-amortizing 30-year loan has an 8% interest rate.
The factor is 7.3376. Multiply by 150 to derive the monthly principal and interest payment:
150 × 7.3376 = $1,100.64.

B. Type of Loan

1. ☐ FHA 2. ☐ FmHA 3. ☐ Conv. Unins.	6. File Number:	7. Loan Number:	8. Mortgage Insurance Case Number:	
4. ☐ VA 5. ☐ Conv. Ins.				

C. Note: This form is furnished to give you a statement of actual settlement costs. Amounts paid to and by the settlement agent are shown. Items marked "(p.o.c.)" were paid outside the closing; they are shown here for informational purposes and are not included in the totals.

D. Name & Address of Borrower:	E. Name & Address of Seller:	F. Name & Address of Lender:

G. Property Location:	H. Settlement Agent:	
	Place of Settlement:	I. Settlement Date:

J. Summary of Borrower's Transaction		**K. Summary of Seller's Transaction**	
100. Gross Amount Due From Borrower		**400. Gross Amount Due To Seller**	
101. Contract sales price		401. Contract sales price	
102. Personal property		402. Personal property	
103. Settlement charges to borrower (line 1400)		403.	
104.		404.	
105.		405.	
Adjustments for items paid by seller in advance		**Adjustments for items paid by seller in advance**	
106. City/town taxes to		406. City/town taxes to	
107. County taxes to		407. County taxes to	
108. Assessments to		408. Assessments to	
109.		409.	
110.		410.	
111.		411.	
112.		412.	
120. Gross Amount Due From Borrower		**420. Gross Amount Due To Seller**	
200. Amounts Paid By Or In Behalf Of Borrower		**500. Reductions In Amount Due To Seller**	
201. Deposit or earnest money		501. Excess deposit (see instructions)	
202. Principal amount of new loan(s)		502. Settlement charges to seller (line 1400)	
203. Existing loan(s) taken subject to		503. Existing loan(s) taken subject to	
204.		504. Payoff of first mortgage loan	
205.		505. Payoff of second mortgage loan	
206.		506.	
207.		507.	
208.		508.	
209.		509.	
Adjustments for items unpaid by seller		**Adjustments for items unpaid by seller**	
210. City/town taxes to		510. City/town taxes to	
211. County taxes to		511. County taxes to	
212. Assessments to		512. Assessments to	
213.		513.	
214.		514.	
215.		515.	
216.		516.	
217.		517.	
218.		518.	
219.		519.	
220. Total Paid By/For Borrower		**520. Total Reduction Amount Due Seller**	
300. Cash At Settlement From/To Borrower		**600. Cash At Settlement To/From Seller**	
301. Gross Amount due from borrower (line 120)		601. Gross amount due to seller (line 420)	
302. Less amounts paid by/for borrower (line 220)	( )	602. Less reductions in amt. due seller (line 520)	( )
303. Cash ☐ From ☐ To Borrower		**603. Cash** ☐ To ☐ From Seller	

Section 5 of the Real Estate Settlement Procedures Act (RESPA) requires the following: • HUD must develop a Special Information Booklet to help persons borrowing money to finance the purchase of residential real estate to better understand the nature and costs of real estate settlement services; • Each lender must provide the booklet to all applicants from whom it receives or for whom it prepares a written application to borrow money to finance the purchase of residential real estate; • Lenders must prepare and distribute with the Booklet a Good Faith Estimate of the settlement costs that the borrower is likely to incur in connection with the settlement. These disclosures are manadatory.

Section 4(a) of RESPA mandates that HUD develop and prescribe this standard form to be used at the time of loan settlement to provide full disclosure of all charges imposed upon the borrower and seller. These are third party disclosures that are designed to provide the borrower with pertinent information during the settlement process in order to be a better shopper.

The Public Reporting Burden for this collection of information is estimated to average one hour per response, including the time for reviewing instructions, searching existing data sources, gathering and maintaining the data needed, and completing and reviewing the collection of information.

This agency may not collect this information, and you are not required to complete this form, unless it displays a currently valid OMB control number.

The information requested does not lend itself to confidentiality.

HUD-1 FORM   511

L. Settlement Charges

700. Total Sales/Broker's Commission based on price $ @ % =	Paid From Borrowers Funds at Settlement	Paid From Seller's Funds at Settlement
Division of Commission (line 700) as follows:		
701. $ to		
702. $ to		
703. Commission paid at Settlement		
704.		
800. Items Payable In Connection With Loan		
801. Loan Origination Fee %		
802. Loan Discount %		
803. Appraisal Fee to		
804. Credit Report to		
805. Lender's Inspection Fee		
806. Mortgage Insurance Application Fee to		
807. Assumption Fee		
808.		
809.		
810.		
811.		
900. Items Required By Lender To Be Paid In Advance		
901. Interest from to @$ /day		
902. Mortgage Insurance Premium for months to		
903. Hazard Insurance Premium for years to		
904. years to		
905.		
1000. Reserves Deposited With Lender		
1001. Hazard insurance months@$ per month		
1002. Mortgage insurance months@$ per month		
1003. City property taxes months@$ per month		
1004. County property taxes months@$ per month		
1005. Annual assessments months@$ per month		
1006. months@$ per month		
1007. months@$ per month		
1008. months@$ per month		
1100. Title Charges		
1101. Settlement or closing fee to		
1102. Abstract or title search to		
1103. Title examination to		
1104. Title insurance binder to		
1105. Document preparation to		
1106. Notary fees to		
1107. Attorney's fees to		
(includes above items numbers:)		
1108. Title insurance to		
(includes above items numbers:)		
1109. Lender's coverage $		
1110. Owner's coverage $		
1111.		
1112.		
1113.		
1200. Government Recording and Transfer Charges		
1201. Recording fees: Deed $; Mortgage $; Releases $		
1202. City/county tax/stamps: Deed $; Mortgage $		
1203. State tax/stamps: Deed $; Mortgage $		
1204.		
1205.		
1300. Additional Settlement Charges		
1301. Survey to		
1302. Pest inspection to		
1303.		
1304.		
1305.		
1400. Total Settlement Charges (enter on lines 103, Section J and 502, Section K)		

The Undersigned Acknowledges Receipt of this Disclosure Statement and Agrees to the Correctness Thereof.

_____   _____

_____   _____

          Buyer or Agent   **Seller or Agent**

Web Sites

Chapter 1

Statistical Profiles of Cities

www.usacitylink.com

http://ww.moving.com/Find_a_Place

Neighborhoods

realestate.yahoo.com/Neighborhoods

Data on local schools

www.schoolmatch.com

Cost of living compared to your current home

www.bankrate.com/brm/movecalc.asp

Data on home values

www.zillow.com

realestate.yahoo.com/Homevalues

www.homegain.com

Get copies of credit reports and explains how to read one

www.annualcreditreport.com

www.experian.com

www.transunion.com

www.econsumer.equifax.com

Fico scores

www.myfico.com

Prequalification calculator

www.dinkytown.net/java/LoanPrequal.html

Special programs from local housing counseling agency

www.hud.gov/offices/hsg/sfh/hcc/hcs.cfm

Chapter 3

The National Association of Realtors

www.realtor.com

Nehemiah Down Payment Assistance Program for down payment grants

www.getdownpayment.com

Home Price Web site

www.zillow.com

Mortgage Calculator at Mortgage 101 site

mortgage101.com/Calculators/Afford.asp?p=mtg101

Web site with calculator that lets you see how your score may affect your ability to buy a house

www.myfico.com/myfico/CreditCentral/LoanRates.asp

Chapter 4

Copy of the Contract form used for most home mortgage loans

www.efanniemae.com/sf/formsdocs/forms/1003.jsp

Department of Veterans Affairs—"VA" or "GI" loans

www.homeloans.va.gov

Special loan programs

www.fanniemae.com/homebuyers/homepath/index.jhtml

www.freddiemac.com

Chapter 5

Current limits for loans in the area that you are buying

https://entp.hud.gov/idapp/html/hicostlook.cfm

Loan rates

www.bankrate.com

Chapter 6

Major Search Engines

www.google.com

www.yahoo.com

www.msn.com

Multiple Search Engines

www.compernic.com

www.dogpile.com

U.S. Department of Housing and Urban Development

www.HUD.Gov/buying/index.cfm

National Association of Realtors

www.realtor.org

NJ Realtor's Association with links for information @ schools, transportation, etc.

www.njar.com

State Governmental sites

www.state.xx.us (substitute the xx with the two-letter state designation)

The National Association of Home Builders

www.homebuilder.com

National Association of Exclusive Buyers Agents

www.naeba.com

American Bar Association

www.findlegalhelp.org

National Academy of Building Inspection Engineers

www.nabie.org

American Society of Home Inspectors

www.ashi.org

National Association of Home Inspectors

www.nahi.org

National Association of Certified Home Inspectors

www.nachi.org

National Mortgage Broker's Association

www.namb.org

Toll Brothers—Large Builders/Developers

www.tollbrothers.com

KHovnanian—Large Builders/Developers

www.khov.com

National Association of Home Builders

www.nahb.org

Chapter 7

HUD Housing, Frequently Asked Questions
www.hud.gov/offices/hsg/sfh/reo/reobuyfaq.cfm
Main HUD Web site
www.hud.gov/homes/homesforsale.cfm
Current list of HUD Houses for Sale
www.hud.gov/offices/hsg/sfh/reo/homes.cfm
National Register of Historic Homes
www.cr.nps.gov/nr/about.htm
Federal Emergency Management Agency (FEMA)—Flood maps
www.fema.gov
Log Home Book Store
www.lhgic.com

Chapter 8

Community Associations Institute—Condos, Co-ops, & Other Planned
Communities
www.caionline.org

Chapter 9

Internet Source of Maps
www.mapquest.com
Source of Realtors Working in Specific Towns
www.realtor.com
Zip-top Tote Bags
www.landsend.com
www.llbean.com

Chapter 10

Home Price Web site
www.zillow.com

National Association of Realtor's—List of Homes for Sale
www.realtor.com

Chapter 11

NABIE, National Academy of Building Inspection Engineers
www.nabie.org

ASHI, American Society of Home Inspectors
www.ashi.org

NAHI, National Association of Home Inspectors
www.nahi.org

NACHI, National Association of Certified Home Inspectors
www.nachi.org

U.S. Department of Housing & Urban Development
www.hud.gov

U.S. Department of Environmental Protection
www.epa.gov

Exterior Design Institute (EDI)—EIFS Inspection Certification Programs
www.exterior-design-inst.com

FEMA, Federal Emergency Management Agency
www.fema.gov

"Fortified… for safer living" weather resistant fortified homes building code requirements
www.ibhs.org

U.S. Government Web sites for weather resistant homes
www.noaa.gov
www.hud.gov
www.earthquake.usgs.gov

Chapter 15

Utility Transfers to New Homeowners
www.connectutilities.com
FEMA—Are You Ready Guide
www.fema.gov/plan/index.shtm
FEMA—"How to" Guides
www.fema.gov/plan/prevent/howto/index.shtm
Free Guides to Checking for Interior and Exterior Electrical Safety
www.hud.gov/owning/index.cfm
Government Programs for Energy Efficiency
www.energystar.gov

Chapter 17

"Residential Construction Performance Guidelines for Professional Builders & Remodelers"—by the National Association of Home Builders
www.BuilderBooks.com
The International Code Council—Building Permits, Codes, Regulations, etc.
www.iccsafe.org

Chapter 18

To Locate a Real Estate Investment Club
www.REIClub.com
Professional Engineers & Architects for Home Inspections
www.nabie.org
Tenant Rights—U.S. Department of Housing and Urban Development
www.hud.gov/renting/tenantrights.cfm

Index